JOHN DUDLEY
DUKE OF NORTHUMBERLAND

JOHN DUDLEY

Duke of Northumberland
1504–1553

DAVID LOADES

CLARENDON PRESS · OXFORD

1996

Oxford University Press, Walton Street, Oxford OX2 6DP
Oxford New York
Athens Auckland Bangkok Bombay
Calcutta Cape Town Dar es Salaam Delhi
Florence Hong Kong Istanbul Karachi
Kuala Lumpur Madras Madrid Melbourne
Mexico City Nairobi Paris Singapore
Taipei Tokyo Toronto
and associated companies in
Berlin Ibadan

Oxford is a trade mark of Oxford University Press

Published in the United States
by Oxford University Press Inc., New York

British Library Cataloguing in Publication Data
Data available

Library of Congress Cataloging in Publication Data
Data applied for

ISBN 0–19–820193–1

1 3 5 7 9 10 8 6 4 2

Typeset by Jayvee, Trivandrum, India
Printed in Great Britain
on acid-free paper by
Biddles Ltd.
Guildford & King's Lynn

To the memory of
Geoffrey Elton
with homage and affection

Preface

IN the four and a half centuries since his death, chroniclers and historians have dealt severely with John Dudley. Within a few weeks of his fall Robert Wingfield was writing of

John Dudley, or as others will have it, Sutton; he was famous for the renown of his exploits and was duke of Northumberland, but he was an ambitious man descended of an ambitious father. After a notable victory on Norwich heath against the peasants ... he sought with excessive impudence to control both the king and the kingdom ...

Half a century later John Hayward characterized him as

A man of ancient nobilitie, comely in stature and countenance, but of little gravitie or abstinence in pleasures ... He was of great spirit and highly aspiring, not forbearing to make any mischief the meanes for attaining his ambitious endes ...

This theme of military prowess and unscrupulous ambition had become an orthodoxy long before Froude and Pollard conveyed it into the twentieth century. As recently as 1970 Professor Jordan interspersed his meticulously reconstructed narrative of the reign with pejorative comments upon Dudley's competence and integrity which were sometimes at odds with the evidence which he was presenting. One of the reasons for this was the attractiveness of the simplistic 'good duke'/'bad duke' contrast in the presentation of Edward VI's two mentors, a contrast which was rooted in contemporary mythology. Somerset was a hero to those humanist ideologists known as the 'commonwealth men', whose intervention in the public affairs of the Protectorate was as disastrous as that of intellectuals in any day and age. The circumstances of his fall thus made him a martyr to the cause of social justice as they perceived it. Northumberland, on the other hand, was twice or thrice a loser. It was he who took the necessary but unpopular steps to hold the minority regime together and suppress dissent, a vital and successful operation for which he received small thanks either at the time or since. He then made the fatal error of opposing the lawful order of succession, a step which cost him both his head and his honour. 'Right heirs for to displace I did detest' as Sir Nicholas Throgmorton is alleged to have commented in justifying his own less than glorious role in the crisis of July 1553. In an aristocratic society acutely sensitive to the issues of inheritance, it was hazardous to make such an attempt, and disastrous to fail. The horns of Richard of Gloucester became fastened upon his brow, which is perhaps why so many people became so irrationally convinced that he had caused Edward to be poisoned. Nor could his reputation be redeemed by the accession of Elizabeth, and the eventual triumph of that brand of protestantism which he had worked so hard to promote during his years in power. By publicly renouncing the faith which he had then professed, he effectively earned the contempt of both parties, and was unable to benefit from the rehabilitation which most of Mary's victims enjoyed after 1558. Gilbert Burnet, writing at the end of the seventeenth century, condemned him in measured but familiar terms

Whether he had been always in heart what he then professed, or whether he only pretended it, hoping that it might procure him favour, is variously reported; but certain it is that he said he had always been a Catholick in his Heart; yet this could not save him. He was known to be a man of that temper, so given both to revenge and dissimulation, that his enemies saw it was necessary to put him out of the way ...

Only over the last twenty years or so has this almost unanimous chorus of condemnation become muted and uncertain. In 1973 Barrett Beer argued that Northumberland was less a villain than a pragmatist who believed that what was good for the house of Dudley was good for England. In 1975 Michael Bush took a cool and deflationary look at the career of the duke of Somerset, and the following year Dale Hoak's important work on Edward's Privy Council compared Dudley very favourably with his predecessor as a head of government. More recently Professor Hoak has followed this up with further articles defending Northumberland's reputation, while Dr Glyn Parry has let some more wind out of Protector Somerset's balloon. However, it is significant that John Dudley is always remembered as the duke of Northumberland, a title which he held for less than two years, and his career is judged by his actions on a handful of critical occasions. In fact his importance to an understanding of Tudor government lies less in the dramatic events of 1551 or 1553, than in the nature of his political experience over a quarter of a century. He is always described as a soldier, but by comparison with Spinola, or Chatillon, or the duke of Savoy, he was the merest amateur. Apart from a vigorous apprenticeship in 1522–4, when he was little more than a boy, the bulk of his campaigning was against the Scots, or against English rebels. As Robert Wingfield hinted, massacring peasants in Norfolk was no great feat of arms, important as it may have been at the time. Although he was ashore briefly at the seige of Boulogne, by far his most important military service was at sea. It was as an energetic vice-admiral between 1537 and 1542 that he first came seriously to the king's attention, and began to earn significant rewards. From 1543 to 1547 he was an innovative and distinguished Lord Admiral, at a time when the navy was undergoing one of the most important developments of the century. Although he spent a great deal of time in and around the court, he was not a conspicuous courtier, and the great household offices which he eventually held were the result of his growing political power, rather than the cause of it. John Dudley was principally a politician and a man of business, who made himself useful in public affairs, and who dealt shrewdly in the land market. William Paulet, John Russell, and William Paget were others of the same ilk. Their commitment to the service of the king was no doubt genuine enough, but it also created that context of principled self-interest within which they all operated so successfully.

This was a different world from that of the traditional nobleman, such as the duke of Buckingham, the earl of Northumberland, or the marquis of Exeter. It was also different from that of the boon companion, such as the duke of Suffolk or Sir Nicholas Carew. Henry liked them because their loyalty to himself was uncomplicated by either ideology or private agendas. They had no family traditions to live up to, or provincial expectations to satisfy. Apart from the fact that he was not as intelligent, and had no legal training, John Dudley was not unlike Thomas Cromwell, and his self-abasement when disaster struck had a very similar flavour. Land for Dudley was a source of wealth, and not a direct source of power. Until 1537 he was described as 'of Sussex', and thereafter, until he acquired his peerage, as 'of Dudley castle, Worcestershire'. In spite of the store which he appeared to set by the Lordship of Warwick, he complained that the castle was partly ruinous, and does not seem to have lived there, although there was a large stable establishment at the time of his attainder. After 1542, when he was in England, he seems to have spent most of his time at his London house, Ely Place in Holborn, and later at Durham Place and Syon, which was where the bulk of his goods were located when the inventory was taken. He held significant property in Kent for most of his life, but did not reside in the county, and the massive estates which he acquired in Yorkshire and Northumberland, towards the end of his career, were visited only briefly, if at all. He served on commissions of the peace at different times in Kent, Sussex, Worcester, Shropshire, Staffordshire, and Warwickshire, and held important regional commissions in both the Welsh Marches and the Scottish borders. Between 1547 and 1553, it would be difficult to say where his 'country' should be located, and his extensive affinity did not have a clear regional identity. In short Dudley treated land very much as a modern business man would treat stocks and shares. 'Good Lordship' in the traditional sense meant little or nothing to him, and that may have been one of the reasons for his sinister reputation. He lacked the magnanimity and *noblesse oblige* which were expected of a great nobleman. Far from being an overmighty subject, in many respects he was not mighty enough for the position which he came to occupy. His own obsessive concern with his 'estimacion' probably reflects a consciousness of that fact. Unlike Wolsey, or Cromwell, he was a man of respectable aristocratic pedigree, but he thought and behaved more like the Tudor parvenus among whom he operated.

This study is an attempt to examine the whole of Dudley's career, and not just the last five years of it, on the assumption that he grew to his ultimate role, and that it is hard to understand the duke of Northumberland without knowing the young knight who had to make his way in the 1520s and 1530s. I have done this to the best of my ability, using source material which is, for the most part, familiar enough. There appear to be no hidden caches of Dudley archive, and consequently no means of reconstructing the early history of either the estate or the affinity in the same detail as has been possible for some other noblemen, such as the duke of Suffolk. This may obscure an important development, but it appears from the evidence which does survive that there may be no very coherent story to tell. John Dudley certainly had some servants who served him long and faithfully, but equally he seems to have picked up and dropped allies and associates in accordance with the priorities of the moment, in much the same way as he did lands and other properties. In other words he was as much an opportunist in the creation of his private fortune as he was in the building of his public career. Such tactics were skilfully deployed, and served him well, but they left him an extraordinarily rootless figure, both in material and cultural terms. Both his father and his sons make guest appearances, but whereas I started with the conviction that the story of the relationship between Dudley and Tudor would make a coherent whole through three generations, I have ended by doubting that, and relegating his well-studied sons to a virtual postscript. Edmund Dudley's career, and his fate, were significant for his son, but I am not convinced that John Dudley's great achievements, and total fall from grace, determined the fortunes of either Ambrose or Robert. In spite of Simon Adams's excellent work upon the Dudley affinity, I now believe that Robert was very much his own man (or possibly Elizabeth's), and that his father's career was a burden to him in a way which his grandfather's had never been. John Dudley was a product of the Tudor style of government, and particularly of Henry VIII's style of government. His was a career which looked forward to the business and political world of the seventeenth and eighteenth centuries, where his particular blend of skill and amorality became more usual and more accepted. In 1553 he not only miscalculated the political forces with which he was dealing, he also underestimated the forces of conventional morality, which were so well symbolized by the vulnerable and uninspiring figure of the Princess Mary.

In preparing this study I have inevitably incurred a number of debts of gratitude. First and foremost to the British Academy for a grant from its small projects research fund, and second to Tony Morris of Oxford University Press, who not only took my project on board several years ago, but who has been consistently patient and encouraging. Over the last few years I have shared John Dudley and his problems with friends, colleagues, and students, who have always been understanding, and sometimes helpful. Above all, however, I owe thanks to my wife, Judith, who has inspired me to further efforts by reminding me how many other things I have to do when it is completed! Finally, as this book was going to press, all Tudor historians, and many others, were saddened and dismayed by the death of Sir Geoffrey Elton. For over thirty years I have been honoured by Sir Geoffrey's friendship, and everything that I have written has been due in some measure to his initial guidance and ongoing support. Such a debt may be acknowledged, but can never be repaid. As a small token of my esteem and gratitude, I am dedicating this work to a great historian, tutor, and friend.

D.L.

Bangor
December 1994

Contents

Prologue

Edmund Dudley: Councillor and Scapegoat

WHEN Edmund Dudley faced his executioner on 17 August 1510 he was, in all probability, not long past his thirty-eighth birthday. His career in the royal service had lasted less than a decade, and although it had brought him great notoriety, had conferred neither wealth nor high rank. Apart from the splendid sounding but insubstantial position of President of the king's council, he had held no great office, and it may well be that the power which was conveniently ascribed to him was largely illusory. The date traditionally allotted to his birth, 1462, is almost certainly too early by a decade, and seems to depend upon an error originally made by Dugdale. An Inquisition taken on 3 November 1508 declares that his mother, Elizabeth, had died on 12 October 1498, at which point Edmund had been 'aged twenty six years and more'.[1] This form of words was used, not to mean 'any age over twenty six', but 'more than twenty six and less than twenty seven': that is, he was born at some point between 13 October 1471 and 13 October 1472. His father was John Dudley of Atherington in Sussex, the second son of John Sutton, Lord Dudley, who had enjoyed a distinguished career under both Henry VI and Edward IV.[2] His mother was Elizabeth Bramshot, the heiress of a modest estate upon the Isle of Wight. Virtually nothing is known about his childhood, and Anthony Wood's assertion that he spent some time at the university of Oxford 'about 1478' is based upon a mixture of error and guesswork.[3] His uncle William, the bishop of Durham, was briefly Chancellor there for a few months before his death in 1483, and he

---

[1] *Inquisitions Post Mortem of the Reign of Henry VII* (London, 1955), iii. 489. This inquisition related to Elizabeth's land on the Isle of Wight, which John had held by 'courtesy of England' after her death. John had died on 6 Feb. 1501, and immediately afterwards Edmund 'intruded into the premises without suing them out of the king's hands'. This was a strange mistake for a lawyer, and one for which he was obliged to sue a pardon.

[2] The first Lord Dudley had been born in 1400. He served Henry VI as Lieutenant of Ireland from 1428 to 1430, and received the order of the Garter in 1459. He made his peace with Edward IV, and may have gone with him into exile; he was not summoned to the readeption parliament, although his barony had been created by writ in 1440. From 1470 to 1483 he served in the sensitive role of Lieutenant of the Tower. He had also served as Chamberlain to Queen Elizabeth. Edmund's father, John, had been fee'd at Petworth by the earl of Northumberland, and had attended the parliament of 1478 as the earl's retainer (Michael Hicks, *False, Fleeting, Perjur'd Clarence* (Bangor, 1992), 200–1).

[3] Anthony Wood, *Athenae Oxoniensis*, ed. P. Bliss (Oxford, 1813), i. 11. Wood's estimate of Dudley's date of matriculation is based on the assumption that he was born in 1462. No registers for the period survive.

attempted to make provision for poor scholars of Divinity in his will, but neither of these facts amount to evidence of his own membership.

He was certainly a member of Gray's Inn by the Lent term 1496, when he was appointed Double Reader, but what seniority he held is not known.[4] The fact that such an appointment normally required a good deal of experience prompted Dorothy Brodie to conclude that Edmund must have enrolled as a student in either Staple Inn or Barnard's Inn before 1480. However such a conclusion does not seem to be required. By 1496 he would have been 24, and, if he had entered one of the Inns at the age of 16 or 17, would have been well past his student days. As Sir John Fortescue had observed several years before, Gray's Inn was very expensive, and '… there is scarcely any learned man skilled in these laws who is not a gentleman by birth or fortune'.[5] Edmund Dudley was well off, well connected, and almost certainly very able. A precocious legal career seems entirely plausible. Later, when he was already established in the royal service, he held property for the Inn in trust, which again suggests that he was a highly respected member.[6] His readings were apparently upon the Quo Warranto proceedings and upon the application of the Assize of Novel Disseisin to incorporeal heritaments. Perhaps these exercises made a big impression, or perhaps Dudley's friends were efficiently mobilized, for in November of the same year, 1496, he was chosen as one of the Under Sheriffs of London.[7] This was his first public office, but it was not quite his first appearance on the public stage. In 1493 he had appeared alongside his father upon the commission of the peace for Sussex—an appropriate way for the son of an important local gentleman to mark his majority, especially if he was already learned in the law.[8] He was a popular and effective Under Sheriff, and when he came to the end of his term of office in December 1502 he was granted a pension and a livery in recognition of the faithful discharge of his duties.[9]

At what point or by what means Edmund entered the king's service is not known, but Dr Brodie's conjecture that it was via the patronage of Sir Reginald Bray is probably correct. Bray had known Edmund's grandfather, the first Lord Dudley, who had died in 1487, and had been a lifelong friend and associate of his father, John. Sir Reginald died in 1503, two years after John Dudley, and is known to have shown an interest in Edmund's career. In the

---

    [4] D. M. Brodie (ed.), *Edmund Dudley's Tree of Commonwealth* (Cambridge, 1948), 2; citing UCL MS Hh.3. 10, fo. 96b. The admission register is not extant.
    [5] *De Laudibus Legum Angliae,* ed. S. B. Chrimes (London, 1942), c. XLIX.
    [6] William Dugdale, *Origines Judicales* (London, 1680), 271, where the date is given as 15 Feb. 22 Henry VII.
    [7] Guildhall Record Office, Journal 10, fo. 81d; see also *The Chronicles of London,* ed. C. L. Kingsford (London, 1905), 348.
    [8] *Calendar of the Patent Rolls, Henry VII,* ii. 67.
    [9] Guildhall Record Office, Repertories 1, fo. 116; cited Brodie (ed.), *Tree of Commonwealth,* 2.

1490s he was an extremely busy and influential councillor, holding a large number of offices of a financial nature.[10] Whether Edmund was influenced by his patron's interests, or Bray was attracted by young Dudley's combination of legal and financial acumen we do not know. In 1501 he made his first appearance in what may have been royal service, as a commissioner for concealed lands in Sussex.[11] In the same year he was also named to the commission of the peace for Hampshire, which does not indicate royal service, but the extension of his activities into a new county, following his father's death and the acquisition of his mother's inheritance on the Isle of Wight, in which John had had a life interest.[12] In 1503 he received a royal writ instructing him to assume the degree and status of a Sergeant at Law, and this seems to have marked a turning-point in his life. On 4 October in the same year he bought himself out of the dignity at a cost of £46. 13s. 4d.[13] As the coif was one of the highest honours of the legal profession, and the assured gateway to the most lucrative commissions, some explanation for this decision is needed. For a man who had already been Under Sheriff of London the costs of installation, although high, can hardly have been daunting. However the Sergeantry was a part of the judiciary, and the Sergeants constituted the pool from which judges were appointed. Presumably at this point Dudley must have opted for an administrative rather than a judicial career, and unless he was a reckless gambler he must have known far more about his prospects than can now be reconstructed from the records.

When Henry's seventh parliament was convened on 25 January 1504 he was chosen to be Speaker of the House of Commons.[14] This appointment was always made on the king's initiative, and means that Dudley was *persona grata* at court, but it does not necessarily mean that he was high in royal favour. A better indication is provided by the fact that he appears on a list of royal councillors drawn up during the autumn of the same year.[15] In 1504 this was not a significant political appointment, as membership of the privy council was to be a generation later, but it does indicate that Dudley had become an important royal servant. Thereafter his rise to notoriety was rapid. As a member of the council his specific functions were nearly all discharged through that group known as *consilium domini regis in lege eruditum*. The status of the 'council learned in the law' is still somewhat uncertain. It used to be described as a committee of the king's council, but

[10] He was Chancellor of the Duchy of Lancaster, and was also described as 'under treasurer of England' (S. B. Chrimes, *Henry VII* (London, 1972), 121). See also *DNB*.

[11] *Cal. Pat.*, ii. 263: 21 Oct. 1501.　　[12] *Cal. Pat.*, ii. 67. See above, n. 1.

[13] PRO E101, 413/2, iii, fo. 46; Brodie (ed.), *Tree of Commonwealth*, 3.

[14] J. S. Roskell, *The Commons and their Speakers in English Parliaments, 1376–1523* (London, 1965), 298–308.

[15] *Cal. Pat.*, ii. 388: 17 Dec. 1504, when he was one of 43 councillors recorded as being present at the exemplification of a judgment in Star Chamber concerning the Merchants of the Staple.

Stanley Chrimes pointed out several years ago that, as it did not report back to the main council, the committee analogy is inappropriate.[16] It seems to have been simply an undifferentiated group of councillors which normally carried out certain functions, but did not have any exclusive right to them. If that is the case, however, and it had no institutional existence, then it is difficult to see in what sense Edmund Dudley could have been its President, as he is described in two charters issued in July 1505.[17] Chrimes believed that Dudley presided over the whole council, but that seems unlikely from the position of his name in the charters cited, as well as from his lack of status for such a position. Brodie argued that he was President of the king's household council, but such a body, if it existed at all, remains extremely shadowy.[18] Whatever the status of the 'council learned' its composition remained stable throughout the five or six years of its recorded existence, and somebody must have prepared its business and chaired its meetings. Perhaps the Chancery clerk used a little licence in describing this situation. The evidence is so slight that it would be unwise to build too much on it.

The function of this group of councillors is much clearer than its organization. They adjudicated some private suits, for reasons which are not entirely clear, drew up indentures and recognizances which defined the duties of officials, and settled the terms of the king's loans.[19] Every aspect of the king's financial prerogative was scrutinized, and methods of effective enforcement devised. Dudley and his somewhat older colleague, Sir Richard Empson, were the hands and feet of the council learned, as well as acting in some cases on their own initiative. Polydore Vergil called them *judices fiscales*, and, whether that was a recognized designation or not, it describes their function very accurately.[20] Dudley's own description of this situation, drawn up after his fall, and when he was already under sentence of death, is almost certainly truthful.

the kinges grace whose soul god pardon was much sett to have many persons in his danger at his pleasure, and y^t aswell spirituall men as temporal men, wherefore divers and many persons were bound to his grace or to others to his use in great somes of money, some by Recognizances, and some by obligacon wth out any condition, but as a simple and absolute bonde payable at a certayne day, for his grace would have them soe made ...[21]

---

[16] Chrimes, *Henry VII*, 99 and n. 3.

[17] D. M. Brodie, 'Edmund Dudley: Minister of Henry VII', *Transactions of the Royal Historical Society*, 4th series, 15 (1932), 133–47.

[18] Brodie (ed.), *Tree of Commonwealth*, 3 n. 7. There is no clear evidence that Henry had anything which could be called a 'household council', although the Board of Greencloth may have functioned in such a way. Nor did Dudley hold any household office.

[19] R. Somerville, 'Henry VII's "Council Learned in the Law"', *English Historical Review*, 54 (1939), 427–42.

[20] *The Anglica Historia of Polydore Vergil*, ed. Denys Hay, Camden Society, 3rd series 74 (1950), 133.

[21] C. J. Harrison, 'The Petition of Edmund Dudley', *EHR* 87 (1971), 82–99. The original

No agent, however trusted, would have dared to act in the way Dudley and Empson did act between 1505 and 1509 without the king's full knowledge and approval. Francis Bacon was almost certainly right when he declared a century later that Henry had been entirely responsible for the oppressive fiscal policies which had characterized his later years.[22] Bacon's circumstantial stories about the king signing every page of Empson's accounts, and about a pet monkey tearing up Henry's dreaded notebook to the secret delight of his courtiers, cannot now be substantiated, but the impression which they give is probably a fair one. Polydore Vergil believed that this policy was simply the result of avarice, and it has since been attributed to a deterioration of character brought on by age, ill health, and the removal of the benign influence of his queen, who had died in 1503.[23]

Dudley's petition, however, points to a chronic sense of insecurity as the real motivation. No doubt the money itself was welcome, but the solvency of the Crown did not depend upon it. A few years before it had been said that Henry was very reluctant to believe evil of anyone to whom he had once given his confidence. If that was the case, then his character had certainly deteriorated, but there were understandable grounds for that. The treason of his Chamberlain, Sir William Stanley, in 1495 seems to have shaken him profoundly, and the deaths of two sons in 1499 and 1502 had left the succession hanging by a thread. Henry's remedy was 'to have many persons in his danger at his pleasure'. Edward Hall's account is consistent with Dudley's own:

Kyng Henry, now drawynge to age, and before this tyme, ever punched, stimulated and pricked with the scupulous stynes of domesticall sedicion and civile commocion, in so much that he more detested & abhorred intestine and private warre, then death or any thynge more terrible. Wherefore he determyned so pollitiquely to provyde that all ye causes of suche unquyetnes and mischief to come, should be eradicate and extirped; which ymaginacion and purpose he doubted not to compasse and brynge to effect. If he made lowe and abated the courage of his subiectes and vassalles, and especially of the richest sorte, remembrynge the olde proverbe, that men throughe abundaunce of ryches waxe more insolent, hedstronge and robustius …[24]

The king's choice of two learned but not particularly eminent common lawyers to execute this policy is understandable. It was prudent to use

document was written in July or Aug. 1509, and probably sent to the addressees, Bishop Fox of Winchester and Sir Thomas Lovell. It was then copied into a register by John Young, the Master of the Rolls, and the existing document is a later 16th-cent. transcript. It is unlikely that the king ever saw it. The MS was found among uncatalogued material belonging to the Marquis of Anglesey at Plas Newydd.

[22] *Bacon's History of the Reign of King Henry VII* (1892), ed. J. R. Lumby; cited by Harrison, 'Petition', 85. See also Chrimes, *Henry VII*, 310–14.

[23] G. R. Elton, 'Henry VII: Rapacity and Remorse', *Historical Journal*, 1 (1958), 21–39; J. P. Cooper, 'Henry VII's Last Years Reconsidered', *HJ* 2 (1959), 103–29; G. R. Elton, 'Henry VII: A Restatement', *HJ* 4 (1961), 1–29.

[24] Edward Hall, *The unione of the two noble and illustre femelies of Lancastre and Yorke*, ed. H. Ellis (London, 1809), 499.

correct legal forms, and mere functionaries could not afford the luxury of conscientious scruples. Dudley's account book survives, and records in meticulous detail the transactions which he conducted on the king's behalf, and the sums of money which he received.[25] This money was paid into the treasury of the chamber, which had for some years been the king's main accounting department.

We can only guess how Dudley saw this work while he was actually conducting it. The petition which he drew up after his fall makes it clear that he then realized that many injustices had been perpetrated:

In primis certayne obligacons of 300 markes of the Abbott of Norton wch he delivered for the temporalities whereas he ought to have payed non ...

Item the kinges grace had of one Hubbard for ye office of waighinge of wolls at Hampton 50 markes wch Hubbard never had the office, But one Troyes had it ...[26]

A total of eighty-four such instances are quoted, some much more explicit than others. As soon as Henry VII was dead, it was, of course, convenient to pretend that these abuses had been inflicted by Dudley and Empson on their own initiative. They did sometimes act as independent agents in the spirit of the king's instructions, but Dudley's petition was designed to set the record straight. That was no doubt the main reason why it was allowed to disappear into a private archive, and to remain unknown until 1970. At the same time it would be a mistake to see the petition as self-justification. Dudley knew that he could not save himself by laying the blame where it actually belonged, and he may well have accepted throughout that the policy was justified in principle, if not always in detail. He was intensely loyal to his old master, and his real concern seems to have been to make on Henry's behalf the confession which he should have made himself before his death. A king may need to do private wrongs in the interest of the greater good of his realm, but they are still accountable in the sight of God. Dudley therefore addressed what was in effect a memorandum to Richard Fox, the bishop of Winchester, and Sir Thomas Lovell

for the helpe and Reliefe of his [Henry's] soule, and dischardge of their owne conscience, they will not forgett but wth all dilligence indeavour to the uttermost of there power to performe and execute, as thinges yt they are bound to doe by the trust he put them in ...[27]

Henry's will had indeed specified that restitution should be made to all persons who had been wronged contrary to the order of law, and Dudley's memorandum identified as many such people as he was able to find by reference to his records.

The picture which the petition presents of the work of the *judices fiscales* is interesting in a number of ways. They conducted hundreds of transactions over a period of nearly five years, so the majority presumably gave Dudley

---

[25] British Library, Lansdowne MS 127.   [26] Petition, fo. 2^v.   [27] Ibid., fo. 2.

no qualms, even when he was about to face his maker. It is difficult to see why the king should have bothered to swindle or bully the aulnager of Southampton out of 50 marks, but in some cases the alleged injustice was clearly a matter of political judgement. The notorious fine of £70,650 imposed on Lord Abergavenny for unlawful retaining can never have been intended literally. It was a dire threat to deter others from an offence which the king believed with some justification to present a danger to the state. Even if the whole of his lands had been sequestered their value would have come nowhere near such a sum. Similarly the fine imposed upon the earl of Northumberland after his conviction in Common Pleas was out of proportion to the offence, and was designed to draw the political teeth of a potentially dangerous magnate. Henry's direct involvement in some of these transactions is made clear by circumstantial detail. The glimpse of the king saying goodbye to Sir John Pennington, and then fining him 200 marks for leaving the court without licence, has its lighter side, although it may be doubted whether Sir John saw the joke.[28] The policy which was embodied in these transactions was deeply resented, but probably no more than aggressive taxation would have been. It was the obvious unease with which the king looked back upon his actions in the face of death which gave his son and his son's advisers their cue. His agents could easily be represented as evil councillors in order to give Henry VIII a good start. In Dudley's case this seems to have been a duty which he discharged loyally and (almost) uncomplainingly.

In detailing the circumstances of Dudley's fall, Professor Chrimes described him as having no powerful relatives or friends.[29] Certainly none came forward to speak on his behalf in 1510, but that is hardly surprising. Men like Sir Thomas Lovell had been his close associates, and must have been breathless with apprehension lest the lightning which was consuming him should strike them also. However, as we have seen, Dudley had not lacked friends in the past, and certainly did not lack family. He was the cousin rather than the nephew of the second Lord Dudley, because his uncle and namesake had died before 1487 without ever coming into his inheritance. Edward, Lord Dudley, had been born about 1459 and was to live until 1532, but there seems to have been little contact between the two men, and the relationship between their sons was to be strained.[30] On the other hand Edmund had married twice and acquired important contacts from both his wives. The first was Anne Windsor, the sister of Andrew, later Lord Windsor. The date of their wedding is uncertain, and the *Complete Peerage* assumes that she was dead by 1494.[31] However, she is referred

---

[28] Petition, fo. 6ᵛ. Pennington had actually been discharged of his bond for 500 marks before the end of Henry VII's reign, but not, presumably, before he had paid 200 (*Cal. Pat.*, ii. 622).

[29] *Henry VII*, 17 and n. 2.

[30] G. E. Cockayne, *The Complete Peerage*, rev. V. Sibbs (London, 1910–49), iv. 479. See below.

[31] Ibid. The date given for Edmund's second marriage.

to as living in the will of her father-in-law, John Dudley, which was dated 1 October 1500, at which point their daughter is also described as 'little Elizabeth Dudley',[32] and was presumably an infant. Edmund and Anne were therefore probably married soon after he achieved his majority in 1493, and she died at some point before the end of 1503. By 10 April 1508 Elizabeth was betrothed to Peter, the son and heir of the 4th Lord Stourton, whose wardship Edmund had purchased, but he had died by November of the same year, and she subsequently married his brother William, 5th Lord Stourton.[33]

Edmund's second wife was also called Elizabeth, and she was the sister and co-heir of John, Lord Lisle. John died in August or September 1505, at which point Elizabeth is variously described as being 20 or 23.[34] Lisle himself had married Miriella, a daughter of Thomas Howard, earl of Surrey, and after his death she bore him a posthumous daughter—another Elizabeth. The date of Edmund's second marriage is not known, but when their eldest son, John, was restored in blood in February 1512, he was described as being 'not yet eight years old'.[35] Consequently he must have been born between February 1504 and February 1505, which probably indicates a wedding in the summer of 1503, when Elizabeth would have been somewhere between 18 and 21 years old. Far from being a self-made man, therefore, Edmund Dudley was a member of the upper gentry, hovering on the fringes of the peerage, linked by blood or marriage to several substantial county families, and to the inner circle of the court through his father's friendship with Reginald Bray. The later sixteenth-century myth that he was the son of a carpenter was born of the hatred and jealousy aroused by three generations of Dudley success. By comparison with such a genuine self-made man as Thomas Cromwell, Edmund belonged to the upper reaches of the establishment.

He was arrested on 24 April 1509, the second day of the new reign, in what must have been a premeditated gesture.[36] It is hard to avoid the con-

---

[32] *Staffordshire Historical Collections*, William Salt Archaeological Society, ix. ii. 74. Cited in the *Complete Peerage sub* Stourton.

[33] *Complete Peerage*, xii. 206.

[34] *Inquisitions Post Mortem*, ii. 794, gives Lord Lisle's death as 7 Aug. 1505, and Elizabeth's age as '20 and more'; ibid., ii. 893, gives the date of death as 6 Sept. 1505, and Elizabeth's age as '23 and more'. I know of no way to resolve these discrepancies.

[35] Statute 3 Henry VIII, c. 19; *Statutes of the Realm*, ed. A. Luder *et al.* (London, 1810–28), iii. 41–2.

[36] Henry died late on 21 Apr., but his death was not announced until the evening of 23 Apr. This delay, which was not mentioned by Hall, is clear from a recently discovered account written by the herald Thomas Wriothesley (British Library Additional MS 45131, fos. 52ᵛ–53, printed with a commentary by S. J. Gunn as 'The Accession of Henry VIII', *Historical Research*, 64 (1991), 278–88). Empson and Dudley were arrested early on the morning of 24 Apr. In a further discussion of the same subject, Gunn comments 'While he [Henry VII] discussed with his "secret servants" the changes that would come over his kingship "yf yt plesed God to send hym lyfe", those same servants were preparing to keep his death secret long enough to be able

clusion that the old king's more powerful councillors used the unpopularity of the *judices fiscales* as a lightning conductor to protect themselves. However, it was one thing to arrest them amidst general applause, and quite another to decide what to do with them. Nothing less than death would satisfy their enemies, but both had been careful to operate within the law, and, even if extortion could be proved, it was not a capital offence. When Dudley was indicted, therefore, and brought before a commission of oyer and terminer at the London Guildhall on 16 July, he was charged with high treason, but not for any offence which he had committed in the previous reign. Instead it was alleged that on 22 April 1509 at his house in Candlewick Street, he had

falsely, feloniously and treacherously conspired, imagined and compassed how and in what manner he, with a great force of men and armed power might hold, guide and govern the King and his council against the wishes of the king ...[37]

This implausible plot was supported with circumstantial details. In order to carry out his nefarious intention, and to 'make and move discords, divisions and dissentions among the magnates and councillors of the King and his kingdom', he was alleged to have written letters to nine named individuals, including Edward, Lord Sutton, and Sir Francis Cheyne

requiring that they, with their servants and adherents and all their power arrayed in manner of war, should come together and speedily repair to London, and adhere to and follow his will ...

These letters he was supposed to have given to Richard Page and Angel Messenger, who had duly delivered them the same day, whereupon 'a great multitude and power of people arrayed in manner of war, came to London in the parish and ward aforesaid'. All this, it might be thought, was pretty fast work within a space of about forty-eight hours, and the charges have normally been dismissed as a total fabrication. None of those who allegedly responded to his summons seem to have been charged, and certainly not the friends upon whose support he apparently thought he could rely. Nevertheless to have invented letters which did not exist, and to have named the persons to whom they had never been sent, would not have been characteristic of a Tudor prosecution. On 21 April no one could be absolutely sure that the succession would be peaceful and unchallenged. A sensible man might well have thought that a little discreet mobilization would be a safeguard against eventualities.[38] A man of Dudley's status was expected to

to spring a coup against Empson, Dudley and Smith, apparently orchestrated by their fellow counsellors' ('The Courtiers of Henry VII', *EHR* 108 (1993)). There may well have been other and less sinister reasons why some delay was desirable.

[37] *Report of the Deputy Keeper of the Public Records*, III. ii. 226; Baga de Secretis, KB8, 4, fos. 54–5.

[38] Gunn, 'Accession of Henry VIII', makes clear the good reasons which Dudley had for apprehension.

have a modest military capability, even if he was a lawyer rather than a soldier, and when his goods at Candlewick Street were later inventoried they included 'VII score and XLII bowes', thirty-five sheeves of arrows, twelve complete harnesses 'lacking one head piece', forty black bills, and other odds and ends.[39] This was not provision for a *coup d'état*, but merely what any substantial gentleman would have kept in his house to meet the king's needs and to protect his family if events should so require.

However, given the political need to convict Dudley of a capital offence, his sensible precaution could easily be given a most sinister interpretation. No fair-minded person could seriously have believed that he intended to abduct the king and overthrow the government with the backing of half a dozen friends of very moderate means, but if he had suggested some measure of mutual protection in the uncertain hours as the old king lay dying, then he had given his enemies sufficient leverage to work his ruin.[40] He pleaded not guilty, and was tried and convicted on 18 July. Richard Empson, arrested with Dudley, was not indicted until 8 August, and was tried at Northampton on 2 October. The charges were very similar, alleging that he had sent letters to his son Thomas Empson, and to a number of other named men, to summon friends and supporters and to be ready upon immediate warning.[41] In this case the time scale was a little more realistic, since the letters were alleged to have been sent on 20 March, and the first assembly to have taken place in London on 12 April. Others, it was claimed, had joined them on 24 and 25 April, but the total assembled only amounted to seventeen, and by 24 April Empson was already in custody.[42] The basis of these charges was probably the same, and the treasonable intention need not be taken seriously. In all probability every member of the council had acted similarly, but the late king's council had also acquiesced in the policies which had become so violently unpopular, and they were determined not to suffer for that either.[43]

The two scapegoats were left in prison for over a year before the decision was finally taken to execute them. It seems unlikely that the king suffered from conscientious scruples about the flimsiness of the convictions. Henry was always scrupulous about due process, but once that had been followed the justice or otherwise of the outcome never troubled him. Perhaps once the storm had subsided Dudley's numerous friends summoned up the courage to try and get him off. Perhaps the king considered that so useful a

---

[39]   PRO E154/2/17; an indenture dated 17 Aug. 1509 between the king, Sir Henry Marney, and Sir John Digby in respect of the goods taken from Dudley's house in Candlewick Street and inventoried.

[40]   Gunn, 'The Courtiers of Henry VII', see above n. 36.

[41]   *Report of the Deputy Keeper*, III. ii. 227.   [42]   Ibid.; Gunn, 'Accession of Henry VIII'.

[43]   Whatever they may have said afterwards, there is no evidence that at the time any of Henry's more senior councillors attempted to dissuade him from the exploitation of bonds and recognizances. Dudley's political patron had been Sir Reginald Bray, and neither he nor Empson were close to more important councillors at the time of the king's death.

man was too good to lose. It may be significant that the bill confirming their attainders was allowed to die in the parliament of 1510. According to Edward Hall their agents, or 'promoters', who were also objects of popular hatred, were rounded up at the time of their arrest, but were punished merely by being exhibited on the pillory.[44] Perhaps, as Hall believed, their fate was sealed by a fresh storm of complaint stirred up during the royal progress in the summer of 1510. Both were beheaded on Tower hill on the same day, but their heads were not exhibited, so there was no particular attempt to make further political capital out of their deaths. It was more in the nature of a tidying-up operation.

According to his own testimony, Dudley seriously considered attempting to escape from the Tower. This must have been in January or February 1510, and he abandoned the idea when he learned that his attainder had not been confirmed by parliament.[45] Presumably he took that as a sign that he would eventually be pardoned, and it was with some bitterness that he realized that he had deceived himself with hope. When he wrote his last will, after he had been warned of his impending death, he was anxious to exonerate two of his former servants, Thomas Michell and William Frank, to whom he had confided his intention. Both had declined to assist, but they had not betrayed his secret, and he was concerned that they might be in danger for his 'lewd demeanour'.[46] Many other people were in his thoughts as he strove to set his affairs in order, but some of them are no more than names—'my near kinsman Jas. Beaumont', 'Marion Raylegh ... bound apprentice with the wife of Mr. Warren, broderer', people who seem to have been the objects of Dudley's kindly interest or generosity. The will is badly mutilated, and because of his attainder it was never proved, but it enables at least a partial reconstruction of his circumstances to be made.[47] Lands in Sussex, Dorset, and Lancashire were enfeoffed to Sir Andrew Windsor and others to the use of his wife, with remainder in tail to his sons John, Jerome, and Andrew, his daughter Elizabeth, and his brother Peter. Other lands in Lincolnshire were to be held to the use of his son Jerome, who was intended for the priesthood, and to his heirs if that intention did not take effect. A distinguished panel, consisting of

---

[44] Hall, *Unione*, 506.
[45] Harrison, 'Petition'; Dudley's will, PRO SP1/2, fo. 4; *Letters and Papers ... of the reign of Henry VIII*, ed. J. S. Brewer *et al.* (London, 1862–1932), I. i. 559.
[46] SP1/2, fo. 4.
[47] It is not, however, very informative about how his lands were acquired. The reversion of the manor of Barerch, Sussex, was 'bought of Copley'; some of the lands in Hampshire were purchased from Sir A. Fortescue; other lands in Sussex and Surrey came from Roger Lewkenor by the same method; and some in Lancashire from Lord Dacre of the South. Dudley did not, apparently, receive any land grants from the Crown. He was granted one wardship jointly with Andrew Windsor, and an annuity of 100 marks on 29 Oct. 1506. Apart from those, his grants were all stewardships of royal manors. The Patent Rolls record six in all, from Warbington in Hampshire to Wythern in Lincolnshire. These were no doubt lucrative appointments but Dudley was not rewarded on a lavish scale, and the value of his lands ranked him only as a substantial gentleman (SP1/2, fo. 4).

Richard Fitzjames, the bishop of London, Dr John Colet, Sir Andrew Wind-sor, and Dr Younge, was entrusted with the task of supervising Jerome's upbringing in learning until he reached the age of 22, and any surplus revenue from the lands assigned to him was to go to the support of divinity students at Oxford. Lands in Norfolk, Suffolk, and Wiltshire were to be held to the use of his son Andrew and his heirs; those in Surrey to the use of some person whose name has now disappeared, possibly Peter, and those in Cheshire for John and his heirs. Dudley also seems to have held other lands for which purchase agreements were incomplete, and some were to be conditionally returned to one Roger Lewkenor, probably for that reason. Elizabeth Martin subsequently petitioned successfully for the return of lands which had been similarly purchased, and not completely paid for, but which the Crown had nevertheless seized on Dudley's attainder.[48] The value of his estate is not specified, but at the time of his conviction he was found to be in possession of lands worth 500 marks per annum, which would be reasonably consistent with the number of manors and other parcels mentioned in his will.[49]

About a dozen named debtors were to be discharged; Sussex neighbours like Edward Lewkwnor, a variety of London tradesmen owed unspecified sums for silks, tailoring , and candles; and William Pellett of Steyning and his wife from whom, for some mysterious reason, he had borrowed £60. Spiritual bequests were similar in number, and were to be supervised by his cousin, Richard Dudley. The largest was for £50 to poor priests of Oxford and Cambridge, to pray for the souls of his parents, his uncle William, and himself and his two wives. Smaller sums were bequeathed for other memorials, and a plea which cannot now be deciphered to 'my lord Steward' (the earl of Shrewsbury), which seems to be related to the ward-ship and marriage of his eldest son, John. His conscience was still troubling him about the discharge of a recognizance for £1,000 in which Sir William Sandes had been bound to the late king, and which had not featured in the list attached to his petition. Some other items of outstanding business can-not now be reconstructed, but the phrase 'if my pardon be had …' is legible, suggesting that, even at the end, Dudley could not really believe that he would suffer a traitor's death for the alleged offences which had led to his conviction. He requested burial in Westminster abbey, and asked his wife to find a priest to sing for him for three years. It was an entirely conven-tional document, but the surviving portions make no reference to substan-tial bequests in cash, nor to the disposal of his goods, which had been valued at the very substantial sum of £5,000.[50] This may be because of the imperfections of the document, or because his goods had already been seized to the king's use. There are no references to his cousin Lord Dudley,

---

[48] Statute 3 Henry VIII, c. 21; *Statutes of the Realm*, iii. 44–5.
[49] KB8 (4) fo. 55; *Deputy Keepers Report*, iii. ii. 226.   [50] Ibid., SP1/2, fo. 4.

nor to the kindred of his second wife, although Sir Anthony Windsor features prominently. The earl of Arundel received one of the very few specific bequests, a cup valued at £8, but that appears to have been an undischarged obligation from his father's will of ten years before.

In addition to his petition and his will, Edmund Dudley also left a third testament, a political treatise called the 'Tree of Commonwealth'. His modern editor has rightly pointed out that this work has no particular originality, and little intrinsic merit.[51] It is altogether lacking in the elaborate classical and scriptural citations with which learned contemporaries ornamented their writings. But it is not without interest, given the author's circumstances and history. He starts with a commendation of Henry VIII for determining to right the wrongs of the previous regime 'willing the comfortt and relief of the souls of his father, to see the will of his said father and king to be truely performed, to his marvelous grete mede and honour'. After some conventional observations upon the duty of a prince to promote virtuous churchmen and to suppress simony, Dudley continues rather surprisingly

Also it were a graciouse and a noble acte that the Churche of England were restorid to hur free election after thold manor, and not to be lettyd therof by meanes of you, oure sovvereigne lord ...[52]

It had been, he fairly observes, the custom of the king's progenitors to write to their subjects, lay and spiritual, demanding the 'disposicions of ther promocions', which was 'A great discourage for Clerkes'. A king should take counsel of grave and experienced men, not listening to young or rash heads. Nor should he listen to the advice of the covetous, because

The covetous counsell will shew there souvereigne his suertie standith mutche in plentie of treasure, but ... the profyte of every christen prince dependith in the grace of god which is won by marcie and liberalytie ...[53]

Covetous counsel, he added, perhaps ruefully 'shall lose the hartes of the subiectes'. He was in a good position to know. Riches are worse than useless without the grace of God. Henry III had been guilty of covetousness, and 'all his realme reiosyd at his deth'. 'Peradventure', he continued, 'of that apetite have ther bene some other of late tyme, and wer in a maner withowt fault, saving only yt; But how such a king shal have the loving hartes of his subiectes late experience may plainly shew hit.'[54] The allusion is clear enough, and so is the message. Cruel, covetous, and 'fleshly' kings all have their just nemesis. The cruel die untimely deaths, the covetous lose the love and respect of their subjects, and the lustful are unfortunate in their

---

[51] Brodie, *Tree of Commonwealth*, 14. Dr Brodie comments that the work is of interest because of the light which it sheds upon the practical problems confronting governments. It is also interesting as an expression of its author's attitude, both to politics in general and to his own career.
[52] Ibid. 25. [53] Ibid. 28. [54] Ibid. 29.

issue. It is a sufficiently conventional message, but taken in conjunction with the petition, shows how aware Dudley was of the faults of his late royal master. The 'Tree of Commonwealth' is a sermon on the arts of virtuous rule, of the sort commonly offered to new monarchs, but deriving an additional force from the experience of its author. It is a little like the warning of Marley's ghost.

Contrary to the received wisdom of his own years in office, the wealth and prosperity of a king lie in the wealth and prosperity of his subjects, because God has ordained his office to protect his people, not the other way round. Amid the somewhat platitudinous urgings to virtue and justice, Dudley's own experience continues to break the surface from time to time.

peradventure oftetymes the Prince shall have counsellors and servauntes yt in his owne causes will do further then conscience requirith, and further then hym self wold shold be done, oftetymes to wynne a speciall thank of the King ...[55]

Servants will use the king's authority to settle their own private quarrels if they are not carefully watched. The king must set an example in the truth and honesty with which he observes his promises and obligations, because if he does not do so, he cannot expect his subjects to be honest towards each other, nor towards him. In respect of truth and faithfulness 'this tree of comen wealth is welnie utterly fayllid and deade' in England, and can only be revived because now 'ye have a prince and kinge in whom was neither spott nor bleamysshe of untroth knowen'.

Justice similarly lies, not in severity of an indiscriminate nature, but in cherishing the good and punishing the bad. Rather surprisingly in view of his professional background, Dudley places little emphasis upon the quality of the law, but a great deal upon the conscience of the prince in its administration. And in this connection too, he has a contemporary message. A king should

in causes tochcing him self ... mynister his Iustice discretely medlyd with marcye, or els his iustice wilbe sore, yt it will oftetyme appere to be crueltie rather than iustice. And I suppose ther is no christen Kinge hath more nede so to do than our prince and souvereigne lorde, consyderinge the greate number of penall Lawes and statutes made in his realme for thard and straighte ponyshement of his subiectes ...[56]

His purveyors should pay truly for what they take, and his servants should be truly paid their wages. By such means will confidence in his liberality be restored, and, when he needs to call for financial support, it will be freely and willingly given. Justice also lies in the due observance of priority and place. It is not just for the nobleman to disdain his inferiors, nor for them to envy him, or to seek to climb into his place. Nevertheless Dudley laments that too many noblemen are unworthy of their blood, and it is consequently right that the prince should promote the learned and industrious man of

---

[55] Brodie, *Tree of Commonwealth*, 37.   [56] Ibid. 41.

humble origin to the place which the nobleman's son is not worthy to occupy.[57]

As might be expected, he is severe alike upon the acquisitiveness of merchants and the idleness of the poor. His values, although extremely traditional, are interlaced with humanist priorities, and in many places he prefigures the 'commonwealth men' of a later generation. Good education, outward peace, and above all the fear of God; these are the criteria for a flourishing tree of commonwealth. As Dudley's treatise progresses, it becomes increasingly schematic, and detached from the real world of politics in which it started. Laments about the decay of hospitality, and about the dishonesty of wool merchants and clothiers, who are ruining England's reputation amongst her neighbours, bear little relation to what we know of the real social or commercial history of the period.[58] They were to be repeated endlessly by self-appointed Jeremiahs well into the seventeenth century. As the author refines his imagery of the tree, its roots, its branches, its fruit, and the bitter cores which all the fruit contain, we move increasingly into a world of abstract moralizing, and away from the sharp observations of personal experience which seem to have launched him on his enterprise. Like many of his contemporaries, Edmund Dudley believed that God was just. He had served his master loyally, and to the best of his ability, but he had been a party to avarice and injustice, and his conscience, like Henry's own, needed purging. Whether this would have troubled him if the old king had lived longer, and he had died in peaceful possession of a peerage and a great estate, we may well doubt. But Henry had been denied the time for amendment which he had craved at the last,[59] and although Dudley continued to deny vehemently that he was guilty of the treason for which he had been convicted, he probably regarded his fall as the *stipendium peccati*. He had not played the part of a true counsellor in warning his master of the evil of his ways, and he was being punished. The only thing he could do was to perform his neglected service for the new king, whether he should be heeded or not.

The fate of Dudley's family in the immediate aftermath of his death can only be pieced together. By February 1512 his widow had married Arthur Plantagenet, the illegitimate but acknowledged son of King Edward IV, to whom she eventually conveyed her father's title of Viscount Lisle.[60] Whether she still had custody of her younger sons, Jerome and Andrew, at

---

[57] Ibid. 45. By the Elizabethan period this was conventional wisdom: 'Alasse, you will be ungentle gentlemen if you be no schollers; you will do your prince but simple service ...' (G. Pettie, *The Civile Conversation of S. Guazzo* (1586) sig. Aᵛ). Dudley was an early advocate of this position.

[58] The early 16th century was a period of steadily expanding English trade, particularly in cloth, and there are no indications that English credit was generally low.

[59] Gunn, 'Courtiers of Henry VII'; see above n. 36.

[60] *Complete Peerage*, iv. 480. Edward Grey, Lord Lisle, had also received the title through his mother, Elizabeth Tailoys.

this point is not clear. Jerome probably did not outlive childhood, and his father's hopes for his education came to nothing. Andrew certainly survived, but the circumstances of his childhood are obscure. John, the eldest, was placed by the king in the care of Edward Guildford, an Esquire of the Body to Henry VII, and the son of Sir Richard Guildford, sometime controller of the household, who had fallen from favour and died on a pilgrimage to the Holy Land in 1506.[61] Guildford was granted John's wardship and this arrangement was confirmed by statute in Henry's second parliament, at which point Edmund's attainder was reversed and John was restored in blood.[62] It certainly could not be said that Henry VIII pursued the Dudleys with malice. He seems to have acknowledged that Edmund's execution had been an act of political expediency. The feofments referred to in Dudley's will were carried out in accordance with his wishes, and Sir David Owen was awarded the sum of £100 'to be levied and taken of the lands late put in feofment to the use of the performance of the will and of the payment of the debts of the said Edmund Dudley …'.[63] His property was restored to his son, with certain provisos, and presumably the provisions which he made for his children were honoured, to the immediate benefit of their lawful guardians. Whether his brother Peter, who makes his sole appearance in the will, was similarly supported, we do not know. In these circumstances it seems highly unlikely that young John, who can have known his father only slightly, would have grown up in the shadow of treason. Nor was he any less well provided for than the sons of many other substantial gentlemen on the fringes of the court who had the misfortune to die while their heirs were still minors. The Dudleys were not stained or discredited in any way by Edmund's treason, and there is no reason to suppose that the unpopularity which attended Henry VII's 'fiscal judge' in the last years of his life transferred itself in any way to his children.

---

[61] *DNB*; Gunn, 'Courtiers of Henry VII'.   [62] Statute 3 Henry VIII, c. 19.
[63] SP1/2, fos. 5–6. It is significant that Sir David Owen should have been given this responsibility. Owen had been Henry VII's Chief Carver, and a leading courtier. Dudley was never noted as a courtier himself, but he clearly had friends at the highest level (Gunn, 'Courtiers of Henry VII').

1

John Dudley

The Young Soldier

VIRTUALLY nothing is known about John Dudley's upbringing, although a certain amount can be deduced. Although his father held numerous manors, only the contents of his house in Candlewick Street were inventoried on his attainder, and it is therefore reasonable to suppose that it was his normal residence.[1] All his children were under 6 at the time of his arrest, and would have been in the care of their mother and her servants. So when his prospects in life were temporarily destroyed, John would have known nothing but the nursery in Candlewick Street, and such elementary instruction as would normally have been given to a little boy 'among the women'. During the uncertain period between Edmund's arrest and his execution over a year later, presumably he and his brothers remained with their mother, but it is not known where, or with whom, she lived during this period. Both her father and her brother were dead, and her nearest kin was her elder sister, Anne, the wife of John Willoughby. She may have taken refuge there, but there is no means of knowing.[2] On 12 November 1511 she remarried, her second husband being Arthur Plantagenet, the illegitimate son of King Edward IV. The following day Arthur received a grant of some of the lands which remained in the king's hands following Edmund Dudley's attainder, but no mention was made of John's wardship, or of the custody of any of the boys.[3] Instead, in February 1512 Edward Guildford petitioned for, and was granted by statute, 'the wardship ... of the said John Dudley while under age without account to the king', and with permission to enter without suing livery.[4] At 7, John would have been just about old enough to have been sent to another household, even under normal circumstances, and so we do not know whether this arrangement was amicable, or the result of a dispute.[5]

[1] PRO E154/2/17.
[2] Anne and Elizabeth were co-heirs, and the lands which Elizabeth had inherited from her father were not touched by her husband's attainder, so she would not have been without resources. On the other hand it cannot be assumed that any of her properties were available for occupation at short notice.
[3] *Letters and Papers of the Reign of Henry VIII*, ed. J. S. Brewer *et al.* (London, 1862–1932), i. 1965.
[4] Statute 3 Henry VIII, c. 19.
[5] There were hints later that his new stepfather, Sir Arthur Plantagenet, felt that he should have had custody of the boy.

In consideration of the good service 'which the said John Dudley is likely
to do', his father's attainder was annulled, and he himself restored 'in name
and blood' by the same Act. A number of provisos then protected the rights
of named individuals, presumably those who had already received grants
of former Dudley property, but also including Elizabeth, 'now wife to
Arthur Plantagenet Esquire'. It seems that little could have been left to
reward Edward Guildford for his guardianship, unless it was those lands
which had already been enfeoffed to John Dudley's use before his father's
fall.[6] Elizabeth may well have felt that Guildford would give her son a
better start in life than could be hoped for from her second husband, a man
of some substance and affectionately regarded by the king, but without
either energy or political ambition. Edward and Henry Guildford were the
sons of Sir Richard, who had been high in Henry VII's favour until his
rather mysterious fall from grace in 1505.[7] Edward was a close friend of
Charles Brandon, had attended his secret wedding in 1508, and stood god-
father to his daughter.[8] By 1512 both the Guildford brothers were Esquires
of the body, and members of that close group of boon companions with
which the young Henry VIII surrounded himself in the early years of his
reign. Henry Guildford had been a member of the king's household before
his accession, and Edward may have been. They were both prominent in
the jousts and other entertainments of the court, and received frequent
small gifts for their pains. The political importance of these companions
may be doubted at this early stage. They were soldiers by talent and inclination, but Edward already held the significant office of Warden of the
Cinq Ports in 1511, and must have appeared to be a rising man. He played
a prominent part in the campaign of 1513, and was knighted at the seige of
Tournai.[9] His principal seat was at Halden in Kent, and it was there that
John Dudley must have spent most of his boyhood.

In such a household he would have been brought up in the traditional
manner of an English gentleman, with much emphasis upon outdoor
sports and martial skills. It would have been very unusual at such a date for
him to have been sent either to school or university, and there is no evidence that he did either. Nor was he encouraged to follow his father's calling of the law.[10] No doubt he shared the services of a tutor with Sir
Edward's own son, Richard, and his daughter Jane. In later life he was to be
literate, and able to hold his own at court, but he was never to show any particular enthusiasm for learning, nor to be noted for his patronage of scho-

---

[6] PRO SP1/2, fos. 5–8.

[7] They were half-brothers rather than full brothers, Edward having been born to Sir
Richard's first wife, Anne Piper, and Henry to his second wife.

[8] PRO C24/28, 29; S. J. Gunn, *Charles Brandon, Duke of Suffolk, 1484–1545* (Oxford, 1988), 6.

[9] E. Hall, *The unione of the two noble and illustre famelies of York and Lancastre*, ed. H. Ellis
(London, 1809), 566.

[10] B. L. Beer, *Northumberland* (Kent, Oh., 1973), 7, says 'John Dudley, like his father, became
a lawyer and used his profession for self gain.' I have been unable to find any evidence of this.

larship. His model was his guardian and his academic training, if not exactly neglected, was no more than conventional. At 9, he would have been far too young to have witnessed Sir Edward's knighting, or to have played any part in the war which ended in the summer of 1514, but the war was one of great importance for the Guildford family. When Sir Thomas Knyvett and Sir Edward Howard were killed in action in 1512 and 1513, some of their offices came to Edward and Henry, most notably the position of Standard bearer to Sir Henry. Their friend Charles Brandon also succeeded Howard as Master of the Horse. By the summer of 1517 Sir Edward had become Master of the Armoury and *ex officio* judge of the jousts which the king staged for the benefit of visiting ambassadors.[11] As the chief performers were the king himself, and Brandon, who had been created duke of Suffolk in 1514, this was a position of no mean trust and responsibility. There is no evidence that young John accompanied his guardian to court when the latter was discharging his duties there, but at 13 he would have been old enough to make himself useful. Sir Edward seems to have treated him very much as a son, and may have betrothed him to his daughter at an early stage, so an introduction to the court, like an introduction to warfare, would have been a natural part of his education.

A courtier's life, however, had its hazards as well as its benefits. In May 1516 the king's sister Margaret, the dowager queen of Scotland, paid a visit to London. She was sumptuously entertained with the inevitable jousts, and the nobility, led by the marquis of Dorset and the earl of Surrey, were called upon to play a leading role. Soon after they found themselves in trouble for unlawful retaining.[12] Lord Chancellor Wolsey had taken careful stock of the retinues with which they had attended upon the king, and found them excessive. Dorset, Surrey, and Lord Abergavenny were temporarily excluded from the council, the earl of Northumberland was proceeded against in Star Chamber, and Sir Edward Guildford was among several members of the household who were indicted in King's Bench. He does not seem to have been tried, and a fine in Star Chamber was the worst that any of them suffered. Wolsey's purpose was to remind his master's courtiers that the king's favour did not place them above the law, and Henry was wise enough to allow that lesson to be administered without protest. Sir Edward's overenthusiasm does not seem to have cost him any part of the king's confidence, and in 1518 he became a founder member of the Privy Chamber. This inner circle of the court had existed since the latter day's of Henry VII's reign, but had consisted only of humble servants. Henry VIII's young friends were knights and esquires of the body, and as such members of the Chamber staff, under the authority of the Lord

---

[11] Hall, *Unione*, 592. Sir Edward is first described as Master of the King's Armoury on a receipt which he issued in Feb. 1513; *L. and P.*, i. 1629.

[12] E. Lodge, *Illustrations of British History* (London, 1838), i. 13, 16, 23, 27–8.

Chamberlain. However in 1518 Francis I sent an embassy into England to negotiate the return of Tournai as a part of a long-term peace settlement. Among those who came were six of his *Gentils hommes de la Chambre*. In the ceremonies which followed these young noblemen were naturally paired with Henry's 'minions' who thereafter were known as the Gentlemen of the Privy Chamber.[13] The formalization of this group into a distinct department of the court was a development of great importance. Once they had established control over the premises of the Privy Chamber, they could control, to some extent at least, access to the king. The king's council soon made it clear that they considered this to be an undesirable development, and when some of the gentlemen made fools of themselves on a return visit to France, the council informed Henry that his honour was being tarnished by the familiarity which he allowed to these irresponsible young men.[14]

Wolsey may have been behind this move, but there is no contemporary evidence to indicate that he was. The king took his councillors' advice in good part, and Nicholas Carew 'with divers other also of the privy chamber' were banished from the court in May 1519. 'And they that had offices were commaunded to go to their offices; which discharge oute of the courte greved sore the hartes of these younge menne.'[15] It is not clear whether Edward Guildford was one of those banished in this way—he was not particularly young—but he was appointed Knight Marshall of Calais later in the same year, and seems to have gone to his post. John Dudley was about 15 by this time, and may well have accompanied his guardian across the channel. He was old enough to be useful, and his serious military apprenticeship was about to begin. Unfortunately there are no specific references to him between 1513, when Guildford obtained an *inspeximus* of the statute granting him the wardship, and 1521 when, as a youth of 17, he joined Wolsey's retinue during his abortive mediation between France and the Empire.[16] The John Dudley who appears among the feofees of several manors of the earl of Worcester in South Wales, and was a knight of the body in 1516, was the son of Edward, Lord Dudley, and was to succeed him in the title in 1532. He was several years older than our subject, and had been an esquire of the body at Henry VII's funeral.[17]

Edward Guildford's ward began his career in 1523 when, at the age of 19, he served as a lieutenant under his guardian in the duke of Suffolk's army. This was a large expeditionary force of about 11,000 men, which landed at Calais in September. The lateness of the season can be explained by the fact that it had almost not been sent at all. Although Henry had entered into an

---

[13] Hall, *Unione*, 293–4; D. Starkey, 'Intimacy and Innovation: The Rise of the Privy Chamber, 1485–1547', in *The English Court from the Wars of the Roses to the Civil War* (London, 1987), 80–2.

[14] Hall, *Unione*, 598.   [15] Ibid.

[16] A. Wood, *Athenae Oxoniensis*, ed. P. Bliss (Oxford, 1813), i. 12; C. Sturge, 'John Dudley, Earl of Warwick and Duke of Northumberland', Ph.D. Thesis, University of London, 1927, 15.

[17] G. E. Cockayne, *The Complete Peerage*, rev. V. Sibbs (London, 1910–49), iv. 480.

aggressive alliance with the emperor in 1521, committing himself to war in 1522, when it came to the point he was less than enthusiastic. Wolsey had never wanted the war in the first place and England's only contribution during 1522 was a raid on the Breton coast.[18] When Charles reproached his ally with slackness, Henry urged the advantages of a year's truce. There seemed to be a threat building up in Scotland, and money was in short supply. Throughout the winter of 1522–3 the emperor continued to urge action with increasing annoyance and frustration. By April 1523 Henry had agreed to send over a small contingent later in the summer, but nothing happened except some small-scale raids into Scotland which were no help to Charles at all. What altered this situation was a violent quarrel between Francis I and Charles, duke of Bourbon, the Constable of France. This had arisen over the duchess's inheritance, and by the end of 1522 had driven the duke into treason. He entered into negotiations with both Charles V and Henry, offering to support the allied war effort with his own substantial affinity. At the end of July 1523 a new treaty was signed by the duke and the two monarchs, committing them all to an immediate joint campaign.[19] Both Henry and Wolsey scented a real chance of profit and success, and the English contribution duly appeared some six weeks later. The plan was for Margaret of Austria, the regent of the Low Countries, to support the English with troops and supplies, but this undertaking had been made by the emperor, and Margaret was following her own agenda in Friesland. The result was further delay, and it was well into October before the joint Anglo-Imperial force began to move south, hoping to link up with the duke of Bourbon's following on the far side of the Somme.

This rendezvous had played a large part in sustaining the morale of Suffolk's men, who were already suffering from disease and the deteriorating weather. As Edward Hall recorded

In these iorneys was comonly spoken that the duke of Burbon with his x M Almaynes would have invaded Fraunce and so ioyned with this army, but ye truth was contrary, for he turned his host another way and went into province and layde seige to Marcelles, whero the duke being advertised not a little mused, and also seyng his menne daily fall sick was sory ...[20]

In spite of this reverse, the campaign so far had gone well. Numerous towns and fortifications had been taken, supplies of ordnance seized, and the townsmen sworn to the service of the king of England. Francis was seriously alarmed, and hastened to pour reinforcements into Paris. Suffolk was not a dashing commander, but he was competent and well supported, particularly by William, Lord Sandys. Among those 'mentioned in despatches'

---

[18] Hall, *Unione*, 462; D. Loades, *The Tudor Navy* (Aldershot, 1992), 105; J. J. Scarisbrick, *Henry VIII* (London, 1968), 94–5.

[19] *L. and P.*, iii. 2333, 2360.

[20] Hall, *Unione*, 670; S. J. Gunn, 'The Duke of Suffolk's March on Paris in 1523', *English Historical Review*, 101 (1986), 596–634.

for feats of skill or gallantry was Sir Edward Guildford, who on 14 November captured the castle of Bohen or Boghan 'whiche ever was thought to be impregnable', taking advantage of the early frosts to assault it across the marshes. Already, on 1 November, the duke had dubbed fourteen knights, including Edward Seymour, the future duke of Somerset, and on 7 November John Dudley and Robert Ughtred.[21] What particular feats of gallantry either of them had performed to earn this recognition is not recorded. Although this was Dudley's first major campaign, it was not his first taste of military action. The French had been probing the defences of Calais since the spring of 1522, and Sir Edward Guildford had led a number of counter-attacks. John is not specifically mentioned in the surviving accounts of these small actions, but that is almost certainly where he gained his initial experience of warfare, and earned the right to accompany his guardian on the expedition which was to bring him his first major opportunity. He had obtained the regular position of Lieutenant of the Spears at Calais in August 1523, before the campaign began, and as that post would have been in the gift of the Lord Deputy rather than the Marshall, his advancement cannot be attributed to mere nepotism. He was a very promising young soldier.

Suffolk's campaign had fizzled out by the end of the year, and the effort was not repeated. Henry had good cause to be disappointed with his allies, and the caution of 1522 returned. Parliament had reluctantly voted an inadequate subsidy, and even if the king had been more bellicose than he was, he could not have afforded much in the way of active campaigning. The defeat and capture of Francis at Pavia in February 1525 briefly rekindled an ardour which looked suspiciously like greed, but not only was the emperor unwilling to allow his sluggish ally any share in the fruits of his victory, Wolsey's strenuous efforts to raise the necessary money also failed humiliatingly.[22] So, for ardent young men like Sir John Dudley, it was back to skirmishing around the Calais Pale. How much time he actually spent in that congenial occupation we do not know. By the end of 1524 the king had appointed him an Esquire of the Body, and he must have spent a part of the year at court. Since the rise of the Privy Chamber such a position no longer had the significance which it would have had twenty years earlier, but it was still a mark of especial favour, particularly for so young a man who was not of noble blood. At Christmas 1524 fifteen of these esquires, John Dudley being one, 'enterprised a chalenge of feactes of armes', which resulted in one of those elaborate tournaments so beloved by the king, and so lovingly described by Edward Hall.[23] The group included John and Leonard Grey,

---

[21]   Hall, *Unione*, 671. According to another source Dudley's companion on this occasion was Robert Barber (*L. and P.*, iii. 3516; BL MS Add. 10110, fo. 236).

[22]   This was the so-called 'Amicable Grant', discussed at length by G. W. Bernard in *War, Taxation, and Rebellion in Early Tudor England* (Brighton, 1986), *passim*.

[23]   Hall, *Unione*, 688.

the brothers of the marquis of Dorset, William Cary, Thomas Wyatt, Sir Edward Seymour, Oliver Manners, and Francis Sidney. Henry's jousting days were coming to an end, but on this occasion he led the answerers, incognito, supported by the Duke of Suffolk and a team drawn from his Privy Chamber. This was select company for the son of an attainted traitor who had still not achieved his majority, but given his guardian's position and influence, not a situation which should occasion any surprise.

Over the next few years Dudley remains an elusive figure. In 1525 he reached his majority, and presumably took livery of his lands, although there does not seem to be any record of the fact. He was not to feature on any commission of the peace for another six years, but apparently held lands in Surrey, Sussex, Hampshire, and Warwickshire. There were a number of John Dudleys about, in addition to Lord Dudley's heir, and identification is not always certain. He was probably not the man of that name whom Henry Chauncey had consulted about the manor of Bedworth, as he reported to Sir Arthur Plantagenet in February 1523, nor he who received an annuity in Wales in 1526.[24] Collecting rents in Coventry in 1524 is a shade more plausible, but that was probably also a different person. Only in 1527 do authentic references begin to appear. By that time Sir John was a young man of some substance; and he had also taken a wife. No doubt this marriage had always featured in Sir Edward Guildford's calculations, since the bride was his daughter Jane, who had been about 3 when her father had obtained the wardship. She had been born at some time during 1509, and was thus about five years younger than John. They may well have been betrothed as children, but were probably not married until a sensible age of cohabitation, which would have been some time between 1525 and 1527. Their third son, also John, had been born by 1528 but it is not possible to identify any of the dates more precisely.[25] It appears to have been a congenial arrangement for both parties, since they produced thirteen children, eight of them sons, and Jane was to survive her husband's execution by less than eighteen months, dying in January 1555 at the relatively young age of 46.

Where they lived in the early days of their marriage is not apparent, but it was probably upon one of Dudley's own properties in Surrey or Sussex. He did not at first make any mark in local affairs, and seems to have remained principally a courtier. In May 1527 he was licensed to alienate the manors of Bury and Swavelyng in Hampshire, and was named as one of a distinguished body of feoffees, headed by the earl of Northumberland, and

---

[24] *L. and P.*, iv, App. 1.

[25] The chronology of John and Jane's children presents a number of problems. The eldest, Henry, had already been knighted when he died, apparently during the seige of Boulogne in 1544. He can hardly have been less than 18 at that point, which would place his birth at some point in 1526. A second son, Thomas, who died as an infant, also has to be fitted in between Henry and John. It is probably safest to assume that the parents were married either late in 1525 or early in 1526 (*Complete Peerage*, ix. 726); BL MS Stowe 652 (Dudley pedigree).

including both Stephen Gardiner and Thomas Cromwell, which was set up
to administer the manors of Staunton Drew and Staunton Wykes.[26] This
was probably an arrangement set up by Wolsey, because both Gardiner
and Cromwell were in his service at that time, and Dudley was one of half
a dozen courtiers brought in to give the scheme a necessary weight and
credibility. Sir John's relations with the cardinal are not known to have
been close, but they were never hostile, and from Wolsey's point of view he
had the great advantage of not belonging to any of the great noble affinities.
He was friendly with both Dorset and Suffolk, but not dependent upon
either of them. Like Sir Edward Guildford, he was the king's man. Consequently when the international situation demanded a major embassy by
Wolsey to France in the summer of 1527, Sir John Dudley was one of over
nine hundred noblemen and gentlemen who formed his imposing
entourage.[27] The cardinal's task was to mediate a peace between Francis
and Charles, hoping that the shock recently administered through the sack
of Rome by an army operating in his name would have made the latter
more amenable to pressure. There was also a hidden agenda, which was
beginning to give everyone nightmares. After a great deal of soul searching, the king had come to the conclusion that his eighteen-year-old marriage to Queen Catherine was unlawful. Wolsey, who thought that he knew
all about the king's conscience, had made reassuring noises about his own
ability to secure an annulment from Rome.[28] Privately he may have been
less confident, but the pope's imprisonment seemed to offer a solution to
this as well. Wolsey drafted a bull for Clement to sign, conferring full
authority upon the cardinal of England to exercise the papal office for the
duration of his constraint. He would then convene as many cardinals as
were at liberty in Avignon, and set up an interim government for the
Church, which would mediate peace and resolve the king of England's
dilemma at the same time.

In spite of Wolsey's confidence, this was an extremely hopeful programme. Even if he managed to obtain plenary power, it would be essential
to secure the peace before the emperor found out about Henry's intentions.
As Catherine's nephew he would be implacably opposed to any annulment, which would have been a blow both to his family honour and his
political interests. Moreover, it soon became apparent that Wolsey no
longer had Henry's full confidence. Instead of keeping the matter secret, as
they had agreed, the king had already informed Catherine of his intentions,
a month before the embassy set out.[29] It was not in the queen's interests to
broadcast this news, and Wolsey did not know what had happened, but
Charles was swiftly informed by way of his ambassador in England. He

[26] *L. and P.*, iv. 3119: 15 May 1527.   [27] Ibid. 3216: 1 July 1527.
[28] Ibid. 3140; PRO SP2/Ci; Scarisbrick, *Henry VIII*, 155.
[29] Nicholas Pocock (ed.), *Records of the Reformation: The Divorce, 1527–1533* (Oxford, 1870),
i. 11.

had consequently already declared his position, and informed Clement, before Wolsey's bid for temporary authority was made. By the time that he crossed to France on 22 July, his mission was already hopeless. Henry may have realized this, because he compounded his envoy's problems by making a direct approach to the pope at the same time, without informing him. While Wolsey was meeting Francis at Amiens on 9 August, and apparently making splendid progress, William Knight, the king's secretary, was on his way to Rome with the very peculiar request that the king of England should be licensed to commit bigamy.[30] The cardinal got wind of what was afoot in time to stop Knight, but not to frustrate his mission. While Henry wrote smooth letters to his minister, reaffirming his confidence in him, he also secretly ordered Knight to proceed, not with the demand which Wolsey had detected, but with another of which he continued in ignorance. Whatever the king might say, it was obvious to Wolsey that for the first time in over a decade, his voice was not supreme in Henry's council. The king had obviously decided to dissemble before Wolsey had set off for France, but he would only be able to remedy the situation by returning. At the end of September he was back in London, having achieved nothing except a sumptuous exchange of courtesies. Sir John Dudley's diplomatic baptism had been very mild. As a middle-ranking member of the entourage it is unlikely that he was called upon to do anything other than participate in courtly ceremonies. As the head of his mission was an ecclesiastic, jousting would not have been considered a suitable form of entertainment, and he would certainly not have been privy to any of the high-level discussions. The cardinal had played his cards very close to his chest, perhaps in an attempt to reassert the uniqueness of his position. On his return

he cam to Richmond, to the king of England, and there ascertained the kyng of all his doynges, but so could no lord that then was in Commission with him, for they knew nothing of all his doynges, which sore greved their stomackes.[31]

Neither Guildford nor Dudley was closely associated with Wolsey, and if anything the reverberations of his fall benefited them. At some point between 1523 and 1528 John's mother Lady Elizabeth Plantagenet died. This should have conferred the barony of Lisle upon her son, but the title had already been bestowed upon her second husband, who had been created Viscount Lisle on 27 April 1523, and John's right was neither recognized nor claimed.[32] Whether he inherited any property from her is not apparent, but his father's alleged misdeeds still surfaced from time to time. In 1527 one John Maryng claimed that the late Edmund Dudley had fraudulently obtained possession of some of the lands in Sussex and the Isle of

<hr>

[30] *State Papers of Henry VIII*, vii. 3. The text of the original request does not survive (Scarisbrick, *Henry VIII*, 159).

[31] Hall, *Unione*, 732.

[32] *Complete Peerage*, viii, 64–5. Elizabeth was certainly dead by 1529, when Arthur married Honor Grenville. She probably died in 1525 or 1526.

Wight which Sir John was presently holding, and petitioned Wolsey for redress.[33] It may have been Elizabeth's death which determined the timing of this petition, although there is no suggestion that she had obtained the lands after her husband's attainder, and we do not know the outcome of the suit. By 1528 the court was already beginning to divide over the king's Great Matter, and Dudley began to be associated with the Boleyn party. We do not know when this happened, because he was not important enough at this stage for anyone to have commented upon his behaviour, but by 1532 he was clearly in favour, and increasingly associated with Thomas Cromwell, then just beginning his spectacular rise in the king's service. John first appeared upon the commissions of the peace for Surrey and Sussex in February 1531.[34] This recognition was not connected with any identifiable change in his status or prospects, but it can be taken to mean that he was *persona grata* with the council, and was thus preferred to other men of similar rank and wealth. In March 1532 he obtained his first office, a joint grant in survivorship with Sir Francis Bryan of the constableship of Warwick castle, and of the lordship and borough of Warwick. Bryan had previously held this position jointly with the marquis of Dorset, who had died in 1530, and the fact that Dudley was foisted on him in this way may have been a small sign the erstwhile minion was beginning to find his favour eroded. A number of lesser offices were attached to the constableship: keeper of the manor of Gooderest, keeper of Weggenoke Park, and master of the hunt there. The fees attached to these various posts amounted to about £45 a year, and most of the duties were presumably discharged by deputy. When the commissions of the peace were issued in the same year, Dudley added Warwickshire to Surrey and Sussex, the office of constable giving him status in a county where he had little, if any, land.[35]

Also in March 1532 he obtained his first wardship, that of Anthony, son of the late Richard Norton of Worcestershire. Whether this was purchased or granted as a mark of favour is not clear, but it carried with it 260 acres of land in Kingsnorton, Feckingham, and Clevys, all in Worcestershire, together with two burgages in the City of Worcester.[36] In July he stood surety, along with Sir Arthur Darcy and Richard Rich, for the repayment of £1,000 which Sir Edward Seymour had borrowed from the king, an arrangement which seems to have been made by Sir Brian Tuke, the Treasurer of the Chamber, and Thomas Cromwell.[37] Dudley was clearly recognized as a man of substance by this time, and his career at court was developing satisfactorily, in spite of the fact that there had been no more war, and that Henry's jousting days were over. He probably gave up his post in Calais at the end of the war, as there are no further references to him in that connection. In 1532 also he began a tangled and acrimonious series

---

[33] *L. and P.*, iv. 3727.   [34] Ibid., v. 119 (52).   [35] Ibid. 909, 1694.
[36] Ibid. 909   [37] Ibid. 1205.

of transactions with his kinsman and namesake. Edward, Lord Dudley, died in debt, and his son John, who succeeded him, already had debts of his own. 'To keep myself from prison', he later complained to Cromwell 'I was constrained to make shift with such lands as he left me in fee, of which I made bargain with Sir John Dudley for £2,000'.[38] This sum he bound himself to repay in annual instalments of £400, due on 12 May each year. By the following year he was complaining vigorously that he had received only £1,400 and that Sir John was dunning him for repayment. When this episode is commented upon, it is normally taken to have been an early example of that unscrupulous greed for which Dudley is supposed to have been later notorious. However, the truth may have been rather different. It would have been quite reasonable to have loaned Lord Dudley £1,400 on the security of some of his lands, and then bound him to repay £2,000 over five years. That would have amounted to an interest charge of 30 per cent spread over the whole repayment period—or 6 per cent per annum, which was not at all usurious. Lord Dudley's indignation may have arisen from his own failure to understand the nature of the transaction rather than from any malpractice on Sir John's part.

Sir John was not the only creditor. The new baron was also bound in 'certain obligations' to Sir John Alen, having apparently borrowed £200 upon the security of the manors of Swynford and Hembley. He also seems to have mortgaged the balance of his lands to Sir John for £6,000. 'I am', he lamented 'also bound to him in the forfeiture of all my lands to the sum of £6,000, according to certain covenants, to the undoing of me and my family.'[39] In the circumstances his plea to Cromwell that the king should take his lordship of Sedgely, and discharge the £2,200 which he owed Alen and Dudley was extremely ingenuous. His fortunes were in such terminal decline that it is not surprising that he did not dare to show his face at court. The excuse 'that Sir John Dudley lays wait for me in the City of London, to keep me afore the days of payment', probably reflects his unwillingness to face his creditors rather than any threat of physical violence, since there would have been little point in bullying a man who was already so helpless. On 11 May 1533, the eve of another payment day, he wrote again, begging Cromwell to make his payment for him, and offering him the surety of four manors worth £40 a year which were part of his wife's jointure, and therefore not already mortgaged to his cousin.[40] This time the excuse was that he had been 'marvellously deceived' of £400 which he had been promised by some other kinsman unnamed. It is not surprising that the mortgage was eventually foreclosed, and the bulk of his inheritance, including Dudley castle, passed into Sir John's hands.[41] The wretched Lord Dudley soon

---

[38] Ibid. 1727   [39] Ibid.   [40] Ibid., vi. 467: 11 May 1533.
[41] This must have happened between May 1537, when there is a record of a sale of land by Lord Dudley to Sir John Dudley 'of Sussex', and Feb. 1539 when the latter is described as 'of Dudley, Staffordshire' when entering into a recognizance (*L. and P.*, xii. 1537; ibid., xiv. i. 357).

became known as the 'lord quondam', and seems to have been something
of a laughing stock. He was never summoned to parliament, or called upon
to perform any of the other duties which would normally have been associated with his rank. This may well have been because of his poverty rather
than because of mental deficiency, which is the usual reason given. He had
been sufficiently *compos mentis* to command a company during the Flodden
campaign in 1513 and his letters, pathetic as they are in some ways, are sufficiently lucid. He seems to have blamed his successful cousin for his misfortunes, but this was less than fair. Lord Dudley was the author of his own
shipwreck, and the worst that can be said of Sir John is that he treated his
kinsman as a normal business client rather than a suitable case for charity.
These transactions are significant, not so much for the demise of Lord Dudley as for the light which they cast upon Sir John's affairs. At the age of
about 28, having come into a modest inheritance some seven years before,
he was in a position to lend over £7,000. Wealth, or credit, on that scale carries power, and it may be significant that Richard Fermour, merchant of the
Staple, had been one of his fellow sureties when he stood bound for Sir
Edward Seymour. By 1533, in addition to being a courtier and a soldier, Sir
John Dudley was a shrewd man of affairs with access to significant
resources of capital. Among the papers which Thomas Cromwell's office
generated at some point during the year was a valor of Sir John Dudley's
lands.[42] The all-powerful Secretary was becoming distinctly interested in
this promising young man.

Anne Boleyn was crowned with exceptional magnificence, the festivities
lasting for five days from 29 May to 2 June. The reasons for this were purely
political, as Henry flaunted his defiance of the pope, and mobilized in the
most visible manner the support of his courtiers, nobles, and subjects. As a
Knight of the Body, Dudley was naturally called upon to play his part. Even
if he had been unsympathetic to the Boleyns he could hardly have avoided
the duties which were laid upon him. So the facts that he served as Archbishop Cranmer's cupbearer at the coronation banquet, and bore christening gifts to the infant princess Elizabeth in September, although interesting,
are hardly significant of his political allegiance.[43] More indicative, probably, is the relationship which he was beginning to develop with Sir Edward
Seymour. Before her death his mother Elizabeth had made a settlement of
her lands, whereby John was entitled to inherit most of them after the death
of her second husband, Lord Lisle. By 1532 he had begun to sell these
reversionary rights. It is not surprising that he felt no attachment to places
which he had never seen, and which he might wait long to possess, and he
probably needed the money for his transactions with Lord Dudley. For
whatever reason, he sold reversions in Devon to the marquis of Exeter, in
Gloucestershire to Thomas Cromwell, and in Somerset to Sir Edward Sey-

---

[42] *L. and P.*, vi. 299, ix G.   [43] Ibid. 562, ii. 1111.

mour.[44] Seymour then rented the Somerset lands from Lisle for £140 a year. At Easter 1533 a dispute arose. Lisle's title to the estate was secured by a recovery, followed by a release made by the feofees to use, and confirmed by an agreement between Lisle and Dudley. Because of an oversight, part of the land had not been secured in this way, and Seymour witheld £60 of the agreed rent on the ground that so much of the land was legally now his, since he had purchased Dudley's right. Lisle threatened to sue Seymour for the missing rent, and Sir Edward counter-claimed that Lisle had not disclosed encumbrances upon the estate.[45] In November he offered to purchase Lisle's life interest for £500, but the latter refused and lodged a complaint in Chancery. In February 1534 both sides agreed to arbitration, and in March Lisle wrote to Cromwell, complaining bitterly of the wrong which was being done to him. He clearly regarded Seymour and Dudley as being in conspiracy against him, and denounced the latter for filial ingratitude.[46] When Cromwell and Audley eventually arbitrated in July 1534, the Secretary was fairly sharp with Seymour, telling him that he had handled Lisle 'very craftly' over the £60. If Dudley had disclosed the true legal situation to Seymour at the beginning, then it would appear that the latter had never intended to honour his rental agreement with Lisle, and a conspiracy, or at least an understanding, seems likely. However, when Cromwell confronted Dudley with this charge, he denied it upon his honour as a gentleman. If he spoke the truth, then Seymour was a rather unscrupulous opportunist, but not a conspirator.[47]

Sir Andrew Windsor, who reported this exchange to Lisle, believed that the Secretary had been scrupulously fair. The law would support Seymour over the £60, but he might have a remedy against Dudley, presumably for not disclosing the defect in the release at the time when he made his agreement. This suggestion does not seem to have been followed up, and a Chancery award was finally made in February 1535. Such disputes were part of the everyday life of a man in Dudley's position, and it is by no means clear that he behaved reprehensibly. Although Cromwell was clearly sympathetic to Lisle over this issue, Dudley continued to grow in his favour. In April 1534 one of the Secretary's innumerable memoranda pencilled him in for the prestigious office of Vice-Chamberlain.[48] In the event Sir John Gage continued to hold the post until 1536, when he was replaced by Sir William Kingston, but the fact that Dudley could be seriously considered for such a

[44] Ibid., xiii. ii. 28: Henry Polsted to Cromwell on the conclusion of the Gloucestershire transaction, 3 Aug. 1538; M. L. Bush, 'The Lisle–Seymour Land Disputes', *Historical Journal*, 9 (1966), 255–74.

[45] Sir Edward Seymour to Lord Lisle, 4 Feb. 1534 (*L. and P.* viii. 159); Bush, 'Lisle–Seymour Land Disputes'.

[46] Lisle to Cromwell, 10 Mar. 1534 (*L. and P.*, viii. 309).

[47] Sir Andrew Windsor to Lord Lisle, July 1534. Seymour apparently claimed that Dudley had told him (*L. and P.*, viii. 92).

[48] Ibid. 583.

responsibility is an eloquent testimony to his standing in the court. The office which he did receive on 11 June was that of Master of the Armoury of the Tower of London, less significant, but still a major mark of favour.[49] It had fallen vacant just a week earlier, through the death of his father-in-law and former guardian, Sir Edward Guildford.

Guildford's death was a major event for Dudley, because he died intestate and without a direct heir, his son Richard having predeceased him. This led to an immediate conflict between John Dudley and John Guildford, the son of Sir Edward's brother George, who had died two years earlier. Sir John Gage, who was a close and long-time friend of the dead man, had visited him at Leeds castle just a few days earlier, and finding him 'sick and in doubt of his recovery', had urged him to make his will. Sir Edward had agreed, and sent for a lawyer.[50] Meanwhile, as Gage later reported, 'He told me his mind in everything that afternoon', and Gage in turn confided in Sir Edward Wotton, John Crowmer, and John Guildford—presumably the intended executors. However, Sir Edward died without accomplishing his intention, and John Guildford immediately set out for Halden, where Sir John Dudley was then living. He may have been simply intending to inform the latter of Sir Edward's last wishes, but he probably went to lay claim to the property, believing it to be a part of his inheritance. Gage anticipated trouble, and urged that 'an indifferent person' should be placed in charge of the manor until the question of right was resolved.[51] He also asked that Lord La Warr should be sent down to Leeds castle itself to 'be a stay' between Guildford and Dudley. Christopher Hales, writing to Cromwell on the same day, identified the same need, and urged that the responsibility be given to Anthony St Leger, who was a near neighbour.[52] If violence was anticipated, it did not arise. Sir John remained in possession of Halden, from whence he wrote to Cromwell a few days later, asking for the custody of Sir Edward's goods once they had been properly inventoried. The Secretary could not prevent the parties from going to law, but at the end of June his remembrances included bills and warrants to be signed for Sir Edward Guildford's affairs, and one for Guildford and Dudley. Dudley, like many other courtiers at this point, professed to see Cromwell as his 'good master', and it was by exercising favour in cases of this kind that the Secretary recruited clients for his other purposes. On 11 October Dudley wrote to him again, reporting extensive flood damage in Gilford marshes. Both he and John Guildford had suffered heavily, he reported, but Guild-

---

[49] *L. and P.*, viii. 1026 (15). The office carried a fee of 12*d*. a day, with 6*d*. for a page, and the use of certain designated buildings on Tower wharf and Tower hill.

[50] Gage to Norfolk, 4 June 1534. The lawyer for whom he sent was his kinsman Baron John Hale, but he did not arrive in time (*L. and P.*, viii. 789).

[51] Ibid. La Warr was John Guildford's brother-in-law, and his impartiality might be questioned.

[52] Ibid. 788.

ford was doing nothing to help repair the damage. Part of the damaged land belonged to the king, having been taken in payment of Sir Edward Guildford's debts to the Crown. 'I beg you', he concluded, 'to be my good master in this, that my enemies may take no advantage against me'.[53] At the same time Sir John was demonstrating his value to the government by denouncing to Cromwell certain 'lewd priests' who were failing to display sufficient enthusiasm for the royal supremacy. One good turn deserved another.

When parliament reconvened in November 1534, Sir John followed his father-in-law as a knight of the shire for Kent.[54] This may have been a recognition of his status by the county community, or it may have been another piece of Cromwell's patronage. Probably it was a bit of both. Clearly by this time anyone who wanted to put pressure on Dudley could only do so through the Secretary. Desperate creditors like Thomas Pope wrote twice in a month complaining that he had been delayed 'from time to time as no one would have treated the lewdest fellow', and begging Cromwell to intervene.[55] However, Dudley was a useful man and his toughness as a man of business added to his value rather than the reverse. Bullying Lord Lisle's tenants, as he seems to have done during Seymour's dispute with Lisle, or making the wretched Thomas Pope wait for his money, or even frustrating his father-in-law's testamentary intentions, were the kind of tactics which brought no discredit. At this stage in his career Dudley does not impress as an amiable man, but he seems to have been one who played his games within the rules. In February 1535 his counsel was still busy 'perfecting his book' against John Guildford, and he wrote to Cromwell asking him to request the dowager Lady Guildford, Sir Edward's mother, to provide copies of the documents securing her own jointure.[56] This case seems to have ground on with inevitable slowness, and one of Dudley's tactics involved a reconciliation with Lord Lisle. Lisle had been appointed Lord Deputy of Calais in June 1532, and had resided in the town since that date. On 16 June 1535 Dudley wrote to him announcing that the king was going on progress towards Bristol, and might wish to visit one of Lisle's manors, either Painswick or King's Lisley. If Lisle would give him authority, he would be willing to act as host and 'welcome him in your absence'.[57] His stepfather must have agreed, and indeed he would have had little choice if the king's itinerary had been determined, because on 8 August Dudley wrote again, reporting on the visit. While Henry had been at Painswick, he had enquired whether any wood sales had recently been authorized within the lordship. The bailiff had replied no, not since the sale of 400 trees some

---

[53] Ibid. 1251.   [54] S. T. Bindoff, *The House of Commons, 1509–1558* (London, 1982), ii. 64.

[55] *L. and P.*, viii. 1146, 1207: 13 and 30 Sept. 1534.

[56] Dudley to Cromwell, 25 Feb. 1535 (*L. and P.*, ix. 264).

[57] This was presumably Kingston Lisle, over which there was later to be dispute (*L. and P.*, ix. 882).

time before, which had not yet been felled. The king had then desired that the transaction should be cancelled, and no further sales undertaken, as they would ruin the lordship. Dudley may indeed have been passing on a message from Henry, but he had himself been trying to prevent Lisle's tenants from felling timber, and it seems likely that Henry's somewhat improbable concern was prompted.[58]

If that was the case, Lisle seems either to have suspected nothing, or to have taken no offence. He testified in Chancery on Dudley's behalf, and on 8 October Sir John sent him a copy of his statement to sign, with a note of urgency as the case was to be heard the following week. 'There is no matter altered', he continued, 'except that I put in that you bore my father in law partly a grudge for disinheriting me, being within age ... '.[59] Lisle seems to have been offended by Sir Edward Guildford's disposal of some part of his ward's lands, although nothing else is known about this transaction. Dudley also hints that his stepfather may not have been too pleased about his marriage, either, but that was hardly an argument which would have served his purpose in this case. Various other documents relating to Sir Edward's handling of his ward's affairs were also laid before the court, and the outcome was a judgment in Dudley's favour. Occasional friendly exchanges with Lisle followed thereafter. Quite apart from their real feelings, each stood to gain by being on good terms with the other. Dudley's land transactions over these years were numerous and complex. In less than a decade he sold most of his original inheritance, as well as the reversions to his mother's lands, and shifted his main base to the midland estate which he acquired by foreclosing Lord Dudley's mortgage. Shortly after winning his case against Guildford he sold Halden and other lands in Kent to Cromwell, and began to make extensive purchases in Staffordshire and the Welsh marches. For this purpose he borrowed 2,000 marks from the Secretary in September 1535, and bound himself to repay £2,000 'at Christmas next', asking at the same time that the king should help him to find the repayment 'so that I may save a little land'.[60] That debt he would repay at £200 a year on the security of all his lands. It looks as though this was a convenient transaction whereby both could profit at the expense of the Crown. Clearly the partnership between Dudley and Cromwell was in good working order, although Sir John never did secure the Vice-Chamberlainship.

Over the next year or two Dudley can be sighted from time to time, going about his business. In August 1535 he was issuing harness from the Tower

---

[58] *L. and P.*, ix. 53; see also Leonard Smith and Sir William Kingston to Lisle, 26 May 1534 (ibid., viii. 717).

[59] Ibid., ix. App. 6.

[60] Dudley to Cromwell, 27 Aug. 1535 (*L. and P.*, ix. 193). Cromwell's hold over Dudley at this point was not only that of a patron over a client. Thomas Broke, reporting the completion of a transaction with Dudley on 24 Aug., mentioned that he had taken the opportunity to point out to Dudley 'how small in value of his goods he assessed himself unto the king', which 'to him was nothing pleasant'. Broke to Cromwell, 24 Aug. 1535 (ibid. 172).

armoury and accounting for it. In February 1536 he reported to Cromwell on the trial of a horse thief in Lichfield in which he had participated, and which for some reason had attracted the Secretary's attention.[61] The Reformation parliament was dissolved on 14 April 1536, and Anne Boleyn's dramatic fall occurred just over two weeks later. On 9 May twenty-two gentlemen of the household, including Dudley, Sir John Russell, and Sir John Gage, were summoned, presumably by Cromwell, to a consultation of unknown purpose. In view of the rumours which were rife in the wake of the queen's arrest,[62] he may have felt it wise to present the official explanation for what had happened, and to dampen down political speculation. In June the Secretary reminded himself that Dudley's bond was due to fall at Christmas, and pencilled him in for the office of King's Carver. By this time parliament had been reconvened, and in spite of his relocation, Dudley again sat for Kent. The main purpose of the session, he informed his stepfather just before it met, would be to settle the matter of the late queen. In July or early August he seems to have visited Lisle in Calais, and to have been robbed on the way.[63] Nothing else is known about this visit, which must have been a private one, for no diplomatic representations followed his misfortune. Instead Lisle wrote in some indignation to the Captain of Gravelines, complaining that a group of his men had been responsible. The Captain responded soothingly on 24 August, asking for further particulars of the place and manner of the assault, and promising to send his provost marshall to investigate.[64]

In September a combination of factors, including dissatisfaction with the recent statute against the lesser monasteries, uncertainty about the king's intentions, and dislike of Cromwell, sparked a major rebellion in Lincolnshire. The duke of Norfolk was placed in charge of the countermeasures, and on 9 October he received the 'prests' for his campaign. Among the fifteen commanders named to serve under him was Sir John Dudley, who was to lead 200 men of Sussex, one of the largest contingents.[65] By the time Norfolk arrived in the north the trouble in Lincolnshire had subsided, but he was confronted instead by the much more formidable Yorkshire rebellion—the so-called Pilgrimage of Grace. At its height this movement, which saw itself as a massive demonstration rather than a rebellion, numbered 30,000 men. Had it come to a battle Norfolk's modest force might well have been overwhelmed, but the Pilgrims were not looking for a fight. They

---

[61] Ibid. 187, 199, 229; ibid., x. 272, 291.

[62] Ibid. 834; 9 May was also the day upon which the jury was empanelled for the trial of Weston, Norris, Brereton, and Smeaton. For a discussion of these trials and their aftermath, see E. W. Ives, *Anne Boleyn* (Oxford, 1986), 382–420.

[63] Jehan de Jovar, Captain of Gravelines, to Lord Lisle, 24 Aug. 1536 (*L. and P.*, xi. 357).

[64] Ibid.

[65] Ibid. 580, 623. Dudley was also listed to be leading 100 men from Kent (ibid., App. 8). The references to Dudley during the campaign show him carrying letters between Norfolk and the king. There was no fighting.

knew what they wanted—the reversal of many recent royal policies—but they had no idea how to achieve it, and time was not on their side.[66] By a mixture of blandishments and false promises, and by exploiting their obvious reluctance to be seen in arms against their prince, Henry persuaded the Pilgrims to disperse early in December. No shot had been fired in anger, and as far as we know John Dudley's 200 men of Sussex were home in time for Christmas. However, it is unlikely that their captain was with them. In the middle of October he had been pricked as Sheriff of Staffordshire, and it is almost certain that by then his normal residence was in the West Midlands. The Pilgrimage had done nothing to enhance Dudley's reputation as a soldier, but it had demonstrated that he was considered to be a reliable supporter of the 'King's proceedings'. He was a man marked out for further responsibilities, and in January 1537 his career took a new and significant step when he was named as a vice-admiral and given the command of a small fleet which was shortly to be sent out to patrol the Narrow Seas.[67]

As far as we know, Dudley had no previous connection with the sea, but that was no disqualification for a vice-admiral, who was intended to be a military commander and administrator rather than a seaman. There was no war, and indeed Henry had recently declared his neutrality in the renewed struggle between France and the Empire. So Dudley's instructions related to the keeping of the seas rather than military operations proper. This seems to have represented a new departure in English naval strategy, and one which was to be of long-term significance.[68] On 16 February Henry Huttoft wrote to Cromwell, reporting that French pirates were active around the Isle of Wight, and suggested that Dudley's small fleet, which was known to be preparing for the sea, should be sent against them. That seems to have been Cromwell's intention, and Dudley's instructions, issued on 7 March, required him police the area between the Solent and Spithead.[69] By that time he was already at sea, having set out on 24 February accompanied by Sir Thomas Seymour, the brother of Sir Edward and of the current queen, Jane. Anxious eyes were cast on his progress. John Hussee wrote to Lord Lisle that one Popley, who had bought a manor of Dudley, was now terrified that 'if any ill happens to him, all the money adventured will be lost'. However, nothing dramatic occurred. Dudley and Seymour sent back regular reports, but the only action seems to have been

---

[66] The basic work for a study of the Pilgrimage of Grace is still M. H. Dodds and R. Dodds, *The Pilgrimage of Grace and the Exeter Conspiracy* (Cambridge, 1915), but more recent publications include C. S. L. Davies, 'The Pilgrimage of Grace Reconsidered', *Past and Present*, 41 (1968), 54–76; and G. R. Elton, 'Politics and the Pilgrimage of Grace', in *Studies in Tudor and Stuart Politics and Government*, iii (Cambridge, 1983). For the most recent summary, see J. A. Guy, *Tudor England* (Oxford, 1988), 149–53.

[67] John Hussee to Lord Lisle, 6 Feb. 1537 (*L. and P.*, xii. 353).

[68] Loades, *The Tudor Navy*, 103–38, which discusses the 'keeping of the seas' during this period.

[69] *L. and P.*, xii. 601; Loades, *The Tudor Navy*, 118.

an engagement on 15 March which resulted in the taking of a Flemish pirate.[70] Although Dudley commanded only four ships they were well equipped, and, warned of his coming, most of the pirates, both French and Flemish, transferred their operations to the Straits of Dover, and menaced the Thames estuary. They were shortly dispersed by other royal warships.

Dudley's brief foray was probably over by the end of March, but the king was well satisfied with the first effort of his fledgling admiral. On 31 July his instructions were repeated and extended.[71] Seconded this time by Sir Gawain Carew, he was to keep the whole coast westwards from the Downs to the Isle of Wight, and thence to St Michael's Mount, Ushant, Scilly, and Lundy. He was to succour English merchants, and to apprehend any French or Flemish ships acting as pirates, reporting his doings regularly to the king. This sweeping commission did not, however, signify the deployment of a larger force. Dudley seems to have had the same four ships as before, and by 18 August he was complaining that Carew's ship was leaking so badly that she was not fit to be at sea at all.[72] The early reports from Dudley and Carew reek of frustration. No one will venture to cross their path: 'we are the heaviest men that ever bare lives to have done so little service in so long space'. By 21 August their ships were in the Solent, only awaiting a fair wind to return to the Thames.[73] However, that very day there were reports of 'Breton shallops' marauding off the Scillies, and Dudley set off in pursuit. On 22 August he caught up with the intruders in Mount's Bay, Cornwall, and a sharp engagement followed 'from 5 o'clock until dark', which resulted in the capture of two of the Bretons.[74] According to one eyewitness, Dudley would have had all four if his spritmast had not broken when the wind got up during the action. It was a very creditable baptism in naval warfare, and by the end of August he could return to Deptford with something to show for his efforts. Unfortunately the matter did not end there, because within a fortnight the French ambassador was complaining of the vice-admiral's action, declaring that the ships seized were lawful traders who had been driven into an English port by bad weather.[75] The Lord Admiral, Sir William FitzWilliam, confessed to Cromwell that there was no proof that the captured ships had been engaged in piracy, except perhaps that they had resisted arrest. As a result

[70] *L. and P.*, xii. 602, 603, 656.

[71] The council had ordered a full mobilization of the fleet in Apr., and Dudley's preparations had gone on throughout June and July (*L. and P.*, xii. i. 815–16; ibid., ii. 393, 535).

[72] Ibid. 416, 535.

[73] Henry Huttoft to Cromwell, 21 Aug. 1537 (ibid. 556).

[74] There seems to have been some confusion about this action subsequently. On 22 Aug. Dudley and Carew reported to the king that they had captured two Breton pirates 'lying in wait for ships of Cornwall', and on 28 Aug. Sir William Godolghen reported the action to Cromwell with circumstantial details. However, later references to the captured ships refer to them having been taken at Portsmouth. Probably they were taken to Portsmouth after their capture (ibid. 563, 595).

[75] Fitzwilliam to Cromwell, 12 Sept. 1537 (ibid. 680).

of these representations, by the end of September the ships had been released and no prize money was paid. It looked as though frustration had made Dudley and Carew a little over-zealous. However, on 5 October Henry wrote angrily to his ambassador in France, Stephen Gardiner, protesting that no sooner had these ships been released than they had set upon a trader out of Calais and robbed her.[76] He was to demand in no uncertain terms that French ships should be instructed 'to know a friend from an enemy'.

Meanwhile Dudley had finally secured a court office which lifted him out of the ranks of mere Knights of the Body. It was not the often mooted Vice-Chamberlainship but the rather less prestigious post of Chief Trencher, with a fee of £50 a year.[77] He also kept up his pressure on Lord Dudley, who had not finally abandoned hope of saving something from the wreck of his fortunes. In June Cromwell again reminded himself of Sir John's affairs, but for what purpose we do not know. Throughout the summer the whole court had been awaiting with anguished expectation for the laying in of Queen Jane. After so many desperate expedients to secure the succession, and so many disappointments, the importance of the outcome could hardly be overemphasized. Finally, on 12 October the queen gave birth to a son, and the whole country exploded with rejoicing. For Henry it was God's vindication of his proceedings over the previous eight years, and even those who could not take so positive a view were relieved that there was at last a male heir to the throne. Sir John Dudley, as his position required, was one of the seventy-five knights and gentlemen who attended Prince Edward's christening on 15 October.[78] Over the next few days, as Jane Seymour sickened to her death, the king's ambassadors set off to bear the tidings to the courts of Europe. The emperor was at Valladolid, and to him was sent Sir Thomas Wyatt, recently rehabilitated after his supposed involvement in the indiscretions of Anne Boleyn. Dudley's inclusion in this mission may have been an afterthought, because he did not set off with Wyatt, but rather followed him with instructions to bring back Wyatt's report of his reception.[79] He was not included in Wyatt's commission, and seems to have been little more than a glorified messenger. On 25 October he wrote to Cromwell from Paris, reporting that the talk there was of peace between France and the Empire, while the Picards expected war with England. When he had landed at Boulogne his diplomatic immunity had almost been infringed by some of those Bretons whom he had arrested in English waters two months earlier, and whose presence in Boulogne at that

---

[76] Fitzwilliam to Cromwell, *L. and P.*, xii, ii. 832.
[77] Grants in Feb. 1537 (ibid., i. 539 (29)).   [78] Ibid., ii. 911.
[79] Cromwell to Wyatt, 20 Oct. 1537 (ibid. 950). For Wyatt's involvement with Anne Boleyn, see Ives, *Anne Boleyn*, 87–99, and Retha Warnicke, *The Rise and Fall of Anne Boleyn* (Cambridge, 1989), 64–8.

moment can hardly have been coincidental.[80] Nevertheless, he had been saved both injury and embarrassment by the governor of the town, and arrived safely in Spain in the first week of November. About ten days later he drew up his own report of the ambassador's interview with Charles, which had been sufficiently friendly, and then set off back. At Lyons on 26 November he was stopped, as he was told on the orders of the French king, although no reason was given.[81] It was being rumoured in that city that Wyatt had been arrested on the emperor's orders. There was no foundation for the report, but it looks suspiciously as though Franco-Imperial peace feelers were beginning to cool Francis's relations with Henry. Such trivial gestures were the small change of diplomacy; the minor flags planted to signal a possible change of policy. Twelve days later Dudley was allowed to proceed. The cardinal of Tournon, he was told, had misunderstood the king's instructions; apologies were offered. Before Christmas he was back in England, and Henry was writing to Wyatt relating his misadventures in France.[82]

Dudley's first taste of diplomacy could hardly be described as distinguished. On the one hand, he had done what was required of him, and could hardly be blamed for the cardinal of Tournon's 'mistake'. On the other, the affair of the Breton ships refused to go away. In January 1538 the owner of one of them, the *Coucou*, petitioned Cromwell for its release, professing his innocence of all piratical intentions, and enclosing character references.[83] On 21 February Germain Gardiner, the bishop of Winchester's nephew, then on mission in France, reported that he had quarrelled violently with one of the French king's secretaries, who had used the case of the *Coucou* as the pretext for a denunciation of the inadequacies of English justice.[84] Probably the ship was released soon after, because there are no further references to her, and her comparatively small value was not worth a serious diplomatic incident. Sir William FitzWilliam, the Lord Admiral, seems to have believed that Dudley had acted precipitately, but piracy was a major and intractable problem, and he had probably felt it better to err on the side of severity. If he failed to establish that the *Coucou* was a lawful prize, then neither he nor his men would have made anything out of her capture, but there is no sign that his action was felt to have been misjudged, or that Cromwell was embarrassed by the fuss which the French were prepared to make.

After a year of active royal service, Dudley's preoccupations during 1538 seem to have been of a mainly domestic nature. He had a rapidly growing young family, Jane having presented him with approximately one child a year from their marriage until 1534, but they are seldom alluded to in the sur-

[80] *L. and P.*, xii. ii. 987.   [81] Ibid. 1053, 1133.
[82] Henry to Wyatt, 23 Dec. 1537 (ibid. 1449).
[83] Jehan Bertre to Cromwell (ibid., i. 186).   [84] Ibid. 327.

viving sources. His relations with his stepfather continued to be close and
reasonably amicable. Lisle was under pressure to sell the lordship of
Kingston Lisle, but this was the *caput honorem* of the barony of Lisle and Sir
John held the reversion, and no transaction seems to have taken place at this
time.[85] At the same time Dudley was concerning himself about the welfare of
his half-sisters, Bridget, Frances, and Elizabeth, Sir Arthur's daughters by
Elizabeth Grey. On 23 February he wrote of his anxiety lest Elizabeth, who
was the younger, might be unfairly treated. It was being rumoured, he
declared, that Lisle was proposing to leave his whole estate to Frances, and
this was having an adverse affect upon Elizabeth's marriage prospects.[86] If
Lisle took offence at this fraternal intervention, we have no record of it. Nor
do we know whether there was any justification for Dudley's concern, but
the letter indicates an aspect of his personality which was to appear again in
later life; a sensitivity to the interests of his kindred, even when they did not
directly affect him. At the same time that he was taking his stepfather to task
in this manner, he was also sending presents of game across to Calais, and
trying to persuade Lisle to exchange the manor of Kybworth for lands in Kent
to the same value.[87] On 14 March he sent his stepfather the latest news of the
court: 'It is said we shall have a great master of the household, as in France,
and that the old ordinary shall be altered … '. He was right, but it would be
two years before the change took effect, and he had probably picked up a discussion of the possibility rather than a decision.[88] The old band of Spears was
also to be revived, fifty in number, and that duly occurred with the creation
of the band of Gentlemen Pensioners in the following year. He was, he confessed, not as well informed as he would like to have been because he was not
a member of the council—a hint of the ambition which was always evident
from his actions, if not always reflected in his words. Courtiers lived by hints
and suggestions, so if Dudley was feeling at all frustrated by his failure to
gain a seat on the council, he should have been encouraged by standing god-
father to the infant son of the earl of Sussex at the end of March, when his fellow 'gossips' were the king, Cromwell, and Princess Mary.[89]

   In July, however, there was a mild hiccup in his relationship with his

---

[85]   John Hussee to Lisle, 6 Feb. 1538 (ibid. 226). It subsequently appeared that these manors
had also been settled on Lisle's second wife as her jointure. Cromwell wanted them because he
desired to favour Sir William Kingston. See below, p. 39.
   [86]   Bridget was probably already married to Sir William Cawarden. Elizabeth subsequently
married Sir Francis Jobson, so his fears seem to have been unfounded (BL MS Stowe 652; *L. and
P.*, xiii. i. 337, 510).
   [87]   Hussee to Lisle, 6 Mar. 1538. Dudley was also involved in another transaction at Holy-
well in Flintshire, probably a purchase (*L. and P.*, xiii. i. 430, 584).
   [88]   Dudley to Lisle (ibid. 503). Charles Brandon, duke of Suffolk, became Lord Great Master
in 1540. The intention was to discontinue both the Lord Stewardship and the Lord Chamberlainship, but the latter office was filled again in 1543 by the appointment of Lord St John. The
Lord Great Mastership was discontinued in 1553 (D. Loades, *The Tudor Court* (Bangor, 1992),
203–5).
   [89]   Hussee to Lisle, 28 Mar. 1538 (*L. and P.*, xiii. i. 614).

patron. Cromwell wished to buy the manor of Drayton Bassett in Stafford-shire from Dudley. The latter was anxious to sell in order to obtain available cash for another transaction, but does not seems to have understood Cromwell's interest. Before Henry Polsted, Cromwell's receiver, could reach him with a bid, he had sold the manor to one Thomas Pope. On 27 July he wrote to the Lord Privy Seal explaining what had happened, and offer-ing to sell other interests which he had in Gloucestershire instead.[90] At the same time Pope wrote to Sir Thomas Wriothesley, offering to sell to Cromwell, but explaining that the matter was now complicated by the interest of a third party from whom he had, presumably, borrowed most or all of the purchase money. Cromwell was obviously very put out by this mischance. Perhaps he was too accustomed to having his own way over such transactions, but he sent Dudley a sharp rebuke. His letter does not survive, but Sir John's response, dated 30 July, is eloquent both of his anxi-ety and of his sense of injustice. 'I have not deserved your displeasure', he wrote, and added, truthfully enough, that he had 'trusted in your Lordship for my preferment before all others'.[91] As long as his favour with the king remained intact, the Lord Privy Seal was a man who had to be placated. He was also a hard man to deny. Having obtained Dudley's interest in Painswick and Morton Valence he began to press Lord Lisle for immediate possession. In a weak moment, of which he had many, Lisle seems to have promised to sell. He then remembered that the manors were a part of his wife's jointure, and that he could not lawfully dispose of it in her lifetime without her consent.[92] Cromwell therefore began to turn the screws on Lady Lisle, exploiting her affection for her husband and his desperate need for money. Lisle could only leave the matter to her discretion, urging some-what feebly that he was confident my Lord Privy Seal would make sure she was no loser.[93] At the end of November she yielded to overwhelming pres-sure. Cromwell got his manors, and immediately sold them at a profit to Sir William Kingston, which had been his intention from the beginning.

Lisle's relations with the Lord Privy Seal remained strained, but Dudley does not seem to have suffered at all for his contretemps. By the middle of August he was writing to express profuse thanks for his 'bill newly signed' for the abbey of Halesowen in Shropshire, the grant of which was finally confirmed in September for a reserved rent of only £28. 1s. 3d.[94] Halesowen

---

[90] Polstead to Cromwell, June 1538; Dudley to Cromwell, 27 July 1538 (ibid. 1310, 1473).
[91] Pope to Cromwell, 27 July 1538; Thomas Pope to Wriothesley 29 July 1538; Dudley to Cromwell, 30 July 1538 (ibid. 1472, 1488, 1498).
[92] Lord Lisle to John Hussee, Sept. 1538: 'The indenture between Sir John Dudley and me purports that I shall make jointure to my wife during my life' (ibid., ii. 479).
[93] Lord Lisle to Lady Lisle, 11 Nov. 1538 (ibid. 798).
[94] Halesown had not been dissolved under the terms of the 1536 Act, because its annual value was £293. William Taylor, the last abbot, had surrendered the house on 9 June 1538. It is reasonable to suppose that Cromwell had earmarked it for Dudley before that date. The reserved rent equalled the tithes (*Valor Ecclesiasticus*, iii. 206–8; *L. and P.*, xiii. i. 431).

was a major acquisition, including four manors as well as the site of the abbey itself, all its buildings, and the advowsons of a number of dependent rectories.

In the late summer and early autumn the court was wracked by a new crisis, usually referred to as the 'Exeter conspiracy'. It arose partly out of the king's awareness of the continuing undertow of discontent among the more conservative of his nobles, and partly from the continuing insecurity of the succession, dependent upon a single infant life. The target of Henry's suspicions were the prominent south-western families of Pole and Courtenay, descendants through the female line of Edward IV and his brother, the duke of Clarence.[95] Once the king had decided that they must be destroyed, it fell to the Lord Privy Seal to prepare a case against them. Geoffrey Pole, Lord Montague's younger brother, was arrested and terrified into producing evidence of a sort. On 3 November Lord Montague and the marquis of Exeter were arrested. They were tried at the end of December and condemned, much as the duke of Buckingham was condemned in 1520. Cromwell was already receiving petitions for the marquis's lands before he had even been tried, let alone executed. Rather surprisingly Lord Lisle was one of the first to apply.[96] Perhaps he was trying to escape suspicion of complicity. He had some cause to be alarmed, because the opportunity was taken to remove some others who had been prominent in their distaste for certain aspects of the king's proceedings. Sir Edward Neville, the brother of Lord Abergavenny, was arrested with Montague and Exeter, and Sir Nicholas Carew, the Master of the Horse and a former favourite of the king, followed in January. On 14 February, when Carew was brought to trial, Sir John Dudley was empanelled as a juror, and sworn, which means that he actually served.[97] Carew's condemnation was important to Cromwell, and Dudley was clearly regarded as a reliable man.

Another of those imprisoned at this time was Thomas West, Lord La Warr. La Warr was certainly of a conservative inclination in religion, but he had assiduously and successfully petitioned Cromwell for grants of monastic land, and had paid the Lord Privy Seal a retainer for his 'good lordship'. However he came under suspicion, it was probably not Cromwell's doing.[98] On 22 December he was released on the large recognizance of £3,000 to appear before the council when summoned. His sureties, who must have been chosen for their unimpeachable loyalty as

---

[95] Margaret Pole, Countess of Salisbury, was the daughter of George, duke of Clarence, and the mother of Henry Pole, Lord Montague. Henry Courtenay, marquis of Exeter, was the son of Catherine, daughter to Edward IV. The king had also been outraged by a work attacking his ecclesiastical position, *Pro ecclesiasticae unitatis defensione*, written by Reginald Pole, another of Margaret's sons.

[96] Lisle to Cromwell, 5 Dec. 1538 (*L. and P.*, xiii. ii. 990).

[97] Ibid., xiv. 290.

[98] Ibid., xiii. ii. 1117; xiv. ii. 782; H. Miller, *Henry VIII and the English Nobility* (Oxford, 1986), 228 and n.

well as their wealth, included the dukes of Norfolk and Suffolk, the earl of Sussex, and Sir John Dudley.[99] La Warre prudently increased his retainer to Cromwell, and the bond was finally cancelled without any further repercussions in November 1539. Dudley, meanwhile, continued to buy and sell land in a manner which makes it hard to deduce any coherent strategy. In February 1539 he completed the sale of his Kentish lands to Cromwell for £3,490. At some point in 1538 he bought the manor of Acton Burnell from the duke of Norfolk, and that of Penkridge in Staffordshire from Sir Richard Lister. In February 1539 he enfeoffed the manor of Halesown to his own use and that of his wife. By this time he had also acquired the lands of the 'late priory of Dudforde', because in March he sold them to his brother Andrew and his wife.[100] There seem to have been many other transactions, and some lawsuits, which have left few surviving records behind, and the impression created is that of a busy and ambitious man making the most of his influential court and council connections. He may also have been more than a little frustrated by his failure so far to secure any office or commission of major importance. In June we find him acting as Sir Thomas Wyatt's agent, collecting from the Treasury of the Chamber the arrears of his diets as ambassador to the emperor, and in July he wrote to Cromwell, begging to be included in the commission for the Council in the Marches of Wales. This was a strange letter coming from a man in his middle thirties, with a powerfully established position in the West Midlands and a string of sons to continue his dynasty.

I have spent a great deal of my life and my youth in the court about my master, and am now drawing homewards where I trust to make an end of my life in God's service and his ...[101]

Whether this should be seen as self-pity, or an early example of the hypochondria for which he was later to be notorious, it does not seem to have moved the Lord Privy Seal. Dudley continued to be named in the commissions of the peace for Kent and Staffordshire, and to discharge his duties as Master of the Armoury. In November 1539 he was named as Master of the Horse to Henry's latest queen, Anne of Cleves, and he played a prominent part in the ceremonies which attended her ill-omened arrival in January 1540. Jane was also appointed to the new queen's household, but more substantial and satisfying promotion continued to elude Sir John, and the success of his private affairs was ceasing to be any comfort to him.

[99] *L. and P.*, xiii. ii. 1117.   [100] Ibid. 491; ibid., xiv. i. 191, 403.
[101] Ibid. 1062; ibid. 1267.

2

Lord Lisle, 1540–1547

JANUARY 1540 was the month of Anne of Cleves. On 3 January she was received with elaborate ceremonial at Blackheath, and escorted towards
London.

next followed the ambassadors, then the Lord Privy Seal and the Lord Chancellor,
then the Lord Marques with the Kynges sworde, nexte followed the king himselfe,
equally ridyng with his faire Lady, & behind him rode syr Anthony Browne with
the kyngz horse of Estate as you hearde before, and behind him rode syr Iohan Dudley Master of her horses leadynge her spare palfrey ...[1]

'I thynke no creature could see them but his herte reioysed', commented
Edward Hall loyally. Unfortunately Henry's heart did not rejoice. With the
boyish impetuosity which was sometimes characteristic of him, he had
waylaid her incognito as she travelled through Kent, and had been deeply
disappointed by what he found.[2] The courtesies on Blackheath, and the joy-
ful procession which followed were a hollow sham, as the king strove
behind the scenes to avoid his impending, and now deeply distasteful,
nuptials. In that he failed. The contracts had been too tightly drawn, and the
last possibility of escape—a precontract going back over twenty years—
was finally scotched by Anne herself on 5 January. The next day Henry
went to his doom in the queen's closet at Greenwich in a mood of rage and
despair. Unsurprisingly in these circumstances the wedding night was a
fiasco, to which Anne's own total innocence added an overtone of farce. She
had no idea that there was anything wrong at all, and was not in the least
disconcerted by the king's failure to consummate their union because she
had no idea what consummation involved.[3] Over the next few days Henry
raged at his ministers and complained in circumstantial detail to his physicians; but to Anne herself he remained studiously polite.

By the end of the month she was almost alone in her undisturbed security. The king's council and his whole court knew that he was determined
to be rid of her. The only questions were how and when. This was

---

[1] E. Hall, *The unione of the two noble and illustre fameIies of York and Lancastre*, ed. H. Ellis
(London, 1809), 835.
[2] Charles Wriothesley, *A Chronicle of England during the Reigns of the Tudors, from 1485 to
1559*, ed. W. D. Hamilton, Camden Society (1875), i. 109.
[3] M. St Clare Byrne, *The Letters of Henry VIII* (London, 1968), 186. For a full reconstruction
of Anne's disastrous innocence, see Antonia Fraser, *The Six Wives of Henry VIII* (London, 1992),
310–13.

extremely bad news for the Lord Privy Seal who had masterminded the match in order to get his monarch out of a European isolation which no longer seemed to matter. It was also bad news for the 126 people who made up the new queen's household. Their preferments, and in some cases their livelihoods, hung by a thread.[4] There was always great pressure for places at court, and the creation of a household for the new consort in December 1539 had rejoiced many hearts. If she was dismissed the search would have to begin all over again. Both John Dudley and his wife held such threatened places, because she had been named as a member of Anne's privy chamber. As far as we know this was her first court appointment, and represented a foot in the door. Her husband's foot was already firmly in, but the Mastership of the Queen's Horse was his most prestigious appointment to date, and there are signs that he relished the proximity which it gave him to the royal couple. In December 1539 when the king had dined with the earl of Hertford Dudley had been a member of the small and extremely select group which had accompanied him.[5] Having been twice passed over for the Vice-Chamberlainship, Queen Anne represented an opportunity which was not to be taken lightly. For the moment the storm hovered, but did not break. On 5 February Henry took his new wife from Greenwich to Westminster by river. They did not process through the City of London, so there was no ceremonial function for Dudley, but her whole household seems to have accompanied her, so he was probably still in attendance. By the middle of March he was back home at Dudley, where his house was briefly but dangerously visited by the plague.[6] The victims were visitors from Gloucestershire and the infection does not seem to have taken hold, but he may well have felt it prudent to remain in the country until that fact was firmly established. So far Sir John had not run to a London house. Like many lesser courtiers he probably took lodgings in London or Westminster when he was on duty. His Mastership of the Horse may have entitled him to accommodation in the court itself, but by April 1540 he clearly felt in need of something more substantial and secure. On his return from Staffordshire he lodged with Sir Thomas Cornwallis, and wrote thence to Sir Ralph Sadler, the Principal Secretary, asking to rent one of his houses in Hackney. As Sadler had several such properties, he probably had no difficulty in obliging.[7]

By the end of April Henry had made no significant progress in his quest to get rid of Queen Anne, but he had found himself a consolation. This was Catherine, the 19-year-old daughter of Lord Edmund Howard, and niece of the duke of Norfolk. She had been brought to court, like Jane Dudley, to

---

[4] *Letter and Papers of the Reign of Henry VIII*, ed. J. S. Brewer *et al.* (London, 1862–1932), xiv. ii. 572; Fraser, *Six Wives*, 313.

[5] *Historical Manuscripts Commission Report*, 58; Seymour Papers XVIII, 341: Kitchen accounts.

[6] *L. and P.*, xv. 386: 21 Mar. 1540.   [7] BL MS Royal 7 C XVI, fo. 151.

attend upon the queen, but her youthful vivacity and somewhat superficial
sex appeal made an instant impression upon the ageing and disgruntled
king. His first recorded gift to her was delivered on 24 April, but by the
middle of May he had become deeply ensnared.[8] Anne's last public appearance as queen came at the May Day celebrations, which went on from 30
April to 7 May. As usual the central theme was provided by ritual combats;
jousting on the Saturday, which was May Day itself, a tourney on the Monday, and barriers on the Tuesday. The challengers, who kept open house at
Durham place throughout the festivities, and feasted the king, queen, and
nobility daily, were headed by Sir John Dudley and Sir Thomas Seymour.[9]
It must have been an expensive week, because parliament was in session,
and on the Tuesday the knights and burgesses of the Common House were
also entertained, followed by the Mayor and Aldermen of London on the
Wednesday. Both the king and the duke of Suffolk had long since retired
from jousting and the defenders were headed on this occasion by the earl of
Surrey, but Henry was still an avid follower of the sport, and Dudley's leading role was a conspicuous mark of favour. The king may well have considered him to be the best lance in the court, but at 36 he was something of
a veteran, and had not managed to capitalize upon his ability in the way
that Brandon, or even Nicholas Carew, had done. He was advancing into
middle age, as he was himself keenly aware, and both title and high office
continued to elude him. He needed something more substantial than a May
Day joust to jolt his fortunes out of the rut into which they appeared to be
settling.

Paradoxically, that jolt seems to have been provided by the fall of the man
whom he had regarded as his principal patron. Thomas Cromwell had collected enemies, as Wolsey had, through jealousy of his influence over the
king and through disparagement of his humble origins. Eventually those
enemies secured the king's ear, and he was overthrown. There was no
simple or rational explanation for this development.[10] The fiasco of Henry's
fourth marriage undoubtedly cost him the rough side of the king's tongue,
but Henry knew perfectly well that it had been his own insistence which
had driven that negotiation forward, and Cromwell was entirely willing to
unpick the knot when he saw that the king was that way determined.
Indeed he could probably have done it faster and more efficiently than anyone. On the other hand he had been playing with fire in his patronage of
radical preachers. Henry's ecclesiastical reflexes were erratic. In spite of the
royal supremacy, the dissolution of the monasteries, the destruction of
shrines, and the simplification of the calendar, he continued to regard him-

---

[8] L. B. Smith, *A Tudor Tragedy* (London, 1961), 124. Smith also argues that Henry commenced sexual relations with Catherine in the middle of May, but that cannot be proved.

[9] *L. and P.*, xv. 617.

[10] G. R. Elton, 'Thomas Cromwell's Decline and Fall', in *Studies in Tudor and Stuart Politics
and Government* (1974), 189–230; id., *Thomas Cromwell* (Bangor, 1991), 38–40.

self as a good catholic.[11] This was largely because of his unwavering faith in the orthodox sacraments, particularly the mass. Protestants were good allies when it came to attacking papal abuses, idle monks, or unprofitable pilgrimages, but as soon as they began to attack the mass they became heretics and their lives were in danger. What Cromwell himself thought about the mass we do not know. He was probably quite orthodox, especially as he knew the king's mind. He certainly raised no objections when the king allowed the duke of Norfolk to push through the Act of Six Articles in 1539, although it must have undermined his position to some extent.[12] On the other hand, he knew, more clearly than Henry himself, that the king would not be able to go on sitting on the theological fence indefinitely. The more orthodox the English Church remained the less justification there was for its schismatic status. So he encouraged support for the royal supremacy by allowing the radical preachers a generous degree of freedom, although there is no reason to suppose that he shared their convictions. This was a very dangerous game to play, because it was on just such matters of conscience that Henry was at his most volatile and unpredictable.

Apart from the little unpleasantness of the Cleves marriage, the spring of 1540 seemed to show the Lord Privy Seal as strong as ever. When parliament convened on 12 April, he was clearly in control of the agenda. On 18 April he was created earl of Essex and Lord Great Chamberlain of the household.[13] Behind the scenes, however, his position was crumbling. Norfolk had long been his enemy, and the king's growing infatuation with Norfolk's niece spelled serious danger. Catherine was a young woman of no particular intelligence and no visible convictions, but she could be relied upon to promote the family interests. If Henry were to divorce Anne and marry her, the duke's influence would be sharing the king's bed. At the same time the king was beginning to listen to voices which told him that the disturbed state of the country's religion was due to the wild sermons which were being preached unchecked, particularly in London and Calais. By the beginning of May the ripples of this conflict were beginning to break the surface. Cromwell's best method of defence was counter-attack, and his obvious line was to accuse his orthodox enemies of popery. Bishop Samson of Chichester was arrested, and then, on 16 May, Lord Lisle was summoned home from Calais. The poor old man seems to have believed that he was destined for an earldom, but when he arrived at Greenwich he found himself accused of secret communications with the arch traitor Reginald Pole. On 19 May the council sent him to the Tower, and a few days later his

[11] L. B. Smith, *Henry VIII: The Mask of Royalty* (London, 1971), 99–117. Until the Council of Trent embarked upon a programme of definition, there could be a good deal of flexibility in the definition of orthodoxy, and Henry always remained convinced of his own rectitude.

[12] J. J. Scarisbrick, *Henry VIII* (London, 1968), 365–7.

[13] *Journals of the House of Lords* (London, 1846), i. 128 ff.; Hall, *Unione*, 838.

wife and children were arrested in Calais.[14] Lisle was certainly innocent of any treasonable intent, but his combination of Plantagenet blood and religious conservatism made him an ideal scapegoat when the Lord Privy Seal was being accused of encouraging heretics in Calais.[15] Less than a month later, on 10 June, Cromwell himself was arrested at the council board, and followed Lisle into imprisonment.

His subsequent fate is well known, and need not be dwelt upon, but the king's suspicions were catholic and it brought no relief to Lisle, who remained in prison after his accuser was dead. Dudley was now in the precarious position of having both his patron and his stepfather in prison on capital charges, although they were on opposite sides. Moreover, on 9 July convocation declared the king's marriage to Queen Anne dissolved. This was confirmed by parliament four days later and her household was stood down.[16] She was given a generous settlement and provision, but had no further need for a Master of the Horse, nor a large entourage of aristocratic ladies. The luckless Sir William Kingston, on whose behalf Cromwell had gone to such lengths to extract the manors of Painswick and Morton Valence from the Lisles, was caught by the earl's fall with the transaction half completed. The lands were declared forfeit to the Crown, and he was forced to sue out a special grant in August, thus effectively barring any attempt on Dudley's part to recover his reversion.[17] Rather surprisingly, we have no means of knowing how he reacted to these dramatic events. According to his final confession in 1553 he had first strayed from the 'true faith' sixteen years before, which would mean that he had become a reformer in some sense in 1536 or 37.[18] As we have seen, his personal relations with his stepfather had varied from cool to amiable without ever being very close. Each knew that the other was upon the opposite side of the great schism which was beginning to divide the court, and when Lisle was imprisoned on suspicion of popish sympathies, Dudley made no move to support or assist him. Cromwell's fall, however, was a different matter altogether. After the court festivities in early May, Sir John probably went home to Dudley, and kept a prudently low profile for the next few months. He had been moderately active in supporting the policies of the Lord Privy Seal, and was a known member of the 'reforming' party.

The next eighteen months or so were remarkably quiet. Henry married

[14] M. St Clare Byrne, *The Lisle Letters* (London and Chicago, 1981), vi. 139: the account of Elis Gruffyd.

[15] Ibid. 61–6: Report by the king's commissioners.

[16] Hall, *Unione*, 839; statute 31 Henry VIII, c. 25; *Statutes of the Realm*, ed. A. Luder *et al.* (London, 1810–28), iii. 781–3.

[17] *L. and P.*, xv. 1027.

[18] Wriothesley, *Chronicle*, ii. 100; *The Diary of Henry Machyn*, ed. J. G. Nichols, Camden Society, 42 (1848), 42; *The Chronicle of Queen Jane*, ed. J. G. Nichols, Camden Society, 48 (1850), 19.

Catharine Howard on 28 July 1540, and was so devoted to her that he seemed to have eyes for nothing else. Once Cromwell was dead his enemies relaxed their efforts, and no concerted attempt was made to root out the servants whom he had placed about the king's person. Consequently, although Norfolk and Gardiner dominated the council, the Privy Chamber continued to be sympathetic to the reforming programme,[19] and Archbishop Thomas Cranmer also retained his personal influence. Consequently the so-called 'reaction' was never more than half-hearted, responding to the king's own changes of mood rather than to the ascendancy of a court faction. Sir John Dudley appeared on the commission of the peace for Worcestershire in September 1540, while continuing to serve in Staffordshire and Surrey, but no longer, it seems, in Kent. In October 1540 his younger brother Andrew is named as being in the service of the duke of Norfolk. By December he had also secured a minor office in the king's wardrobe, but neither position was of sufficient significance to be useful in re-establishing Sir John's court credentials, should that have been necessary.[20] He seems to have spent very little time there during the Howard ascendancy, but was never in the slightest danger. The king, who seemed to have recovered his youthful exuberance in the autumn of 1540, was seriously ill in the spring of the following year. His always uncertain temper became savage and morose, and he began to lament his impetuosity in dispatching Thomas Cromwell. He was, he declared, surrounded by treachery and deceit.[21] A minor conspiracy in Yorkshire in April prompted the execution of the aged Countess of Salisbury, a prisoner in the Tower since 1538. Henry enjoyed his progress to the north which followed, and his health recovered, but the failure of an anticipated rendezvous with James V of Scotland sent him home in October in a bleak mood, for all the charms of his young wife. It was a good time to be away from the court, and worse was to follow. At the beginning of November one John Lascelles, a minor reformer and a committed enemy of the Howards, sought out Cranmer with hair-raising stories of Queen Catherine's dissolute youth.[22] At first the king was inclined to shrug such charges off as mere calumny, but it swiftly became apparent that they were only too well founded. He had been totally deceived in the woman whom he had married, and sank into a morass of fury and self-pity. Arrested on 12 November, a few days later Catherine made a tearful and hysterical confession to Cranmer.[23] When he reported this to Henry, the archbishop, whether from distress of mind or lack of time

---

[19] David Starkey, 'Intimacy and Innovation: The Rise of the Privy Chamber, 1485–1547', in id. (ed.) *The English Court from the Wars of the Roses to the Civil War* (London, 1987), 115.

[20] *L. and P.*, xvi. 169, 402.   [21] Ibid. 284: Marillac to Francis I.

[22] *Proceedings and Ordinances of the Privy Council in England, 1386–1542*, ed. N. H. Nicolas (London, 1834–7), vii. 353. For a full account of these revelations, see Smith, *A Tudor Tragedy*, 178.

[23] *Historical Manuscripts Commission Reports*, MSS of the Marquis of Bath, ii. 8–9; *L. and P.*, xvi. 1325.

to do justice to such a saga, confided the full story to the bearer of his letter, who must presumably have been present throughout the interview. That bearer was Sir John Dudley. How he came to be present at Syon at such a traumatic moment is not explained. Perhaps the king sent him, or perhaps Cranmer chose him to be the confidential messenger, knowing that he would not attempt to mitigate the full horrors of the story. Dudley had hardly less interest than the archbishop himself in bringing the Howard ascendancy to an end. When Catherine's household was broken up he was entrusted with the highly responsible task of escorting the Lady Mary, the king's eldest daughter, to join her brother's establishment at Ashridge.[24] If his connection with Cromwell had ever made him suspect to the council, that phase had passed by the end of 1541.

Meanwhile, in spite of such favourable signals, his career was still making no progress. Business continued as usual. In January 1541 he bought about a dozen manors in Shropshire from the duke of Norfolk, and in March he received a grant of the property of Dudley priory, a cell of Wenlock abbey.[25] This latter he seems to have acquired as a speculation, for he sold it off in parcels over the next few months to men who appear to have been small local gentry. He had no reason to complain of a lack of prosperity or local influence, but the breakthrough which he had hoped for by throwing in his lot with Cromwell and the reforming party had not come. Cromwell had gone, but at the end of 1541 the prospects of the reforming party again looked bright. If he was upon the winning side, it remained to be seen what advantage that would bring him. Ironically, however, his promotion, when it came, seems to have owed nothing to his party allegiance. On 3 March his stepfather, Lord Lisle, died at the advanced age of about 80.[26] Lisle had never been tried, or even indicted, for his alleged treason, and it seems clear that the king intended to release him. It was even being rumoured that Henry had taken a fancy to his stepdaughter Anne Basset. But whatever was the truth, time overtook intention, and the old man died in the Tower. Nine days later, on 12 March, Sir John Dudley was created Viscount Lisle 'by the right of his mother Lady Elizabeth, sister and heir to Sir John Grey, Viscount Lisle, who was late wife to Arthur Plantagenet, Viscount Lisle, deceased'.[27] This was consistent with the terms of the patent which had created Plantagenet's title in 1523, and was clearly considered sufficient by the person who recorded it. Nevertheless Dudley was also granted a new patent, and as though to add to the confusion also assumed the titles of Baron Malpas and Lord Basset of Tyasse at the same time.[28] These titles were not granted, and it is not entirely clear where they came

[24] *L. and P.*, 1331: 11 Nov. 1541.   [25] Ibid. 678.
[26] Francis Sandford, *A Genealogical History of the Kings of England* (London, 1677), 448.
[27] *L. and P.*, xvii. 163; BL Add. MS 46354, fo. 2.
[28] For a discussion of these titles see G. E. Cockayne, *The Complete Peerage*, rev. V. Sibbs (London, 1910–49), v, App. F..

from, but Dudley's right to them was tacitly acknowledged when they were used in official references to him thereafter.

The ceremony was no doubt a standard one, but it was solemn, and has been recorded in full. It took place in the Privy Chamber of the palace of Whitehall;

In primis after the sacring of the mass he and thother lords went into the pages chamber, which is nigh the King's Great Chamber where they donned their robes. And the King's Majestie being ready under his cloth of estate they proceeded towards him in maner following: In primis the officers at armes 2 and 2. The Garter bearing the Letters Patent. Then the Lord Delaware in his parliament robes bearing his mantle having two barons and a clerk then to lead him on his right hand was the Earl of Hertford in his habit of estate and the Lord Admiral in his parliament robe on the left hand and so proceeded into the King's Privy Chamber where he stood under his cloth of Estate with all the nobles of his council. And after due obeisance done Garter delivered the patent to the Lord Great Chamberlain who delivered it to the King's highness and he gave it to Sir Thomas Wriothesley secretary to read, which he did with high voice and at the words Creamus etc. the King put on his mantel and robe assissed with the other lords and then the patent being read out and all things being done the King delivered the patent to the said Viscount, who gave his Majesty most humble thanks. Then the Viscount retired in like order as before to the Lord Great Chamberlain Chamber where he was prepared for his dinner ...[29]

Within a month the new nobleman had been joined in commission with Sir Richard Southwell, and by the end of April was on his way north to inspect the fortifications of Berwick.[30] A new and very important phase of his career had opened. After nearly twenty years of peace, the king was again preparing for war, and the promising young soldier of 1523 could at last look forward to some service worthy of his mettle.

One traditional explanation for this revival of Henry's latent bellicosity is that he was on the rebound from the humiliating fiasco of his fifth marriage, and using war rather than sex as a method of stimulating his flagging self-esteem. However, it seems that such an explanation is too simple. After the Franco-Imperial *rapprochement* of 1539, which had seemed to threaten such danger to England, had begun to cool in the summer of 1540, Henry had been looking for ways of prising his old sparring partners further apart. Towards the end of 1541, when the revelations of Catherine Howard's indiscretions were apparently unsettling his mind, he was already contemplating a closer relationship with the emperor.[31] In June 1542 he sent Thomas Thirlby to Charles as a special ambassador to clinch an agreement for joint campaigns against France in the following summer, and mobilization began.[32] At the same time his diplomatic failures in Scotland still rankled, and impending war with France would almost certainly lead to a

[29] BL Add. MS 46354, fo. 2.
[30] Henry VIII to John Rogers, 28 Apr. 1542 (*L. and P.*, xvii. 277).
[31] Chapuys to Charles V, 29 Jan. 1542 (ibid. 63); Scarisbrick, *Henry VIII*, 434–5.
[32] *L. and P.*, xvii. 441.

revival of the 'auld alliance'. Bearing in mind what had happened in 1513 there was a sound argument for a pre-emptive strike in the north before committing his main forces across the Channel. Just when Henry decided to provoke James V to war is not certain, but the commissioning of Lisle and Southwell is certainly significant. Work had been going on at Berwick for some time, but it was not progressing satisfactorily, and on 28 April Henry instructed John Rogers, the master of the works at Hull, to proceed to Berwick to consult with Lisle and Southwell about what should be done.[33] On 11 May, having consulted Rogers, the commissioners sent in their first report. The plans which had been approved were fine, but they were not being followed, and the controller and the master mason were at logger-heads. About £13,000 had already been spent, and as much more would be required, so it was essential that the situation should be remedied.[34] A fort-night later, presumably to help them in the task of improving discipline, the council sent them a copy of the statutes and ordinances of the garrison. The king decided against severe measures. Anxious as he was to provoke a con-frontation in the borders, he did not want to start by replacing the officers of Berwick. So the commissioners were instructed to summon the officers before them and deliver the king's 'especial commandment' that they were to look to their charges in accordance with the old ordinances, and upon evidence of amendment were to be allowed to retain their places.[35] Even the chief porter, who was particularly singled out for criticism for allowing the gates to fall under the control of 'mean people', was not to be dismissed.

At this stage the Scots had no aggressive intentions. Commissioners were meeting regularly to resolve the endemic border disputes, and there was even talk of James venturing into England to meet his uncle. But Henry had heard that one before, and when Scottish envoys came to York in Septem-ber, they were pressed hard on his instructions. Behind the scenes he was refurbishing his claim to suzerainty over the northern kingdom, and mobi-lizing an army of 20,000 men under the command of the duke of Norfolk.[36] While the Scottish commissioners were still wondering how to respond to this threatening behaviour, the order was given to march, and on 21 Octo-ber Norfolk crossed the border and cut a swathe of destruction through the Scottish East March. This was not intended to be a serious invasion, and eight days later he was back in Berwick, but it was the opening of a serious campaign. Norfolk was accompanied by the duke of Suffolk, and by the earls of Shrewsbury, Derby, Hertford, Cumberland, Surrey, and Rutland. Lisle seem to have returned south after discharging his task at Berwick, and was at court on 1 October. A mission to France was under discussion, and he may even have been briefed for it, because he was described a few weeks

---

[33] *L. and P.*, 277. [34] Ibid. 318. [35] Ibid. 343: 23 May 1542; ibid. 399: 13 June 1542.
[36] Ibid. 862; Gordon Donaldson, *Scotland: James V to James VII* (Edinburgh, 1978), 58–9; Scarisbrick, *Henry VIII*, 434–5.

later as 'already furnished' for that service.[37] However the king changed his mind in the light of the situation in the north. The Lord Warden of the Marches, the earl of Rutland, was a sick man, and no longer able to discharge the duties, and the decision was taken at some point during October to replace him. At first the intention seems to have been to name the earl of Hertford, but on 29 October he wrote to the council from Newcastle pleading his unsuitability.[38] The earl of Cumberland, Lord Parr, or Lord Dacre would all be preferable, he argued, because they had 'great possessions and kindred' in those parts. But that was precisely what the king did not want. He wanted an effective servant in the marches, but one who would be his own man, not some local magnate with pretensions to autonomy. He had not pulled down the Percies to raise up the Cliffords or the Dacres in their place. If Hertford was unwilling, and perhaps better kept for service in France, he would name another court peer with military talents. On 8 November he wrote to Norfolk, discharging the earl of Rutland and appointing Viscount Lisle in his place.[39]

The earl of Cumberland, who was considered too young for the responsibility, was to be sworn of Lisle's council, and because his own experience of the north was so recent the bishop of Durham was to remain and aid him with his advice. Hertford was to remain in the north until Lisle's arrival, and was to raise 1,500 men to serve under the new Lord Warden. Lisle would bring an additional 500 or 600 with him. Two days later the warrant was issued for his 'diets' at 66s. 8d. a day, to commence on 21 November.[40] On 16 November Dudley set out from Hampton Court to assume his first major political and military responsibility, and arrived in Newcastle about a week later having collected most of his retinue in Yorkshire on the way through. By the time that he arrived the situation had been transformed by a single dramatic event. James's honour and the security of his realm would not allow him to ignore Norfolk's provocative action, and on 23 November he launched about 20,000 men into the 'debateable land' north of Carlisle.[41] In so doing he walked into a carefully laid trap. Two days later the raw Scottish levies were confronted by a smaller but much better trained English army at Solway Moss, and put to flight after what was little more than a skirmish. What made this a serious setback was not the casualties, which were light, but the large number of important Scottish noblemen who were captured and sent off to London to become pawns in Henry's political game. When the first news of this victory reached him, Lisle was somewhere between Newcastle and Berwick, and had not yet begun to exercise his authority. It was therefore Hertford who sent the first news to the

---

[37] Hertford to the Council, 29 Oct. 1542 (*HMC Reports*, Bath MSS, Seymour Papers, ii. 29); Henry VIII to Norfolk, 8 Nov. 1542 (*L. and P.*, 17, 1048).
[38] Seymour Papers, ii. 29.   [39] *L. and P.*, xvii. 1048.   [40] Ibid. 1063.
[41] Wriothesley to Hertford, 18 Nov. 1542 (ibid. 1094); Hall, *Unione*, 856; *L. and P.*, xvii. 1117, 1121, 1140, 1142, 1175.

council.[42] On 29 November he wrote again, reporting continued skirmishing in the East March, and the murder of Somerset Herald, who was on his way back from Edinburgh with official letters. There was disarray in Scotland, he wrote with some satisfaction, the temporal lords blaming their 'late overthrow' upon the impetuosity and Anglophobia of the clerical party. The following day Lisle reached Berwick, and received from the treasurer, John Uvedale, the account for which he then assumed responsibility. On 1 December Hertford wrote for the last time, announcing Lisle's arrival and the formal hand-over of responsibility.

The new Warden faced an extremely fluid and confused situation. Henry was furious over the death of his envoy, and demanded the punishment or extradition of the guilty parties. The Scots claimed—truthfully as it turned out—that the murderers were English renegades, but there were objections to yielding to any English pressure, however justified.[43] There were rumours that another great foray was planned 'at the light of the next moon'. Raiding parties were passing backward and forward, sometimes meeting head on in the middle of the night.[44] The whole country, Lisle reported, was 'wonderfully consumed and wasted, especially hay and corn'. He had ordered views to be taken of the state of Tynedale and Redesdale, where it never seemed to be clear which side the dalesmen were on. On 8 December he wrote from Alnwick that the queen of Scots had been delivered of a son. Four days later this intelligence was corrected; the child was not a son but a daughter, 'a very weak child, and not like to live as it is thought'.[45] The English spies may not have been very accurate, but they were certainly quick. Meanwhile Lisle was setting his house in order. Cuthbert Tunstall, the aged but still energetic bishop of Durham, followed him to Alnwick, where he set up his headquarters. Sir William Mallory and Sir Thomas Tempest arrived from Yorkshire, each with 100 men. The earl of Cumberland had sent word that he was on his way with 500 more. On the other hand the bulk of Hertford's force, some 1,100 men, were considered no longer fit to serve and were discharged.[46] Meanwhile there seemed to be little leadership upon the Scottish side. Prisoners, when interrogated, gave the impression that Henry could do what he liked. It was reported that the king, who had not been present at Solway Moss, had gone after the battle to Tyntallen, where he had a mistress 'in the keeping of Oliver Sinclair's wife'.[47] Some construed this to mean that 'he setteth not much store by the queen', others that he was sick. It was soon clear that the latter was the truth, and on 16 or 17 December he

---

[42] *L. and P.*, xvii. 1140.
[43] Lisle to Henry VIII, 4 Dec. 1542 (BL Add. MS 34628 fo. 173); same to same, 7 Dec. 'at four o'clock in the morning' (ibid., fo. 183).
[44] Lisle to the council, 13 Dec. 1542 (ibid., fo. 205).   [45] Ibid., fos. 190, 198.
[46] Lisle to Henry VIII, 7 Dec. 1542 (*L. and P.*, xvii. 1180).
[47] Same to same, 12 Dec. 1542 (*L. and P.*, xvii. 1194; BL Add. MS 32648, fo. 201).

died, leaving the kingdom in the hands of his week-old daughter, without any firm provision for a regency.

In one sense this sudden disaster strengthened Henry's hand, but in another it increased his difficulties. For the time being he did not know with whom he was dealing in the Scottish council. Scottish prisoners or exiles in England could be sent home and bribed or persuaded to act in his interests, but it was impossible to tell whether they would succeed in controlling the situation. At the same time James's death had an inhibiting effect upon Norfolk and Lisle. On 19 December, the latter wrote to the king:

seeing God hath thus disposed his will of the said King of Scots, I thought it should not be to your majesty's honour that we your soldiers should make war or invade upon a dead body, or upon a widow, or upon a young suckling his daughter[48]

A major 'attemptate' in the East March, involving over 2,000 men, had been cancelled. Whether Henry appreciated this squeamishness on the part of his commanders is not clear, but they were not rebuked. In any case it made sense to wait and see what the complexion of the new Scottish government was going to be. Just before James's death there were rumours that he had fallen out badly with Cardinal David Beaton, and that the latter would soon depart to either France or Rome.[49] That would have been good news to the English, and was not now likely to happen, but it remained to be seen whether Beaton and his friends would succeed in controlling the regency. Lisle also had another reason to welcome a suspension of hostilities. He was desperately short of money, and there was not enough in hand at Berwick to pay off those who were due to be discharged. In reporting these circumstances to the king, the Lord Warden also made a significant comment. Contrary to early rumours, the infant queen was 'toward': 'I would that she and her nurse were in my Lord Prince's house', he mused.[50] Whether this possibility had already occurred to Henry or not, it quickly became the cornerstone of English policy in Scotland, and a constant theme of correspondence.

By Christmas Henry seems to have believed that he had the Scottish situation under control. The lords taken at Solway Moss were treated to some lavish hospitality, and required to swear an oath committing them to the support of the marriage policy as a condition of being allowed to return home. A select few also took a secret second oath to uphold the king's claim to the Scottish succession should the young queen 'miscarry'.[51] At the same time Archibald Douglas, earl of Angus, and his brother Sir George, exiles in England since 1528, were encouraged to return and reclaim their lands.

---

[48] *L. and P.*, xvii. 1221; Add. MS 32648, fo. 224.

[49] Sir William Evers to Lisle, 13 Dec. 1542 (*L. and P.*, xvii. 1199).

[50] Ibid. 1221; Add. MS 32648, fo. 224.

[51] *L. and P.*, xvii. 1128; 18, i. 22; *Acts of the Privy Council*, ed. J. Dasent *et al.* (London, 1890–1907), i. 69.

Meanwhile the council of Scotland ruled, and dealt with all those matters
which had been addressed to James V before his unexpected demise.
Threatened it seemed on every side, they were studiously conciliatory
towards their powerful southern neighbour. In formally announcing the
king's death to Lisle on 23 December, they reported also that they had
arrested and were returning the murderers of Somerset Herald, and asked
him to appoint deputies to resolve border disputes.[52] Nevertheless, as Lisle
soon realized, these professions of goodwill needed to be treated with a certain reservation. The council was not in full control. Cross border raids continued and, more irritatingly, Scottish pirates continued their depredations
off the Northumberland coast. The most powerful men in Scotland, Lisle
advised, were the earls of Argyll, Arran, Huntly, and Moray, and Cardinal
Beaton, that determined Anglophobe.[53] As long as Beaton retained any
power, no expressions of goodwill could be taken at their face value. Moreover it soon became clear that, however fearful the council may have been
of Henry's power, they had no intention of allowing him to dictate to them,
directly or indirectly. On 1 January 1543 a Great Council assembled in Edinburgh and named the earl of Arran as Protector for the duration of the
young queen's minority.[54] Henry was furious at this demonstration of independence, and hastened the departure of the 'assured' lords from London,
but in the short term this appointment seemed to work in his favour. Arran
professed sympathy both with the English marriage proposal and with the
reform of the Church. Before the end of January Cardinal Beaton was under
arrest, and the prospect of a dynastic union with England seemed to be
attracting a good deal of support.[55]

In the early weeks of 1543 Scotland was playing a much larger role in
English policy than had been anticipated in the previous autumn. Instead
of defeating an old adversary in order to prevent him from interfering in
the forthcoming Anglo-French war, Henry suddenly found himself confronting what looked like a golden opportunity to assert a long-term dominance over the northern kingdom through a union of the crowns. It is not
surprising that preparations for the French campaign hung fire while the
king of England considered his options in the north. His hope, of course,
was that a mixture of threats and promises, plus the efforts of the 'assured'
lords would enable him to have his way without another major military
effort, but a campaign had to remain a possibility, and continued to be
talked of.[56] Meanwhile Henry was shuffling his pack. The duke of Norfolk

---

[52] *L. and P.*, xvii. 1231.   [53] Lisle to Henry VIII, 24 Dec. 1542 (*L. and P.*, xvii. 1233).
[54] Lisle to the council, 1 Jan., 5 Jan. 1543 (*L. and P.*, xviii. i. 4, 12, 13; Add. MS 32649, fo. 2).
[55] Lisle to Henry VIII, 19 Jan. 1543 (Add. MS 32649, fo. 85); Lisle to Suffolk, 28 Jan. 1543
(*L. and P.*, xviii. i. 88).
[56] Suffolk to the council, 6 Feb. 1543 (*L. and P.*, xviii. i. 123). An 'abstinence' of four months
and the exchange of ambassadors was agreed on 9 Feb. Henry VIII to Arran (*L. and P.*, xviii. i.
132).

was replaced as Lieutenant of the North by the duke of Suffolk, a change which seems to have had no political significance; the earl of Hertford replaced the earl of Sussex as Lord Great Chamberlain; and Viscount Lisle replaced Lord John Russell as Lord Admiral.[57] This did not lead to his immediate recall from the north, and for nearly four months he continued to discharge both functions. They frequently overlapped, because not only did the activities of the Scottish pirates require constant vigilance and frequent representations, but there was a growing anxiety about intervention from France. At first it was believed that the duke of Guise was coming to 'comfort' his sister the queen dowager, and to make sure that the land did not fall into the hands of heretics.[58] On 10 February Henry warned the earl of Angus that, although Guise would not come for a while, the earl of Lennox would shortly be returning from exile in France with designs on Mary of Guise, and possibly on the succession. He would be accompanied by a member of the French king's council who would seek to 'take charge' of affairs in Scotland.[59] Sir Francis Bryan was appointed Vice-Admiral of the North, and in consultation with Lisle did his best to mobilize and deploy sufficient ships from the Humber northward to cope with both these dangers. They enjoyed only partial success, because their resources were stretched, and the weather extremely inclement. On one occasion Lisle reported that there was so much ice in the Tyne that his ships were unable to set out. Towards the end of February the council decided to recall him, and then immediately changed its mind, perhaps in response to some new twist in Scottish politics, concluding that his experience in the borders was for the time being indispensable.[60]

Arran was clearly playing for time, and the messages which were coming out of Scotland would have baffled the best informed. At one moment the Protector was assuring Lisle and Suffolk that the cardinal would be kept securely, and was asking for waggon loads of English bibles to help the process of reform. At the next he was secretly trying to place the kingdom under papal protection.[61] The earl of Bothwell commended himself to the English king, and men as diverse as Sir George Douglas and Oliver Sinclair sent reassurances that the marriage would be negotiated.[62] Early in February the parliament was called, much to the indignation of Henry, who thought he should have been consulted. But at the same time Lisle was instructed to run down the border garrisons, and a three-month truce was negotiated, on the condition that ambassadors should be exchanged.[63] Lisle

[57] Ibid. 36, 100 (27).
[58] Henry VIII to Angus and George Douglas, 10 Feb. 1543 (ibid. 140).   [59] Ibid.
[60] Lisle and Sir Francis Bryan to the council (Add. MS 32649, fo. 97). Suffolk to the council, 23 Feb. 1543 (*L. and P.*, xviii. i. 198; ibid. 213).
[61] Arran seems to have been completely two-faced on the subject of religious reform (*L. and P.*, xviii. i. 324, 542–3, 572); Scarisbrick, *Henry VIII*, 435–8; Donaldson, *James V to James VII*, 63–6.
[62] Add. MS 32649, fo. 85; *L. and P.*, xviii. i. 155.
[63] Add. MS 32650, fo. 12; *L. and P.*, xviii. i. 132.

believed that civil war was about to break out in Scotland, but so complex was the situation that it was impossible to predict who would be fighting whom. In spite of this insecurity, Sir Ralph Sadler was dispatched to Edinburgh in early March, with instructions to support the Protector, and to galvanize the 'assured' Scots, whose lack of commitment was becoming abundantly clear.[64] Skirmishing continued both by land and sea, in spite of the truce, which suggests that neither side was completely in control of its own agents. Nevertheless the garrisons were reduced as planned to 500 men.[65]

In the middle of March the Scottish parliament met in a bellicose mood, immediately demanding the release of Cardinal Beaton, a halt to all ecclesiastical reform, and the cancellation of all embassies to England. The demands were refused, and may have been misrepresented by Arran in order to increase his credit with Henry, because at the same time he was confirmed in full authority as Protector.[66] Sadler was with Lisle in Berwick when this news reached him, and on 17 March they sent a joint dispatch to the king. Sadler's instructions had been to bring the regency government under English control, but the ratification of Arran's powers, and his declaration as the 'second person' of the kingdom, that is, the heir to the throne, somewhat altered the situation. Although 'much contrary to your majesty's purpose touching the government of that realm', Henry would be well advised to accept the *fait accompli*, lest Arran 'fall to the devotion of the French king', a risk which would be greatly increased if Henry pressed his own claim to the succession.[67] In spite of parliamentary objections, the ambassadors would come as planned, and three days later Sadler arrived in Edinburgh to discharge the remainder of his commission. About a fortnight later he received an indignant missive from his master, dated 30 March, in which he was instructed to denounce the 'assured' Scots for having failed to find a more 'suitable' governor than Arran, and to declare that the English king would no longer 'nourish' men who could deliver only words and no deeds.[68] Sadler interpreted his orders with his customary discretion, knowing perfectly well that, however unsatisfactory the 'assured' party might be, it was the only party Henry was likely to have in Scotland. His main task must be to try and keep the slippery Arran in the Anglophile frame of mind which he had professed since the beginning of the year.

For the time being, however, Arran kept most of his promises. The English renegades, Edward Leigh and John Priestman, who had been responsible for the murder of Somerset Herald were duly delivered to the duke of Suffolk in Newcastle, and were interrogated by him before being subject to the process of law. Scottish envoys also came to Newcastle to 'treat of' the marriage.

---

[64] *L. and P.*, xviii. i. 270.   [65] Add. MS 32650, fo. 12.
[66] Lisle to Suffolk, 16, 17 Mar. 1543 (*L. and P.*, xviii. i. 285, 291); Lisle to Henry VIII, 24 Mar. 1543 (Add. MS 32650, fo. 77).
[67] Ibid., fo. 50.   [68] *L. and P.*, xviii. i. 334.

Henry had demanded that, as a preliminary step, the young queen should be sent to England for her upbringing. There could be no question of Arran yielding to such a demand if he wished to retain any credibility with his own people, and it does no credit to the king's intelligence that he appears to have been unable to understand that. Lisle, who should have known enough about the realities of Scottish politics to have expected the outcome, nevertheless wrote to Henry with a show of indignation on 24 March that he understood the envoys to have no adequate commission to treat of the delivery of the child 'which thing considered moveth me to think that they go not so frankly with your majesty as they ought to do'.[69] No doubt that was what a loyal subject was expected to say. He was probably nearer the mark when he suspected Arran of stalling, and sending 'unto Denmark and France to make themselves strong'. Nor did he trust the Douglases, and in that too he was probably correct. Lisle's tour of duty in the north was, however, coming to an end. By 21 April he was back in London, and on 29 April Lord William Parr, the brother of Henry's last queen, Catherine, was instructed as his replacement.[70] He was to support the duke of Suffolk, who remained as the king's lieutenant in the north, to aid Sir Ralph Sadler, and obtain redress for border grievances by 'the law of the borders'. At the same time sub-wardens were appointed for the three marches, and Sir Ralph Ever was given the thankless task of overseeing Tynedale and Redesdale.

With his appointment as Lord Admiral, John Dudley had become one of the great officers of state, a fact which his continued discharge of his responsibilities in the marches tends to conceal. He was an *ex officio* member of the Privy Council, but did not attend his first meeting until 23 April, when he was sworn. On the same day, St George's day, he was also created a knight of the Garter, along with Lord St John and Lord William Parr.[71] Within a year of his elevation to the peerage, he had become a major political figure. This rested upon no very striking success, either diplomatic or military. He had not even been present at Solway Moss, let alone in command, and there had been no action of any significance during his months as Warden. On the other hand he had been competent and assiduous, and single-minded in his loyalty to the king. He was by this time fairly wealthy, with extensive estates mainly in Shropshire and Staffordshire, but he was a service nobleman, not a magnate. Like Cromwell he was not afraid of hard work, often writing his dispatches into the small hours of the morning, and travelling constantly between Newcastle, Alnwick, and Berwick. Nor did he overestimate the discretion open to him. Several of his key letters to the earl of Arran were actually drafted by the council in London, and sent to him to copy over his own signature.[72] As an administrator he was thorough,

---

[69] Add. MS 32650, fo. 77.   [70] *L. and P.*, xviii. i. 468.   [71] Ibid. 450, 451.
[72] For instance that of 11 Jan. 1543, warning him that the fitting out of the *Salamander* and the *Unicorn* would be regarded as a hostile gesture, which seems to have been drafted by Gardiner and corrected by Wriothesley (*L. and P.*, xviii. i. 27).

reliable, and disciplined. At this stage it is misleading to think of him as a soldier, because his only active service had been twenty years before. On the other hand he had served successfully at sea much more recently, and had shown there something of the panache which had earned him his knighthood in 1523. As Henry entered his last great war with France, John Dudley was extremely well placed to take advantage of the opportunities which such campaigns always offered.

As Lord Admiral, Lisle's chief concern during the early months of 1543 was with the north-east. Sir Francis Bryan commanded the ships at sea, but it was Lisle who had to persuade the council to make enough money available for keeping six to eight ships patrolling between the Humber and the Forth.[73] It is hard to judge how effective they were, because there were only a couple of small-scale actions, both poorly recorded. There were constant reports of Scottish ships off the Tyne or Holy Island, and a number of small English coasters seem to have been taken. The French were a bigger worry, because they were not only pirates. They might be bringing money or men to support the queen mother, who was assiduously countermining English influence in Scotland, but who was seriously short of resources. Rumours of the coming of the duke of Guise himself turned out to be a false alarm, but Matthew Stuart, earl of Lennox, successfully eluded the English patrols and was with the queen mother at Linlithgow by 5 April.[74] Ships were also needed to safeguard the supply lines. Grain for the garrisons had to be brought from Hull and Grimsby, and should that be taken by marauders, the consequences would be serious indeed. However, by the early summer the focus of attention was shifting south. On 27 May the king ratified his treaty with the emperor on oath, a ceremony at which Lisle was one of the council witnesses, and a month later delivered an ultimatum to the French ambassador. This was in substance, although not in form, a declaration of war. The main English fleet, some twenty-two vessels, was already mobilized, and had fought its first engagement in the Narrow Seas on 6 June. A few weeks later about 5,000 English troops under Sir John Wallop were sent across to Calais for the defence of the Low Countries.[75]

On 15 June Lisle briefed Sir Rees Mansell as his Vice-Admiral for the Narrow Seas, with instructions to 'go upon' the French, but not to molest any ship of Spain, Flanders, Portugal, or Scotland. Danish and Hanse ships were to be searched for contraband, but not otherwise detained.[76] At this point the Scottish ambassadors were on their way to London to sign a treaty of amity and marriage, and Henry was anxious not to destabilize such a

---

[73] Bryan's Instructions, 27 Jan. 1543 (*L. and P.*, xviii. i. 83); Lisle to the council, 22 Jan. 1543 (ibid. 68).

[74] Donaldson, *James V to James VII*, 65.

[75] *L. and P.*, xviii. i. 603; Scarisbrick, *Henry VIII*, 440–1.

[76] *L. and P.*, xviii. i. 712.

favourable situation by risking incidents at sea. However, it was already too late to start planning a major campaign for 1543, so the top-level discussions were for a joint invasion of France in June 1544. On 1 July the treaty of Greenwich was signed with the earl of Arran, and it seemed that at last the way was clear for the king to pursue his main objective. The expectation was for a run-down of the forces still in the north, and for an autumn and winter of raiding and counter-raiding around the Calais Pale. Lisle would keep ships at sea as a precaution against any surprise, but the serious business of mobilizing the fleet would not begin until about February. However the reality turned out to be rather different, because the Scots again emerged as a rogue factor. It was all very well for Arran to sign a treaty, but his grasp of the situation was becoming extremely fragile. In spite of assurances to the contrary, Cardinal Beaton had been virtually set at liberty by being transferred to his own castle of St Andrews at the end of March. By the middle of July the pro-French party had rallied to him, and he was able to move the young queen and her mother from Linlithgow to Stirling by the end of the month.[77] Arran ratified the treaty of Greenwich on 25 August, but it was a meaningless gesture. At the same time Henry had made his own and Arran's task more difficult by attempting to insist that Mary should be handed over at once, and that the Scots should formally break off their alliance with France. Sadler warned him that such pressure would end by driving Arran into the French camp, and he was right.

Fearing the imminent onset of civil war in Scotland, on 31 August Henry ordered Suffolk to mobilize an army of 16,000–20,000 men to aid the regent against his enemies. The duke responded with some enthusiasm, asking that he might be given the assistance of the Lord Admiral to lead the vanward and the earl of Derby to lead the rearward.[78] Dudley's military reputation had clearly benefited from his time in the marches, but the expedition did not take place, because before it could be mobilized Arran's position had collapsed, and he had joined the other side. Henry was furious, but even he could see that there was little point in launching an army into such a political jungle. Paradoxically, Arran's defection did not leave the king of England without a party in Scotland. The earl of Angus and his brother had always had difficulty in working with Arran, and were much happier working against him. More surprisingly, the same was true of Matthew Stuart, earl of Lennox, who had been specifically sent from France to strengthen the cardinal's party. No sooner had Arran defected to the French than Lennox defected to the English.[79] However, this realignment was not in itself sufficient to redeem the situation, and on 11 December the Scottish parliament formally repudiated the treaty of Greenwich, and

[77] *Concilia Scotiae Ecclesiae Scoticanae*, ed. J. Robertson, Bannatyne Club, 113 (1866), pp. cxlii–cxliii; Donaldson, *James V to James VII*, 65.

[78] Suffolk to Henry VIII, 2 Sept. 1543 (*L. and P.*, xviii. ii. 118).

[79] Donaldson, *James V to James VII*, 68–9.

renewed the alliance with France. A year after the victory at Solway Moss Henry had precisely nothing to show for it, and his northern border was, if anything, at greater risk than before.

Lisle spent the second half of 1543 mainly about his business as Lord Admiral, but he was not at sea. English ships were operational throughout the late summer and autumn, but in small squadrons which did not require the Admiral's presence. Sir Rees Mansell reported an inconclusive skirmish with the French on 9 July, in which the enemy showed an unexpectedly clean pair of heels.[80] Privateers were licensed, such as Miles Middleton, Yeoman of the Guard, who was authorized to 'go upon' the king's enemies with two ships, at his own expense.[81] It was not until the end of November that the last of these 'enterprises' was called home, when William Woodhouse brought ten very storm-battered ships back to the Thames. The Admiral's sights were rather set upon the following year, when a 'navy royal' on the grand scale would probably be needed, and all the capital ships of 300 tons and over would need to be ready for mobilization. During these months also Lisle was a frequent attender at court and council. On 1 July and again on 23 December he carried the sword of state at the creation ceremony for new peers. On the latter occasion the beneficiaries were his friends the Parrs. Lord William became earl of Essex and Sir William Lord Parr of Horton.[82] By this time Dudley was sufficiently important to make prolonged absence from the court undesirable, and he was no doubt glad of the opportunity to put right any consequences of his earlier absence in the borders. One of the problems of serving the king at a distance was that you had to ask for your rewards through intermediaries, and benefits tended not to come to those who did not actively seek them. It was much better to present your own requests if you were in a position to do so. It was more effective, and created fewer obligations. On 3 July Lisle obtained a very lucrative licence to export 400 tons of tallow and 400 dickers of calfskins without paying the normal customs dues; and on 22 July he was granted the stewardship of the royal manors of Bromsgrove, King's Norton, Oddingly, Clifton, and Droitwich, all in Worcestershire.[83] Such unspectacular but profitable acquisitions were the staple diet of successful courtiers and office-holders, among whom Dudley must now be ranked. He also continued to buy and sell land through the Court of Augmentations, but it is difficult to be sure how far his position enabled him to secure preferential treatment.

The king's last marriage, which took place on 12 July 1543, may also have contributed to the Lord Admiral's rising political profile. Catherine, the widowed Lady Latimer, who caught Henry's eye in the spring of that year,

---

[80] *L. and P.*, xviii. i. 849.   [81] Patent under the Admiralty seal, 4 Aug. 1543 (ibid., ii. 8).

[82] Ibid., i. 803; ibid., ii. 516.

[83] Ibid., i. 981 (25); ibid., ii. 107. These lands are described as being in the king's hands by the death of the late Queen Jane.

belonged to the reforming circle of those who had looked to Thomas Cromwell. Her brother, Sir William, had received a barony by patent in 1539, when Cromwell still had a major say in such promotions, and the marriage was recognized as a major setback for the religious conservatives at court. Still reeling from the fiasco of the king's fifth marriage, the sixth effectively denied them a way back. As Henry's health deteriorated, and his temper became increasingly volatile, it was always possible that he would turn against his latest queen and her friends. But the odds were on their side, and as Prince Edward was not yet 6 in July 1543, a royal minority seemed increasingly likely. It was a time for those who were good at political arithmetic to start doing their sums, and both self-interest and his own recent background prompted Lord Lisle to align himself with the Parrs and the Seymours against the Howards and their allies. On 20 June he wrote from Greenwich to Lord Parr at Alnwick, sending him news of the doings of the fleet, and the latest gossip of the court, adding significantly, 'My Lady Latimer your sister is here with the Lady Mary ...'.[84] The promotion of Parr to the earldom of Essex was thus a good political omen for Lisle. After a period during which his future at court must have been in some doubt, he was now again upon the winning side. On 28 January 1544 it was to the Lord Admiral that Eustace Chapuys confided a message from the emperor to the council which he did not wish to trust to writing.

Charles was willing to declare war upon the Scots in support of his ally, and this was welcome news to Henry faced, as he now was, with the necessity for a major campaign against France in the summer. Either he could trust Angus and Lennox to keep the Scottish council too busy to think of marching south, or he could try to repeat the tactics which had worked so well in 1542. In January 1544 he was not inclined to trust anyone. By the end of that month he had already nominated the duke of Suffolk to carry out an 'enterprise' against Edinburgh in March which would deploy 15,000 men, in addition to placing an extra 2,000 in garrison.[85] On 2 February Suffolk wrote, welcoming the mission, and asking for Lisle, Hertford, and Sir John Gage to assist in its execution.[86] By the middle of February Lisle was assessing the number of ships available, and the talk was of an army royal; it was even rumoured that the king would take the field in person. In reporting these aggressive gestures to the emperor, Chapuys also expressed the view that the French were not interested in intervening in the north. Henry was determined to subdue the Scots, and would put out 150 sail to transport his army. The king had apparently accepted that Angus and Lennox had not betrayed him over the repudiation of the treaty, and there was therefore no case for making them the particular targets of his wrath, but the 'treachery'

[84] Ibid., i. 740.
[85] Suffolk to Henry VIII, 2 Feb. 1544; same to the council, 11 Feb. 1544 (*L. and P.*, xix. i. 86, 103).
[86] Ibid.

of the Scots in general must be severely punished.[87] At that point, however, Henry modified his plans. Suffolk was recalled, ostensibly because he would be required to accompany the king to France, and on 11 March Hertford was briefed to take his place, necessitating the postponement of the enterprise by several weeks. On 20 March Lisle took his leave of the king and set out for Harwich, where the fleet was assembling. The following day all those ships that had rendezvoused in the Thames departed for the same destination. On 30 March Hertford reported that they had begun to arrive in the Tyne, having been scattered by fog on the way. A fortnight later the main fleet had still not arrived, causing confusion and some irritation in Hertford's headquarters.[88] On 12 April the council assured him that the ships had been off Yarmouth on 8 April, and should have reached him before their letter, but they did not. On 17 April Lisle was alleged to be at Hull, and the following day at long last he arrived at Tynemouth.[89] No adequate reason was ever offered for this delay, which seriously disrupted plans for the campaign, and there is no suggestion that the Admiral was responsible. Naval warfare in the sixteenth century was a slow and uncertain business. Hertford meanwhile was somewhat at odds with the king over stategy. In his view the English should aim to establish certain strong points on a long-term basis, to maintain an element of control. Specifically he advised the fortification and garrisoning of Inchkieth to control the Firth of Forth. Henry, however, intended his forces to be in and out again as quickly as was consistent with doing serious damage. His eye was still on the main campaign against France, and he wanted his Admiral back in the south as soon as possible to keep the Narrow Seas.

By 21 April Lisle had joined Hertford in Newcastle, and every nerve was being strained to embark the remaining troops. The commanders were also complaining vigorously of defective and fraudulent victualling, for which they held the chief commissioner, the bishop of Winchester, responsible.[90] Gardiner defended his own competence and integrity convincingly, but the complaints may well have been justified, and the opportunity for Lisle and Hertford to undermine a political enemy was too tempting to resist. Money was also in short supply, and there were tactical problems presented by the need to co-ordinate a strong raid against Haddington with the main operation. At the end of April Lisle's accounts show that Chapuys's estimate of 150 sail was well wide of the mark: 68 ships were paid for one month, of which only 11 were the king's own;[91] 12,000 men had been embarked, plus another 4,000 who were going overland via Haddington. In

---

[87] Chapuys to the emperor, 2 Mar. 1544 (ibid. 147).
[88] Hertford to the council (ibid. 264).   [89] Ibid. 317, 348, 350.
[90] BL Add. MS 32654, fo. 141. For a discussion of the justice of these charges, see G. Redworth, *In Defence of the Church Catholic* (Oxford, 1990), 210–1.
[91] On 25 Apr. 1544, 'An estimate for ships against Scotland' (*L. and P.*, xix. i. 396; Add. MS 32654, fo. 164).

spite of all the fuss, and the size of the stake in Scotland, this was still only a sideshow in the eyes of the king. On 3 May the English force landed about two miles from Leith and immediately put themselves in battle order, with Lisle commanding the vanguard and Hertford the main army. They were challenged by a Scottish force about half their size led, ostensibly, by Cardinal Beaton. This may well have been no more than a delaying tactic, but the English descriptions all made a point of mocking the cardinal's allegedly precipitate flight.

but when he saw the vanward march down towards him, and that he might perceive they had a great devotion to wet their shoes to come to his Holiness, like a valiant champion he gave his horse the spurs and turned his back,[92]

as Lisle wrote a few days later to Paget. More significantly the expedition captured the town of Leith with very little resistance, 'and there they found such riches as they thought not to have found in any town of Scotland'. Some ordnance was also taken, and two substantial ships, the *Salamander* and the *Unicorn*, which happened to be in the haven.[93] While the English warships occupied themselves by taking a number of small coastal forts in the area, the army advanced on Edinburgh. The citizens offered to surrender on terms, which Hertford rejected, declaring that he had come to punish earlier Scottish treachery, and had no desire to be subjected to any more. He was clearly determined to sack the city, and the inhabitants made what defence they could. Lisle attacked the main gate on the morning of 8 May, blowing it in with a culverin. Thereafter the city was an easy prey, but the attackers took a number of casualties from the guns of the castle, which they had neither the time nor the resources to beseige.[94] Hertford still hankered after holding Leith, but on 15 May he was thanked for his services and instructed to return at once, having razed the defences of Edinburgh.[95] It remained to be seen what Hertford's exploit had accomplished; meanwhile he was to send 2,900 of his men straight to Calais for the French campaign, and Lisle was to appoint ships and 2,000 men to keep the Narrow Seas. By 18 May the whole expeditionary force was back at Berwick, having returned overland burning and destroying everything in their path. The ships had been sent on ahead 'laden with spoil and gunshot', and Lisle scarcely paused before sailing straight for London. Hertford's enthusiastic commendations preceded him to the council.

The immediate effect of this incursion upon Scotland was low-key, but significant. Both Arran and Beaton were considerably discredited, and at a special convention summoned to Stirling in June the Governorship was

[92]   Hertford and Lisle to Henry VIII, 4 May, 6 May 1544 (Add. MS 32654, fos. 168, 173); Lisle to Paget, 8 May 1544 (*L. and P.*, xix. i. 481; Hall, *Unione*, 860).

[93]   *L. and P.*, xix. i. 481; Add. MS 32654, fo. 173.

[94]   Hall, *Unione*, 860. Hertford, Lisle, and Sadler to Henry VIII, 9 May 1544 (*L. and P.*, xix. i. 483).

[95]   Council to Hertford and Lisle (ibid. 508).

transferred to the queen mother, Mary of Guise.[96] This may not have seemed much of a gain from the English point of view, but Mary was able to work with Angus and Lennox in a way which neither Arran nor Beaton could have done. On 6 July Lennox married Margaret Douglas, strengthening his ties with Angus, and bringing him (or rather his children) into the problematic English succession. Henry continued to rely on him, and in one sense he was justified because Mary made no attempt to come to the aid of her French kindred in the southern war. On the other hand by the end of 1544 there had been a general reconciliation of the warring factions in Scotland, leaving the English no nearer accomplishing the marriage alliance which they had so strenuously sought.

By the time that the Lord Admiral returned to court, most of the preparations for 'wafting' Henry's last great army royal were already complete. On 10 June the emperor instructed his own officers to afford Lisle every assistance, but the French offered no resistance on the sea, and by the middle of the month over 30,000 men had been shipped across to Calais. There they were divided into two armies, one commanded by the duke of Norfolk, and the other by Suffolk. The only thing that was lacking was a campaign strategy. Charles wanted English men and money to support his own priority of a direct thrust to Paris, and he did not want his ally encumbered with an ailing king. On the latter point he had the support of most of the English council. Henry, on the other hand, wished to campaign in person, and was determined to have something to show for his efforts at the end of the day. On 20 June Norfolk was instructed to besiege Montreuil, while Suffolk waited on the borders of the Calais Pale.[97] The siege was a shambles, and Norfolk complained bitterly of a lack of supplies and support of every kind. He may well have been justified, because by the time Henry arrived at Calais on 14 July, it was clear that Montreuil was only a sideshow. He joined Suffolk, and they moved directly against Boulogne, investing the town on 19 July. Thereafter the king remained deaf to all pleas from his ally, and to all complaints from Norfolk. He had set his heart on taking Boulogne, and was not to be diverted by any consideration whatsoever. The earl of Hertford had already been summoned from the north, where his place was taken by the earl of Shrewsbury, and Lisle was brought ashore once the fleet had performed its main task, to accompany the king to the siege. By 28 July, as the council reported to Norfolk, he was responsible for the 'quarter between the green bulwark and the Bullen gate'.[98] Henry was clearly concentrating his resources, and anxious to have all his best soldiers deployed to secure his main objective. Contrary to what had been expected, it proved

[96] Donaldson, *James V to James VII*, 70.
[97] *L. and P.*, xix. i. 741; Hall, *Unione*, 861; Scarisbrick, *Henry VIII*, 447.
[98] *L. and P.*, xix. i. 1003.

a therapeutic experience. The king enjoyed himself hugely and his health was better than it had been for years. However, all good things come to an end. On 11 September the castle was blown up, and the following day a general assault commenced. Two days later the town surrendered and on 18 September Henry made his ceremonial entry.[99] On the same day the emperor, totally disgusted with his ally's preoccupation, and lack of interest in the joint campaign, signed the peace of Crespy with Francis, and left the English to continue the war on their own. It looked as though Boulogne was going to be a very expensive acquisition.

However, for the time being Henry was so pleased with himself that he seemed not to mind Charles's defection. For nearly a fortnight he remained within the captured town, making detailed dispositions for its future government and defence. However, it quickly became apparent that complacency would be misplaced. Within a few days of the fall of Boulogne the Dauphin moved swiftly to the relief of Montreuil, and Norfolk had considerable difficulty in extricating himself.[100] With the emperor's withdrawal his German mercenaries had become distinctly unreliable, and he had a lucky escape. On 30 September the king returned quietly, almost secretly, to England, leaving the two dukes and the bulk of his army in Boulogne. His intention seems to have been to winter the army there in strength, and to resume the offensive as soon as weather permitted in the spring. On the day of his departure he named Lord Lisle as Captain of the town and Senechal of the Boulonnais, with a fee of 40s. a day.[101] Lisle was less than delighted by this evidence of his master's confidence, fearing, apparently, that he was being shunted into a political siding. There remains among the state papers a single page, written in his own hand, folded and endorsed on the outside 'My Lord Admiral's requests'. It carries no superscription, and was clearly not a letter to either the king or the council. Perhaps it was an *aide-mémoire* for a letter which was never written, or has not survived. More likely it was a brief for Sir William Paget, the Principal Secretary, who returned to England with the king, and with whom Lisle was on terms of close friendship.

Although brief, it is a remarkably frank and revealing document:

My trust is that I shall have the King's Majesty's favour t'enjoy the office of High Admiralty of England, for it is an office of honour, of estimacion and of profit, and within the realm; and having his gracious favour thereunto I may occupy it with a deputy and serve in this (as Captain of Boulogne) notwithstanding, which I beseech your lordships to consider.[102]

He went on to request that in Boulogne he might have 50 footmen and 50 horsemen, counted as his household servants, and an additional 400

---

[99] Hall, *Unione*, 862; *L. and P.*, xix. ii. 221.
[100] Ibid. 278, 285; Scarisbrick, *Henry VIII*, 448–9.   [101] *L. and P.*, xix. ii. 337.
[102] SP1/193, fo. 15; *L. and P.*, xix. ii. 338.

footmen commanded by his own nominees. He already had the leadership
of the largest single contingent (700) among the garrison, and this extra provision seems to have been intended to place his authority beyond any possibility of challenge. He was also prepared to look beyond the immediate
requirements of the military situation, and seek to establish himself in suitable state.

Item, to have some arable land, pasture, mead and woods for the provision of my
house at reasonable rent.
Item, to have the choice of the gentlemen's sporting houses or pyles in the country,
with the demesnes, to be for recreation in time of peace ... To have admiral jurisdiction ... To have provision of my house shipped here or to Calais, custom free ...

Lisle was clearly a man who did not miss a trick when it came to promoting
his own interests, although given the insecurity of the English hold on
Boulogne, many of his requests could be classed as highly optimistic. How
much was communicated to the council we do not know, but he retained
the Admiralty, which was probably his chief concern. It may never have
been the king's intention to leave him in Boulogne once the immediate fear
of a French counter-attack had receded. At the end of January 1545 he was
recalled to deal with the mobilization of the fleet, and replaced by Sir
Thomas Poynings.[103]

The four months which he spent in Boulogne cost Lisle considerable
trouble and anxiety. Within a few days of the king's departure both Norfolk
and Suffolk decamped to Calais with their forces, leaving only the basic
garrison behind. The reason alleged was that they feared the Dauphin, with
nearly 50,000 men, was about to launch an attack upon the Pale.[104] If they
really believed that, their intelligence was defective because the prince,
with plague decimating his camp, was in fact about to retire and disband
his army. More likely the two dukes disagreed with the king's strategy, and
decided to force his hand. Henry was furious, and ordered them to return
to Boulogne, but that was now manifestly impossible as the Dauphin was
indulging in a final flurry of activity, and no one on the English side seems
to have had any understanding of his predicament. No sooner did they
reach Calais than Norfolk and Suffolk started shipping their armies home-
ward, and Henry was forced to accept the *fait accompli* although with a very
bad grace. Lisle got some of the backlash from this. He was probably not
reluctant to see his powerful colleagues depart, because they would have
been bound to confuse the command structure, but no sooner had they
gone than he found himself involved in an acrimonious correspondence,
first with the council and then with the king himself on the subject of victuals. Lisle complained that he was inadequately provided, and on 19 Octo-

---

[103] Instructions to the Earl of Hertford, 31 Jan. 1545 (*L. and P.*, xx. i. 121).
[104] Ibid., xix. ii. 353. Henry's response was furious but unavailing (*State Papers of Henry VIII*,
x. 104).

ber the council wrote sharply, telling him to be more careful with his supplies, because the French were too strong at sea for him to be resupplied.[105] Three days later Henry wrote in a similar vein, telling him that he was supposed to have been provided for six months, and would have to be more careful in future.[106] A few days later the Captain must have complained again; some provisions had arrived, but they were not adequate. In what can only be described as a very tetchy response on 29 October, the council disclaimed responsibility for the supplies, which had been sent independently, and proceeded to lecture him on the deployment of 2,000 reinforcements who were being sent, and upon his alleged failure to fortify 'Base Bolleyne'.[107] Two days later the extra men were dispatched under the command of Sir Thomas Poynings, together with the much needed victuals, and £2,000 in cash to cover the new commitments.

Lisle's problems were not over, however. Early in November he seems to have picked up a report of French troop movements, which he interpreted as a possible threat to his garrison. Given the Dauphin's known determination to recover Boulogne, and the recent failure of an attempted Anglo-French negotiation, this was not an unreasonable fear. The French had in fact walked out of the negotiations in Calais precisely because Henry had refused to contemplate abandoning his conquest.[108] Nevertheless on 18 November Lisle received a severe rebuke from the council for heeding alarmist tales. The king, they informed him, thought it 'very strange' that he should believe any French army to be threatening him at such a season. He was to get on with the task of fortifying his perimeter, and not to divert men to confront a non-existent threat.[109] At some point during these months he also lost his eldest son. There were two Henry Dudleys involved at Boulogne. One, usually referred to as 'Harry Dudley', was captain of 100 infantry, and this was probably Lisle's second cousin, a son of the 'lord quondam'. The other was his son, a youth of 18 or 19, who was one of those knighted by the king before his departure on 30 September.[110] Whether he was really as promising a soldier as this would seem to suggest, or whether the knighthood was a compliment to his father we do not know. Within a few weeks he was dead, of disease, apparently, rather than enemy action, but nothing is known of the circumstances. Lisle never referred to his son in any surviving letter and no one else at the time commented upon his loss,

---

[105] *L. and P.*, xix. ii. 457.

[106] Henry VIII to Lisle, 22 Oct. 1544. The same day he received another similar rebuke from the council, of which the surviving draft is in Gardiner's hand (*L. and P.*, xix. ii. 473, 475).

[107] Council at Calais to Lisle (*L. and P.*, xix. ii. 500).

[108] Hertford and Paget had been commissioned to conduct these negotiations, which had begun on 18 Oct., but no progress was made on account of the king's intransigence (Scarisbrick, *Henry VIII*, 450).

[109] *L. and P.*, xix. ii. 629.

[110] *State Papers of Henry VIII*, x. 75; *L. and P.*, xix. ii. 258. On the death of Henry Dudley, see the epitaph of 1545 printed ibid. xx. ii, App. 1.

but some personal distress must have compounded the difficulties of his situation.

At some point between 30 November, when he wrote to the king from Boulogne to reassure him about the state of the fortifications, and 26 December when he signed a council letter at Greenwich, he must have returned to England. This may well have been to demand in person part at least of the arrears of pay due to his garrison, because when he returned to his post on about 7 January he took with him £3,000, which he reckoned was less than half of what was owing.[111] As we have seen, on 31 January he was recalled and replaced, but he did not leave at once. On 12 February the council wrote to the earl of Shrewsbury, reporting that a French attack upon Boulogne had been repulsed by the Lord Admiral 'Lieutenant there', with assistance from Calais. It must have been an attack in some force if the French really suffered six or seven hundred casualties as the council alleged, and suggests that the king's rebuke in November had been misplaced.[112] In spite of the difficulties, Lisle was not recalled because of any deficiencies in his conduct at Boulogne, but because as Lord Admiral, he needed to give his whole attention to the navy in what was already promising to be a very dangerous summer. After the defection of the emperor Henry had no allies, and a war on two fronts. His forces continued to raid across the Scottish border, but achieved nothing except the conversion of the earl of Angus from an ally into an enemy. It was Angus who, on 27 February 1545, inflicted a rare defeat upon the English at the battle of Ancrum Moor. However, the real danger in the north came not from the Scots but from the French. Relieved of the emperor's hostility, Francis seemed to have both the means and the opportunity to intervene. By the spring there were constant reports that French troops would be sent to Scotland by both the eastward and the westward routes. At the same time the likelihood of a renewed assault upon Boulogne and the possibility of a large-scale invasion of the south of England had to be provided against.

By April 1545, when the naval preparations were in full swing, Henry was desperately short of money, and his search for allies among the protestant princes of Germany was no more successful than it had been five years earlier. They knew that the king of England would do nothing to help them if their quarrel with the emperor should come to a head, and were not prepared to do anything to help him, beyond allowing him to recruit some mercenaries. England's resources were dangerously overstretched, and for the first time it was proving difficult to recruit enough seamen for the king's ships. Wages were raised from 5s. per month to 6s. 8d., and fierce proclamations threatened death by martial law for desertion, but during the winter of 1544/5 it was not possible to put enough ships to sea to cover all

---

[111] *L. and P.*, xix. ii. 683, 777; ibid., xx. i. 39.   [112] Ibid. 180.

commitments.[113] Newcastle and Bristol were told that they would have to provide for their own defence, because all the ships that could be mobilized were needed in the narrow seas.[114] Only a promising growth in privateering activity since the summer of 1544 had offered any relief in the general gloom, and even that had contributed to the difficulties of naval recruitment. Benevolences and forced loans had been levied in 1542 and 1544, heavy parliamentary subsidies in 1543 and 1545. Relations between the emperor and the king of France remained ominously cordial, and although there was no sign of a joint crusade against the schismatic islanders, there were distinct signs that the long-threatened General Council of the Church might at last become a reality. The panic of 1539 had turned out to be a false alarm, but 1545 was to be the supreme test of Henry's kingship.

On 7 May an imperial agent reported that the French plan was to launch a fleet of over 300 ships and galleys against 'an island'—probably the Isle of Wight—establish a bridgehead there, and then proceed to the reduction of Boulogne.[115] He was probably misinformed, because such a scheme makes little tactical sense, but the French were forced to improvise their tactics. The main objective was Boulogne, but Admiral d'Annebaut had between 120 and 300 ships of various sizes assembled at Le Havre, Harfleur, and Honfleur long before the army was ready to move. Rather than keep this large force consuming money and victuals in idleness, it was decided to use it for a large-scale raid on the English coast. The English seem to have believed that a serious invasion was intended. Commissions of array were issued between 7 May and 14 June, and regional military commands set up under the dukes of Norfolk and Suffolk, Lord Russell, and the earl of Arundel.[116] By the end of May the mobilization of the English fleet was completed, and the Lord Admiral had decided upon a pre-emptive strike. On 19 June he presented a plan to the king for the destruction of a large part of the French fleet at its moorings in the Seine estuary. On or about 25 June he tried to enter the Seine with 160 ships and some 12,000 men, but the weather frustrated him. At first there was no wind, and his ships exchanged fire at a disadvantage with the French galleys, and then a wind arose which forced the galleys into shelter, but also threatened to drive the English ships on to the shoals, so they stood out to sea with their mission unaccomplished. All Lisle had to show for his pains was an encounter with twenty-one French galleys near the island of Alderney where, in spite of the fickle winds, he managed to sink several and put the rest to flight.[117] By 15 July he was back at Portsmouth, and

---

[113] P. L. Hughes and J. F. Larkin, *Tudor Royal Proclamations* (New Haven and London, 1964–9), i. 347: 25 Jan. 1545; ibid. 346–7: 24 Jan. 1545.

[114] D. Loades, *The Tudor Navy* (Aldershot, 1992), 129.

[115] St Mauris to Covos (*L. and P.*, xx. i. 682).

[116] Hall, *Unione*, 863; Scarisbrick, *Henry VIII*, 454.

[117] Hall, *Unione*, 862–3; *L. and P.*, xx. i. 823, 987, 1023, 1184.

attending meetings of the council, which was with the king as he inspected his coastal defences.

Meanwhile d'Annebaut had got his fleet to sea, and on 19 July appeared at the entrance to the Solent, no attempt having been made to intercept him. He now had the same advantage that Lisle had enjoyed some three weeks earlier, but equally failed to turn it to account. Probing attacks were made against the Isle of Wight, but the local defenders were ready and repulsed them. The absence of wind did not worry d'Annebaut. He organized his fleet in squadrons, and sent his galleys forward to bombard the English ships. A fitful breeze then arose, and several of the largest of Henry's war-ships moved out to the attack. The resulting engagement was complex and inconclusive, owing more to the wind than to the tactical skill of either com-mander, but confronted by a fleet which was almost as numerous as their own, and fully prepared to fight, the French backed off. This was to prove the decisive turning-point of the campaign, although neither Lisle nor the king could have known that at the time. In the short term they were con-cerned about where d'Annebaut would strike next, and shaken by the dra-matic loss of the *Mary Rose*, which had gone down like a stone as she moved out to battle stations. Reporting this incident a few days later, Chapuys cor-rectly declared that she had been lost because the lower gunports had been left open 'for firing', and when the ship had keeled over under a sudden gust of wind, the water had rushed in through the open ports.[118] At the time it was the loss of 500 lives rather than the loss of the ship which caused com-ment. The water was not deep, and it was fully expected that both the ship and the guns would be salvaged. Meanwhile the danger of invasion was not over, and d'Annebaut moved along the Sussex coast, launching further probes against Brighton and Newhaven, but always finding the defenders prepared. Whether by design or accident of the wind he then crossed over to Boulogne, landing some 7,000 men to join the army which had by then advanced to the seige. A blockade of the harbour may have been intended, but if so it was again frustrated by the weather, which made it impossible for him to hold his ships on station. By 10 August an easterly gale had driven him back to the Sussex coast.

Lisle, meanwhile, had been struggling to get his fleet to sea in order to go in pursuit. He was delayed, not only by determined efforts to salvage the

---

[118] Van der Delft to Charles V, 24 July 1545 (ibid. 1263). William Harrison's Chronology, written in the 1580s but apparently repeating an oral tradition, gives the following account: 'At the same time also certain of the king's navy setting forward to go forth of the haven of Portsmouth to encounter with them [the French] the Mary Rose a noble ship was lost through oversight by reason that her portholes were left open and her ordnance unbreched for certain hours after the king had dined in her, some of the officers were so drunk that the master gunner killed the carpenter because he meddled with his office, whereupon ye rest fell together by the ears. Whilst this was toward the vessel sank ...' (BL Add. MS 70984 *sub* 1545). The only problem with this attractive story is that Henry almost certainly dined on the *Henry Grace a Dieu*.

Mary Rose, but also by sickness among his crews and a shortage of experienced captains. By 3 August Suffolk was satisfied that Portsmouth was sufficiently garrisoned to withstand an attack in the absence of the fleet, and Lisle was considering his options.[119] He was reluctant to set out without reliable information of d'Annebaut's location, in case he should allow the French to get between him and the English coast. A suggestion from Paget to isolate the French galleys was dismissed as too risky, but Lisle was far from being a cautious or conservative tactical thinker. The fleet orders which he eventually issued on 10 August show him to have been fully abreast of the latest French and Spanish thinking. Not only had he organized his ships into squadrons, determined by their size and firepower, but he also clearly envisaged manœuvring in formation, which had been considered impossible only fifteen years earlier.

It is to be considered that the ranks must keep such order in sailing that none impeach another. Wherefore it is requisite that every of the said ranks keep right way with another, and take such regard to the observing of the same that no ship pass his fellows forward or backward nor slack anything, but [keep] as they were in one line, and that there may be half a cable length between every of the ships ...[120]

The purpose of these manœuvres was still to bring his ships to boarding stations in the most favourable circumstances, but tightly controlled and co-ordinated gunfire was now seen as a necessary means of bringing that about. Even in 1530 gunfire had been seen principally as a way of causing alarm and confusion.

When these orders were issued, Lisle had 69 ships and 10,390 men ready for the sea. He had also abandoned immediate attempts to salvage the *Mary Rose*, having recovered most of her rigging and some of her guns.[121] The Venetian experts had succeeded in breaking off her mainmast, and the large hulks which were being used in an attempt to lift the wreck were required for active service. On 7 August an English patrol clashed with prowling French galleys off St Helen's point, but the main fleet was some way away. On 11 August, when d'Annebaut was off Rye with a total of nearly 200 ships, the Lord Admiral was finally authorized to move, and he left Portsmouth on the morning tide the following day. On 15 August he made contact with the enemy, and reported that they had exchanged over 200 shots, with little damage to either side.[122] After a day of somewhat desultory manœuvring in light and fickle winds, both fleets hove to. On the morning of 17 August Lisle reported in total frustration that the French had slipped away under cover of darkness, and there was insufficient wind to

[119] *L. and P.*, xx. 2, 13, 16, 24, 26, 27.
[120] *Fighting Instructions, 1530–1816*, ed. J. S. Corbett, Navy Records Society, 29 (1905), 20–3. The original is among the Le Fleming MSS in the Cumbria Record Office.
[121] Suffolk, Lisle, and St John to Paget, 5 Aug. 1545 (*L. and P.*, xx. ii. 38).
[122] Ibid. 61, 94, 108, 136, 142. The muster of Lisle's fleet is contained in Salisbury MS 137, fo. 76, calendared in *L. and P.*, xx. ii. App. 27.

make search for them.[123] Three days later he wrote again to say that his scouts had discovered that the French had retreated and were unlikely to return. At first sight d'Annebaut's lack of effectiveness is puzzling, given the huge efforts which had been invested in preparing his armament, but a dispatch from Lisle on 21 August probably provides the explanation. By that time his spies had located the enemy on the Normandy coast, where they were disembarking many sick men. It seems that plague, or some similar epidemic, had brought the French effort to nothing.[124] Lisle's attempt to exploit this situation led to another skirmish, but his own victuals were running out by then, and by 24 August he was back at Portsmouth. There, on 27 August, fresh instructions reached him. Once he was sure that the main French fleet had broken up, he was to send some of his ships to 'keep' the narrow seas. The remainder he was to victual for a fortnight, and make some 'enterprise' against the French coast.[125] On 2 September he crossed to Normandy, where he captured and burned the town of Treport, destroying thirty ships in the harbour there. It was a small enough success, but all that either side had to show for a massive outlay of money and effort. On his return he discovered that plague had broken out in his own fleet and it was all he could do to find enough 'clean' ships to send to Dover, let alone the 5,000 men whom he was required to send on to reinforce the Calais garrison.

On 18 September, having wound up his operation at Portsmouth and left the Channel guard to Sir Thomas Seymour, Lisle returned to court. The previous day he had written an intriguing letter to Sir William Paget, with whom he was clearly on terms of the closest confidence.

Tomorrow I intend to be with the king and ready to serve … I would the king had appointed me to serve in the meanest room under some nobleman of reputation, for all the world knows I am not of estimation for so weighty a charge. I should do better service as directed rather than director, for directions in great affairs appertain to such as have great credit and are feared …[126]

What this great responsibility may have been is not obvious, because Dudley did not secure any other major office in 1545. However, in another letter to the same confidant a few days later he hinted broadly that he was fishing for the Lord Great Mastership of the Household, vacant by the death of the duke of Suffolk on 22 August.

Whether to move or omit it I leave to your discretion. Albeit the thing is no higher than what I have, its being before occupied by such a personage would give it more estimacion to the world …[127]

In spite of his modest disclaimers of ambition in both letters, it seems that the hidden agenda in his letter of 17 September was that the time had come

[123] Lisle to Sir John Gage, 17 Aug. 1545 (ibid. 151).   [124] Ibid. 183, 184, 185.
[125] 'An order devised for the proceedings of my Lord Admiral' (ibid. 229; Hall, *Unione*, 864).
[126] *L. and P.*, xx. ii. 391.   [127] 22 Sept. 1545 (ibid. 427).

for him to be given that higher rank that would give him the 'credit and esti-macion' for the post which he coveted. He felt himself to be, as he put it, 'bound to continual service', and in need of constant enhancement to fit him for that role. Nor was Lisle the only person who felt that he should have been destined for greater things. In reporting the death of the duke of Suf-folk to the President of the Council of Flanders, the sieur d'Ecke, a member of the emperor's council, commented specifically upon the increasing influ-ence of the Lord Admiral, as though he expected the late duke's functions to devolve upon him.[128]

The king does not seem to have shared that view. As Lord Admiral Lisle received bouge of court and membership of the Privy Council, while in his personal capacity he was a gentleman of the Privy Chamber, but he never approached the degree of intimacy with Henry which Charles Brandon had enjoyed. Nor did he receive any further military responsibilities. When Lord Poynings, the Captain of Boulogne, died on 18 August Lord Grey was moved from Guisnes to take over his command, and the earl of Surrey appointed to Guisnes.[129] On 21 September Lisle wrote to Paget from Green-wich, mainly about the ships which he was preparing to take supplies to Boulogne. In the course of this letter, however, he also alluded to the fact that he had retained 200 hagbutters from the dissolved 'army of Ports-mouth', commanded by a kinsman of his, and 80 of his own servants whom he had sent for 'out of my own country'. What were these men now to do?[130] It seems clear that he was expecting some major promotion, probably of a military nature, and was prepared both with his personal retinue and with his 'nolo episcopari'. If he was disappointed in such a way, it was not for lack of favour. He had done well over the previous eighteen months. In April 1544 he was in receipt of three separate annuities in Augmentations, and in the following month received a very substantial grant of lands, including the hospitals of Burton St Lazarus (Leicestershire) and St Giles in the Fields, in reward for his services.[131] At about the same time he gave up his first preferment, as Master of the Royal Armoury, and was succeeded by Sir Thomas Darcy, but there is no suggestion that he considered that to be a setback. When the army royal was summoned in March 1544, Lisle had been rated for the large contribution of 100 horsemen, and later in the year he was listed as the owner of two 200-ton ships, the *Falcon* and the *Anne Lisle*, which had been taken up for royal service.[132] The Lord Admiral was not suffering from hubris when he suggested that his 'estimacion' lagged behind his resources. When the first part of the 1545 subsidy was assessed on 1 March 1546, Lisle was rated at £1,376 in lands which made him the eighth or ninth richest peer, just behind the earl of Hertford (£1,700) but way ahead of the earl of Westmorland (£600).[133]

---

[128] 24 Aug. 1545 (ibid. 203).   [129] Paget to Norfolk, 25 Aug. 1545 (ibid. 209).
[130] Ibid. 421.   [131] Ibid., xix. i. 368, 610.   [132] Ibid. 273; ibid., ii. 502.
[133] E179/69/54. The richest baron in this assessment was Lord Scrope at £900.

The records of the court of augmentations show what a persistent and large-scale trafficker in land John Dudley had become by 1541. Some he received in reward for his services, without request; some he petitioned for, and was allowed to purchase. A very large transaction of that kind was approved on 10 December 1545, when he received the manors of Birmingham, Richards Castle, Kidderminster, and five other places covering seven counties.[134] How much he paid for these properties is not apparent, and the transaction may have represented the rather unsatisfactory outcome of a campaign which he had been pursuing for several months. On 19 September he had written to Paget:

Pray remember my suit to the king whereof I spoke to you yesterday. It was answered before my going to the sea, at his grace's being at Greenwich, first for a college worth £400 a year, I offering 1000 marks in money and to found a free school in his Majesty's name, which would ask £60 a year, besides that pensions for term of lives would amount to £140 or £160 a year. The king thinking it a great matter for me to pay so much ready money and so great pensions, answered my friend that it were better for me to have a portion of land; and so my suit has ever since remained unmentioned ...[135]

Such an approach seems to have been a standard court tactic. A college worth £400 a year should have cost Lisle £8,000 on the open market, so we may wonder whether Henry's alleged response was entirely free from irony. Nevertheless on 5 April 1546 the Lord Admiral seems to have petitioned successfully for the gift of the site of the late priory of St John of Jerusalem in Clerkenwell, and several other properties formerly belonging to that house.[136] At the end of September 1545 he also sold some property at Kayo, Surrey, to Sir William Paget. Considering the extent to which he depended upon Paget to smooth his way at court, it is to be hoped that he gave him a bargain. In spite of his own anxieties, and apparent frustration at not being 'called to serve', all the indications are that Lisle's stock stood very high at the end of 1545. On 30 November one of his daughters, probably Margaret, was christened. The sponsors were the imperial ambassador, Francois Van der Delft, who had recently succeeded the ageing Chapuys, the Lady Mary, and the widowed duchess of Suffolk, who hosted the occasion.[137] Everyone was there except, it would seem, the king himself. The Lady Elizabeth attended upon her half-sister, and everyone was studiously courteous to Van der Delft, as well they might be considering that England was still at war with France. It was a court event of the first importance, well beyond what might have been expected for the younger daughter of a viscount, and an indication that d'Eyck may well have been right in his assessment of the Lord Admiral's standing.

Much of the Admiral's work was routine, and connected with the juris-

---

[134] E318/393, which contains a full list of the properties.   [135] *L. and P.*, xx. ii. 412.
[136] E318/715. This 'gift' nevertheless cost him £1,000. See below, App. 1.
[137] Van der Delft to the Emperor, 30 Nov. 1545 (*L. and P.*, xx. ii. 899).

diction of the Admiralty court. Lisle was assiduous, and constantly in correspondence with the council, particularly over the endless complaints presented by the imperial ambassador, which arose partly from the predatory habits of English seamen, and partly from genuine uncertainties about contraband in time of war. He defended the actions of his servants strenuously, and challenged the council directly in August 1545 when Anthony Huse, his Admiralty judge, was summoned for contempt.[138] In January 1546 Van der Delft reported upon several such cases, which he used regularly as a pretext for seeking access to the council when he was trying to find out what they were doing about other matters which he believed to affect his master's interests. On 17 February he complained that such approaches were proving increasingly fruitless, but that the Lord Admiral was dealing well and promptly with 'our claims'.[139] This seems to have been because Lisle was efficient and conscientious rather than because he was particularly sympathetic to the emperor's subjects. By the end of January preparations for the new season's campaign were well in hand, and Lisle was again writing obliquely about 'a place of service and pain', telling Paget that he would gladly accept the post for much less than the reward offered, because of its 'credit'. Probably he was angling for the overall command of the army royal which Henry was intending to send across to France—the lieutenancy of the 'Parts beyond the seas' which the duke of Suffolk had held the previous summer. If that was his hope, then it was to be disappointed, and when Paget wrote to Christopher Mont in Germany on 25 February, it had already been decided that the earl of Hertford was to be Lieutenant, Henry Grey, marquis of Dorset, was to command the 'forward', and the earl of Surrey the 'rearward'.[140] The Lord Admiral was to command upon the seas with 16,000 mariners and men-of-war—a sufficiently honourable service, but not, apparently, what he was looking for.

Henry's intentions at the beginning of 1546 are not entirely clear. His council had decided months before that Boulogne was not worth the price of defending it, but the king did not agree, and broke off negotiations with the French when they proved insufficiently amenable. The German protestants had attempted to mediate, hoping that peace between England and France would bring one at least of the warring kings to their aid against the emperor; but Henry seems to have been attempting to renew his imperial alliance with a view to continuing the fight. For that purpose he began to drop hints about a Habsburg marriage for Prince Edward, irrespective of the fact that he was still lambasting the Scots for having repudiated the treaty of Greenwich. Charles was not impressed, but it suited him for the Anglo-French war to continue while he dealt with the League of

---

[138] Lisle claimed that Huse had acted directly on his orders, and that as the jurisdiction belonged to him, the council was acting *ultra vires*. As the matter was not pursued, presumably his argument was accepted (ibid. 4).

[139] Van der Delft to Granvelle, 17 Feb. 1546 (ibid., xxi. i. 235). [140] Ibid. 121, 272.

Schmalkalden, and his agents were not averse to encouraging the more bellicose English nobles, such as the earl of Surrey. Van der Delft was almost certainly wrong when he suggested in March that England's military preparations were mostly for defence,[141] but it could well have been that the aggressive preparations were intended mainly to build a strong negotiating platform. Early in the same month the king was ill; not a serious fever, but given his age and generally deteriorating health, not an encouraging sign. For several days he passed his time playing cards with a group of his intimates, of whom Lisle was one; but on 13 March the Admiral was commissioned to go to sea. About a week later he went to Portsmouth to organize the escorts for the Staplers' fleet, and to take command of the forty Great Ships which had been assembled, manned, and equipped.[142] This he did, not simply *ex officio* but by virtue of a special appointment as Lieutenant-General of the 'army and armada upon the seas in outward parts against the French'. Why this should have been considered necessary is not clear, unless it was intended to separate his command from that of Hertford, in which case it may have been engineered by Paget to alleviate his disappointment. On 30 March he embarked on his flagship, the *Pauncey* of 450 tons. But whatever the drift of his commission he did not confine his service to the sea. Within a few days he was with Hertford inspecting the fortifications of Ambleteuse in the Boulonnais, and thereafter divided his time about equally between the command of the fleet and an undefined function ashore.

The first tactical decision which had to be made was whether to launch an attack upon Etaples, which commanded the sea approach to Boulogne. The king was eager, but his commanders on the spot pointed out the difficulties and no assault was attempted. One of the reasons for this lack of aggression may have been that very delicate negotiating feelers were already being put out. Henry must have sanctioned this, but it was made to appear that these moves originated with the Lord Admiral. On 1 April an alert imperial agent noticed that a Venetian merchant, Francisco Bernado, had been sent by Lisle to his opposite number Claude d'Annebaut, the Admiral of France.[143] Over the next few weeks both sides manœuvred with one eye on a possible peace and the other on a vigorous prosecution of the war. D'Annebaut sent a fleet of seventeen galleys to menace the English coast, and Henry abused Hertford and Lisle for not pressing the attack upon Etaples. A few days later later Lisle was back in England, organizing 'wafters' to protect his supply ships coming from East Anglia, and arguing with Paget about the allocation of funding.[144] His role in the events which followed was central,

---

[141] Van der Delft to Charles V, 10 Mar. 1546 (ibid. 365); Scarisbrick, *Henry VIII*, 460.

[142] Scepperus and Van der Delft to Charles V, 22 Mar. 1546 (*L. and P.*, xxi. i. 439).

[143] St Mauris to Covos (ibid. 515).

[144] Lisle to Paget, 2 Apr.; Paget to Lisle, 3 Apr.; Lisle to the council, 4 Apr.; Lisle to Paget, 6 Apr. 1546 (ibid. 520, 527, 538, 553).

but extremely hard to define. On 17 April he was joined in commission with Paget to negotiate for peace, without being superseded in either of his other functions.[145] Talks began near Guisnes on 24 April, but Lisle seems to have moved in and out of them in an unpredictable manner, writing to the council now from Calais and now from 'the camp' near Ambleteuse. Henry's demands were extremely tough: the retention of Boulogne, the resumption of his French pension, with arrears, a war indemnity of 3 million crowns, and French assistance to enforce the Scottish marriage.[146] It is not surprising that the English commissioners should have been less than optimistic of success, but Bernado was indefatigably positive, and seems to have known more about the French negotiating position than they were willing to disclose to their opposite numbers.

The truth probably was that both Henry and Francis wanted peace, and that the English position was marginally stronger in that they had already taken the initiative, both by land and sea. Whether the commanders on either side were equally in earnest is more open to question. Hertford and Lisle were full of aggressive contingency plans if the negotiations should fail, and on the French side the Dauphin was more anxious to win his spurs on the battlefield than around the negotiating table. By the end of April plans for an attack on Etaples were being revived. D'Annebaut suggested a cease-fire, which Henry was extremely reluctant to concede, and Lisle and Paget sought an amplification of their commission.[147] At the beginning of May imperial observers believed, probably rightly, that the English still had the upper hand, not least because they continued to ship reinforcements across to Boulogne. On 6 May, however, Lisle got wind of French naval manœuvres which might put the whole peace process in jeopardy. D'Annebaut disclaimed any such intention, and Paget strove to reassure his colleague, but on 10 or 11 May the Lord Admiral suddenly quit the peace conference, alleging the king's permission to do so, and took to the sea.[148] Reports of what actually happened are conflicting, but it appears that a number of French galleys had returned to the English coast near Rye, where they had captured a few small victuallers. D'Annebaut at first denied all knowledge of this, and then claimed that he had recalled them. However, they remained on station, and on 12 or 13 May Lisle attacked them, capturing one and driving the rest off.[149] He then left the fleet under the command of Lord William Howard and returned to the negotiations. Van der Delft believed that his action had reduced the prospect of peace, but in that he appears to have been mistaken.

The French Admiral was trying his opposite number's metal, and having satisfied himself that no advantage was to be gained that way, the negotiations quickly reached a level of mutual understanding. On 15 May Lisle

[145] BL Egerton MS 2603, fo. 31; *L. and P.*, xxi. i. 610.   [146] Ibid.
[147] Ibid. 632, 685, 693, 707, 710.   [148] Ibid. 751, 806.
[149] Van der Delft to Charles V (ibid. 825).

confided to Sir William Petre that he found d'Annebaut 'a very proper man', and obviously enjoyed the game of bluff and counter-bluff in which they then engaged. 'You know how commodious this peace is for us', he continued, 'and will not reckon that I mean my own commodity, being a poor gentleman made by my master ...'.[150] For whatever reason, by the middle of May it was clearly Lisle rather than Paget who was controlling the negotiations on the English side, and receiving most of the credit. On 17 May the council reassured the commissioners that the king approved their proceedings, and added 'The king has even now seen your letters, my lord Admiral, touching the French Admiral's message from the Dolphyn, and prays you to signify he takes it thankfully ...'.[151] In spite of last-minute alarms about a renewed French naval threat and a mutiny in the English army, which the commissioners feared might 'mar all', the discussions at Guisnes were now edging towards a satisfactory conclusion. Skirmishing continued around Boulogne, as much because the troops needed an occupation as in any hope of advantage, and d'Annebaut made a great show of wrath about the loss of his galley, but on 24 May a cease-fire was finally agreed, and Lisle suggested that it would be a good idea if Hertford, who was the ranking English commander, also signed the articles which were then in preparation.[152] By 25 May the final round of discussions, the 'fine tuning', had begun. As late as 2 June there was a quiver of indignation about French unreasonableness, but by 6 June agreement had been reached, and on the following day both sets of commissioners signed the articles. Paget was then recalled, while Lisle and Wotton were instructed to go to Paris for the process of ratification, and Wotton to remain there as resident ambassador.[153]

This treaty, known as the treaty of Camp from the actual place of its signature, was a remarkable achievement for the English. On 27 May, when he was fishing around, trying to discover what had been agreed, Van der Delft believed that Boulogne would be returned in exchange for the French abandoning Scotland to its fate.[154] It was an intelligent guess, but underestimated the effectiveness of English pressure. Boulogne and the Boulonnais remained in English hands, pending payment by the French of the massive sum of 2,000,000 crowns in compensation and arrears of pensions going back to 1515. This was supposed to be accomplished by 1554, but given the state of Francis's revenues, it may well have been doubted on both sides whether it would ever be accomplished at all.[155] The English merely agreed to refrain from further attacks upon Scotland 'without fresh occasion'. Henry VIII had managed to hang on to the spoils of his last great war with-

---

[150] Van der Delft to Charles V (*L. and P.*, xxi. i. 837).   [151] Ibid. 849.
[152] Ibid. 881, 909.   [153] Hall, *Unione*, 865–6; *L. and P.*, xxi. i. 913.
[154] Van der Delft to the Emperor (ibid. 938).
[155] It seems that both Henry and Charles V were privately of that opinion (Scarisbrick, *Henry VIII*, 464).

out any assistance from the emperor, and although time was to show that Boulogne was an expensive liability, in June 1546 he had every reason to feel pleased with himself and his negotiators. The Admiral's political standing and favour undoubtedly increased as a result of this success, which was rewarded immediately with the grant of the dissolved hospital of St John of Jerusalem, Clerkenwell, for which he paid £1,000 into the king's hands.[156] The earl of Hertford's nose seems to have been somewhat put out of joint by these developments. Although he was the king's lieutenant in France he had played only a marginal role in the negotiations, and indeed d'Annebaut had more than once made it clear that he preferred to deal with Lisle. At the same time it was Hertford rather than Lisle who was the leader of the 'reformed' party at the English court, and there are some indications that they may both have lost ground as a result of being continually occupied on the other side of the channel, in spite of Henry's satisfaction with their achievements.

July saw a very determined attempt by the conservative party, led by the bishop of Winchester, to recover the initiative which they had lost with Henry's last marriage, to the evangelically minded Catherine Parr in 1543. Their foil was a Yorkshire gentlewoman named Anne Askew, a sacramentarian heretic of pronounced opinions and forceful personality. Anne undoubtedly had court connections in the queen's circle, if not with Catherine herself, and Henry was occasionally irritated by his wife's notions of spiritual domesticity.[157] According to Van der Delft, Gardiner was the councillor most in favour with the king at the beginning of July, and he seems to have decided to seize the opportunity presented by his own ascendency and the queen's vulnerability to strike a decisive blow.[158] Neither Hertford nor Lisle were involved, but both their wives were named among the contacts whom the regretable Askew had cultivated, along with the duchess of Suffolk and a number of other ladies of the Privy Chamber. Anne herself was tortured and eventually executed without making any incriminating revelations, but it appears that a direct attack was also made upon the queen. The only source for this story is Foxe, and it is well known, but if Catherine's successful reconciliation with the king is authentic it would help to explain the sharp decline in Winchester's fortunes which was to occur during the autumn.[159]

In spite of a carefully cultivated air of euphoria, which lasted until after the ratification of the treaty, the Anglo-French peace was followed by a long period of mutual fear and suspicion. Even before the ink was dry on the

---

[156] E318/715.

[157] D. Loades, *The Politics of Marriage: Henry VIII and his Queens* (Stroud, 1994), 141–4.

[158] John Foxe, *The Acts and Monuments of the English Martyrs*, ed. S. R. Cattley and George Townsend (London, 1837–41), v. 553. For examination of Anne Askew, see *L. and P.*, xxi. i. 1181.

[159] Redworth, *In Defence of the Church Catholic*, 230–7.

original treaty Hertford and Lisle were being warned not to disband their forces, and the latter was instructed to put on a show of strength to deter any possible second thoughts on the part of the notoriously Anglophobic Dauphin.[160] It seems to have been feared that the French would eventually wake up to how much they had conceded, and seek to go back on the agreement. Van der Delft certainly believed that Henry had won hands down, and the king could not, perhaps, quite trust his good fortune. In spite of his earlier instructions, Lisle did not proceed direct to Paris for the ratification. After a short period of consultation with Hertford he returned to England, and it was not until 2 July that he received his passport and fresh instructions to proceed to France.[161] He was then joined in commission with Cuthbert Tunstall, bishop of Durham, Nicholas Wotton, and Sir Henry Knevett, to receive Francis's oath to the treaty. It was fitting that the Admiral should complete what he had been so instrumental in beginning, but he also seems to have been *persona grata* at the French court, thanks perhaps to his good relations with d'Annebaut. Most of his entourage, numbering about thirty and including his brother Andrew, set off from London on 10 July, but Lisle himself was not with them. For some unexplained reason he did not leave until 12 July, which caused Tunstall, who was already in Boulogne, a fit of panic.[162] According to the terms of the original treaty, it should have been ratified within forty days; Lisle's delay now made that impossible, and a fresh clause would have to be added to their commission. In the event it did not matter, the French were even slower off the mark, and the Admiral made a stately progress towards Fontainebleau, exchanging elaborate courtesies by letter with the French court as he advanced upon it. His instructions were duly amended on 17 July, and the time for ratification extended, but it was 30 July before he reached the court, where his colleagues had been awaiting him for several days. Francis was not the least disturbed, and the ratification duly took place on 1 August. On the same day d'Annebaut set off for London to perform the same mission.[163]

On his way back, Lisle wrote a rare personal letter to Paget, lamenting the expense of the trip: 'I assure you this journey hath been extremely chargeable, after such sort as I think I shall be fain to hide in a corner for vii years.' His wife had asked him to bring back 'some goldsmith's work' from Paris, but he had already borrowed £500 in the French capital, and even so would have barely enough to get him home.[164] Curiously, there is no mention of any expensive gift, such as was normally bestowed upon an ambassador upon such an occasion. Lisle's lamentations were routine among ambassadors, and perhaps should not be taken too seriously. Certainly he had sold a number of parcels of land over the previous three months, and there

---

[160] *L. and P.*, xxi. i. 972, 1008. [161] Ibid. 1177.

[162] De Selve to Francis I, 10 July 1546; Tunstall to Lisle, same day (ibid. 1251, 1253).

[163] Hall, *Unione*, 867; *L. and P.*, xxi. i. 1292, 1295, 1299, 1306, 1325, 1337, 1340, 1352, 1394, 1405.

[164] Lisle to Paget, 3 Aug. 1546 (ibid. 1406).

are later references to unspecified, but apparently substantial debts to the Crown incurred at this time, but he received all his regular fees and diets on time, and there is no suggestion of real financial embarrassment.[165] In reporting the Admiral's return to London on 16 August, Van der Delft again assessed the relative importance of Henry's councillors as it appeared to him. Winchester, Paget, and Wriothesley, the Lord Chancellor, headed the list; but it is noticeable that Winchester did not feature among the leading councillors who authorized Sir Anthony Denny, John Gates, and William Clerc to use the king's dry stamp at the end of that month.[166] By the beginning of September the imperial ambassador was changing his tone. Both Gardiner and Paget were sympathetic to his master's interests, but on 3 September he wrote to Louis Schore complaining that certain people were trying to get into favour 'who will not suit our purposes'. These malign influences he named in another letter as Hertford and Lisle, wishing them 'as far away as they were last year'.[167] The cause of his agitation was the sympathetic reception accorded to John Sturmius and Hans Bruno, who had come to England to solicit the king's support for the protestant princes of Germany.

In fact neither Henry nor his council was quite as committed to 'the true faith' as Van der Delft would have wished. Not only were Bruno and Sturmius given 'countenance', but a secret emissary from Paul III, Guron Bretano, was given remarkably short shrift when he tried to reopen discussions on ecclesiastical jurisdiction and tempt Henry into sending representatives to the Council of Trent. Moreover, while entertaining Admiral d'Annebaut for the ratification of the Anglo-French treaty, he had spoken in all apparent seriousness of his intention to abolish the mass throughout his realm and replace it with a communion service—urging his 'good brother' of France to do the like.[168] He may have been bluffing, but it is difficult to see what he could have expected to gain by such a deception. The diplomatic situation was extremely fragile. Lisle and d'Annebaut fell out noisily over the galley which the former had taken, and Henry was so ostentatious about his continued naval preparations that de Selve, the French ambassador, was convinced that the war would soon be resumed.[169] The Admiral, he reported, was the strongest supporter of peace, and much would depend upon his influence. However, it was suddenly announced at the end of September that Lisle was departing into 'his country' for a month. There were hints that he was ill, so sick that he could not peruse a

[165] E315/252, fo. 48; Lansdowne MS 2, fo. 34; *L. and P.*, xix. i. 135; ibid., xx. ii. 496, 1068; ibid., xxi. i. 1235, 1383.

[166] Van der Delft to the emperor, 16 Aug. 1546 (ibid. 1463); grants in Aug. 1546 (ibid. 1537).

[167] Van der Delft to Mary of Hungary, 3 Sept. 1546; same to Louis Schore, same day (ibid., ii. 14, 15).

[168] Ibid., i. 1215, 1309; Foxe, *Acts and Monuments*, v. 568 ff.; Scarisbrick, *Henry VIII*, 472–8.

[169] De Selve to Francis I, 10 Sept., Privy Council to Nicholas Wotton, 31 Aug., De Selve to D'Annebaut, 14 Sept. 1546 (ibid., xxi. ii. 63; ibid., i. 1530; ibid., ii. 91).

letter, it was said, but the real reason seems to have been a bitter confrontation with Gardiner, which had caused him to strike the bishop in full council.[170] Had the king been present that would have been a capital offence, and
a month's rustication was in fact a very light punishment, confirming that
the reformers already had the lion's share of the royal favour. By the beginning of November, when the Admiral returned to court, the international
tension had eased a little. The military preparations, de Selve decided, were
aimed against Scotland. Henry had agreed in the treaty of Camp not to
make war upon the Scots without fresh 'occasion', but occasions were easy
to find in that volatile situation, and it is very likely that the king was
intending to launch another major expedition to the north as soon as the
winter was over.

Domestic tensions, on the other hand, were as bad as ever, and encouraged by Henry's visibly deteriorating health. By the first week in December
Hertford and Lisle were sufficiently in command of the situation for the
council to be meeting at Hertford's London residence, and then on 13
December they struck.[171] The duke of Norfolk, Lord Treasurer and long-
term political survivor, was suddenly arrested, stripped of his office and of
the Order of the Garter, and lodged in the Tower. His son, the earl of Surrey,
joined him on the same day. The fall of the Howards was very reminiscent
of the destruction of Thomas Cromwell, or of the Boleyns. They had been
skating on thin ice since the lamentable disclosures of Catherine's infideli-
ties in 1541, and the duke, thoroughly frightened by that experience, had
been consistently discreet. Not so his son. Henry Howard had been in
trouble on a number of counts in the recent past. He had made a mess of his
command at Boulogne, and had been recalled. During the last orthodox
ascendancy in June and July 1546 he had been questioned about his connections with sacramentaries; and he made no secret of his contempt for the
'upstarts' by whom the king had so frequently been guided—Wolsey,
Cromwell, Boleyn, Seymour, Dudley, and Parr.[172] It was this aristocratic
hubris which finally gave his father's many enemies their chance. He was
accused of having boasted what a fine regent the duke would make for the
young prince, and of having quartered the arms of Edward the Confessor
with his own, which implied a claim to royal blood and hence possibly to
the succession.[173] The truth seems to have been that he was loud-mouthed

---

[170] Council with the king to that in London, 18 Sept., council in London to that with the king,
20 Sept. 1546 (ibid. 122, 134); de Selve to d'Annebaut, 4 Nov. (*Calendar of State Papers, Spanish*,
viii. 556). The story of the blow is derived only from de Selve, and is unconfirmed by English
sources, but that is not surprising in the light of the political circumstances. The chronology,
however, presents some difficulties. The episode is discussed thoroughly in Redworth,
Defence of the Church Catholic, 239 and n.

[171] *L. and P.*, xxi. ii. 605. On the fall of the Howards, see Smith, *The Mask of Royalty*, 252–4;
Scarisbrick, *Henry VIII*, 482–4; Redworth, *Defence of the Church Catholic*, 239–41.

[172] Various depositions against Surrey are calendared in *L. and P.*, xxi. ii. 555.

[173] Ibid. (17).

and boastful, and that his only real talent was for writing poetry. As early as 12 July he had been offering hostages to fortune, when Lisle sent Paget a letter which he had received from him 'so full of parables that I do not perfectly understand it', with the advice that it should be shown to the king.[174] A monarch as suspicious as Henry did not need much encouragement to scent conspiracy, especially when the whiff came from that quarter. However they had achieved it, by mid-December Hertford, Lisle, and probably Paget, had succeeded in convincing the king that the earl of Surrey was a traitor, and that his father knew of, and had condoned, his treason.

As the enquiries were pressed ahead, and a sordid story of intrigue was woven out of disjointed and circumstantial fragments, the ascendancy of the earl of Hertford and the Lord Admiral (now generally linked together) becomes increasingly clear. On Christmas eve Van der Delft reported gloomily to the emperor that English affairs changed almost daily.[175] The persecution of heretics and sacramentarians had ceased abruptly when Hertford and Lisle had returned to court in the autumn. It seemed certain that they favoured 'the sects', and that the ambassador's attempts to mobilize council opposition to them had failed. Instead the waverers were drifting into the 'heretical' camp, thus demonstrating that Hertford and Lisle had gained the king's ear. They were ill-disposed towards the emperor and his subjects, and many believed that 'this misfortune to the house of Norfolk may have come from that quarter'. It was even to be feared that the custody of the prince and the government of the realm might be entrusted to them. 'The majority of the people', he went on, 'are of these perverse sects, and in favour of getting rid of the bishops, and they do not conceal their wish to see Winchester and other adherents of the ancient faith in the Tower with the Duke ...'. It was probable that parliament, which had been convened for January, would pass some strange acts. The king was still in favour of maintaining the emperor's friendship, but his death would throw everything into confusion. In some respects, Van der Delft's appraisal of the situation was extremely shrewd. Gardiner, although not in the Tower, was certainly out of favour, a situation which ostensibly arose from a trivial-seeming misunderstanding with Henry over the exchange of some lands.[176] His rustication had nothing to do with the fall of the Howards, but his notorious irascibility had probably exposed him to misrepresentation, and the king was not in a tolerant or understanding frame of mind.

By the time Henry's will was completed and stamped on 30 December it was clear that the faction at court led by Hertford and Lisle was completely dominant. Its members included Sir Anthony Denny, the Chief Gentleman of the Privy Chamber, Sir William Paget, and Thomas Cranmer, the archbishop of Canterbury. All of these men were among the sixteen named

---

[174] Ibid., i. 1263.   [175] Ibid., ii. 605.
[176] Redworth, *Defence of the Church Catholic*, 237–40.

executors of the will, and formed the largest coherent group. How protestant they were at this stage is arguable. In spite of Van der Delft's clearly
expressed views, none of them had openly departed from the doctrine laid
down in the King's Book of 1543. Earlier in the year Paget had described
Lisle as 'God's knight', which suggests the evangelical affinities of both of
them. More tellingly, the forthright Anne Askew had written in July

> Then came my Lord Lisle, my Lord of Essex [William Parr] and the bishop of Win-
> chester requiring me earnestly that I should confess the sacrament to be flesh, blood
> and bone. Then said I to my Lord Parr and my Lord Lisle that it was great shame for
> them to counsel contrary to their knowledge. Whereunto in few words they did say
> that they would gladly all things were well ...[177]

Rightly or wrongly she believed them to share her sacramentarian views,
and to lack the courage to say so. As long as Henry was alive and conscious
he set the agenda, and no one who wished to remain in favour crossed him.
On 29 January the aged but still shrewd Eustace Chapuys wrote to the
queen of Hungary from his retreat at Louvain, confirming most of his successor's diagnosis. Hertford and Lisle were 'stirrers of heresy'. The queen,
instigated by the duchess of Suffolk, the countess of Hertford, and the
Admiral's wife, was showing herself similarly affected. The earl was
known to be an enemy of the Lord Chancellor, Sir Thomas Wriothesley,
and the Admiral an enemy of the bishop of Winchester.[178] Meanwhile the
king's illness, which had been advancing since early December, had
become increasingly desperate. Perhaps it was only his determination to
settle with the Howards which kept him alive. Throughout the Christmas
season, in spite of a fluctuating fever, he followed the interrogations of the
earl and the duke with passionate and minute interest. On 13 January 1547
Surrey was brought to trial before a commission of oyer and terminer in
London, not before his peers because his title was one of courtesy.[179] From
Wriothesley's jottings of his examinations, it seems clear that the earl
believed himself to have been framed by Hertford, Paget, Lisle, and Denny,
and at his trial his only defence was that nobody should believe the words
of such dishonourable upstarts in preference to those of a true nobleman.[180]
The jury deliberated for a surprisingly long time, not because they were
swayed by such effrontery but because there was, in truth, little hard evidence. In the end he was found guilty of treasonable intent, and went to the
block on 19 January, denouncing the king for his favours to 'low people'. It
may be wondered whether he was entirely sane.

   The old duke was not tried, but proceeded against by act of attainder,
which received a special royal assent by dry stamp on 27 January, the last
day upon which the king was sufficiently conscious to know what went on

---

[177] Foxe, *Acts and Monuments*, v. 544; *L. and P.*, xxi. i. 1181 (1).   [178] Ibid., ii. 756.
[179] Ibid. 697.
[180] Wriothesley, *Chronicle*, i. 177; *Chronicle of the Greyfriars of London*, ed. J. G. Nichols, Camden Society, 53 (1852), 53; Smith, *Mask of Royalty*, 256–8.

around him. The final version of his will was stamped on the same day. As the old king slipped into unconsciousness, the Lord Admiral was one of the two or three most powerful men in the kingdom. Whether he had achieved that position on merit or by skilful intrigue cannot be fully resolved from the surviving evidence, nevertheless over the last two years of the reign his merits had been abundantly apparent. He was not only a good soldier, as he had shown at Boulogne, but a diplomat worthy of the trust which had been accorded him. He was also an excellent Lord Admiral, who had devoted himself to the routine of his office as well as being a dashing commander at sea. His fleet orders of 1545 show a man who was thoroughly versed in the latest tactical thinking, and an innovator in terms of English naval warfare. He was also in all probability responsible for turning the miscellaneous collection of officers who had previously cared for the king's ships into the Council for Marine Causes, which came into existence between 1545 and 1546.[181] This council gave Henry, and his successors, the most efficient naval administration in Europe, and brought Henry VIII's naval revolution to a fitting climax. He had, of course, done well for himself on the way, and he continued to collect rewards and offices to the day of Henry's death. A wardship and a land purchase in Augmentations in May 1546; the reversion to the captaincy of Beaumaris castle in September; several profitable sales to the Crown; and in December the very valuable right to sell 3,000 fothers of lead, and to defer the purchase price—£13,000—for six years.[182] In spite of his debts to the Crown he was a rich man as well as a powerful one, and he had manœuvred himself into an excellent strategic position for the regime which was about to emerge. Despite his disclaimers, he was clearly ambitious, but there is no reason to doubt his honesty when he declared that his honour was to serve the king. Unlike the Howards, or the Percies, or the Courtenays, all of whom had fallen under Henry's jealous wrath, he was a service nobleman of the new sort, and it remained to be seen what advantages could be extracted from that service during a royal minority.

---

[181] Loades, *Tudor Navy*, 81–4.   [182] *L. and P.*, xxi. ii. 647.

3

The Earl of Warwick, 1547–1549

HENRY VIII's will has been described as a 'forensic conundrum'.[1] The final version was dated 30 December 1546, and ostensibly signed by the king, but most modern experts who have examined the document believe that it was stamped. If this was the case, then two further questions follow. Was the will altered after its contents were last discussed with Henry on 30 December, and did the fact that it was stamped make any difference to its validity?[2] The letters patent authorizing the use of the stamp were undoubtedly valid, and many important documents were authenticated in that way, including the Duke of Norfolk's attainder on 27 January. No one seems to have challenged the will at the time, and it was not until 1566 that the Scottish lawyer Maitland of Lethington claimed that the stamp did not satisfy the condition laid down in the succession act of 1543 that the king's will should be 'signed with his most gracious hand'.[3] He was pleading a special case, because he was trying to argue that his mistress, Mary, queen of Scots, had not been lawfully barred from the English succession. Mary had been ignored, both in the will and in the act itself, and Maitland's letter made little impression upon Sir William Cecil, to whom it was addressed. Consequently there is little reason to doubt that the final version of Henry's testament, as it now survives, was fully valid in law. That, however, does not guarantee that it represented the old king's last conscious intention. Ostensibly he left the minority government of his young son in the hands of a body of sixteen executors, who were expected to make decisions and enforce their will collectively. On the other hand he also empowered those executors to take whatever steps they deemed to be necessary for the safeguard of the king and the realm. Those who believe that Henry intended a collegiate form of government argue that the second clause was an insertion, designed by those who subsequently seized power as a justification for their action.[4] Given the circumstances

---

[1] E. W. Ives, 'Henry VIII's Will: A Forensic Conundrum', *Historical Journal*, 35 (1992), 779–804.

[2] There are references to conversations with Henry about the will after 30 Dec., but no conclusive evidence that alterations were made. The will would only have been invalid if it had actually been stamped after Henry's death. This was never suggested at the time, and would be incapable of proof.

[3] Maitland of Lethington to Sir William Cecil, 14 Jan. 1566(7) (G. Burnet, *The Historie of the Reformation of the Church of England* (London, 1694), I. ii. 267–8).

[4] W. K. Jordan, *Edward VI: The Young King* (London, 1968), 52–9, which contains a very

surrounding the last few days of Henry's life, however, the implied conspiracy is an unnecessary hypothesis. The king changed his mind over a number of things, and was totally unwilling to recognize the imminence of his own death. It is therefore quite probable that he thought of his will as still being in a provisional form when he was last aware of it. What he might have prescribed had he lived a few more days, we cannot know, but his executors were perfectly entitled to believe that Henry had left an indeterminate situation rather than a determinate one, and that it was up to them to give the regency government a workable form.

The fact that the earl of Hertford and his friends were in political control when the king died was less the result of successful intrigue than of Henry's own wishes. At no point did he become senile, or deranged, or any more suggestible than he had been during most of his life.[5] Not only had he made it perfectly clear that the destruction of the Howards was his own work, he had also been swift to assure Sir Anthony Browne that the exclusion of Stephen Gardiner from the body of executors was entirely deliberate.[6] As Van der Delft noted ruefully, there was little chance of any effective challenge being mounted against Hertford's ascendancy, however little the emperor might relish the prospect of such a regime. When Henry died, late on the night of 28 January, Hertford left Westminster immediately, accompanied by Browne, to secure the person of the new king, who was living at Hatfield House. Meanwhile the late king's death was concealed until such time as his successor should reach London. There was nothing sinister about such a delay; a similar thing had happened when Henry VII had died, and it had more to do with seemliness and formality than with politics. Parliament, which was in session at the time, held a meeting on the morning of 29 January, and meals continued to be carried to the Privy Chamber with the sound of trumpets.[7] Meanwhile the executors themselves had been informed, and most of them gathered at Westminster on 30 January to consider the implementation of Henry's will, which was in the custody of Sir William Paget. It was proposed to accompany the proclamation of the new king with a general pardon, perhaps designed to reassure those who feared a continuing vendetta from the struggles of the past few months. Hertford, however, who by this time was with Edward and Elizabeth at Enfield, sent word that he did not believe that either the executors or

detailed examination of the will and its implications, but refutes both Maitland of Lethington and the contemporary common law lawyer Edmund Plowden by arguing, rather unconvincingly, that the will was actually signed on 27 Jan.

[5] See above, pp. 44–5; also L. B. Smith, *Henry VIII: The Mask of Royalty* (London, 1971), *passim*.

[6] John Foxe, *The Acts and Monuments of the English Martyrs*, ed. S. R. Cattley and George Townsend (London, 1837–41), vi. 163–4; Glyn Redworth, *In Defence of the Church Catholic* (Oxford, 1990), 245–6.

[7] J. Strype, *Ecclesiastical Memorials* (London, 1721), II. i. 17; *Calender of State Papers, Spanish*, ed. Royall Tyler *et al.* (London, 1862–1954), ix. 6–7.

the wider council (which included the twelve assistant executors) had the power to issue such a pardon until they had clarified their own position. It would be much better to wait until the coronation, as was customary. On the morning of Monday, 31 January, Lord Chancellor Wriothesley announced the king's death to parliament, and formally dissolved the session. At about noon Edward entered London, accompanied by Hertford, and proceeded to the Tower where the royal apartments had been hastily prepared to receive him. There the nobility hastened to greet him, and the executors immediately got down to business.[8]

The record of their deliberations was formally entered into the Council Book, and conveys an impression of unanimity which may be misleading. However, the air of inevitability which it also conveys is probably accurate enough.

And forasmuche as in the consideracion and debating of the several poyntes of the charge by the saide wille committed unto us, and of the grete accompte which we have to rendre to God, to our Souveraigne Lorde that nowe is, and to the whole worlde for the same, it appeared unto us aswell uppon thoccasion of the depeache of sundry letters … as uppon sundry other grete and urgent thinges … that being a greate number appoyncted to be executors with equal and like charge, it shuld be more then necessarie aswel for thonour, surety and gouvernment of the moste royal persone of the King our Souveraigne Lorde that nowe is, as for the more certaine and assured order and direction of his affayres, that somme special man of the nombre and company aforesaide shuld be preferred in name and place before others, to whome as to the state and hedde of the reste all strangers and others might have accesse …[9]

It was therefore decided that two offices should be created, that of Lord Protector of the Realm and that of Governor of the King's Person. Whereupon 'by oone hole assent, concorde and agreement' it was resolved to confer both these offices upon the earl of Hertford 'uppon mature consideracion of the tendreness and proximitie of bludde between our Souveraigne Lorde that nowe is and the saide Erle of Hertforde, being his uncle …'. In the context, no other decision was possible. Corporate government was unrealistic, even if Henry had seriously intended it, and in the absence of any adult prince of the blood the only possibilities were the king's maternal uncles, Hertford and Sir Thomas Seymour, or the widowed queen, Catherine Parr. Catherine had indeed been named by Henry as regent during his last brief absence in France in 1544, but she was devoid of ambition and was passed over without comment.[10] Of the two Seymour brothers, Edward was not only the elder and the senior in rank, but also much the more substantial in terms of leadership and the confidence of his colleagues. Dissent, if there

    [8] *Cal. Span.*, ix. 20–2; *Acts of the Privy Council*, ed. J. Dasent *et al.* (London, 1890–1907), ii. 3–4, 17.

    [9] Ibid. 4–5.

    [10] Catherine's latest biographer, Susan James, says 'without doubt she expected to be named to the regency council', but Dr James cites Henry's second succession act of 1536, and there is no contemporary evidence to that effect (S. James, *Queen Catherine Parr* (forthcoming)).

was any, may well have concentrated less upon the identity of the Protector than upon the nature of the powers which the office would convey. There was at this stage no will to create a regency with full powers, and it was decreed that Hertford should enjoy his office 'with this special and expresse condicion, that he shall nat do any Acte but with thadvise and consent of the reste of the coexecutors in suche maner and fourme as in the saide wille of our saide late Souveraigne Lorde ... is apoynted and prescribed'.[11]

The next day, 1 February, the executors waited upon the king to obtain his formal assent to their proceedings before announcing their decision to the rest of the council, and to the assembled peers. Letters were then dispatched to the emperor, the regent of the Low Countries, and the king of France, notifying them of Henry's death and of the accession of his son. No dispatch was sent to the pope, thereby indicating that the Protectorate intended to commence its policies where the old king had left off; and no dispatch was sent to Venice, because nobody remembered to do so.[12] Charles V was so unenthusiastic that he refrained for some time from returning the greetings which had been sent to him in Edward's name. As far as he was concerned the true heir of England was Mary, because she was the only one of Henry's three surviving children who had been born in lawful wedlock.[13] Once the realm had gone into schism in 1533, no valid marriages could be contracted, and therefore Edward was as illegitimate as Elizabeth, or Henry Fitzroy. However, it was not in his nature, or his interest, to persevere in such a view once it had become clear that nobody in England shared it, not even Mary. After a few weeks, and firmly holding his nose, he began to do business with the Lord Protector. Until 14 February the old king lay in state at Westminster, and council business was ostensibly kept to a minimum. The coronation was fixed for 19 February, and the preparations, including a court of claims, occupied a fair amount of time. Less visible, but much more significant in political terms, was the attention which began to be given to a list of promotions and rewards which had been drawn up before Henry's death. This matter was first brought to the council on 6 February when, as a result of claims which were beginning to be made, Paget, Denny, and Herbert were required to testify as to their knowledge of the late king's intentions.[14] The testimony which mattered was that of Paget, who declared that Henry had disclosed to him his anxiety that the nobility of the realm was 'greately decayed', and a plan for remedying that situation, using partly

---

[11] *APC*, ii. 5–6; *The Chronicle and Political Papers of King Edward VI*, ed. W. K. Jordan (London, 1970), 4; Burnet, *Historie*, ii. 40.

[12] *APC*, ii. 489–90, App. A letter was finally sent to Harvell on 8 Mar. According to the record it had been 'omytted thrugh forgetfulness emonges soo many other urgent affayres ...'.

[13] Mary of Hungary to Van der Delft, 6 Feb. 1547 (*Cal. Span.*, ix. 15); emperor to Van der Delft, 20 Feb. (ibid. 38).

[14] *APC*, ii. 15–22.

the lands recently come to the Crown through the attainder of the Howards: 'he willed me to make unto him a book', the Secretary went on, 'of such as he did chose to advance; which I did.'[15]

It was probably this 'book' which now survives among the State Papers Domestic. It is a heavily amended and not very coherent document, but that would be consistent with its alleged provenance, having been discussed and altered as the king's mind or mood had fluctuated.[16] The list is considerable, and contains a number of rewards of a routine kind—grants of land, annuities stewardships, and other offices. Its significance, however, lies mainly in the list of peerage creations with which it starts. The earl of Hertford to be duke of Hertford, Exeter, or Somerset; the earl of Essex to be marquis of Essex; Viscount Lisle to be Great Chamberlain and earl of Coventry; Lord Russell to be earl of Northampton; Lord St John to be earl of Winchester; Lord Wriothesley also to be earl of Winchester; Sir Thomas Seymour to be Lord Seymour and Lord Admiral; and Sir Richard Rich, Sir John St Leger, Sir William Willoughby, Sir Edmund Sheffield, and Sir Christopher Danby to be barons. In presenting this list to the council, Paget simplified it a little by removing the specific titles, but he also gave a long and circumstantial account of the discussions which he had had with Henry, going into considerable detail about the deployment of particular lands.[17] The council declared itself to be satisfied as to the genuineness of the intentions, some knowledge of which had presumably provoked the claims which had already been made, but postponed action until a more seemly time. Once Henry's body was safely on its way to Windsor, and the plans for the coronation had been completed, that time had come. On 15 February, with only four days to implement its decisions in time for the crowning, the council returned to the issue of new peerages.[18] For some reason, possibly because they declined the proffered honours, St John, Russell, St Leger, and Danby were not promoted as had been proposed. Hertford became duke of Somerset, Essex became marquis of Northampton, Lisle became earl of Warwick, Wriothesley became earl of Southampton; and Seymour, Rich, Willoughby, and Sheffield became barons. The ceremonies of creation were decreed to be held at the Tower on the following day, and the Lord Chancellor was instructed to get busy on the Patents.

In the event the creations did not take place until 17 February because on 16 February the old king was finally laid to rest, with suitable pomp 'as to the dignity of such a mighty prince it appertaineth'. The chief mourner was the marquis of Dorset, the husband of Henry's niece, Frances, but among the very large attendance listed, the principal councillors of the new regime do not feature.[19] Presumably they remained in attendance upon the new king who would not, by custom, attend his father's obsequies. On the

---

[15] *APC*, ii. 16.   [16] PRO SP10/1, no. 11.   [17] *APC*, ii. 17–20.

[18] Ibid. 34–5; *Chronicle of Edward VI*, 4–5.

[19] Strype, *Ecclesiastical Memorials*, II. ii. 289–311; PRO SP10/1, no. 17.

following day they duly received their new dignities, and the tangible rewards which went with them—£800 a year in lands to Somerset, and £200 each to Northampton, Southampton, and Warwick. Paget, whose role in the whole process had been so crucial, received no dignity but 400 marks a year in lands, so he was hardly unrewarded for his pains.[20] However much this may look like the party in power feathering their own nests, there is no serious reason to doubt that Henry had intended more or less what transpired. Too many people, particularly members of the Privy Chamber, had had access to some at least of the information to make significant misrepresentation possible. The only man who was seriously aggrieved, as it later transpired, was Thomas Seymour, to whom a barony and the office of Lord Admiral seemed paltry by comparison with what his brother had received. As far as we know, the new earl of Warwick was sufficiently content. He had hankered after the Great Chamberlainship for some time, and he now had the greater 'estimacion' of an earldom. On the other hand, he had lost the Admiralty, by which he had set such great store. If he harboured any resentment on that account he kept it to himself, but his relations with Seymour do not seem to have been particularly good.

By the time these things had been accomplished, the coronation was imminent, and the council had already spent a considerable time debating the correct format. Not only was it nearly forty years since the last such event, but the central actor was a young child, to whose 'tenderness' a number of concessions had to be made. Most of the changes which were made in the traditional rite can be attributed to this consideration, rather than to any desire to signal impending religious change. The psalms and collects used, and the high mass celebrated, were all in strict accordance with precedent. Only in the archbishop's oration to the king was the revolution of the last twenty years clearly expressed.

The promises your Highness hath made here at your coronation to forsake the devil and all his works are not to be taken in the bishop of Rome's sense, when you commit anything distasteful to that see, to hit your majesty in the teeth ... We, your majesty's clergy, do humbly conceive that this promise reacheth not at your highness's sword, spiritual or temporal ... Your majesty is God's vicegerent and Christ's vicar within your own dominions, and to see with your predecessor Josiah God truly worshipped, and idolatry destroyed, the tyranny of the bishop of Rome banished from your subjects, and images removed ...[21]

In retrospect Cranmer's speech looks like a protestant manifesto, but it is unlikely that many at the time heard it in that sense. The emphasis was very much upon the supremacy which Henry VIII had created, and the message was that the king's minority was not going to make any difference to his ecclesiastical jurisdiction.

---

[20] *Calendar of the Patent Rolls*, Edward VI, ed. R. H. Brodie (London, 1924–9), i. 45–6.
[21] PRO LC2/3; *APC*, ii. 29–33; J. E. Cox, *Cranmer's Miscellaneous Writings* (Parker Society, 1844–6), 126.

Being bound by my function to lay these things before your royal highness, the one as a reward if you fulfil, the other as a judgement from God if you neglect them; yet I openly declare before the living God, and before these nobles of the land, that I have no commission to denounce your majesty deprived, if your highness miss in part or in whole of these performances much less to draw up indentures between God and your majesty, or to say you forfeit your crown with a clause.

Perhaps because the ceremonies were shortened, the coronation cost less than half the outlay on Henry VIII's funeral, but it was nevertheless a very spendid public spectacle, and conveyed visual as well as oral messages. As a concession to Edward's youthful sensibilities, he was closely followed in procession by the 12-year-old duke of Suffolk, by a group of half a dozen noble youths of similar age, and by John Anthony, his 'tumbling boy', who seems to have been a particular favourite.[22] The duke of Somerset, Earl Marshall for the day as well as Lord Protector, was deliberately conspicuous, and the gentlemen of the Privy Chamber were led by the earl of Warwick.

On 19 and 20 February the emphasis was all upon joy and harmony: 'Sing up heart, sing up heart and sing no more down, but joy in King Edward that weareth the crown ...'. However, the contrived appearance was deceptive. Within a few days of the coronation Cranmer had petitioned for new commissions to be issued to himself and his fellow bishops in the name of King Edward. The logic behind this was impeccable, since bishops under the royal supremacy were primarily royal officers, but it came as a nasty shock to some conservatives, including the bishop of Winchester. Gardiner was far too astute to object to the issuing of commissions as such, but on 1 March he wrote to Secretary Paget, protesting that the draft which he had seen described him as a 'delegate' and not an 'ordinary'.[23] The point was far from pedantic, because the latter term implied that the bishop's authority derived, in part at least, from his consecration. As a delegate his whole jurisdiction depended upon his appointment, and consecration could be regarded as redundant. Paget replied politely, but the commissions were issued unchanged on 2 March.[24] More seriously, on 3 or 4 March a carefully primed charge exploded under the Lord Chancellor, the earl of Southampton. Apart from the earl of Warwick, Thomas Wriothesley was the only man on the minority council with the political skill and status to challenge the Protector. There is no evidence that he had resisted the creation of the Protectorate at the end of January, but a man who could criticize Henry VIII to his face, and earn his gratitude was a man to be reckoned with, and he had crossed swords with Edward Seymour before. Seymour was not satisfied with the limited powers which he had been given on 31 January, and discussions were going on among his fellow councillors to provide an

[22] PRO LC2/3.
[23] PRO SP10/1, no. 25; J. A. Muller, *The Letters of Stephen Gardiner* (Cambridge, 1933), 268–72.
[24] PRO SP10/1, no. 26; *APC*, ii. 14–15.

amplification. It seems likely, both from what happened and from things which were subsequently said, that the Lord Chancellor made clear his opposition to any such move.[25] Whether this was prompted by ambition on his part, or by loyalty to Henry VIII's intentions as he understood them, cannot be deduced, but he was perceived to be a formidable obstacle.

He had, however, exposed himself to attack in a manner which is surprising for one of his habitual shrewdness. On 17 February he had issued a commission to four well-qualified civil lawyers to hear cases in Chancery in his absence, or when he should be preoccupied with the work of the Privy Council.[26] The Chancellor's jurisdiction was partly in equity and partly in common law, and there was an immediate outcry from the common lawyers about the impropriety of his action. On 5 March the case was called before the council, the offending commission having already been examined by the judges, who were not exactly disinterested parties. The substance of the complaint was that the commissioners 'being civilians and nat lerned in the Comen Lawes, setting aside the saide Commen Lawes [would] determyne the waighty causes of this realme according either to the saide Lawe Civile or to their owne conscience; which Lawe Civile is to the subjectes of this realme unknowne'[27] but this was a matter of policy or opinion, and the judges concentrated upon the legality of the commission itself. This was a grey area. The judges advised that the commission was unlawful because it had been issued without warrant from the council, but it was at least arguable that the Chancellor had authority *ex officio* to issue such a process relating to the discharge of his own office. There were plenty of precedents from the time of More and Audley, and Wriothesley himself had issued similar commissions during Henry VIII's reign.[28] However, he had then been granted specific power to do so, and that power had not been renewed in the name of Edward VI. So the precedents may not have been strictly applicable, and the Chancellor's convictions may have been mistaken. According to the council record Wriothesley made no defence, and submitted himself to judgment.[29] He may have been persuaded of the weakness of his ground, or he may simply have recognized a political defeat when he saw one. He had been careless at worst, and in other circumstances might have suffered a mild rebuke or an instruction to withdraw the commission. The judgment that he should be dismissed from

[25] 'I have perceived plainly from the Lord Chancellor that the Protector did not obtain by the will the elevation in the matter of titles that he desired, and he ascribed this to the influence of the Lord Chancellor. The latter also would not consent to any innovations in the matter of government beyond the provisions of the will ...', Van der Delft to the emperor, 16 June 1547 (*Cal. Span.*, ix. 100).
[26] *APC*, ii. 48–57; A. J. Slavin, 'The Fall of Lord Chancellor Wriothesley: A Study in the Politics of Conspiracy', *Albion*, 7 (1975), 265–85; BL Harley MS 284, fo. 9.
[27] *APC*, ii. 49.　　[28] Slavin, 'Fall of Wriothesley'.
[29] *APC*, ii. 56. It has also been suggested that Wriothesley's fall was prompted by his anticipated resistance to the Protector's religious policy (Jordan, *Edward VI*, 69–72).

office, and suffer fine and imprisonment at the king's pleasure, was totally disproportionate to the offence, even if an offence had been committed, and reflected the determination of the Protector and his allies to be rid of him.

The reason for this became apparent just a week later when, with Lord St John acting as Keeper of the Great Seal, the executors petitioned the king for a grant of

his royal assent for their establishment and confirmacion in the romes of his High-nes Counseillours, and that it wold like please his Heighnes to graunte unto them by a Commission to be signed with his Graces owne hande such powre and auc-torite as to their saide romes ... apperteigned.[30]

At the same time the Protector's own powers were significantly amplified. He was given the crucial authority to appoint new councillors, and the requirement that he should consult his fellow councillors was to be inter-preted

amplissimus [*sic*] liberalissimo ac beneficentissimo modo pro amplificacione, aug-mentacione ac manutenencia auctoritatum, potestatum, preeminenciarum et digni-tatum dicti avunculi nostri in quantum verba ac sententia ac verborum et sententiarum vero [*sic*] intenciones in dictis literis nostris patentibus expresse et specificate construi et extendi possint.[31]

In other words it was waived for all practical purposes, giving the duke of Somerset full regency powers until the king came of age. It was these patents rather than the decisions of 31 January which truly constituted the Protectorate. They certainly went far beyond anything which had been envisaged in Henry VIII's will, and appeared to contradict its spirit totally, but they were perfectly lawful, and probably necessary to give adequate authority to a government which could potentially last for nine years, and which was bound to languish in the shadow of the great king.

The earl of Warwick had played a full part in all these proceedings, being one of the half-dozen or so councillors who was present at every meeting between 29 January and 12 March. Along with Russell, St John, Denny, and Herbert, he was one of Somerset's closest allies, as Van der Delft had noticed before Henry's death.[32] At the same time his signature is noticeably absent from the proceedings of 13 March, when the above-mentioned amplification was approved. It is very unlikely that this was a gesture of dissent. Denny and Herbert were also missing on that day, when only six councillors apart from Somerset himself signed the register. Since the minority council, unlike the Privy Council of an adult king, had a collective responsibility for its actions, it did not matter greatly who was present on any particular day. Van der Delft at this point predicted a rift between Warwick and Somerset, on the grounds that both were ambitious, and that Warwick enjoyed higher popular esteem, but he also believed that Wrio-

---

[30] *APC*, ii. 63.   [31] Ibid. 522–33; *Cal. Pat.*, i. 97.   [32] See above, pp. 83–4.

thesley and Paget were the two most powerful men in the council a few days before the former's fall.[33] He subsequently revised his opinion of Warwick, some time before events justified it, and his assessment of the situation during these formative days is not worth a great deal as evidence. A better indication is provided by the fact that on 4 March the earl was commissioned, along with Russell, Thomas Seymour, and Paget, to follow up the treaty of Camp by settling the boundaries of the Boulogne Pale, and to remove by a fresh treaty of amity the kind of alarms which had beset relations between England and France in the autumn of 1546.[34] Warwick and Paget had been the architects of the original treaty, and had the confidence of their French equivalents, so it was logical to employ them in this way, but the Protector would hardly have done so if he had suspected their loyalty. The negotiations took place in London during March, and the draft treaty was forwarded on 1 April by the council to Nicholas Wotton in Paris for Francis's ratification. Unfortunately the French king had died on the previous day, and his successor Henry II refused ratification and repudiated the whole proceeding.[35] By early April it began to look as though the fears of attack which had been expressed by Lord Grey in February were about to be realized, and Somerset's policy during the summer has to be seen in that light. To counter the French threat, he appealed to the Anglo-Imperial treaty of 1543. Charles responded very reluctantly. He had enough problems in Germany, and the last thing he needed was another round with the Valois. He categorically refused to extend his protection to the 'new conquest' of Boulogne, while agreeing to intervene if Calais should come under attack.[36]

In spite of this setback to English diplomacy, Henry's bark turned out to be worse than his bite. He refused to honour the indemnity due for Boulogne under the treaty of Camp, but reports that he had sent 4,000 troops to Scotland were mistaken. His own financial situation precluded large-scale aggression, and in spite of Guise influence, and Wotton's pessimistic predictions, for the time being nothing happened. Somerset, however, did not know this, and in the circumstances his pursuit of a 'final solution' in Scotland has to be seen as a rash gamble. On 24 July he informed Van der Delft that the Scots had mobilized 25,000 men against him, and that French galleys were operating in the Firth of Forth.[37] Both these statements seem to have been incorrect, and were primarily a justification for his own

[33] Van der Delft to the emperor, 10 Feb. 1547 (*Cal. Span.*, ix. 19–20); B. L. Beer, *Northumberland* (Kent, Ohio, 1973), 59–60.

[34] *APC*, ii. 47–8. Van der Delft had to be reassured that no threat was intended to his master's interests: 18 Mar. 1547 (*Cal. Span.*, ix. 58).

[35] On the death of Francis I and its immediate consequences, see R. J. Knecht, *Francis I* (Cambridge, 1982), 416–25.

[36] *Venetianische Depeschen vom Kaiserhofe*, ed. Gustav Turba (Vienna, 1892), ii. 298–302, 2 July 1547; Jordan, *Edward VI*, 237–8.

[37] Van der Delft to the emperor, 24 July 1547 (*Cal. Span.*, ix. 126–7).

mobilization, which was already going ahead. Somerset had risen to favour, not just as the brother of Henry VIII's favourite queen, but as a soldier, and he had been particularly successful in Scotland. If he could cap that success by forcing the Scots to accept the marriage which Henry had failed to impose, it would surely give his Protectorate an instant credibility which could not be obtained by any other means. The dying king may, or may not, have urged another Scottish campaign upon him; but the decision to undertake it should not be seen either as an example of his far-sighted idealism, or as a mere piece of wanton aggression. If he wanted to 'busy giddy minds with foreign wars', then Scotland was by far the safest bet—or it would have been if it had not been for the death of Francis I. War always raises soldiers to political prominence, and, although he had achieved some note as a diplomat, Warwick was also primarily a soldier. His kinsmen and friends followed the same bent. His cousins Edward and Henry were both serving under Lord Grey at Boulogne, where it is reasonable to suppose that he had been instrumental in placing them. Henry, indeed, had cut a great dash at the tournament held there to celebrate Edward's coronation.[38] At the same time Warwick's younger brother Andrew had been appointed as early as 27 February to command a fleet 'addressed into the North Sees aswel for annoyance of the Skottes bruted to prepare to passe towardes France, and for the interruption of suche municion as is loked to be brought for Skotland owte of Fraunce ...'.[39] On 12 March he reported a notable success to the Lord Admiral, Thomas Seymour. He had taken the *Lyon*, and with it many Scottish prisoners, although documents which he had also been anxious to secure had been cast into the sea.

After 20 March Warwick virtually ceased to attend council meetings, probably because he was busy with military affairs in France and the north. On 28 May he received £42. 10s. 'for so muche by him imprested in Frenche crownes to James Walshe, sent aboute the Kinges Majestes affayres into the partes of Fraunce',[40] but there are few other indications of his activity in the early summer. He was, however, not neglectful of his own interests, and his manner of pursuing them gives some insight into the workings of the patronage system at this stage of the Protectorate On 24 March he wrote, not to Somerset but to his old familiar Paget, setting out his case for a grant of the 'lordship' of Warwick as a part of the £300 a year in land which he was due to receive under the terms of the February creations. He was already constable, high steward, and master of the game there, and 'because of the name and my descent from one of the daughters of the rightful line I am the more desirous to have the thing'.[41] He offered to remit part of the fees which he already enjoyed in Warwick in return for the farm of the manor, castle, and town. The castle was in any case, he pointed out, partly ruinous and 'unable to lodge a good baron with his train'. 'Move the rest of the lords to

[38] PRO SP 68/13, no. 47.   [39] *APC*, ii. 44.   [40] Ibid. 96.   [41] PRO SP 10/1, no. 30.

this effect', he wrote 'and be friendly to [Sir Anthony] Denny, according to his desire for the site and remains of Waltham.' If he could not have Warwick, then Paget was to put in a bid on his behalf for Tonbridge, Penshurst, and Canonbury. At the same time he was mindful that Sir Anthony Browne was keen to have 'the lordship in Sussex that was Lord De La Warr's', and that it would be well bestowed upon him because he would keep a household there.[42] If Somerset's was the only voice which counted in such matters, then Warwick was clearly ignorant of the fact. He was prepared to bargain for support, and to be beholden to his friends; nor was he taking anything for granted. Paget presumably advised him to present his request in due form, because on 27 March he submitted a very large petition, running to twenty-nine membranes, to the court of Augmentations, listing lands in twelve counties, which must have amounted to the whole £300 of his entitlement, and headed by the manor, castle, and town of Warwick.[43] Much negotiation must then have followed, because the grant which he eventually received on 22 June was different in many respects from the grant requested, but it included the Warwick 'lordship' by which he set so much store.[44]

No sooner was this grant made than Dudley began to alienate some of the properties which he had received: the site of the hospital at Ludlow to William and Edward Foxe; the monastery of St John at Colchester to Francis Jobson; the manor of Ramborough, Suffolk, to Sir Edward North.[45] Over the following two years he was to distribute much land in this way, and although we do not know the terms, it is very likely that these were preferential sales, or even gifts, intended to built up an affinity and a network of friendships. The names of the recipients—Sir Thomas Darcy, Francis Jobson, Sir Thomas Palmer, George Harper, and Thomas Culpepper—suggest no less. In spite of a noble lineage, as a service peer Dudley had no natural manred. He had shifted his main base at least twice, and, although the earldom gave him a position of some strength in the West Midlands, he needed an affinity to sustain the political position to which he aspired, especially in the uncertain circumstances of a minority. On 7 July he received the £500 which had been bequeathed to him under the terms of Henry VIII's will, and had every reason to be satisfied with a profitable few weeks,[46] but his gains were as nothing by comparison with those of the duke of Somerset, who on 9 July caused himself to be granted a massive annuity of 8,000 marks.[47] At £5,333 per annum he thereafter received what was in effect a salary as chief minister equivalent to the landed revenues of the richest peerage in the country—over and above the revenues of the duchy of Somerset. For the next two years his income from all sources was probably in

---

[42] Ibid.   [43] PRO E318/2042: 27 Mar. 1 Edward VI.
[44] *Calendar of the Patent Rolls*, Edward VI, i. 252.   [45] Ibid. 4, 204, 200.
[46] *APC*, ii. 106.   [47] *Cal. Pat.*, Edward VI, i. 184; PRO E315/258, fo. 49.

excess of £10,000 a year. He also used his position to extract lands from the Church by way of profitable exchanges. The bishop of Lincoln was licensed on 18 August to grant him the manor of Woburn.[48] Nor did he fail to extract other rewards from a vulnerable Crown estate. On 11 July 1548 he was to receive a further £500 worth of land for his services in Scotland where the situation by then would rather have merited a refund.[49] On 19 August 1547 his brother Thomas also received land to the annual value of £500.[50] Perhaps it is only fair to add that the Seymours, unlike the Dudleys, did not in addition nibble away at the court of Augmentations. Apart from two small grants to the Protector's son after his death, their profits were taken on a large scale.

By the beginning of July preparations for war in the north were far advanced. As early as 24 March the council was deliberately exaggerating the report of an 'attemptate' by the Scots of the West March, received from Lord Wharton.[51] In April the northern counties were warned about aggressive Scottish and French intentions, and muster commissioners in all counties were required to survey their available men, making returns by 20 May.[52] Warwick was one of those busied in this way. He was still available in London on 2 July to be one of those commissioned to take Sir Anthony Denny's account. His instructions for the north were eventually dated 12 August, but they seem to have been drafted about a month earlier, and to have been the subject of some negotiation. On 22 July Paget replied to a letter from the earl, in which he had clearly objected to some part of his orders, including the daily rate of his 'diet', which was set at 5 marks. Paget agreed that £5 would have been more appropriate, but regretted that he was unable to reply more satisfactorily 'For both my Lord Protector's Grace is absent at London, and I here at Drayton also absent from the court ...'. He suggested that Dudley should leave his unsatisfactory commission with one of his servants, until Paget could acquire a more satisfactory one to send after him.[53] It was presumably the amended version which was issued on 12 August. Warwick's authority was that of 'Lieutenant and Captain Generall' of the North Parts. At the same time Lord Thomas Seymour was given a similar commission for the South, and a number of other peers were given authority to levy men within particular counties.[54] The Protector

[48] *Cal. Pat.*, Edward VI, i. 184.   [49] *Cal. Pat.*, Edward VI, ii. 27.

[50] *Cal. Pat.*, Edward VI, i. 25–33.

[51] Wharton was instructed 'that by one letter apart he should enfourme them of the very certeintie of their nombre and damage by them done at that tyme, as truely as he himself was instructed therein, and by another letter to enlarge the matter, describeng their nombre to have bene upon a vii[c], and that they burned iii or iiii villages on our Borders, toke notable prays, prisoners and catell away, with such other aggravacions of that their rode as his wisdom in that behalfe could set furthe'. This tactic was described by Jordan as a 'monstrous deception' (*APC*, ii. 461, App.; Jordan, *Edward VI*, 248).

[52] *APC*, ii. 471; PRO SP10/1, no. 36.   [53] PRO E315/475, fo. 52.

[54] The marquis of Northampton in Essex, Norfolk, and Suffolk, the earl of Arundel in Surrey, Hampshire, and Wiltshire, and Sir Thomas Cheney in Kent. Warwick's commission

himself was appointed 'King's Lieutenant and Captain General for wars both within the realm and without' with the power to hire mercenaries and to exercise martial law at his discretion. The impression given by these commissions is that of a realm preparing to defend itself against a mighty adversary, rather than that of one preparing to launch a medium-sized campaign of brief duration against a recalcitrant but not particularly formidable foe. Perhaps this was done to deter the French from intervening, or perhaps to strengthen the council's hand for dealing with possible trouble at home. It certainly appears unnecessarily comprehensive for the campaign which followed.

By this time there was little in the way of an English party in Scotland, but there was a growing protestant element which looked to England for protection, particularly as the Protector's religious policy began to surface in the summer of 1547. Over a year before, in May 1546, a protestant 'commando' group had broken into St Andrews castle, murdered Cardinal Beaton, and defied all attempts to remove them.[55] The raising of that seige does not seem to have been high on Somerset's agenda, and the naval protection which Henry had accorded to the garrison was inadequately maintained. On 31 July 1547 a squadron of French galleys under the command of Leo Strozzi bombarded the castle into surrender, and English credibility among the Scottish reformers was heavily undermined. Just two days later, on 2 August, Somerset sent orders to the muster commissioners of all shires to send their contingents to rendezvous at Newcastle on August 28.[56] Because the Lord Admiral was also Lieutenant of the South, the fleet was placed under the command of Lord Edward Clinton. By 1 September Somerset had about 18,000 men and 24 fighting ships mustered at Berwick, while Lord Wharton at Carlisle was poised to lead 2,500 raiders across the western border as a diversion. On 2 September the earl of Warwick, leading a vanguard of about 4,000 men, crossed the river Tweed and entered Scotland. Behind him Somerset commanded the main army, and Lord Dacre the rearguard. Whatever his original commission may have indicated, when the campaign actually began, Warwick was the Protector's second in command, and entrusted with the most responsible position in an advancing army. William Patten, whose account, published in January 1548, provides a detailed narrative of the campaign, is fulsome in his praise of the Earl's skill and courage. Admittedly Patten's work is a eulogy of the whole English command, and his comments may be discounted, but the incidents which he describes are circumstantial and convincing. On 7 September, while the army was crossing the north Tyne in a thick mist, Warwick, with

covered Yorkshire, Cumberland, Westmorland, Kendall, Northumberland, Cheshire, Lancashire, Nottinghamshire, Derbyshire, Shropshire, and Staffordshire (*APC*, ii. 118–19).

[55] S. Haynes and W. Murdin (eds.), *A Collection of State Papers … left by William Cecil, Lord Burghley* (London, 1740–59), i. 43–54.

[56] E. Lodge, *Illustrations of British History* (London, 1838), iii. 9, App.

a small band of horsemen, lingered behind to deter a Scottish attack upon the rearguard, and fell into an ambush. Unintimidated and seizing his lance, .

with so valiant a courage he charged at one (it was thought Dandy Carr a captain among them) that he did not only compel Carr to turn, but himself chased him above twelve score together, all the way, at spear point; so that if Carr's horse had not been exceeding good and wight, his Lordship had surely run him through in this race. He also, with his little band, caused all the rest to flee amain.[57]

The panache which had earned the 19-year-old John Dudley his knighthood was still there in his mid-forties. Neither advancing years nor the responsibilities of command had dimmed his appetite for a good fight. Patten's account of this incident is also interesting for the names of some of those who were the members of his 'band', presumably a kind of personal bodyguard; Henry Vane 'a gentleman of my Lord's', and the French mercenaries Jean de Bertheville and Jean Ribaut, both of whom were to have chequered careers over the next few years.[58]

On 9 September, as the advance continued to the Esk, Warwick was again tempted to let his youthful zeal outrun his mature discretion. George Gordon, earl of Huntly, one of the Scottish commanders, sent a challenge to Somerset offering to reduce the effusion of Christian blood by fighting him man to man in limited or personal combat. The Protector took the opportunity to deliver the herald a public lecture on Scottish responsibility for the confrontation, and declined Huntly's somewhat quixotic offer on the grounds of his own superior status and responsibility. Warwick immediately offered to accept the challenge in Somerset's place, 'but my Lord's Grace would in no wise grant to it'.[59] The argument that Warwick was also superior to Huntly in status is unconvincing, but the Protector was undoubtedly right not to risk his valued second in command in a chivalric gesture which would have resolved nothing. Whether he was also unwilling to allow Dudley to obtain extra prestige by winning such a combat must remain an open question. The battle which was fought on the following day, was at first a close and bloody contest because the Scots, instead of standing on the defensive, attacked, taking the English by surprise. However, good discipline and superior firepower turned the day, which ended in a devastating Scottish rout. Although Patten does not expressly say so, it seems from his account that this was a victory won by hard fighting captains and soldiers rather than by skilful commanders. Somerset receives

---

[57] William Patten, *The expedicione in Scotlande of ... Edward, Duke of Somerset* (London, 1548), in E. Arber (ed.), *An English Garner* (London, 1877–96), iii. 91.

[58] Both Bertheville and Ribaut continued in Dudley's service. The former spent some time in the Tower later in the reign, and the latter was to transport Thomas Stafford on his ill-fated expedition to Scarborough in 1557. Ribaut eventually died trying to establish a French Huguenot colony in Florida.

[59] Patten, *Expedicione*, 101.

nothing but praise and 'My Lord Lieutenant' is vividly portrayed inspiring the vanguard with noble words,[60] but once the battle was joined there was little that either of them could do to influence the outcome. According to Patten, some 13,000 Scots were killed in the battle and the pursuit which followed it. The figure is certainly an exaggeration, but this was no repetition of Solway Moss, and the casualties were certainly heavy. Nor did the English escape lightly, although their dead may have been numbered in hundreds rather than thousands.

Having won his victory, Somerset did remarkably little with it. He moved towards Leith, and began some desultory seige works but more to keep his pioneers occupied than with any serious intent. Clinton's ships took the island of Inchcolm in the Firth of Forth, and the castle of Broughty, further north on the Firth of Tay, but no attempt was made against Edinburgh, and on 20 September the English army began to withdraw towards the borders. Somerset was well aware that Henry VIII's policies in Scotland had achieved nothing, and fear of a similar failure haunted his dreams.[61] The battle of Pinkie had destroyed Scotland's military capability for the time being, but unless he could devise a better follow-up strategy than the old king, it would amount to no more. His intention, as it soon emerged, was to plant strategic garrisons across the Lowlands, and by a constant military presence to apply coercive pressure and to make future large-scale invasions unnecessary. In the immediate aftermath of the battle such garrisons were established at Hume castle, Roxburgh, Eye mouth, Castlemilk, and Moffat in the Scottish marches, at Inchcolm, and at Broughty.[62] Somerset made no secret of his intentions. The French and imperial ambassadors were well aware of them, and so were the Scots themselves. The ultimate objective of all this coercion was, of course, to resurrect the treaty of Greenwich and to bring about a personal union between England and Scotland. By the beginning of October Somerset was back in London, leaving the earl of Warwick and Sir Ralph Sadler, with other commissioners, in Berwick to meet with the promised representatives of the council of Scotland. Two other Dudleys also remained behind, Andrew (who had been knighted during the campaign) as Captain of Broughty, and Sir Edward, the earl's cousin, as Captain of Hume castle.

Over the following weeks it transpired that Warwick was wasting his time. The promised Scottish commissioners 'neither came, nor, belike, meant to come'. This was probably due not, as Patten believed, to deliberate Scottish perfidiousness, but rather to the chronic divisions among the Scottish aristocracy.[63] These were partly occasioned by personal and family feuds of long standing, and partly by the steady growth of the Reformation.

[60] Ibid. 119.   [61] Ibid. 80.

[62] A complete list of these garrisons, both actual and contemplated, is provided by M. L. Bush, *The Government Policy of Protector Somerset* (London, 1975), 14–15.

[63] Patten, *Expedicione*, 146; G. Donaldson, *Scotland: James V to James VII* (Edinburgh, 1978).

A number of border lairds pledged their allegiance to Warwick as the king's Lieutenant, and there were English supporters of similar rank in both Fife and Angus. The earl of Bothwell, Patrick Hepburn, who had been captured at Pinkie, offered to surrender his great border castle of Hermitage in return for an English marriage. However, since he had his eyes on the two royal princesses, Mary and Elizabeth, thinking 'if he liked them, they would not mislike him', either his judgement or his seriousness must be suspected.[64] How long Warwick remained in the north after the end of September is not apparent. He is not noted as having been present at the parliament which convened on 4 November, nor does he appear again among the attenders at the Privy Council until January 1549.[65] Neither of these records can be relied upon, however, and it is likely that he was back in London well before Christmas. On 22 December he received a grant of lands to the value of £108 for his services in Scotland, which had presumably been completed by that date; and on 25 December he was licensed to grant his manor of Ramborough in Suffolk to his fellow councillor Sir Edward North.[66] On 8 January 1548 he wrote to the Protector from Ely Place, asking the latter to authorize an exchange of lands with the bishop of Worcester. 'This is the first exchange I ever desired at any of [the bishop] hands' he wrote righteously, 'and shall be the last. I desire no disprofit to the bishop …'.[67] He had extracted Lincoln Place in Holborn from the bishop of Lincoln back in August, but that, presumably, did not even pretend to be an exchange.

On 24 December Somerset had caused his patent of 12 March to be renewed 'forasmuch as by his [the king's] said uncle and council, affairs have been well managed …'. He was now to hold office during the king's pleasure rather than for the duration of the minority, and he was confirmed in his office of Lieutenant-General of the kingdom.[68] It has been pointed out that Warwick did not set his hand to this, but that is of no significance because, unlike the original patent, this confirmation was not recorded in the council register, and was authorized directly by the king. In spite of Warwick's absence from the council board during these months, there is no evidence of a rift, or even of strained relations, between himself and the Protector. He saw himself as a person of influence with Somerset and was so perceived by others. On 22 January Sir Henry Long wrote 'It may please your Grace to understand thant I have written unto my Lord of Warwick, desiring his lordship to be a mean for me unto your grace, whereby I trust

[64] Warwick to Somerset, 30 Sept. 1547 (*Calendar of State Papers*, Scotland, ed. J. Bain *et al.* (Edinburgh and Glasgow, 1898–1952), i. 22).

[65] Acording to Patten he left Newcastle on 5 Oct., but there is no indication of where he went, and it is possible that he spent some time in the Welsh marches before returning to London.

[66] *Cal. Pat.*, Edward VI, i. 200.   [67] PRO SP10/3, no. 1.

[68] *Cal. Pat.*, Edward VI, ii. 96.

the sooner to know your grace's pleasure'; and on 1 February the earl himself wrote to William Cecil, Somerset's private secretary, urging the Protector's favour for a group of 'poor folk' who were desirous of founding a free grammar school.[69] Warwick's developing relationship with Cecil is of considerable interest, because by the spring of 1548 he was writing to the secretary in very much the same manner as he had addressed Sir William Paget when the latter had been the king's secretary in 1545 and 1546. Like Paget, Cecil was the man with immediate access to the source of power. Paget was still an important councillor, and there is no reason to suppose that Warwick had fallen out with him, but his influence was declining. He continued to bombard the Protector with good advice, but Somerset was no longer listening. This was eventually to prove a mistake, but it explains the change in the pattern of Dudley's correspondence. There are some references in the early part of 1548 to suggest that Warwick's health may have been poor. Both de Selve and Van der Delft commented upon his frequent indispositions in explanation of his absence from the council; but the former also reported that his influence with the Protector was unimpaired.[70] It is possible that having observed the increasingly marginal role to which the council was being relegated in the decision-making process, Warwick simply did not bother to attend, preferring to maintain his role by other means. The key to that strategy may again lie in his developing relationship with Cecil.

At the end of June he was appointed President of the Council in the Marches of Wales. There is no trace of his commission either in the Patent Rolls or in the council register, so the exact date is unknown, but on 2 July he wrote to Cecil 'to know my lord's resolution concerning the commission of marches'.[71] In many ways he was an appropriate choice, because his principal seat at Dudley castle was within easy reach of Ludlow, and he held a number of properties within the marches. Nevertheless his old anxiety about 'estimacion' still seems to have troubled him. He was willing to serve, but doubted whether his 'liveries' would be sufficient. 'Without honest and sound associates,' he wrote, 'the President will be able to do little good with the froward and ignorant.'[72] His doubts must have been overcome, because he certainly did serve, but very little is known about his activity in that capacity. Even his title is open to some doubt. In July 1549 he was formally described as President of the Principality of Wales and its Marches, whereas the usual title was President of the Council in the

[69] PRO SP10/3, no. 6.

[70] Germain Lefèvre-Pontalis (ed.), *Correspondance politique de Odet de Selve* (Paris, 1888), 307, 353; *Cal. Span.*, ix. 383. References to Warwick's poor health are somewhat confusing. In Mar. 1548 Odet de Selve referred to a leg ailment for which a doctor had been treating him for months, but when he alluded to his own ailments, it was nearly always his stomach that he complained of.

[71] PRO SP10/4, no. 22.   [72] Ibid.

Marches of Wales, which was the designation applied to his successor, Sir William Herbert.[73] None of his surviving correspondence is dated from the marches, and if he ever went there in an official capacity it has escaped notice. Despite his professions of willingness, a distinctly sour note was struck within a few days of his appointment. On 7 July he wrote to Cecil complaining that his attempt to remove a corrupt Justice and some unsuitable councillors had been blocked in spite of earlier assurances from the Protector that his wishes would be respected.

By whose persuasion this happens I know not, but I am sure I have base friends who smile to see me so used. But I trust, despite my charges and pains, I have made provision there. Despite mockery I shall be as ready to serve as those who have now won their purpose, not the first or last to be worked with my lord. If they work no more displeasure I will be more willing to forgive.[74]

It is difficult to know how seriously to take this display of ill humour. Warwick may have believed that he had influential enemies at court, who were endeavouring to poison his relationship with Somerset, or he may have been suffering from a fit of temporary pique. There is no suggestion of a serious rift with the Protector himself, and his requests to Cecil for small favours from the duke's patronage continued without interruption.

Until the end of July Warwick was at Pendley in Hertfordshire. While the council concerned itself with the recurring French threat to Boulogne, and with reliable reports of Henry's intention to intervene in Scotland, England's most dashing and successful soldier seems to have stayed quietly at home. Barrett Beer's conjecture that this was due to a prolonged period of ill health is probably correct, although the sparsity of comment to that effect is rather surprising.[75] For whatever reason he was not on active service during the summer of 1548; nor was he at court. The earl of Shrewsbury commanded on the Scottish borders, and Lord Grey of Wilton at Boulogne. There was plague in London during the summer, 'a great mortalitie by pestilence' as Grafton recorded. Warwick was at Ely Place in Holborn during September when he reported that his wife 'had had her fit again'. This was clearly not plague, but it caused him to defer a planned return to the court.[76] His occasional references to his own health are more suggestive of hypochondria than of serious indisposition. He complained of falling ill while on a visit to the earl of Southampton, and of being unable to eat.[77] Wriothesley was not the most obvious man to be playing the host, as the former Lord Chancellor was still excluded from the council and was deeply aggrieved by the way in which he had been treated in the previous year. However, they were colleagues of long standing, and he does not seem to

[73] *APC*, iii. 427; *Cal. Pat.*, Edward VI, iii. 300.   [74] PRO SP10/4, no. 26.
[75] Beer, *Northumberland*, 66–8.
[76] Richard Grafton, *A Chronicle at large* (London, 1568), ed. H. Ellis (London, 1809), 506; BL Add. MS 32657, fo. 49.
[77] Beer, *Northumberland*, 68.

have held Dudley responsible for his humiliation. The continued friendship which this visit suggests was to be significant for the events of the following year. Warwick's return to active and visible participation in affairs
came with the convening of Edward's second parliament of 27 November.
This was the parliament which saw the introduction of the first bill of uniformity, which was the culmination of the Protector's ecclesiastical policy.
Warwick had been noted long before Henry's death as a supporter of the
new learning—a heretic in the eyes of Van der Delft—and he had done
nothing during the first year of the reign to indicate a change of heart.[78]
Indeed the imperial ambassador noted with disfavour that mass was no
longer celebrated in the earl's household by December 1547.[79] As this was
some months before the public introduction of Cranmer's interim provision for an English language communion, it would be interesting to know
what liturgy was used at Ely Place. Unlike Somerset, Warwick seems to
have had no interest in doctrinal issues. He did not, at this stage, corres-
pond with leading reformers, or receive the dedications of their works. He
did take part in December 1548 in one of the debates on the Bill of Uniformity of which a record has survived, but his contribution serves only to reveal
an unsophisticated and distinctly secular mind.

On the first day he intervened only to point out that what was looked for
was uniformity, not theological debate. He accused Thomas Thirlby, the
bishop of Westminster, who disagreed with the doctrine of the proposed
Prayer Book, of speaking a 'perilous word', and of stirring up discord.[80] The
clergy, he continued, echoing the well-remembered words of Henry VIII,
were looked to for leadership in consensus, to set an example of obedience
to the laity, 'Seeing there is but one truth and verity... calling therein for the
aid of God'. On the second day Dudley was somewhat more ambitious,
challenging Bishop Nicholas Heath of Worcester on the question of tran-
substantiation. His question was actually answered in a protestant sense by
Nicholas Ridley of Rochester, whereupon the Earl exclaimed 'Where is
your scripture now, my Lord of Worcester? Methink because you cannot
maintain your argument neither by Scripture nor doctors, you would go
now with natural reason and sophistry ...'.[81] The best that can be said for his
interjection is that it shows an understandable anxiety to bring the rather
pointless exchange to an end. Conservatives and reformers were actually
talking at cross purposes on this issue, having different philosophical pre-
misses, but there is no sign that Warwick understood that.[82] He was clearly

[78] See above, p. 83.
[79] Van der Delft to the emperor, 5 Dec. 1547 (*Cal. Span.*, ix. 221).
[80] BL Royal MS 17B, XXXIX; F. Gasquet and E. Bishop, *Edward VI and the Book of Common Prayer* (London, 1890), 395–443.
[81] Ibid.; see also Beer, *Northumberland*, 70.
[82] The ubiquity of the divine presence, which is fundamental to the catholic position, could only be comprehended on the basis of a strict separation of substance and accident, which was

out of his depth in intellectual terms, but understood clearly that the outcome of the debate depended upon political power rather than persuasive argument. If the Protector could muster enough votes in the House of Lords, then the validity or otherwise of the dissenters' views would count for nothing. On 15 January 1549 seven bishops and three lay peers voted against the Bill of Uniformity, which passed comfortably in a House of some seventy-five members. Warwick voted with the majority.[83]

It is possible that his low-profile summer may also have been connected with the desire to pay some attention to the management of his estate. In July he sold 40 acres of marsh in Poplar to Sir Francis Jobson, and on 17 August paid £1,286 into the court of Augmentations for the manor of Chedworth in Gloucestershire, and a long list of other lands.[84] According to a subsidy assessment taken in the first year of the reign, his income from lands at this point was £1,200 per annum.[85] This represents both an absolute and a relative decline from his position four years earlier. Not only was he now behind the Lord Protector (£1,700), but he was also exceeded by Lord Russell the Lord Privy Seal (£1,396), the marquis of Dorset (2,000 marks), and the marquis of Northampton (also 2,000 marks), as well as by other major peers, such as the earls of Derby and Shrewsbury, whose assessments at this time are not recorded. The absolute decline was probably of no significance, because the assessments were already beginning to lose touch with the reality which Henry had always insisted upon, but Warwick's failure to gain on his peers indicates a lack of competitive edge which he may well have been attempting to remedy. He certainly spent some time upon his estates in Warwickshire, probably during July and August, because it was there that he brushed with the commission of enquiry into enclosures, headed by the zealous John Hales of Coventry. These commissions had been launched by the Protector in the previous summer, in pursuit of what he considered to be his social duty.[86] While population levels were low in the previous century, a fair amount of arable land had been taken out of use and converted to profitable sheep pasture. When the population began to rise again, after about 1480, holdings became scarce, and resentment against 'depopulation' began to be voiced. Cardinal Wolsey had been sufficiently concerned by the evidence of agrarian unrest to launch a series of enquiry commissions in 1517. No very

impossible from the nominalist position shared by most protestants (J. McGee, 'The Nominalism of Thomas Cranmer', *Harvard Theological Review*, 57 (1964), 189–206; T. F. Torrance, *Space, Time, and Incarnation* (London, 1969), 25–6).

[83] *Journals of the House of Lords* (London, 1846), i. 331.

[84] *Cal. Pat.*, Edward VI, i. 277; ibid., ii. 29. Warwick received a large number of licences to grant, which presumably means to sell, land, which raises the suspicion that he was using his political position to broker a number of profitable deals.

[85] PRO E179/69/51.

[86] Bush, *Government Policy*, 43–8. These commissions had no authority to hear or determine cases, but only to report.

resolute action had resulted, but Henry VIII had accepted an anti-enclosure culture, which had been expressed in a series of statutes for the protection of tillage. By the end of his reign the overall economic situation had deteriorated because of the advent of inflation, and the consequent need felt by landlords to maintain their real income by raising rents and converting land to more profitable use wherever possible. There is no reason to suppose that there had been an orgy of depopulating enclosure since 1520, indeed all the evidence points the other way, but a group of zealous preachers and pamphleteers who are sometimes known by the misleading collective term of 'the commonwealth men', set about launching a moral crusade in the early days of the Protectorate.[87] Their targets were gentle and aristocratic landlords, whom they accused of irresponsible economic exploitation, and of wilful disregard of the rights and interests of the poor. Modern research has shown most of their specific arguments to have been spurious, but they held the moral high ground at the time, and Somerset was convinced by their thesis. It was the king's responsibility to protect his humble subjects against oppression by the rich and powerful, and that responsibility devolved upon him as Protector. He therefore let it be known that he intended to continue with the traditional Tudor policy of protecting arable farming, and sent out commissioners to collect complaints and evidence of abuse. It was such a commission that aroused the ire of the earl of Warwick.[88]

Warwick's protest to Hales does not survive, but he obviously accused him of stirring up agrarian unrest by promising remedies which could not be implemented, and by undermining that deference to the gentry upon which so much of the fabric of social discipline depended. John Strype, nearly two centuries later, commented disparagingly that 'he grew much displeased with Hales, who acted very honestly in this commission, and favorably to the commons'.[89] However, it was not Hales's honesty that was in question, but the political sense of what he was doing. Writing to Warwick during August, he protested that he had no intention of 'stirring up' the people against the nobility and gentlemen, nor of inciting anyone to violence. It is clear from his instructions, and from the Protector's proclamations, that he was theoretically right. It was very carefully pointed out that no private citizen, however justly he may feel aggrieved, was entitled to

---

[87] These men, some of whom were leading protestant preachers, like Hugh Latimer, were primarily concerned to reawaken social consciences, in accordance with the ancient Christian teaching of the stewardship of wealth. Typical of their writings is the tract entitled 'The Decay of England by the Great Multitude of Sheep' (in R. H. Tawney and E. Power, *Tudor Economic Documents* (London, 1924), iii. 51–7). By concentrating their attacks upon aristocratic landowners they exposed themselves to charges of social and political subversion.

[88] P. L. Hughes and J. F. Larkin, *Tudor Royal Proclamations* (New Haven and London, 1964–9), i, no. 327. See also I. S. Leadam (ed.), *The Domeday of Enclosures, 1517–8* (London, 1897), ii. 656 ff.

[89] Strype, *Ecclesiastical Memorials*, ii. i. 149–52; BL Lansdowne MS 238, fos. 321–5.

take the law into his own hands.[90] However, it is also clear from the sporadic riots which broke out during the summer of 1548, and from the storms of the following year, that that is exactly what happened. However virtuously Hales, or Somerset, might deny it, or disclaim any such intention, there was a direct connection between the expectations aroused by the commissions and the spread of agrarian violence. Warwick was right to be both angry and alarmed by these developments, and the fact that his own interests were threatened is no good ground for dismissing the validity of his fears. He was to return to the same theme in the more threatening circumstances of the following summer.

By the end of 1548 the Protectorate was in difficulties. Somerset had started the year in Scotland by attempting to build on the strong position which the victory of Pinkie and the establishment of the garrisons had given him. His first weapon was persuasion, and in January he published, both in Latin and in English, *An epistle or exhortation, to unitie and peace*, in which he set out with eloquence and conviction the advantages which would accrue to both kingdoms from a union of the crowns.[91] This work was widely circulated in southern Scotland, but the fact that it was published simultaneously in Latin meant that the Scots were not its only target. It was intended to persuade the international community, and perhaps most particularly the imperialists, of the righteousness of the English cause. The Protector's arguments found an echo in the north, not only among the protestant reformers who dreaded the revival of French influence, but also among mercenary intellectuals like James Harrison, who endeavoured to sell the union line to his fellow countrymen in return for a pension.[92] Unfortunately such propaganda, however good, did not convert readily into serious politics. In January and February 1548 a diplomatic battle was raging in Scotland between England and France, and the principal weapon was gold. At first it seemed that the English would prevail. Lennox, Glencairn, Bothwell, Angus, and even Argyle were apparently taking that side at the end of January. However the French, urged on by the queen mother, Mary of Guise, counter-attacked strongly with an offer of marriage between Mary and the Dauphin. What probably decided the issue in the end was the constant irritant of the English garrisons. However careful the English commanders Grey, Wharton, and Bowes might be (and they were not always particularly careful) the reinforcement of these fortresses, and the desultory fighting which they inevitably provoked, con-

[90] Hughes and Larkin, *Tudor Royal Proclamations*, i, no. 309; Strype, *Ecclesiastical Memorials*, II. ii. 359–65: 'We charge and command you all, that be present on the king's behalf, and that ye likewise charge all your neighbours that be absent, that ye nor none of them go about to take upon you to be executors of the statutes …'.

[91] *Epistola exhortoria ad pacem … missa ab … Protectore Angliae … ad populum regni Scotiae*, STC 22269.

[92] James Harrison, *An exhortacion to the Scottes* (London, 1547), STC 12857; Jordan, *Edward VI*, 270.

stantly reminded the Scots of the unfinished war.[93] As late as the end of March the chief French negotiator, Chapelle, believed that he would lose because of the threat of English military power. There was no will to resist; the English raided selectively and at will to intimidate those who refused to adhere to them; and another full-scale English invasion was being prepared.[94] On the latter point his intelligence was faulty, but there was substantial military activity in the borders, and Sir Andrew Dudley was an active, not to say aggressive, commander at Broughty Crag. Somerset's policy, although not pursued with uniform success, was to speak softly and carry a big stick. So impressed was Chapelle that he told Henry that only a full military commitment in Scotland could redeem the situation, and the king believed him.[95]

On 18 June 6,000 French troops were landed at Leith. Lord Clinton and Sir Thomas Wyndham had a substantial fleet at sea off the north-east coast, because the advent of Montalembert's force was expected, but they were in the wrong place, and, although the French were sighted off Dunbar, by then it was too late to intercept. This comparatively modest force transformed the military situation, because the English were not as strong as rumour made them, and the spirit of Scottish resistance revived. Strategically well briefed, Montalembert moved straight to the seige of Haddington, the key English fortress on the road between Berwick and Edinburgh. At the same time he proposed to the assembled Scottish estates the Franco-Scottish marriage which had been mooted in January, together with the suggestion that Mary should be sent immediately to France. Overwhelmed, perhaps, with relief at being freed from English bullying, or not liking to argue with their forceful liberators, the parliament accepted both these proposals in the treaty of Haddington on 10 July.[96] Early in August the young queen left Scotland by the western route, and, evading a rather half-hearted attempt at English interception, landed after a stormy crossing at Roscoff in Brittany on 13 August. Somerset's Scottish policy was ruined at a blow, and over the next few weeks his political limitations were ruthlessly exposed. Instead of cutting his losses, or reverting to a low-key policy of support for the Scottish protestants until the French should outstay their welcome, he resurrected the worst features of Henry VIII's bankrupt strategy. Abandoning the idealism of his January manifesto, he again advanced the ancient English claim to suzerainty over her northern neighbour.[97]

---

[93] Bush, *Government Policy*, 18–20.

[94] M. de la Chapelle to the Duc d'Aumale, 22 Mar. 1548 (A. Teulat (ed.), *Relations politiques de la France et de l'Espagne avec l'Écosse au XVIe siècle* (Paris, 1862), i. 160–2.

[95] Ibid.; *Calendar of State Papers, Scotland*, i. 121.   [96] Jordan, *Edward VI*, 283.

[97] Somerset sent out an urgent plea for evidence to support this position, and received a number of responses which are still extant (BL Cotton MS Caligula B vii, 166, fo. 322; 169, fo. 329 ff.; BL Add. MS 6128). The arguments were then summarized in *An epitome of the title that the King's maiestie of England hath to the sovereigntie of Scotland*, by Nicholas Bodrugan, al. Adams, STC 3196.

Those Scots who had regarded his 'one Britain' rhetoric as opportunist humbug thus appeared to be completely vindicated, and those who had accepted it were embarrassed and undermined. At the same time he prepared to strike another military blow.

There was a good case for trying to neutralize Montalembert, and his presence at Haddington actually created the English threat which he believed he had come to counter. The first attempt, however, led by Sir Robert Bowes and Warwick's protégé Sir Thomas Palmer, was a fiasco. What was intended as a diversionary raid by 3,000–4,000 men was ambushed, thanks to Palmer's foolhardiness, and driven off with heavy losses. Both Bowes and Palmer were captured.[98] The Protector was understandably enraged, because Palmer had deliberately ignored orders, but it was not altogether unreasonable, as Paget pointed out, for the latter to claim that he had been misled by Somerset's own bellicosity.[99] Palmer bitterly resented the anger which was vented upon him, and Paget was troubled, not for the first time, by the fact that his cautious advice had been ignored. The main campaign, led by the sensible Shrewsbury, ran no such risk, but was extraordinarily inconsequential. As 15,000 men crossed the border on 17 August and advanced towards Haddington, the French prudently withdrew, but Montalembert refused to be drawn into a pitched battle. By early September, short of money and supplies, and apparently under orders from the Protector not to tarry, Shrewsbury retreated to Berwick and immediately began to disband his forces.[100] Apart from reinforcing Haddington, he had accomplished nothing. By the end of September the Franco-Scottish siege had again closed around the garrison. The contrast between Somerset's aggressive rhetoric and his faltering performance was stark and disturbing.

By the end of 1548 the Protector's Scottish policy seemed to be drifting. Torn between an obstinate determination not to abandon the hopeless cause of an Anglo-Scottish marriage, and an acute awareness of his mounting debts, he managed to achieve the worst of all possibilities. Sir James Wilford, in command of the key fortress of Haddington, received such indifferent responses to his appeals for assistance that he believed that he had been abandoned. Sir John Lutterell, who had replaced Andrew Dudley at Broughty Crag, shared the same conviction, and yet both in fact remained crucial to the Protector's strategy.[101] He had totally failed to exploit the Franco-Scottish tension which surfaced in the wake of Shrewsbury's raid, and it was the weather rather than English military strength which preserved the *status quo* through the winter. In January 1549 fresh

[98] *Calendar of State Papers, Scotland*, i. 148; *Chronicle of Edward VI*, 9–10.
[99] BL Cotton MS Titus F iii, fos. 273–6.
[100] *Calendar of State Papers, Scotland*, i. 157–8, 164.
[101] Ibid. 166, 167, 170; *The Scottish Correspondence of Mary of Lorraine*, Scottish Historical Society, series 3: 10 (1927), 275–8.

levies were brought to Berwick, and both Haddington and Broughty were revictualled for six months. John Brende, Somerset's personal representative in the north, sent him regular and dispassionate accounts of the situation, so it was not ignorance, or the special pleading of particular officers, which induced the Protector's low-key attitude to what had been his most obsessive programme. The truth is that other pressing issues forced him to reduce the priority of Scotland as soon as an enforced period of inactivity allowed him to do so.

In spite of the war in the north, formal relations with France continued to be correct. Shrewsbury's campaign encouraged Chatillon, the French commander in Picardy, with the king's encouragement, to venture some probes against the defences of Boulogne.[102] These achieved nothing, and neither side wanted an open breach. The English council could not contemplate a second war without imperial support, and Henry was finding his commitments in the north unexpectedly expensive and frustrating. Both sides scored points. The French complained bitterly that Charles was allowing the English to recruit mercenaries in the Empire for use in Scotland, while the English complained that Henry was styling himself king of Scotland by virtue of his son's betrothal to the queen. Both sides stepped up privateering activity—or more properly piracy since there was no state of war—and Lord Admiral Seymour seems to have allowed his enthusiasm for this activity to outrun the limitations of discretion or common sense.[103] At the same time, Warwick was not the only peer to be suffering grave doubts about the wisdom of the Protector's agrarian policy. There had been scattered riots in a number of counties during the summer, which seemed to be directly connected to his sympathetic attitude to petitions. The religious temperature was also rising as the affects of the Chantries Act of the previous year began to become apparent, and as the archbishop's campaign against images became increasingly insistent.[104] In April the abrasive and somewhat unsavoury archdeacon of Cornwall, William Body, had been lynched for a particularly insensitive application of these policies.[105] The ringleaders had been arrested and executed, but their action had commanded a great deal of support. The introduction of the uniformity bill therefore, in December 1548, not only heralded a sharp debate in the House of Lords, but also the possibility of violence in the parishes. Somerset's biggest problem, however, at the end of 1548 was domestic in every sense of the word, because it concerned the conduct of his younger brother, Lord Seymour of Sudely.

---

[102] Somerset to Lord Seymour, 6 Aug. 1548 (PRO SP10/4, no. 38).

[103] PRO SP10/4, nos. 39–41. It was later alleged that the Lord Admiral failed to ensure that the shipping of friendly powers was respected, and accepted inducements to overlook such improprieties.

[104] Jordan, *Edward VI*, 182–7.

[105] A. L. Rowse, *Tudor Cornwall* (London, 1969), 253–9. Body had been imprisoned on the orders of the council in the previous Dec. for stirring up a 'tumult' by his indiscreet and clumsy behaviour (*APC*, ii. 535, App.).

Seymour was a man of some ability and, as it transpired, overwhelming ambition. He had been created a gentleman of the Privy Chamber in 1537, while his sister was queen, and knighted in the same year. In 1543 he became Master of the Ordnance, and was given several commands, mostly at sea, during the ensuing French war.[106] He was a member of the Privy Council during the last year of Henry's life, but to his bitter chagrin was not named as one of the sixteen executors of the king's will. Like several other councillors, he appeared among the twelve assistants. Having received a barony in Edward VI's 'accession honours', he succeeded Warwick as Lord Admiral on 17 February, and returned to the council *ex officio*. From his own subsequent actions, and from testimony relating to them, it appears that he considered such recognition inadequate. He believed that he should have been given the position of Governor of the King's Person, and became increasingly jealous of his dominant and successful brother. Little of this rancour, however, was apparent at the time. What was apparent was the rapid revival of the relationship which had formerly existed between Seymour and the queen dowager, Catherine Parr.[107] Catherine would almost certainly have married Seymour after the death of her second husband, Lord Latimer, if Henry had not intervened. In the early months of 1547, having endured three sexually unsatisfying marriages, the 35-year-old Catherine responded ardently to the advances of her erstwhile admirer. It is easy to be cynical about Seymour's motives, but the courtship seems to have been a passionate one on both sides, and their short-lived marriage was to be happy.[108] The Protector, understandably, was not amused by his brother's passion when he found out about it. Not only did it appear to be a mere cover for political ambition, it also exarcerbated an existing feud between Catherine and the duchess of Somerset, Anne Stanhope, a lady with a highly developed sense of her own importance. Realizing that Somerset would not consent to his intended marriage, and that to proceed without consent would be politically impossible, Seymour circumvented his brother in the only way open to him. He made himself familiar with John Fowler, one of the grooms of the Privy Chamber, who by virtue of his office had unsupervised access to the king. According to Fowler's later testimony

He ... asked me if I had communication with the king soon, to ask him if he would be content he should marry, and if so whom. I agreed, and that night when the king was alone, I said I marvelled that the Admiral did not marry. He said nothing. I asked him if he was content he should do so, and he agreed. I asked him whom and he said my lady Anne of Cleves, and then he said no, but he should marry his sister Mary, to turn her opinions ...[109]

---

[106] For a summary of Seymour's career before 1547, see John Maclean, *The Life of Sir Thomas Seymour, Knight, Lord Seymour of Sudeley* (London, 1869), 1–36.
[107] Ibid. 44–7; PRO SP10/1, nos. 41, 43.
[108] Antonia Fraser, *The Six Wives of Henry VIII* (London, 1992), 400.
[109] Deposition of John Fowler (PRO SP10/6, no. 10).

Having extracted this somewhat flippant response from the 9-year-old Edward, Seymour was poised to exploit his advantage.

Next day the Admiral came again to St. James's, and called me to him in the gallery. I told him all the king had said. He laughed, and asked me to ask the king if he would be content for him to marry the queen, and if he would write in his suit. I agreed and did so that night. The next day the Admiral came to the king; I cannot tell what communication they had, but the king wrote a letter to the queen, and the Admiral brought one back from her ...

Catherine did not need any persuasion, but the king's personal endorsement, obtained in this underhand manner, made it impossible for the Protector to object. He was greatly incensed, however, and if relations between the two brothers had not been strained before, they certainly were after July 1547. A quarrel over Catherine's jewels, for which each must bear a share of the responsibility, made matters even worse.[110]

This story is illuminating in several ways. It shows the young king in an attractive light. He was fond of his stepmother but clearly did not at once associate her happiness with Seymour. On the other hand he was easily persuaded. He must have liked the Admiral, who was a plausible operator, and he was innocent of suspicion. At the same time it shows that the Protector was a negligent guardian. He already knew that his brother coveted the Guardianship, and yet he took no precautions to forestall such an approach. On one occasion Seymour rashly commented to Fowler that the king was so poorly kept that it would have been easy to carry him off.[111] Probably the appointment of Sir Michael Stanhope, the Protector's brother-in-law, as Chief Gentleman of the Privy Chamber in August 1547 was an attempt to lock the stable door after the horse had been stolen. If that was the case the remedy did not work, because Stanhope kept his young master short of money, an opportunity which Seymour, through Fowler, was quick to exploit.[112] The Admiral also had a gambler's reckless confidence. Very early in the reign, probably before his marriage to Catherine, he persuaded the not very bright Henry Grey, marquis of Dorset, to place his eldest daughter, Jane, then aged about 10, in his household, claiming that he would be able to arrange her marriage to the king. Edward liked his cousin, but that Seymour should have made such a suggestion, and that Dorset should have believed in it, suggests that neither had a very firm grasp of political reality.

In spite of his office, Seymour did not command the fleet against Scotland. It was later alleged that he refused to do so, the implication being that he wished to remain at court in order to undermine his brother's influence

---

[110]   Jordan, *Edward VI*, 372; Depositions of William Parr, marquis of Northampton, and of William Wightman (PRO SP10/6, no. 14; ibid. 7, no. 8).

[111]   PRO SP10/6, no. 10.

[112]   Ibid; also Deposition of William Sharrington (PRO SP10/6, no. 13).

during the campaign.[113] However, the true reason seems to have been that he had also been appointed Lieutenant of the South of England, and that the Protector intended him to stay on his command, in case the French should seek to exploit the situation to their advantage. On 18 August, Van der Delft reported to Prince Philip, mentioning the Admiral's marriage, and declaring that it was intended that during the coming campaign 'he will remain here with the council to take the place of his brother'. Once the campaign was over, it was expected that Lord Seymour would be elevated to a dukedom.[114] The ambassador may have been a victim of Seymour's own propaganda, or the Protector may have been naïve, but it certainly does not look as though relations between the brothers had broken down irretrievably at that stage. However, Seymour did not know the meaning of discretion, and jealousy continued to fester. Catherine bore him a daughter, and died in childbirth in September 1548. The marquis of Dorset very properly withdrew his daughter from the widower's household, but was then persuaded to allow her to return.[115] Even before his wife's death Seymour seems to have been attempting to build up a relationship with the 14-year-old Princess Elizabeth, and he subsequently made a wild bid for her hand.[116] Mary was also bombarded with proposals, but she was old enough, and wise enough to have nothing to do with his advances. Elizabeth was almost compromised. All this is a familiar story, and it is difficult to know how much of it was subsequent embroidery, designed to put a treasonable construction upon actions which were, in themselves, merely foolish and irresponsible. The crisis came in January 1549, not triggered by any single event but by the cumulative effect of his behaviour during the second parliament. His intention seems to have been to introduce a bill for the purpose of annulling his brother's patent of office. He talked to a number of his fellow peers, and believed that he had their support.[117] Presumably he also believed that their backing would give him enough clientage to sway the House of Commons as well. By about 10 or 11 January his activities had become so notorious that Somerset summoned him to a private meeting. Fearing a trap he refused to come, and on 17 January the full council deliberated 'siche informations as had bene geven ... of great attemptates and disloyall practises' by the Lord Admiral, and ordered his arrest.[118]

John Hayward, being wise after the event, attributed Lord Seymour's fall and the estrangement between the brothers to the machinations of the duchess of Somerset and the earl of Warwick who 'had his finger in the businesse and drew others also to give furtherance or way to her violent

---

[113] Jordan, *Edward VI*, 369.   [114] *Cal. Span.*, ix. 136.

[115] Deposition of the marquis of Dorset (PRO SP10/6, no. 7).

[116] *APC*, ii. 252; Depositions of Katherine Ashley (PRO SP10/6, nos. 19, 20, 22).

[117] Depositions of Lord Clinton, the earl of Southampton, and Lord Russell (PRO SP10/6, nos. 12, 15, 16).

[118] *APC*, ii. 236–8.

desires. Being well content she should have her minde, so as the Duke might thereby incurre infamy and hate …'.[119] According to this theory, Dudley had long harboured a jealous dislike of the duke, which he had dissembled until the opportunity arose to strike at him through his brother. Seymour's fall then set in train the sequence of events which enabled the earl of Warwick to overthrow the Protector in October 1549, and eventually to bring about his execution in January 1552. All this, however, owes more to Dudley's 'black legend' than it does to contemporary evidence. Seymour certainly disliked and distrusted Warwick. The marquis of Dorset testified that 'the Admiral also advised me to keep my house in Warwickshire, as it is a county full of men, chiefly to match Lord Warwick'.[120] Similarly, according to Sir William Sharrington, 'He [Seymour] often showed me what shires and places were for him, noting where he was the judge of his friends, and where lay the lands of the Protector and Lord Warwick, to whom I know he had no affection …'.[121] From this it seems clear that Lord Seymour regarded the earl as an ally and associate of his brother, rather than as someone who could be cajoled into his own camp. Van der Delft confessed that he had originally believed that Warwick, 'as he is the most splendid and haughty by nature and in high reputation', would have challenged the Protector, but by July 1547 he had changed his mind. Warwick and Paget were Somerset's two principal allies, and the former showed every sign of contenting himself with 'the pre-eminence which he at present enjoys'.[122] While the investigations into Seymour's misconduct were still progressing, in early February 1549, the ambassador also repeated a story relating to Warwick's conduct which is circumstantially convincing. At some point after the feud between the two brothers had become notorious, probably in the summer of 1547, he had set out to affect a reconciliation, 'using strong language to the Admiral, remonstrating with him that he had come to occupy such a high position through the favour of his brother and the council …'. Seymour had been explicitly excluded by the late king from the body of his executors, the earl went on,

'Be content therefore' (these are Warwick's words) 'with the honour done to you for your brother's sake, and with your office of Lord Admiral, which I gave up to you for the same motive, for neither the king nor I will be governed by you, nor would we be governed by your brother were it not that his virtues and loyalty towards the king and country made him the man fittest to administer the affairs of the country during the king's minority'.[123]

Van der Delft does not cite the source of this very precise information, but

[119] John Hayward, *The Life and Raigne of King Edward VI*, ed. B. L. Beer (Kent, Ohio, and London, 1993), 99.

[120] PRO SP10/6, no. 7.

[121] Deposition of Sir William Sharrington (PRO SP10/6, no. 13).

[122] Van der Delft to the emperor, 10 July 1547 (*Cal. Span.*, ix. 122).

[123] Van der Delft to the emperor, 8 Feb. 1549 (ibid. 340).

it may well have been Warwick himself, in which case it reflects the impression which he wished to create, rather than what actually happened. According to the story, Seymour was so abashed by this rebuke that he went off at once and negotiated a cessation of hostilities, at least for the time being.

Whether or not Warwick did play the honest broker in the manner described, he certainly wanted to emphasize his loyalty to Somerset. He had nothing particular to gain from the destruction of the Admiral, and it is not at all clear that anyone at the time believed that the Protector's position had been undermined by his decision to deal resolutely with his brother. The reason why he was proceeded against by act of attainder rather than by a normal trial probably had more to do with his own attitude and the position of the king than it did with the nature of the charges. Edward was fond of Lord Thomas, who clearly had a great deal of charm and plausibility, and if treason was to offend the king, then the Admiral was not guilty. However, the real problem was that he refused to answer the charges against him. The Lord Chancellor, accompanied by five other members of the council, visited him in the Tower to obtain his response, but after admitting that he had at one time sought the custody of the king's person, and had given John Fowler money for the boy, he refused to say any more, and refused to set his hand to a transcript of the statement which he had already made.[124] No efforts could break this impasse, and the council were therefore faced with the possibility of arraigning a peer who would refuse to plead before the court. This interview took place on 24 February, and the bill of attainder was introduced into the House of Lords the next day.[125] By 27 February it had passed on the third reading, and was sent to the Commons. There it suffered considerable argument and delay, not because the Admiral had many supporters in the House, but because the Commons disliked bills of attainder on principle. After some pressure, it passed on 4 March.[126] On 10 March the king gave his assent, with obvious reluctance and using words which had been put into his mouth.[127] It has sometimes been argued that Seymour's crime was simply to plot against his brother, and that his fate was the Protector's personal revenge. 'Seymour was doubtless an ambitious and turbulent man, but there is no evidence whatever to show that he harboured any ill intentions against the state', wrote John Maclean, and such a view has been echoed more recently.[128] However, he was guilty of

---

[124] PRO SP10/6, no. 27; *APC*, ii. 258–60.   [125] *Lords Journals*, i. 346.

[126] *Journals of the House of Commons* (London, 1803–52), i. 9. For a full discussion of Seymour's misdemeanours, real and alleged, and the evidence against him, see Jordan, *Edward VI*, 368–82, which also cites the testimony of Christopher Eyre, Seymour's gaoler in the Tower who had a number of conversations with him, and which is now preserved in the Salisbury MSS.

[127] *APC*, ii. 262.

[128] Maclean, *The Life of Sir Thomas Seymour*, 81. Jordan inclines to the same view. Seymour denied vehemently that he intended any harm to the king, but he did seek, and effect, unau-

treason as that was construed during a minority government, and it was not for that reason that the Commons were temporarily obstructive. According to Hayward 'Many of the nobles cried out upon the Protector, calling him a blood-sucker, a murderer a parracide and a villain ...', but there is no hint of such a reaction at the time, and if they did so they were hypocrites because none of them voted against the attainder.[129]

The solid support which the Protector received from the council over this issue strengthened his position rather than the reverse, but it could not dissipate the other clouds which were gathering about his regime. Suspicions that Seymour had been preparing an armed insurrection led to an investigation of his resources, and that in turn uncovered the large-scale malfeasance of his friend Sir William Sharrington, the under-treasurer of the Bristol mint.[130] Sharrington had not been deeply involved in the Admiral's plots, but Seymour had let it be known that he was aware of his illegal practices, and in return had extracted a promise of large-scale financial backing—to the tune of £4,000—in support of whatever enterprise he might have in hand. It is not known exactly how much Sharrington had already milked out of the mint before these revelations, but his activities were certainly not helping a currency already heavily undermined by debasement, and increasingly discounted on the foreign exchanges. Although the French had failed to carry Haddington by storm in early October, by the end of 1548 the English were on the defensive throughout the borders, with no clear-cut policy and inadequate resources. Henry II hoped that the arrest of Lord Seymour might provoke civil strife within England, and expose the country to French pressure from both sides.[131] His agents seem to have been taking the Lord Admiral too much at his own valuation. There was never the slightest chance of an armed faction attempting to rescue or avenge the Protector's brother, and de Selve would have been wasting his time trying to create one, but the warning of French intentions was worth heeding in case some other dissension should arise. There were well-founded reports that Henry was intending to send reinforcements to the north, but his resolution was extremely fragile. Imperial agents, picking up reports of his dissatisfaction with the Scottish nobility, believed that he was about to pull out

thorized entry to the privy apartments. The most recent, and by far the fullest, account of Seymour's behaviour is given by G. W. Bernard in 'The Downfall of Sir Thomas Seymour' (*The Tudor Nobility* (Manchester, 1992), 212–40). Bernard concludes that Seymour's ideas were confused, but included plans to defy his brother from the stronghold of Holt castle in Denbighshire, which never came near to fruition. The contemporary suggestion that Warwick originally prompted Seymour to demand the Governorship of the King's Person remains unsubstantiated.

[129] *The Life and Raigne of King Edward VI*, 100.

[130] PRO SP10/6, nos. 13, 29; *APC*, ii. 239; Jordan, *Edward VI*, 382–5; Historical Manuscripts Commission, *Salisbury MSS*, i. 62–3.

[131] 'A copy of the instructions to Mons. d'Avoys, the envoy sent to England by the French king on the occasion of the troubles caused by the Lord Admiral' (*Salisbury MSS*, i. 63–4; Bush, *Government Policy*, 32–9).

altogether.[132] If these rumours reached the English, they rightly discounted them. Moreover, even if the French did reduce their military commitment, that did not alter the fact that the Scottish queen was in France and likely to stay there.

Somerset's decision, which must have been taken very early in 1549, to redeem his position in Scotland with a new offensive in the summer was a triumph of hope over experience, and of obstinacy over common sense. Whether he consulted the council at all on the matter is not clear. According to Professor Hoak's persuasive reconstruction, he was scarcely meeting the council at all during these months, except to determine the fate of his brother.[133] Routine business continued to be transacted, but attendance lists are almost entirely missing. On the other hand there is no clear evidence that he was at odds with his colleagues over Scotland until his fall gave an opportunity for retrospective criticism. As early as 20 February Van der Delft picked up a rumour that the earl of Warwick was about to depart to the north 'to look after the English fortresses'; but he added that he seemed to be in no hurry to go, and the report may have been premature.[134] In March and April consideration was being given to the commands in the borders. Lord Grey, who had long since been asked to be relieved of the East March, was replaced by the earl of Rutland, a man of adequate status, but very slight experience. At the same time Lord Wharton was dismissed from the West March, and replaced by his arch rival Lord Dacre, a move which earned the Protector his implacable hostility.[135] By the end of May Rutland had about 5,500 under his command, half of them foreign mercenaries, and a general levy had been ordered to rendezvous at Berwick. On about 25 May Warwick returned to court, after what Van der Delf described as 'a long illness' of an unspecified nature.[136] Three days later he was appointed general of the army against Scotland, although there is no trace of his commission, and it was not until 3 July that he was paid £1,000 'uppon advancement of his journey'.[137]

Within a few weeks circumstances were forcing a complete rethink of the Protector's 'forward' strategy, and it is not clear that Warwick's command ever took effect. As early as 19 March he had written to Somerset's confidential aide Sir John Thynne, outlining his proposals for the government of the Welsh marches in his absence, so he had had plenty of time to prepare himself for his northern command. However by early July civil disorders were breaking out all over southern and midland England, and on 12 July

[132]   St Mauris to the emperor, 5 and 13 Apr. 1549 (*Cal. Span.*, ix. 361, 366).
[133]   D. E. Hoak, *The King's Council in the Reign of Edward VI* (Cambridge, 1976), 20–3.
[134]   *Cal. Span.*, ix. 345.
[135]   M. L. Bush, 'The Problems of the Far North', *Northern History*, 6 (1971), 55; Jordan, *Edward VI*, 296.
[136]   Van der Delft to the emperor, 28 May 1549 (*Cal. Span.*, ix. 383).
[137]   *APC*, ii. 298.

Warwick wrote urgently to Thynne from Ely Place. Either he had never left London, or he had returned in haste as the alarming tidings reached him.

Mr Thynne, I received your letters, being very sorry to hear the continual trouble of my Lord's Grace with these uproars. And wherein I do perceive my Lord's Grace would have had mine advice if I had had therein other notice or knowledge ...[138]

Since leaving the court he had been 'ill in my stomach', and was unable to leave his house that day, however

I do intend to adventure tomorrow to come to his Grace, though it cast me down utterly. For the body that shall not be able to strive at this present were better out of the world than in it, and so if God should not give me health now to stir, I would me to be in my grave ...

It may be that Thynne's letter had expressed some doubt on Somerset's part about his friend's attitude, for Warwick's response seems to be making excuses, 'for my meaning towards his Grace, I would his Grace knew it as God doth ...'. He had heard that very morning of stirs in Warwickshire, and of gentlemen's servants 'gowing from their masters to the rebels, which is a piteous hearing'. He was uncertain whether his own men would be able, or willing, to hold Warwick castle, and he had summoned his friends to come to him.[139] There is no trace of hostility in this letter. The writer is anxious to reassure, and if he held the Protector in any way to blame for the hornets' nest which had been stirred up, he gives no hint of it. In any case as the crisis grew during the remainder of July, it was no time for rifts to appear among the councillors. In the face of this growing emergency Somerset finally abandoned his Scottish priority. Rutland's mercenaries were withdrawn, and no reinforcements were sent. The campaign deteriorated into rather aimless raiding, and by August the Protector had very belatedly decided to cut his losses.[140]

Somerset's unwillingness to accept the seriousness of the domestic situation is understandable. There had been suggestions in the previous year that his sympathetic attitude towards anti-enclosure protesters was undermining the structure of public order. On 23 May he felt constrained to issue a proclamation which, while promising redress 'when his highness sees time convenient' consisted primarily of a fierce denunciation of those who took the law into their own hands instead of waiting for due process to take its course.[141] At some point in June or early July the council summoned as many Justices of the Peace as were able to attend, and the Lord Chancellor harangued them on the need to do their duty more rigorously. Rich

---

[138] HMC, *Bath MSS at Longleat*, Seymour Papers, ii, De Lisle and Dudley Papers, i, fo. 20.
[139] Ibid.
[140] John Stow, *The Annales of England* (London, 1592), 595–6. Thomas Holcroft to Somerset, 2 Aug. 1549 (BL Cotton MS Caligula B vii, fo. 176); Thomas Fisher to Cecil, *Calendar of State Papers Scotland*, i. 179–80.
[141] Hughes and Larkin, *Tudor Royal Proclamations*, i. 461–2.

certainly took his own message to heart, and kept the peace in Essex with remarkable success during the troubled weeks which followed. Thinking that the situation was under control, the Protector then most unfortunately allowed his enclosure commissioners to resume their work. The king's journal expressed the result succinctly:

> the people began to rise in Wiltshire, where Sir William Herbert did put them down, overrun and slay them. Then they rose in Sussex, Hampshire, Kent, Gloucestershire, Suffolk Warwickshire, Essex, Hertfordshire, a piece of Leicestershire Worcestershire, and Rutlandshire, where by fair fair persuasions, partly of honest men among themselves, and partly by gentlemen, they were often appeased, and again, because certain commissions were sent to pluck down enclosures, then [they] did rise again ...[142]

The Protector refused to see these things as cause and effect. According to Van der Delft he informed the council in the middle of June that there was much justice in the commons' complaints, and at about the same time issued another proclamation pardoning all those who had been misled into creating disturbances, provided that they desisted at once.[143] This was hardly the crisis management which Warwick's letter to Thynne had implied to be necessary, and it may be significant that the correspondence ceases at that point. The earl seems to have kept his word and returned to court, illness or no, because by 16 July he was playing a leading role in arming the Tower of London and Windsor castle.[144] By then regular watches had also been organized in London, and an altogether more realistic sense of urgency prevailed in the council. To what extent this may have been Warwick's achievement the evidence is not adequate to show, but it would have been consistent with the kind of advice we know him to have been offering. By the middle of the month artillery had been mounted at the gates of the City, and martial law had been proclaimed.[145]

In spite of the widespread nature of the disturbances, in most places the local gentry managed to suppress or contain the trouble. In Sussex the earl of Arundel, who had no sympathy whatever with most of the Protector's policies, nevertheless managed to impose a peaceful solution in an excellent demonstration of traditional lordship.[146] Although less well recorded, it seems that the earls of Shrewsbury and Derby also succeeded in controlling their 'countries'. Where the situation got out of control, there was either no dominant lord, as was the case in Oxfordshire, or the traditional ruling families had been removed by royal action. This was the case both in the south-west, where the Courtenays had been destroyed by Cromwell in 1538, and in East Anglia, where the Howards had fallen a mere two and a

---

[142] *Chronicle of Edward VI*, 12.

[143] Van der Delft to the emperor, 13 June 1549 (*Cal. Span.* ix. 395).

[144] *APC*, ii. 300–2. This was in a context of extensive security precautions for London.

[145] Jordan, *Edward VI*, 445.

[146] Laurence Stone, 'Patriarchy and Paternalism in Tudor England: The Earl of Arundel and the Peasants' Revolt of 1549', *Journal of British Studies*, 13 (1974), 19–23.

half years before. The earl of Warwick does not seem to have had much faith in his own lordship to control the midlands. His large estates had been recently acquired, and his family had no ancient prestige in the region. Lord Russell, who had taken the marquis of Exeter's place as the largest landowner in Devon, was sent down to the south-west at the end of June, but it soon became apparent that his own manred could accomplish nothing, and that he would need professional soldiers to encounter a rebel army which was beseiging Exeter and controlling virtually the whole county.[147] Russell bombarded the Protector with pleas for resolute instructions, and for the necessary forces to carry them out. It may be that at first Somerset was genuinely anxious to avoid bloodshed, clinging to the hope that the rebels were merely deluded protesters. But it is more likely that he simply did not have the troops to send until those who had been withdrawn from the borders arrived in the south. On 22 June Russell was informed that Warwick would be sent to join him, but the reinforcements which actually left a few days later were commanded by Lord Grey and Sir William Herbert.[148] Once he was adequately supported even Russell, who was an overcautious and indifferent soldier, had little difficulty in defeating his numerous but poorly armed opponents.[149]

The reason why Warwick did not go to Devon seems to have been that he had grasped the nettle of maintaining order in his own country, and gone down to Warwick to rally the local gentry. Despite the relative weakness of his local position, this leadership seems to have been effective, and the midland 'stirs' did not escalate into a major rebellion. Somerset himself seems to have felt obliged to remain at Westminster with the remainder of the council. The only business recorded during these days is the signing of warrants, but their main preoccupation seems to have been the mobilization of troops, and their own physical security.[150] By the middle of July it was clear that Norfolk as well as Devon would require the attentions of a professional army, because the local gentry had fled in confusion before a rebel host rumoured to number 10,000 men. By about 25 July some 2,000 soldiers had been assembled, mostly Italian mercenaries and the retinues of several peers and councillors. With Warwick away in the midlands and Russell, Grey, and Herbert already committed, however, the choice of a commander presented real difficulties. There seems to have been an intention to send the earl of Shrewsbury, but it was not pursued, probably on the grounds that he was urgently needed at home. The only peer who was available because he had very little authority in his home area was William Parr, marquis of Northampton. He was a man with no military experience and no talent, but presumably it was hoped that his professional captains

---

[147] PRO, SP10/7, no. 41; *Chronicle of Edward VI*, 13–14; B. L. Beer, *Rebellion and Riot: Popular Disorder in England during the Reign of Edward VI* (Kent, Ohio, 1982).

[148] Inner Temple, Petyt MS, 538, vol. 46, fos. 439–46.

[149] Ibid. fos. 435–6; Jordan, *Edward VI*, 464–5.   [150] *APC*, ii. 297–312.

would know their job in any case, and that he could have been little more than a figurehead. Unfortunately such hopes proved to be ill-founded. On 30 July Northampton occupied the city of Norwich, encountering no resistance. The same night it became clear that he had walked into a trap, and his force was driven out with heavy losses.[151] As he fell back towards London, the council went into emergency session to decide how to redeem the situation. With the Protector anchored in the capital, there was only one person who could be turned to. On 7 August it was decided to commission the earl of Warwick, and £5,000 was paid to John Hornywold, the treasurer of his army.[152] On 10 August Warwick wrote to Cecil from his title town, to acknowledge receipt of his instructions 'for which I am bound to [the Protector] and council', but also to suggest that Northampton should remain in overall command. 'He has lately had enough misfortune, and this might discourage him forever …', he wrote with remarkable charity,[153] 'No one should be discarded for one mischance, which may happen to us all …'. However, the Protector was less inclined to be sympathetic, and the marquis did not command again in East Anglia. By 15 August the gentry of Essex, Suffolk, and Norfolk were mustered with their retainers, a few veterans were perilously recalled from Boulogne, and Warwick, having set his own country in order, joined them at Cambridge and assumed his command.[154]

His relationship with the Protector at this point appears to have been correct, if not cordial. There had been disagreements between them, and Warwick had occasionally expressed dissatisfaction, notably over the council in the marches, but if there was any deep-seated rivalry or jealousy, it was either not noticed or not commented upon. He conducted an intermittent but perfectly amicable correspondence, partly with William Cecil and partly with Sir John Thynne, who had become Somerset's principal man of business. Most of these letters related to land transactions of one sort or another, or appointments. In March 1548 he commended Edward Peckham to the Protector's attention, and complained that Somerset was not willing to sell him the 'overplus of Aldington lordship'.

I perceive by your said letters that his grace will not condescend to my request in that behalf [but] I assure you that there is neither castle nor manor nor borough nor market town belonging or appertaining unto the lordships land … The lordship of Fecknam is not above £33 a year, and Ardingley that is joined to it is £19 a year. But seeing his grace esteemeth it to be such a thing, it becometh me not to sue further for it …[155]

However, he eventually obtained his desire, receiving both Aldington and

---

[151] Grafton, *Chronicle*, 520; Raphael Holinshed, *Chronicles etc.* (London, 1577), ed. H. Ellis (London, 1807–8), iii. 972–4; Petyt MS 538, 46, fo. 542. There are many accounts of this episode.
[152] *APC*, ii. 309.   [153] PRO SP10/8, no. 38.
[154] Hughes and Larkin, *Tudor Royal Proclamations*, i. 481–2; Jordan, *Edward VI*, 489.
[155] Warwick to Thynne, 19 Mar. 1548 (De Lisle and Dudley Papers, i, fo. 11).

Fecknam as part of a substantial grant on 10 July 1549.[156] This was neither gift nor purchase, but part of an exchange arrangement with the Crown, and it looks as though a long negotiation followed Warwick's original request. In March 1549 he was again requesting changes to the commission of the council in the marches, which needed a fuller authority if it was to cope with the troubles which could be foreseen. 'The people be both subtle and naturally given to sedition ...', he wrote.[157] On 29 March a further letter expressed his pleasure and satisfaction that the commission had been 'amplified'. In April a rather curious letter suggests that Warwick had been angling for a senior post, 'so great an office and meet for the best man in the realm under my lord himself', and was 'the more ashamed to seem to labour for it ...'. Although he had been unsuccessful in his suit, he expressed himself well content with Thynne's 'good answer', and went on 'I did not at any time despair of his grace's friendship towards me ...'.[158] What the object of his ambition may have been is not clear. Both the Admiralty and the Mastership of the Horse were vacant at that point, but neither would merit so fulsome a description. Perhaps he was hoping to exchange the Lord Great Chamberlainship of the household for the more powerful position of Lord Great Master. A week later he wrote again 'touching the office of the pensions', which he had requested either for himself or for one of his friends, and which the Protector had forgotten 'albeit I am out of doubt you had broken with him in it at length'.[159] Early in May further letters commended a 'poor man' for the post of surgeon, and asked for Somerset's decision about another land deal, this time intended to place the Lady Elizabeth 'in Otford or Knole or some other place agreeable to her desire ...'.[160] The tone of all this correspondence was friendly, even intimate considering that Thynne was little more than a servant. It is reminiscent, both in content and manner, of much of the correspondance which Thomas Cromwell received when he was the doorkeeper of the king's bounty, and too much should not be read into it. As long as Somerset was in power everyone was polite to him, but that does not necessarily mean that they were happy with his regime. A good example is provided by Thomas Wriothesley, earl of Southampton. Wriothesley had more cause than most to be the Protector's enemy, but he had been far too sensible to get drawn into Thomas Seymour's insubstantial schemes. His role in that crisis earned him an offer to lead the last-ditch negotiations with France which took place in June. He declined on the grounds of ill health, but in a courteous exchange of letters assured Somerset 'You shall never have cause to repent of your goodness towards me'.[161] He then went on to press an earlier request for the grant of a house 'which is now ten times more important than before ...'.

[156] PRO E318/2047.
[157] Warwick to Thynne, 29 Mar. 1549 (De Lisle and Dudley Papers, i, fo. 12).
[158] Warwick to Thynne, 22 Apr. 1549 (ibid., fo. 14). [159] Ibid., fo. 15.
[160] Ibid., fos. 17, 16. [161] HMC, *Bath MS*, IV, Seymour Papers, 110.

Neither Warwick nor Southampton were displaying any overt hostility to the Protector as the crisis of the summer of 1549 moved towards its climax. However, Paget's letter of 8 May suggests a rather different situation. He had warned the Protector earlier about the need to cultivate the goodwill of his colleagues, and to work with their collaboration, even if the terms of his patent no longer strictly required that. By May 1549 he was close to despair. If Somerset could not control his temper, and deal more rationally with those who disagreed with him, he was going to be in serious trouble.

a subject in great authority, as your grace is, using such fashion, is like to fall into grat danger and peril of his own person, beside that to the commonweal ...[162]

Royal rages were all very well, but he was not the king. Paget was not expressing a remote or hypothetical anxiety. He knew perfectly well that it was not only relatively insignificant men like Sir Richard Lee who were distressed and angered. The growing civil disorder might well expose the Protector to further criticism, but it also gave him an opportunity to redeem himself, and protected him from colleagues who were, above all else, anxious to give no further encouragement to the rebellious commons. If he could not use that opportunity constructively, then he might well face a radical challenge to his authority. Consequently it proves very little that there was no open bickering among the councillors during June and July 1549, or that men going about their business did not pick quarrels with each other's servants. There is no reason to suppose that Warwick had been plotting against the Protector for years, but it would be unrealistic to imagine that, as he took up his command in East Anglia, he was entirely happy with the way in which English affairs were being managed. According to Van der Delft, who was reasonably well informed, a conspiracy against the Protector had already formed by the end of July, and the earl of Warwick was one of the plotters. That would be consistent, both with the cessation of his correspondence with Thynne in mid-July, and with the disparaging remarks which he is alleged to have made about Somerset during the Norfolk campaign. Almost the last news which he received before setting off from Warwick had been of the French declaration of war on 8 August. He might tell Cecil that 'open war seems better than cloaked friendship', but he also went on, 'I wish we had no more to deal with; as it is we must trust in the lord ...'.[163] It may well be that he and his friends already knew what they had to do.

[162] PRO SP10/7, no. 5.   [163] PRO SP10/8, no. 38.

4

The Struggle for Power,
1549–1551

ALTHOUGH it may have had tens of thousands of occupants at its largest
extent, Robert Kett's great camp on Mousehold Heath outside Norwich
was only the tip of the iceberg. The 'camping movement' spread far and
wide through East Anglia during July 1549, from King's Lynn to Bury
St Edmunds and beyond. The grievances which inspired such widespread
anger were mostly connected with the misappropriation of common land,
and with systematic overgrazing, rather than with the conversion of arable
into pasture.[1] The local gentry were the targets, rather than the king's council, and the tone of the gravamina which emerged from the camp was that of
reasonable men much wronged. Kett and his followers professed a loyalty
to the king and his council which was probably genuine, however naïve. On
7 August a deposition was taken in Colchester relating to words spoken in
that town by one Sir John Chandler 'parson of Afristhorp in Norfolk, near to
Lynne', which John 'there said I would the towne of Lynne and all the gentlemen there were on fire …'. He had then gone on to declare that the great
camp at Norwich contained 120,000 men, and 'more he said that there were
six posts sent from their camp unto the king's council, and never one of them
could come to the said king's council …'.[2] Such claims may have been honestly made, and may even have been true, but they were beside the point. No
matter how sympathetic the Protector may have been to their cause, no
Tudor government could treat a mass demonstration of the kind going on in
Norfolk as anything other than rebellion. It was a growing appreciation of
this fact rather than any effective action on the government's part which
broke up the camping movement over most of Norfolk and Suffolk during
August. Local initiatives and negotiations resulted in partial and grudging
settlements; once camps had broken up the majority went home to get in the
harvest, and the irreconcilables drifted off to join the 'great camp' at Mousehold. For Kett there could be no going back. Whatever he may have believed

[1] D. N. J. MacCulloch, 'Kett's Rebellion in Context', in P. Slack (ed.), *Rebellion, Popular
Protest and the Social Order in Early Modern England* (Cambridge, 1984), 39–76; D. N. J. Mac-
Culloch, *Suffolk and the Tudors* (Oxford, 1986), 301–3.
[2] BL Lansdowne MS 2, fo. 60.

about his cause, his brief and bloody repulse of the marquis of Northampton had left him with no alternative but to remain in the field.

Having won a victory, however, he had not the slightest idea what to do next. A march on London would have been feasible, and would have kept his men positively occupied, but it would have been pointless because he did not know what he was trying to achieve. Most of the laws which he wanted were already in place, but were not being enforced. He could not have demanded the dismissal of the entire commission of the peace, even if his mind had been capable of grasping anything so radical, because there was no alternative to the local gentry as the agents of government. All he could do was demand that the council impose a more effective control over its agents—which was not a very inspiring programme for an armed insurrection. Consequently he stayed where he was beside Norwich, maintained his power base as best he could, and waited for the next move to be made against him. Warwick did not waste time. The force which he assembled at Cambridge consisted of about 6,000 foot and 1,500 horse. Most of these men were the somewhat mottley retinues of the East Anglian gentry and of an *ad hoc* group of peers who were available to join him—Lords Powis, Bray, and Willoughby and the chastened marquis of Northampton.[3] Some were his own men, and the followers of his sons Robert and Ambrose. However a hard core of 1,400 mercenaries gave his force a much greater professional stiffening than its predecessor had possessed, and indicated that the council was not prepared to risk a second repulse. By 23 August Warwick had reached Intwood, within a couple of miles of the Mousehold camp, and established his own headquarters. His first action was then to make contact with Kett, who was probably known to him slightly through business connections, and offer a pardon in return for immediate and unconditional disbandment.[4] Whether this was a genuine offer or a tactical manœuvre we cannot tell. Kett wanted to take it seriously, but some of his men were much more sceptical, even derisory. A picturesque story tells how the royal herald bearing Warwick's offer was confronted by a boy making obscene gestures, and how the boy was shot and killed by one of the herald's escort. The herald himself was then subject to a barrage of abuse, and Kett was physically restrained by his own men from returning with him for a conference with Warwick.[5] If the story is true, it serves to demonstrate that in spite of his charismatic qualities, and powers of organization, the rebel leader could not maintain control in a crisis.

---

[3] *The Chronicle and Political Papers of King Edward VI*, ed. W. K. Jordan (London, 1970), 15; W. K. Jordan, *Edward VI: The Young King* (London, 1968), 489–90.

[4] Warwick had sold land to Kett in 1548, although it is not clear that he had ever met him. The supply lines to the camp had already been broken by Warwick's forces before this offer was made (BL Harleian MS 523, no. 43, fos. 53–5).

[5] There are several accounts of this episode; see Raphael Holinshed, *Chronicles etc.*, ed. H. Ellis (London, 1807–8), iii. 977–8, and F. W. Russell, *Kett's Rebellion in Norfolk* (London, 1859), 128–9.

However it came about, the earl's offer was repulsed, and the Mousehold camp was immediately blockaded. The following night, 24 August, with a small part of his force, probably his mercenary infantry, Warwick stormed the rebel-held city. After fierce street fighting Kett's men were driven out, and forty-nine prisoners were hanged on the spot by the earl's orders.[6] By this ruthless and effective action control of Norwich was recovered within a matter of hours, and the camp was cut off from its main source of supply. Two days later, perhaps because his position was untenable, Kett broke up his high fortified camp, and deliberately moved to lower ground to confront the royal army. He may still have had a big advantage in numbers, and he may have been listening to optimistic prophecies, but in truth his choice was to fight at a disadvantage, or to be starved out. As soon as the campaign reached this stage, there could be only one outcome. Kett was not a soldier, and he had no experienced captain with him. He seems to have intended to create a defensible position, but he was too slow, and his men lacked the skill. Warwick attacked with about two-thirds of his force before the rebels could form any sort of array, and what followed was not so much a battle as a systematic slaughter. A large number of prisoners were also taken, and Kett himself was picked up a few miles away the next day, but there was no pursuit and no plunder. Warwick's force remained under admirable control throughout the operation. For several days after the victory martial law was enforced in and around Norwich, but the number of executions carried out was strictly limited, probably no more than a dozen or so, including a number of 'captains'.[7] Warwick was much more successful than Russell in frustrating the desire of the badly frightened gentlemen for vengeance on their enemies. 'There must be measure kept, and above all things in punishment men must not exceed', he is alleged to have said, pointing out very sensibly that if they tried to execute everybody who had been involved in the 'camping movement', they would end up ploughing and harrowing their own land.[8] On 29 August a thanksgiving service was held in St Peter Mancroft, and a day or two later Warwick returned to London. He seems to have left the gentry retinues behind to police the countryside, and to have taken his own men and the mercenaries with him. A commission of oyer and terminer then began to operate in Norfolk, which resulted in a significant number of further executions. The king's chronicle says that 2,000 peasants perished in the main battle, and a modern estimate would add at least 600 for the other skirmishes, particularly on the streets of Norwich, and for the toll of martial and common law.[9] Nor did the royal

[6] Ibid.; Jordan, *The Young King*, 490.

[7] BL Harleian MS 523, no. 43, fos. 53–5; Russell, *Kett's Rebellion*, 146–50, 213–15.

[8] Jordan, *The Young King*, 491.

[9] *Chronicle of Edward VI*, 16. Other contemporary estimates varied from 3,500 to 5,000; 600 is Jordan's calculation, based on Holinshed, *Chronicles*, iii. 982, John Stow, *Annales of England* (London, 1592), 597, and Charles Wriothesley's *Chronicle*, ed. W. D. Hamilton, Camden Society, NS vol. xi, pt. ii (London, 1875–7), 21.

forces escape unscathed. One band of 180 from Northamptonshire lost a third of its strength, and the total may have been as high as 300. A legacy of bitterness was left behind. For the next two years there were to be constant rumours of a new 'camping movement', and mutterings of vengeance against the triumphant gentlemen. Gentry feuds also broke out amidst a flurry of recriminations, and during September William Cecil was bombarded with protests and complaints from those who felt that their actions had been misinterpreted, or their services unrewarded.[10] The one man who undoubtedly gained was the earl of Warwick. He had suppressed a dangerous rebellion with a minimum of fuss, and probably a minimum of bloodshed. His name was remembered with fear and hatred by the commons of Norfolk, but he had been just as effective as Russell in the west, and far swifter. When he returned to London early in September his prestige stood higher than at any time since the Pinkie campaign two years earlier.

Meanwhile the greatest landowner in East Anglia behaved like the dog in the night time. The Princess Mary had received the greater part of the extensive Howard estates in Norfolk, and much of the former Howard affinity seems to have transferred to her.[11] She was at Kenninghall throughout the rising, but seems to have done nothing about it one way or the other. Van der Delft observed that the rebels showed no hostility to her, some of them even claiming that 'she was kept too poor for one of her station', but he also noted that they had broken down some of the fences on her land.[12] She had no sympathy with the religious position taken by Kett, which was supportive of the Protector's reforms rather than the reverse. Some of her servants were allegedly involved in the Devon rising, which had a strongly conservative religious tone, but on her own doorstep no similar accusations were made. On the other hand if she sent any support to Warwick's forces, or contributed to his campaign in any way, it has escaped the record. She was ideally placed to intervene, as the earl of Arundel did in Sussex. Given her status and general popularity her role could have been crucial, but she seems to have been determined to play no part in public affairs beyond the defence of her privileged exemption from the act of uniformity.

By the beginning of September order was restored throughout the country, but the councillors felt that they had few grounds for satisfaction. By 17 September Haddington had been abandoned, and although a few English garrisons remained, the impossibility of reinforcing them meant that English pressure on Scotland effectively disappeared.[13] The only benefit of this,

---

[10]   e.g. Sir William Woodhouse to William Cecil, 6 Sept. 1549, and Sir Thomas Woodhouse to Sir William, 3 Sept. 1549 (PRO SP10/8, nos. 55, 55 i, 55 ii).

[11]   D. Loades, *Mary Tudor* (Oxford, 1989), 137–9.

[12]   Van der Delft to the emperor, 19 July 1549 (*Calendar of State Papers, Spanish*, ed. Royall Tyler *et al.* (London, 1862–1954), ix. 405–9).

[13]   Stow, *Annales*, 595–6; Thomas Fisher to William Cecil (*Calendar of State Papers, Scotland*, ed. J. Bain *et al.* (Edinburgh and Glasgow, 1898–1952), i. 179–80); Jordan, *The Young King*, 298–9.

apart from a saving of money, was that Henry II no longer considered it to be worth his while to divert scarce resources to the north. The great fortress of Boulogne was successfully holding out, but most of the Boullonais, including Ambleteuse, Newhaven, and Blackness, had fallen with very little resistance.[14] The Protector faced defeat on all fronts, because the need to suppress widespread insurrection was in itself a defeat for his social policy. Moreover the fact that he was beholden to others, particularly Russell, Grey, and Warwick, for rescuing his regime from the consequences of its own mistakes weakened his position still further. He was vulnerable to what, in the different political culture of a later generation would have been a vote of no confidence, but which in 1549 could only be a plot for his removal. The genesis of this plot is hard to trace, because so many of the accounts are bedevilled by hindsight. By the early 1560s it was conventional wisdom that the earl of Warwick had been the prime mover, just as it was by then accepted that it had been his machiavellian promptings which had lured the Lord Admiral to his doom, but there is no more contemporary evidence for the one than for the other. He is alleged to have indulged in a hostile exchange of correspondence with the Protector while on campaign in Norfolk, and to have denounced Somerset to his close associates at the same time as 'a coward, a breaker of promises, a nigard, covetous and ambitious ...'.[15] However, the source of this apparently explicit information is a former servant of Somerset's, writing after Elizabeth's accession. None of the alleged letters survives, and no one else admitted having been a party to the conversations.

The most useful contemporary is Francois Van der Delft, who probably got his information partly from his political ally Paget, and partly from the Princess Mary who was under his master's protection. The latter seems to have first told him of a division within the council, provoked by a scheme of Somerset's for the formation of a 'new council'.[16] This presumably meant a select council, consisting only of those whom the Protector felt he could either trust or dominate. He was later accused of operating a 'private council' of his own servants, such as Cecil, Thynne, and Cheke, but that does not seem to have been the issue at this point. The princess named the objectors as Warwick, Southampton, Arundel, and St John. According to what she told Van der Delft, they had solicited her assistance in removing the Protector, but she had told them that she had no desire to interfere in matters of government. Professor Hoak has argued reasonably that this enquiry might have been a veiled offer of the regency once Somerset was overthrown.[17] During the subsequent crisis the Protector accused his opponents

---

[14]   Richard Grafton, *A Chronicle at large* (London, 1568), 521; *Chronicle of Edward VI*, 16–17.
[15]   BL Add. MS 48126, fos. 6ᵛ–16ᵛ; partly published by A. J. A. Malkiewicz as 'An Eyewitness Account of the *coup d'etat* of October 1549', in the *English Historical Review*, 70 (1955), 600–9.
[16]   Van der Delft to the emperor, 15 Sept. 1549 (*Cal. Span.*, ix. 248).
[17]   *Cal. Span.*, ix. 445; D. E. Hoak, *The King's Council in the Reign of Edward VI* (Cambridge, 1976), 247.

of seeking to set up such a regency, but it appears that no such proposal was actually discussed. What did happen was that Van der Delft received a visit from Paget, who confirmed that there was indeed hostility between Somerset and Warwick, and solicited the ambassador's good offices to bring the earl to 'a better disposition regarding religion'.[18] Since Van der Delft was a professional catholic, this could only mean to influence Warwick in a conservative direction. Paget's own inclinations were conservative, but he had never yet let that stand in the way of his support for the Protector. Probably this somewhat cryptic request meant that Paget, realizing which way the wind was blowing, was beginning to distance himself from Somerset, and was anxious that what looked like being the winning side should not divide over that rather sensitive issue. The fact that Warwick had already joined Wriothesley, St John, and Arundel in approaching Mary, would suggest that his position was at least flexible, although if his change of heart had been obvious the ambassador would hardly have been called upon in such a cause. In the event, it was Warwick who made the move, not in search of religious advice but in order to sound out the emperor's attitude to the coup which was now clearly impending. At some point between 15 and 23 September he visited Van der Delft at his country retreat.[19] He was frank with the ambassador about his discontent with the Protector's government, apparently blaming the duchess of Somerset's pride and vindictiveness for much that had gone wrong. Warwick knew perfectly well that Charles did not approve of the direction which religious policy in England had taken over the previous two years, so it was an obvious tactic to hint at his own conservative preferences, and to suggest that any new regime would be looking to mend its fences with the emperor. Van der Delft would also have known that this was Paget's intention as well. So although he was no doubt suitably guarded, he indicated that the conspirators' chosen course of action would not cause his master to lose any sleep.

We do not know who originated the moves against Somerset which were coming to a head by the time that Warwick had his interview with Van der Delft. The 'Black legend' attributes the initiative to Warwick himself, but that is based upon assumptions about his long-term attitude and ambitions which cannot be substantiated. His relations with the Protector had had their ups and downs, but it was probably during the Norfolk campaign, when he was confronted with the tragic consequences of the latter's obsessive agrarian programme, that he finally made up his mind to take action. Others were almost certainly coming to the same conclusion at the same time, and they were not necessarily following a single leader. Warwick may have found additional grievances against the Protector after his return from Norfolk, but they are not necessary to explain his subsequent role. He had

[18] *Cal. Span.*, ix. 445–8.
[19] Ibid. 454; B. L. Beer, *Northumberland* (Kent, Ohio, 1973), 87.

returned to a hero's welcome, and it is unlikely that Somerset would have gone out of his way to antagonize him.[20] More importantly, the core of his army remained, ostensibly for security duties in the home counties, but really to give the council the leverage they needed to bring the Protectorate to an end. By the last week in September, Warwick, Wriothesley, and Arundel were working together, and if Warwick was the leader it was by virtue of the fact that he had these troops at his disposal, rather than because he was the most cunning or ruthless. Either Somerset suspected nothing, or he had decided to outface his critics, because there was a determined air of normality about his actions during most of September, and Cecil's surviving correspondence contains no hint of impending crisis, even as late as 28 September.[21] On 25 September the Protector sent a routine letter to Lord Russell in the west, one of a series about the winding down of his operation there, but added the significant postscript 'we look for you and Sir William Herbert, at the farthest about the 8th day of the next month, about which time we would gladly have you here for matters of importance'.[22] If this was intended as a countermove against the threat of Warwick's forces, it was surprisingly lacking in precision and urgency, and may well have been provoked by some quite different consideration. If Somerset realized at that point that he faced a radical challenge then it is surprising that he did not take more positive steps to rally his own friends who were closer at hand, or attempt a pre-emptive strike against one or more of the conspirators.

It is more likely that he was taken by surprise, and if that is true it is a measure of his diminished grasp upon political reality. The first unmistakable sign of his alarm was a proclamation issued on 30 September, commanding all soldiers who had been mustered to proceed to their appointed commands, and specifically ordering them to 'avoid and depart forth of the city of London and the suburbs of the same'.[23] As late as 4 October the council register shows the Protector and those who were with him at Hampton Court discharging routine business, including passing warrants for the payment of some of those troops which were already being deployed against him. According to the Londoner Richard Grafton, in the first few days of October

> many of the Lordes of the Realme, as well counsaylors as other myslyking the gouvernement of the Protector, began to withdrawe themselves from the Courte, and resorting to London, fell to secret consultation for redresse of things, but namely for the displacing of the sayde Lorde Protector, and sodainely of what occasion many marvelled and few knewe every lorde and counsaylor went thorowe the Citie weaponed, and had their servauntes likewise weaponed ...[24]

---

[20] According to the author of the eyewitness account Somerset had rebuffed more than one request which Warwick had made to him after his return from Norfolk (BL Add. MS 48126, fo. 8).

[21] See e.g. SP10/8, no. 65.   [22] Inner Temple, Petyt MS 538, 46, fo. 466.

[23] P. L. Hughes and J. F. Larkin, *Tudor Royal Proclamations* (New Haven and London), i. 483.

[24] *Acts of the Privy Council*, ed. J. Dasent *et al.* (London, 1890–1907), ii. 329; Grafton, *Chronicle*, 521–2.

Aware at last of these sinister consultations, on 5 October Somerset suddenly sprang to life, issuing a letter over the king's sign manual, commanding all subjects to repair, armed and in haste, to Hampton Court to defend the king's person against 'a most dangerous conspiracy'.[25] Because Grafton's dating is imprecise, we do not know whether the sudden arming of the 'London lords' was a cause or an effect of this summons, but they were undoubtedly connected. The Protector's reaction was both belated and inept. Because he had delayed so long he had no chance of assembling a usable military force before his opponents struck, if they were going to strike. At the same time, by appealing to the king's subjects at large, instead of to his noble allies, he presented his opponents with the opportunity to represent him as a revolutionary, trying to set the commons against their natural lords—a charge to which he was already vulnerable on account of his agrarian policy.

On the following day, 6 October, the self-styled Privy Council met at the earl of Warwick's residence, Ely Place in Holborn. Sir William Petre, the principal secretary, who had been sent to the Lords from Hampton Court the previous day, was with them, having decided to join the protesters.[26] The venue was sufficient recognition of the leading role which the earl had by this time assumed. He seems to have had influential friends in the City, notably John York, but it was his military strength and prestige which placed him in charge at this juncture. However, this could turn out to be a diminishing asset. An armed strike against Hampton Court was out of the question, because of the danger to the king, and the longer the stalemate persisted, the more chance there was that Somerset might be able to match their strength. It was therefore imperative that they should discredit the Protector as generally and thoroughly as possible. They started by solemnly recording their case in their own version of the Council Register.

consydering with themselfes the great rebellion of the people in sundry partes of the realme ... and remembring with all that thies and sundry others great disorders had proceded of the yll gouvernment of the Lord Protector ... [and] that through thonly default of the said Lord Protector, Haddington, being of his owne will first made and fortyfied in Scotland, was abandoned, Newhavon, Blacknesse, and Bullenbergh were lost and possessed of thennemyes ...[27]

They had determined, they declared, 'to have had friendly communicacion with the Lorde Protector about the reformacion of the State ...', but when they had been about to set out for Hampton Court they had been warned that he had raised 'a power of the communes', with the intention of destroy-

---

[25] SP10/9, no. 1. Although included in Hughes and Larkin (i. 483) this is not a proclamation but a letter under the sign manual, countersigned by the duke of Somerset. For a discussion of the dating, see Jordan, *The Young King*, 506; Hoak, *King's Council*, 327 n. 63; and *Calendar of State Papers, Domestic*, Edward VI, ed. C. Knighton (London, 1992), no. 368.

[26] *APC*, ii. 330; F. G. Emmison, *Tudor Secretary* (London, 1971), 75–6.

[27] *APC*, ii. 330–2.

ing them. In support of this claim they then solemnly recorded an inflammatory leaflet, purporting to have been issued on behalf of the Protector, and calling upon the king's subjects in the name of God to defend him against 'certen Lordes and gentilmen and chefe mastres'[28] who were attempting to depose the Protector and injure the king. On the same day the council issued its own letter, announcing that the king was in danger on account of the treason of the duke of Somerset, and commanding all recipients to proclaim 'the truth', and 'repair to us for the king's service'.[29]

At the same time the Protector was warned by his own spies, wrongly it would seem, that the 'London Lords' were about to launch a sudden attack upon the court. He immediately fortified the gates, and armed his own and the king's households. According to the anonymous observer, he then harangued his men, denouncing the treason of Warwick and his accomplices, accusing them of attempting to set up Mary as regent, and announcing 'I myself will be the first that will die in the gate …'[30] in the event of an attack. Such a speech was a trope, and may or may not have been made, but Somerset was certainly busy in other ways. He had already followed up his general summons with specific letters to Sir Henry Seymour, to the earl of Oxford, and to Lord John Russell. Russell and Herbert commanded the only military force actually on foot which could have matched the power assembled by Warwick and his friends, so their role was potentially crucial. In the space of two days the Protector seems to have written to them three or four times, including in one letter the surprising claim that his enemies were accusing him of plotting to restore the mass.[31] Religion had not been mentioned in any of the authentic statements emanating from the council up to this point, and Van der Delft's testimony suggests that their position was generally thought to be conservative, so perhaps this mendacious statement was intended to discredit the lords by attributing to them an obvious falsehood. The only person who is known to have responded to the Protector's pleas is the archbishop of Canterbury, who arrived that same day with sixty men. The fact that Cranmer had not been recruited by the lords, and joined Somerset in good faith may mean no more than that he was thought to be a close friend and ally, who would have denounced the Protector's opponents if he had been aware of their intentions. On the other hand it could mean that the intention of the plotters was to reverse the religious policy of the last two years, which had been as much Cranmer's as Somerset's. In view of what was to happen over the next few days, the archbishop's perception of the crisis is crucial to a proper understanding.

Events moved fast on 6 October. Early in the day, presumably as soon as he received reports of an impending attack, Somerset sent word to Sir John Markham, the Lieutenant of the Tower of London, not to admit any

---

[28] Ibid. 331. [29] SP10/9, no. 10. [30] Add. MS 48126, fo. 10[v].
[31] SP10/9, nos. 3–9.

member of the council without his authorization. Markham, however, was not committed to the Protector's cause, and when the lords received word of what had happened they

> dyd send for the Lieutenant, requyring him to suffer certain others to enter for the good keeping thereof to his maiesties use, whereunto the Lieutenant accordyng, Sir Edmund Peckham, knight, and Leonard Chamberlain, esquire, with their servauntes, were commanded to enter into the Tower as associates to the same Lieutenant for the better presidy and gard of the same ...[32]

Towards evening, realizing that he had lost control of the Tower, that the response to his various appeals was quite inadequate for his purpose, and that Hampton Court was not defensible with the forces at his disposal, Somerset determined to move the king to the stronghold of Windsor castle. This manœuvre is nowhere described in detail. Inevitably the London lords represented it as a virtual kidnapping, and Edward seems to have been genuinely frightened by the experience. Windsor was not properly prepared to receive them, and there was a makeshift air about the hastily relocated court. The king was now Somerset's only powerful card, and began to appear increasingly like a hostage. Late that night yet another missive was directed to Russell and Herbert, instructing them to appear at Windsor and not at Hampton Court.[33] The Protector was not without friends, but they were not of the sort to be much help to him in a crisis. Opinion was very much divided in London, and it was claimed that some 4,000 unarmed and untrained supporters turned up at Hampton Court in answer to his appeal. At the same time a handwritten pamphlet circulated in the capital, denouncing the lords, by whom the authors seems to have meant mainly Warwick, as murderers of the king's subjects, who were now conspiring the death of the Protector because he 'according to his promise would have redressed things in parliament to the ease of the commons'. 'That done', the tract continued, 'they will murder the king because of their ambition and to restore popery ...'.[34] By 7 October the lords held most of the strong cards, but time was not on their side if they were to prevent further bloodshed and avoid danger to the young king.

It was consequently an anxious meeting which convened at the Mercers Hall on the morning of Monday, 7 October, and was told of Somerset's departure to Windsor. Rumours were flying by this time. Somerset had

---

[32] *APC*, ii. 332. According to Grafton the London lords 'concluded to possess the Tower of London, which by the pollecie of Sir Wylliam Paulet, Lorde Treasorer of Englande was peaceably obteyned for them, who by order of the sayde Confederates, immediately removed Sir John Markham then Lieutenant of the Tower, and placed in that rome syr Leonard Chamberleyne' (*Chronicle*, 522). However, that is not the story told by the *Acts*, and Markham was certainly Lieutenant later in the year.

[33] SP10/9, no. 6.

[34] 'Henry A to all true Englishmen', SP10/9, no. 11. Others were on their way to help the Protector, as subsequent evidence makes clear, but were too late; see e.g. John Eason to William Cecil, 24 July 1550 (SP10/10, no. 18).

sent a ship to the French king, laden with gold and silver, presumably to purchase his assistance. He was planning to spirit the king out of the realm. He was swearing that if he were attacked, the king should die first.[35] None of this need be taken seriously. It was designed to brand the Protector as a dangerous traitor, and to counteract the fact that the letters emanating from Windsor still bore Edward's authentic signature. Unable to gain access to the king, the Lords were in a serious dilemma. Later the same day they wrote to him, professing their loyalty;

we take God to wytnes, we have heretofore by all good and gentle meanes attempted to have had your highness uncle, the Duke of Somerset, to have gouverned your Majestes affayres by thadvise of us and of your counsilours ...[36]

They had, however, found him unwilling to listen to reason, and he had responded to their requests by raising forces against them. Quite what they expected this letter to achieve is not clear. Edward had just turned 12, and he had been treated up to this point like an expensive and fragile piece of luggage. They can hardly have expected him to assert himself against his uncle who, if he did not command the boy's affection, certainly exercised a quasi-parental authority. Presumably they hoped to drive a wedge between the king's servants and the duke's which might undermine the latter's position. At the same time a second letter was written, to those members of the Privy Council who were at Windsor, that is, the archbishop of Canterbury and Lord Paget. If the duke were a good subject, as he claimed, they argued, then he should 'be willing to be ordered by reason and justice'. If he would disperse his force 'we will gladly commune with him for the king's safety and the order of all other things'.[37] They then placed the onus squarely upon Cranmer and Paget to bring this about. This was an intelligent move, because Cranmer's integrity was respected by all parties, and Paget was a politician of unrivalled craft and experience. He had been the Protector's right-hand man since before the old king's death, but the state of that relationship in the summer of 1549 is open to some doubt. He had warned Somerset on a number of occasions to be more responsive to advice, and to curb his temper when his ideas were challenged. It seems, however, that his warnings had not been heeded, and on 8 May he had written in genuine distress:

If I did not love you so deeply I might hold my peace as others do; but I am forced to say that unless you show your pleasure more quietly in debate with others, and graciously hear their opinions when you require them, there will be sorry consequences, and you will be the first to repent.[38]

Paget, therefore, knew the justice of some, at least, of the complaints of the London lords, and fully understood the danger of the situation which had

---

[35] *APC*, iii. 337; SP10/9, no. 10.   [36] *APC*, iii. 339.   [37] Ibid. 341.
[38] SP10/7, no. 5. On 7 July Paget had written again, even more urgently, warning Somerset that he would have to be ruthless if he was to maintain his position, and being extremely frank about the error of his ways (SP10/8, no. 4).

arisen. The bearer of these council letters to Windsor was William Hon-
ynges, a groom of the Privy Chamber, but he seems to have been accompanied by Sir Philip Hoby. Hoby was a seasoned diplomat, who had
returned briefly from his posting at the emperor's court, ostensibly on
private business but perhaps summoned as a mediator. He was thought
to have the confidence of both sides, and he was certainly at Windsor on
8 October.[39]

On that day a letter was sent in the king's name, replying to the councillors' representations: 'we think you forget your duty to us ... You charge
our uncle with wilfulness, but we have found him so tractable that we trust
you may come to a peaceful agreement'. This letter was accompanied by a
set of articles from Somerset, justifying his actions as a response to threats,
and offering to negotiate via two commissioners for each side.[40] Sir Philip
Hoby was credited to bear the councillors' response. At the same time
Cranmer and Paget also responded. The Protector, they claimed, was willing to stand down—'He has little regard for his position. He considers he
was called to it by the king with your advice and the consent of all the lords
...'—but he did not accept the justice of their charges, and would not put
himself at their mercy without adequate guarantees.[41] They also accredited
Sir Philip Hoby. While awaiting these replies the lords endeavoured to
strengthen their position by appealing for the direct support of the City of
London. The Lord Mayor, Sir John Amcotes, prevaricated, aware that
opinion was deeply divided. He insisted upon summoning the Common
Council, and there followed an anguished debate, in the course of which
one citizen reminded his fellows what misfortunes had overtaken the City
as a result of having become embroiled in a similar quarrel during the reign
of Henry III.[42] More influenced by the presence of armed retinues than by
this cautious antiquarianism, the Common Council eventually agreed to
provide 500 men, and not to respond to a similar appeal from Windsor.
Their reluctance was manifest, however, and the men were never actually
raised. The Privy Council Register recorded the outcome rather differ-
ently;

And the said Mayor, Aldermen, and Commune Counsaile, with one voyce thank-
ing God for those good inclynacions they perceyved to be in their Lordships,
promised their ayde and helpe to the uttermost of their lieves and goodes ...[43]

At the same time Russell and Herbert removed the last danger of a serious
conflict by allying themselves with the London council. Their letter, dated
from Andover on 8 October, cannot have reached Windsor in time to influence the responses which we have already noticed, but by 9 October what
was left of the Protector's bargaining position had been still further

[39] 'Letters of Richard Scudamore to Sir Philip Hoby', ed. Susan Brigden, *Camden Miscellany*,
30 (1990), 73–86; *APC*, ii. 337–8.
[40] SP10/9, no. 24.   [41] Ibid. 26.   [42] Grafton, *Chronicle*, 523.
[43] *APC*, ii. 337.

eroded.[44] Messages of support were beginning to arrive from other peers, and the councillors sent a circular letter to all sheriffs and justices of the peace, instructing them to maintain order within their jurisdictions, and not in any circumstance to allow forces to be raised on the Protector's behalf.[45]

On 9 October the crisis reached a climax. In the morning the councillors wrote again to the king, lamenting the distress of mind which the situation must be causing him, but also trying a new tactic. Only if they could confront Somerset in the king's presence could the dispute be resolved.

For the ende of this matier towching the Duke of Somerset if he have that respect to your Majestes surety that he pretendeth … let him first quietly suffer us, your Majestes most humble servauntes and true Counsailours, to be restored to your Majestes presence …[46]

At the same time they also wrote again to Cranmer and Paget. The tone of this letter was distinctly threatening, and may have reflected the fact that Lord Russell had now joined them. The archbishop and the Controller would be held responsible if any attempt should be made to remove the king from Windsor, and they were to ensure 'at your uttermost perilles' that the king was attended by his own servants, and not by those of the duke of Somerset.[47] According to Russell and Herbert, only their presence in Wiltshire over the preceding few days had prevented a large force from being raised there on Somerset's behalf. They had 'stayed' all the parts westward, they claimed, and were now looking to the council for further instructions.[48] Since they had also communicated their position to Edward Seymour, the Protector's son, their own letter to him was amply substantiated. Before the end of that day, Somerset decided to surrender. How and by whom this was achieved cannot be precisely described. According to Richard Grafton, Sir Philip Hoby returned to Windsor 'And truely he did so wisely declare his message, and so gravely told his tale in the name of the Lordes, but therewithall so vehemently and so grievously against the Protector, who was also there present by the king, that in the ende the Lord Protector was commanded from the king's presence and shortly was committed to ward …'.[49] Hoby's mission is confirmed by the king's own chronicle, but so simple a solution is intrinsically improbable. If Edward had been capable of resolving the situation himself in the manner implied, why had he not done so long before? Moreover his own account gives no hint that he played a crucial role, and glosses over the whole issue in a few words. Presumably a collusive scene was staged between Hoby and

---

[44] SP10/9, no. 23: 'We much dislike your proclamations and bills put about for raising the commons …'.

[45] SP10/9, no. 28.   [46] *APC*, ii. 337–40.   [47] Ibid. 340–2.

[48] SP10/9, no. 31: 'Had we not arrived 5000 or 6000 men would have gone to Windsor, besides the popular disturbances that might have arisen …'.

[49] Grafton, *Chronicle*, 523.

Somerset for the king's benefit. Someone must have negotiated the terms, but we can only speculate as to who that person was, and exactly what the terms might have been.

The Protector had already indicated his willingness to stand down in return for an amnesty which would guarantee his personal security and that of his property. It seems that some such undertaking was given on behalf of the Lords by Hoby, because Somerset seems to have felt later that Sir Philip had betrayed him.[50] But Hoby alone would not have had authority to give such an assurance, and its true author was probably the earl of Warwick. Among the numerous letters exchanged on 8 October had been an appeal from Somerset to his former friend:

My lord, I cannot persuade myself that there is any ill conceived in your heart as of yourself against me; for that the same seemeth impossible that where there hath been from your youth and mine so great a friendship and amity betwixt us, as never for my part to no man was greater, now so suddenly there should be hatred; and that without just cause, whatsoever rumours and bruits, or persuasions of others have moved you to conceive; in the sight and judgement of almighty God, I protest and affirm this unto you, I never meant worse to you than to myself; wherefore my lord, for God's sake, for friendship, for the love that hath ever been betwixt us or that hereafter may be, persuade yourself with truth, and let this time declare to me and the world your just honour and perseverence in friendship, the which, God be my witness, who seeth all hearts, was never diminished, nor ever shall be while I live ...[51]

No written response to this plea has survived, nor was made in all probability. Warwick may have been touched, but he may equally have perceived an advantage to himself in this situation. He was probably the most important leader of the council, but he was not the only one, and if Somerset could be persuaded to surrender without bloodshed, thought would have to be given to what might happen next. There was much at stake, not least the future of the Protector's religious programme. Van der Delft was not alone in perceiving Somerset's enemies to be religious conservatives. Leading protestant divines awaited the outcome of the crisis with bated breath, expecting the return of 'popish superstitions'. Not only would Somerset himself have been concerned at the thought of such a reversal, Archbishop Cranmer would have been mortified, and possibly placed in personal danger. Although there is not a scrap of direct evidence to support such a thesis, a number of circumstantial indicators point to an understanding between Somerset, Cranmer, and Warwick. If such an interpretation is correct, Warwick would have undertaken to use his best endeavours, not only to protect Somerset's life and estate, but also the

---

[50] At the time of the crisis, Van der Delft had believed that Hoby was devoted to the Protector. He subsequently reported that he had betrayed him out of pique, believing that his services had not been adequately rewarded, but the fact that he was probably summoned back to act as a mediator tells a rather different story.

[51] Stow, *Annales*, 598.

Church which he had created, and Cranmer would have persuaded the Protector to accept these somewhat clandestine assurances as the best deal he was likely to get. When the council met again at the house of Lord St John on 10 October, the members knew that the crisis was as good as over:

by the dilligent travaile also of tharchebisshop of Canterbury and Sir William Paget, then being at Wyndsour, the Kinges Majestes owne servauntes were agayne restored to their places of attendance about his Majestes person, and that the Duke of Somersettes and others of his bandes were sequestered ...[52]

They sent Sir Anthony Wingfield, the Vice-Chamberlain, and two gentlemen of the Privy Chamber, Sir Anthony St Leger and Sir John Williams, to take charge of the situation.

The remaining danger lay, not in anything which Somerset himself might attempt in going back on his word, but in the possibility that others might take advantage of the tension to create 'stirs'. The Lords had already issued several public justifications of their action. They now wrote to the king's sisters, Mary and Elizabeth, and to the earl of Rutland, in command on the northern borders. To him they also sent a copy of their latest proclamation, denouncing those who laboured to maintain 'the traitorous doings of the Duke of Somerset' by misrepresenting the actions of the council.[53] The writers of all such 'bills' were to be sought out and apprehended. The tone of these letters did not suggest any relaxation in the atmosphere of crisis, and until Wingfield reported from Windsor on 11 October, some doubt may have remained in their own minds. However it seems clear that Somerset, and those who were totally compromised by their loyalty to him, had fully accepted their defeat, and had no desire either to escape or resist. Sir Thomas Smith, Sir Michael Stanhope, Sir John Thynne, Edward Wolf, and William Cecil were all placed under arrest by Wingfield as soon as he arrived, and Somerset was moved out of his previous accommodation into the Lieutenant's Tower, to distance him from the king.[54] The duchess was already at Beddington, but rather surprisingly, the young earl of Hertford and his brother were with their father at Windsor. Wingfield sent them away, probably to join their mother, until the council's further pleasure was declared. The king himself was cheerful, but had a bad cold and was very anxious to get away from Windsor. On 12 October the whole body of the London council presented themselves to receive Edward's 'most harty thankes', and orders were given to prepare suitable accommodation in the Tower for Somerset and his adherents.[55] On 13 October a very full council meeting was held at Windsor, attended by no fewer than twenty-four members, including Paget and Cranmer. The luckless Thomas Smith,

---

[52] *APC*, ii. 342.
[53] SP10/9, nos. 33, 34; *Historical Manuscripts Commission*, 12th Report, App. IV: Rutland MSS, iv. 191–2.
[54] *APC*, ii. 342.   [55] Ibid.; SP10/9, no. 42.

whose only real offence seems to have been loyalty to his patron, was removed from office, and from the council 'for sundry his misdemenours and undiscrete behaviours heretofore …'.[56] Smith, Stanhope, Thynne, and Wolf were then committed to the Tower, along with one William Gray, as the 'pryncipall instrumentes and counsailors' of Somerset's misgovernment. Cecil is not mentioned in this connection, and does not feature in a list of prisoners drawn up just over a week later. The evidence about his fate at this juncture is somewhat inconsistent, but in view of his previous easy relations with Warwick, and the favour he was subsequently to enjoy from him, his lot may well have been eased by a discreet word from the earl.[57] Somerset himself was dispatched to the Tower on 14 October, escorted by the earls of Sussex and Huntingdon, and special orders were sent to the Lieutenant that no one except their authorized servants was to have access to any of the prisoners, for fear of 'secret practices and intelligences'. On the same day Edward returned to Hampton Court.

In spite of the continuing air of nervousness, the Protector's defeat had been definitive. However, it was by no means clear what sort of regime would follow his fall. His appointment had been a personal one, so although his office was not formally abolished, it would be a mistake to see the Protectorate as vacant and awaiting a new incumbent.[58] Theoretically Somerset's arrest and the *de facto* annulment of his patent caused the executive power to revert to the fourteen surviving executors of Henry VIII's will, but in practice it was assumed by the Privy Council as it existed on 14 October.[59] No individual leader emerged, but if there were divisions within the council they were, for the time being, remarkably well concealed. The removal of Sir Michael Stanhope necessitated a reorganization in the Privy Chamber 'to give order for the good gouvernement of [the king's] most royall person, and for the honorable educacion of his Hieghnes in thies his tender yeres …', and on 15 October a complete new establishment was put in place. This consisted of six noblemen—Northampton, Arundel, Warwick, Wentworth, St John, and Russell—and four principal gentlemen—Sir Edward Rogers, Sir Thomas Darcy, Sir Andrew Dudley, and Sir Thomas Wroth.[60] Two lords and two principal gentlemen were always to be in attendance. The council clearly had no intention of allowing so important an institution to escape from its control, since all the lords named were also

---

[56]   *APC*, ii. 343–4.

[57]   Cecil was not in the Tower on 22 Oct., when a very full list was drawn up. He was, however, placed there towards the end of November, having apparently been in the custody of Lord Rich. He was released upon recognizance on 25 Jan. 1550 (SP10/9, no. 48; Scudamore letters, 94, 114).

[58]   The Protectorate was not so much abolished as abandoned, as the letters patent do not seem to have been formally rescinded.

[59]   Powers were drafted, but never implemented, conferring on the surviving executors the function of a Privy Council during the king's pleasure, and to conduct business by 'the voice of the greater part of those present' (BL Cotton MS Titus B II fos. 91–5).

[60]   *Chronicle of Edward VI*, 18.

councillors, but the appointments do not appear to have much significance in terms of the conflict which was later to appear, suggesting that it was not present at this stage. For what it is worth Northampton, Warwick, Wentworth, Darcy, Wroth, and Dudley could probably be classed as sympathetic to religious reform, Arundel, St John, Russell, and Rogers as conservative. But at the same time the council itself had a clear conservative majority. The appointment of Sir Richard Southwell and Sir Edmund Peckham, and the reappointment of Nicholas Wotton on 6 October seem to have been designed simply to strengthen that part of the council which was hostile to the Protector's protestant policies, while the death of Sir Anthony Denny, followed by the removal of Smith and of Somerset himself, had correspondingly weakened the reformers' position.[61]

On 17 October Van der Delft remained confident that the restoration of 'true religion' had been one of the principal aims of the coup:

The archbishop of Canterbury still holds his place in the council, but I do not believe they will leave him there unless he improves, and it is probable that they are now tolerating him merely that all may be done in proper order. For the same reason they are not yet making any show of intending to restore religion, in order that their first appearance in government may not disgust the people, who are totally infected. But every man among them is now devoted to the old faith, except the Earl of Warwick, who is none the less taking up the old observances again day by day, and it seems probable that he will reform himself entirely, as he says he hopes his elder son may obtain some post in your majesty's court, where he may serve you ...[62]

This was the sensible view of a well-informed observer, who was not privy to any secrets. In fact the ambassador did not understand Cranmer's position at all, and seems not to have appreciated his special relationship with the king. He probably also overestimated the enthusiasm of Arundel and Southampton for the 'old religion', because there are no other signs from contemporary evidence that the lack of action over religion was causing any anxiety or tension among the councillors themselves. Warwick strengthened his position on 19 October by recovering the office of Lord Admiral, but not much can be read into that since the admiralty had been vacant since January, and he was the obvious man for the job.[63] Meanwhile the council went energetically about its other business. A special embassy was sent to the emperor to raise again the question of support for Boulogne; Sir Richard Cotton was sent on a special mission to survey the state of the Scottish borders; and strenuous efforts were made to raise men, money, and supplies for the war against France. Having loudly denounced the Protector for his neglect of these matters, they could hardly risk encouraging the same charges.

It was not until the beginning of November that the first breath of another political storm can be detected. This centred on Sir Thomas Arundel, a strong religious conservative with ambitions to become Controller of the

[61] Hoak, *King's Council*, 52–5.   [62] *Cal. Span.*, ix. 462–3.   [63] *APC*, ii. 347 n.

Household. Arundel, who may well have been as disappointed as Van der Delft at the lack of action against the 'heretics', seems to have attempted to broker a deal between the council and Princess Mary.[64] The case for having a governmental figure-head was as strong as ever, since Edward was barely 13, and Mary would in many ways have been an ideal choice. She would not have interfered with the normal processes of government, and would have waved a magic wand over relations with the emperor. Moreover, if she had accepted the regency in November, she could hardly be accused of having been a party against the Protector. Arundel was certainly in contact with Mary during the first week in November, although the statement that he was trying to enter her service may be an erroneous perception. He was also being put forward, probably by the earl of Southampton, as a candidate for appointment to the Privy Council. There is no specific evidence that the question of a Marian regency was raised, but if it was, it would have to be seen as a move by those disillusioned with the absence of a clear-cut policy of religious conservatism, and that would certainly not have included the earl of Warwick. On the contrary, there is every reason to suppose that Warwick regarded both Arundel and his activities with suspicion and distaste. Sir Thomas's promotion to the council was blocked, and instead, on 6 November, Thomas Goodrich, the bishop of Ely, appeared for the first time.[65] Goodrich was a protestant, and for that reason his appointment was of the utmost significance. The author of the early Elizabethan account already referred to noted that in early November the earl of Warwick 'procured by the means of the archbishop of Canterbury, great friends about the king ...'.[66] This is a loaded comment, because no one was more 'about the king' than Warwick himself, but if it means that Warwick and Cranmer combined to persuade Edward to make a personal intervention in favour of Goodrich and against Arundel, then it seems clear that the consensus of early October was beginning to break down along religious lines.

As late as 7 November Van der Delft still believed that Southampton was 'head' of the council, but he was becoming increasingly puzzled by the failure of the expected religious reaction to appear. By the same token, the protestants were beginning to breath a little more easily. John Hooper, with cautious optimism, noted 'as yet no alteration has taken place', and ten days later Richard Hilles was more positive, declaring 'we are hoping that Christ may yet remain with us'.[67] One well-informed protestant divine who had left the country before the beginning of November, later claimed to have seen a draft letter or proclamation declaring the continuance of 'Godly reformation'. That could easily have been hindsight, but by the end of November it must have been clear to the conservatives that whatever understanding they thought they had with the earl of Warwick and his friends was not

[64] *Cal. Span.*, ix. 469–70; Hoak, *King's Council*, 245–6.   [65] *APC*, ii. 354.
[66] BL Add. MS 48126, fo. 15ᵛ.
[67] Richard Hilles to Henry Bullinger, 17 Nov. 1549 (*Original Letters*, i. 268).

working, and that he was steadily gaining power at their expense. The earl of Southampton ceased to attend the council after 21 October, probably because of illness, although the fact that he signed a routine council letter on 24 November must leave that in some doubt.[68] Sir Edward Peckham similarly disappeared after 30 October, and it looks as though he may have been a client of Southampton's, who was simply dropped as soon as his patron became incapacitated. On 22 November Richard Scudamore, Sir Philip Hoby's man of business, wrote to his master from the court to tell him (among other things) that he had delivered a letter to Warwick 'who hath bene and yett is troubled with a rume yn the hedd that it caused his lordshyp to kepe his chamber …'.[69] This did not, however, mean that Warwick and Southampton were now in the same situation, because on 27 November Scudamore wrote again, describing how the council had come to Ely Place because of the earl's incapacity, although Southampton remained absent.

On Friday, 29 November, Henry Grey, marquis of Dorset, was sworn of the council and the balance of power tilted critically towards the reformers.[70] Warwick was now clearly in the ascendant, rhume or no rhume, and the possibility of a religious reaction was stalled. There was, however, no open rift, and Warwick seems to have believed that he had maintained the consensus of early October, which also suggests that he did not take the motivation of the religious conservatives very seriously. As late as 5 December, according to Scudamore, Warwick was intending to take the office of Lord Treasurer himself, and bestow that of Lord Great Chamberlain upon the earl of Arundel. Sir William Paget had just been created a baron, presumably in reward for his services at Windsor, and was destined for the Chamberlainship, in succession to Arundel.[71] Within a few days, however, this harmony was disrupted. It seems clear that Warwick had overestimated the complaisance of Arundel and Southampton, and the former at least had come to the conclusion that only a decisive blow could restore that conservative ascendancy which had been progressively eroded over the previous six or seven weeks. The details and extent of the 'plot' which resulted are not entirely clear, but it centred upon an attempt to exploit the interrogation of the duke of Somerset which was then proceeding. These interviews, in which a number of councillors were involved, were designed to extract admissions of misgovernment from the fallen Protector which would form the basis of the charges against him.[72] Southampton, who must have made a rapid recovery after 27 November, was one of

---

[68] BL Harleian MS 284, fo. 56: council to Lord Cobham. Three days later, however, Scudamore reported that he 'lyeth syke at his howse yn London and, as some saye, verye wilde' (Scudamore letters, 93).

[69] Ibid. 95–9.   [70] Ibid. 96.   [71] Ibid. 98.

[72] 'manye of the counsell hath ben dyvers tymes this weke at the Towre with the Duke of Somersett' (Scudamore letters, 101). The charges themselves are listed by Stow, *Annales*, 601–2, and in BL Add. MS 9069, fo. 43ᵛ.

those most actively involved. It seems to have been generally assumed, by Van der Delft among others, that Somerset would be executed, because at this stage nobody was publicly condoning his actions. Whether Warwick was biding his time, or whether he intended to dishonour whatever undertakings he had made on 9 October, we do not know. According to our anonymous source, Southampton was determined to harry the duke to his death 'being hote to be rewenged ... for old groges paste whan he lost his office'.[73] Under questioning Somerset understandably took the line that he had done nothing in respect of his public policy, without the consent of the council. As Warwick had been perceived as his leading ally and supporter, that presented Southampton with a golden opportunity to portray his successful rival as the leading accomplice in the Protector's crimes. 'I thoughte', he is alleged to have said, 'ever we sholde fynde them traytors both; and both is worthie to dye for by my advyse ...'.[74]

Arundel supposedly concurred in this judgement, which must have been made about the end of the first week in December. However, despite the authority's presumed closeness to events, there is an air of unreality about this. A united council could certainly have executed Somerset had it wished to do so. He was politically discredited and his popular support cowed and irrelevant. To have swept Warwick into the net, on the other hand, would have meant overturning his ascendancy in the council and defeating a very powerful political faction. At the same time it would have been possible, by pressing hard for Somerset's death, to force Warwick into the open. If he opposed the execution, then he could be weakened by association with the Protector's guilt. If he concurred, then a rift could be forced between himself and Cranmer, who had guaranteed Somerset's safety and was a man of his word. That Arundel and Southampton should have been accused of plotting Warwick's death seems entirely plausible; that they actually did so seems much more problematic. The reality seems to have been that there was a plot involving a number of conservative councillors and others, to use the ex-Protector's trial and execution as a means of discrediting Warwick and reversing the balance of power within the council. It failed because Lord St John, in whom the plotters had confided, went immediately to Ely Place and told the earl what was afoot.[75] St John was a conservative, but he was also an opportunist. He had perceived a rising tension in the council towards the end of November, and may well have seen the recruitment of Dorset as a sign that, if there were a showdown, Warwick and his friends would win. Armed with this information, the earl then staged a dramatic confrontation, probably on 11 or 12 December. Whether he was really indisposed again, or seeking to put his opponents at a disad-

---

[73] BL Add. MS 48126, fo. 15^v; Hoak, *King's Council*, 255.
[74] Ibid.; H. James, 'The Aftermath of the 1549 Coup and the Earl of Warwick's Intentions', *Historical Research*, 62 (1989), 91–7.
[75] BL Add. MS 48126, fo. 16^r; Hoak, *King's Council*, 255.

vantage, the council was summoned to his residence in Holborn. Southampton then took the initiative to propose 'how worthie the lord protector was to die and for how many high treasons', whereupon

The earle of Warwicke ... with a warlyke wisage and a long fachell by his syde, laye his hand thereof, and said: my lord you seek his bloude and he that seekethe his bloude woulde have myne also ...[76]

According to the only surviving account a stunned silence then descended on the company, and the meeting broke up amazed by Warwick's vehemence. On 13 December Somerset signed a list of thirty-one articles of submission, and the crisis over his fate began to ease. The public rebuff to Southampton had been decisive, because his supporters were neither resolute enough nor numerous enough to recover the lost ground. Russell, like St John, hastened to align himself with the winning side. Others were not quite so quick on their feet. Sir Richard Southwell, who had been brought on to the council to strengthen the conservative interest, was dismissed on 29 December, charged with having written 'certain bills of sedition'.[77] More surprisingly, the usually agile Paget was also wrong-footed. He never obtained the Lord Chamberlainship for which he had seemed destined, and having been 'put out of his controllership' when he received his barony, was left without any office at court. He remained on the council, but his relationship with Warwick never recovered its Henrician closeness, and he progressively lost favour over the following year. Warwick's sudden change of mind about him in mid-December must have been caused by some suspicion of his involvement with Wriothesley and Arundel, but we do not know what the evidence for that may have been.[78]

Parliament had been in session since 4 November, and had systematically, although not without controversy, demolished the Protector's social policy. A bill 'for the punishment of unlawful assemblies and risings of the King's subjects', which broadened the definition of treason, and placed sweeping powers in the hands of the magistrates, was finally approved by the Lords on 28 December.[79] A bill against 'fond and fantastical prophecy' had completed its passage two days earlier, while Somerset's sheep and cloth tax was repealed on 16 January after an elaborate show of petitioning,

[76] Ibid. There are problems about the timing of this episode, because Richard Scudamore, writing on 26 Dec., seems to have known nothing about it. For that reason Professor Hoak dated it to the very end of December. On the other hand Van der Delft, writing on 19 Dec., reported that it was generally believed that the duke's life would be saved, which would seem to have been a consequence of Warwick's outburst (*Cal. Span.*, ix. 489). The picturesque language of the Additional MS need not be taken too seriously. The actual confrontation in council may well have been much less dramatic, although equally decisive.

[77] *Chronicle of Edward VI*, 19.

[78] The only full-scale biography of Paget, S. R. Gammon's *Statesman and Schemer* (Newton Abbot, 1973), ignores the episode entirely.

[79] *Lords Journals*, i. 373.

and replaced with an ordinary subsidy.[80] These measures, and the manner of their passage, are sufficient indication that the council and the parliament were working harmoniously together in the wake of the Protector's fall. A bill 'concerning the improvement of Commons and Waste grounds' revived the statute of Merton, and effectively reversed the long-standing Tudor tradition of anti-enclosure legislation.[81] On the other hand the members seem to have shown no inclination to be vindictive towards the Protector himself. A bill for his fine and ransom, which signified the council's decision not to proceed to his attainder, was introduced on 2 January, and had passed all its stages in both houses by 14 January.[82] If Arundel and Southampton had hoped to preserve their influence by persuading the Lords to reject this measure, then they failed totally, and the conclusion must be that Warwick and his allies had parliament under effective control. The final evaporation of conservative hopes for an end to protestant reform came on 25 December, with the issuing of a proclamation reaffirming the council's commitment to the Act of Uniformity, because

we are informed that divers unquiet and evil disposed persons, since the apprehension of the Duke of Somerset, have noised and bruited abroad that they should have again their old Latin service, their conjured bread and water, with such like vain and superstitious ceremonies, as though the setting forth of the said book [of Common Prayer] had been the only act of the aforenamed duke.[83]

By the time that parliament was prorogued on 1 February, Warwick had moved to consolidate his victory and strengthen his grip on power. His two important new allies, St John and Russell, were rewarded on 19 January with the earldoms of Wiltshire and Bedford respectively. At about the same time Arundel and Southampton were commanded to vacate their chambers at court, and were placed under house arrest in London. On or about 16 January Warwick's loyal supporter Sir Thomas Darcy was sworn of the council, and became Vice-Chamberlain and Captain of the Guard in place of Wingfield.[84] A few days later, on 26 January Walter Devereux, Lord Ferrers, another protestant, became a Privy Councillor, and on 30 January Sir Thomas Arundel and his brother Sir John were committed to the Tower 'for conspiracies in the west parts'.[85] Rumours were rife. On 18 January Scudamore reported—wrongly it seems—that Southampton was not under house arrest, and had been assured that the council had no 'displeaure'

[80] 3 & 4 Edward VI, c. 5; *Lords Journals*, i. 357; 3 & 4 Edward VI, c. 15; *Statutes of the Realm*, ed. A. Luder *et al.* (London, 1810–28), iv. i. 114–15; 3 & 4 Edward VI, c. 23; *Statutes of the Realm*, iv. i. 122–4.

[81] 3 & 4 Edward VI, c. 3; *Statutes of the Realm*, iv. i. 102–3.

[82] 3 & 4 Edward VI, c. 31; *Lords Journals*, i. 379; *Commons Journals*, i. 15.

[83] Hughes and Larkin, *Tudor Royal Proclamations*, i. 485–6.

[84] Darcy first appears on 16 Jan., although there is no record of his oath; *APC*, ii. 370. He had been named as one of the Principal Gentlemen of the Privy Chamber the previous Oct., and was appointed Vice-Chamberlain and Captain of the Guard on 2 Feb.

[85] *APC*, ii. 372.

against him.[86] The duke of Somerset's friends expected his release within six days. The earl and countess of Warwick had removed to Mr York's house, 'and as yet my lorde came not at the courte, the which thyng maketh men to iudge that he dareth not to remayne yn his owne howse', presumably for fear of another plot against him. However on 2 February, the day after parliament had been prorogued, Arundel and Southampton were formally expelled from the council, and Warwick assumed the office of Lord President.[87]

Richard Scudamore was greatly relieved by this turn of events, but not entirely sure that Warwick's victory was conclusive. 'It was high time to take the byrdes [Southampton and his allies]', he wrote, 'for they purposed to have made a popys fflyght …'. Divisions among the aristocracy over religion would only encourage a repetition of the violence of the previous summer.

God shorten theyr evell purpos, for by the devysyon of the greate the madd rage of the idell commoners is much provoked therbye to ffollowe theyr naugh[t]ye pretences, so that {or onlesse God shewe his mercy over us) this yere to come is lyke to be wors then eny was yett.[88]

Events were to prove that his fears were exaggerated, but his perception raises the question of Warwick's motivation since the overthrow of the Protectorate. Did this period represent, as Hayward believed, the culmination of machiavellian ambitions going back before Henry VIII's death, with John Dudley cast in the mould of Shakespeare's Richard III? Or was he, as some more recent historians have believed, merely an opportunist who was forced to defend himself against jealous rivals, and who obtained supreme power more or less by accident?[89] As we have seen, the evidence for Hayward's position nearly all derives from the crisis of 1553 and its aftermath, but it does not necessarily follow from that that power was more or less forced upon Warwick by circumstances. Warwick would have needed to be very innocent not to have understood that the overthrow of the Protector had left him in an immensely strong position. However, much of what followed is imperfectly attested, and the interpretation can only be based upon circumstantial evidence. We know that Cranmer retained his influential position on the council, against Van der Delft's expectations, and we know that no steps were taken to restore the traditional forms of worship. The reasons for this can only be deduced, but the archbishop's mediation with Somerset and his personal influence over the young king must have been the main factors in steering Warwick away from the conservative group with whom he had certainly been in alliance towards the end of September. How serious his consequent rift with the conservatives

---

[86] *Chronicle of Edward VI*, 19; Scudamore letters, 114, 117.   [87] Ibid. 108.
[88] Hoak, *King's Council*, 59; Scudamore letters, 108.
[89] See particularly Beer, *Northumberland, passim*.

was by the end of November is again unclear. We do not even know certainly how conservative Arundel and Wriothesley actually were. Richard Scudamore might talk about a 'pope's flight', and John Hooper speculate darkly about 'popish superstitions', but there is no evidence from the conservative side that they intended to go back before 1547, and speculations about the release of Gardiner and Bonner did not imply that either.[90] Warwick might well have felt that in religious terms the gap between the two sides was not great, and that those who had accepted a reforming policy under Somerset would also accept its continuance under his successor. He had a record as a reformer going back to the mid-1530s, and it is his conversations with Van der Delft before the *coup* which appear to have been out of character rather than his pact with Cranmer afterwards. Inevitably he was later accused of having double-crossed his conservative allies, but we have no idea what sort of an understanding the London lords had among themselves about religious policy, if they had any at all, nor what undertakings Warwick may have made, or may have been thought to have made. We know that there was factional tension on religious lines within the council during November, and that the appointments of Goodrich and Dorset rather than Thomas Arundel were seen at the time to have been significant. On the other hand neither Warwick nor his religious allies saw themselves as being in irreconcilable conflict with the earl of Arundel in early December, when his intended promotion was mentioned by Scudamore without comment. At the same time, we have very little hard evidence about the alleged plot which led to the political demise of both Arundel and Southampton. Scudamore only reports what he was told afterwards, and the main source never alleges that the plotters went beyond indiscreet rhetoric. Were Arundel and Southampton simply framed by St John with Warwick's connivance? As we have already seen, the alleged aim of the plotters seems somewhat far-fetched, and the fact that neither of them was subsequently indicted under the statute which made it high treason to plot the death of a privy councillor suggests that there was no case, even by the flexible standards of the time. The most probable explanation is that St John reported to Warwick conversations which revealed to the latter that the opponents whom he thought he had outmanœuvred were not as reconciled to the situation as he had believed, and were planning a counterstroke of some kind. Using illness, which was never incapacitating and may well have been feigned, as a pretext, he then seized the initiative by causing the council to meet at his house, and wrong-footed his opponents by choosing to make an issue over the fate of the fallen Protector.

The most likely explanation for Warwick's conduct throughout the tur-

---

[90] Neither Gardiner nor Bonner at this stage questioned the validity of the royal supremacy. Gardiner particularly had argued against Somerset that his protestant reforms would weaken the royal supremacy. Even Mary saw herself as defending her father's settlement.

bulent year 1549 is that he had his eye on the future, about five years hence, when the king should attain the age of 18, and assume personal responsibility for his government. Edward showed every sign of becoming a strong, not to say bigotted, protestant,[91] and of developing powerful likes and dislikes. Somerset had treated the boy with a clumsy lack of consideration, and the fact that there was little personal affection between them had made the Protector's overthrow easier. If anyone else placed himself *in loco parentis*, he would run a similar risk of clashing personalities with Henry VIII's strong-minded son. The ultimate prize of power in the coming regime would go to whoever could read the young king's mind best, and win his confidence. Warwick judged rightly that an alliance with Cranmer, and a programme of continuing reform, were essential first steps in that process. At what point he formed that view we do not know. There is no evidence to suggest a long-standing ambition of such a nature, but the events of early October presented an opportunity which was too good to be missed. Dudley was the only man in a position to grasp it; the only man, indeed, who had the political capacity, the standing, and the religious convictions to form a government with which Edward could grow comfortably towards manhood. It is not surprising that he was less than scrupulous in seizing his chance, and he could have argued that he owed it to his king to do no less.

Having shaped the council to his satisfaction, in early February 1550 the Lord President carried out a major reallocation of offices. He abandoned his rumoured intention of taking the Lord Treasurership himself, and bestowed it instead upon the newly created earl of Wiltshire. Instead he took the Lord Great Mastership of the Household, the office previously held by Lord St John. His own previous office, the Great Chamberlainship, he handed on to his friend the marquis of Northampton. The earl of Arundel inevitably lost the Chamberlainship, and was replaced by Thomas, Lord Wentworth.[92] Sir Anthony Wingfield had already replaced Paget as Controller, and he was replaced as Vice-Chamberlain by Sir Thomas Darcy. Richard Rich remained as Lord Chancellor, and there was no further change among the secretaries. Change was balanced by continuity, because Warwick was aware of the need for experience in high office, and did not want to send out signals which would indicate any revolutionary change of direction. A general reconciliation would not only protect him against any further attempt at a counter-*coup*, it would also indicate to both domestic and foreign enemies that there was no factional strife for them to exploit. William Cecil, Richard Whalley, Edward Wolf, and Richard Palady were the first group of Somerset's adherents to be released on recognizance. In reporting this on 25 January, Scudamore observed that it was 'a fayr begynnyng; it is trusted that more shall ffollowe shortelye': and on 23 February

---

[91] On this point see particularly W. K. Jordan, *Edward VI: The Threshold of Power* (London, 1970), 17–27.

[92] Scudamore letters, 116–17.

he added 'Mr Stanhope, Mr Smyth, Mr Thynne, Mr ffysher and Mr Graye are all delyvered the xxii day of ffebruary payeng greate ffynes ...'.[93] Somerset himself confirmed the terms of his submission on 27 January, and on 6 February he was summoned to the council, meeting at John York's house in the City. There his recognizance was fixed at £10,000, and he was released upon the condition that he live within four miles of his house at Syon, and avoid the court.[94] His duchess, who had been briefly imprisoned in the aftermath of the *coup*, had long since been released, and awaited him at the Savoy. On 18 February he was given a full pardon, and the bulk of his estates were restored.[95] No further action was taken against the earl of Southampton, whose death on 30 July following may well have been hastened by the chagrin of having been outmanœuvred twice, first by Somerset and then by Warwick. Arundel was fined a sum which may have been as much as £12,000 on extremely dubious charges of having abused his office of Lord Chamberlain and purloined the king's property.[96] Most of this fine was subsequently remitted, and his estates remained untouched. The political crisis, which extended by some interpretations from the beginning of October 1549 to the end of January 1550, was thus ended without a single treason trial, and without bloodshed.

Those who did suffer were the prisoners already condemned for their role in the events of the previous summer. The Kett brothers, Humphrey Arundell, Wynslade, Bery, and Holmes were arraigned at Westminster Hall on 26 November and condemned to death. The Ketts were executed at Norwich shortly after, and the westerners at Tyburn on 27 January.[97] It was probably felt that Russell had already carried out so many executions in Devon and Cornwall that further exemplary punishments were unnecessary. The message sent out by these executions, and by the proceedings of parliament, was perfectly clear. The new government was prepared to allow territorial lords a considerable measure of discretion over the enclosing of common land, and was not prepared to tolerate any protest or dissent. At the same time the protestant reformation would continue, and conservative religious protest would be handled with a similar lack of sympathy. Over the next three years the council was to show constant concern over social discipline and security—so much so that one scholar has branded it as 'government by fearful men'[98]—but Warwick's policy of working with the grain of local gentry opinion rather than against it probably meant that the danger of renewed insurrection was never as great as some on both sides believed it to be. Nevertheless the pursuit of such a policy simultaneously with the rehabilitation of the duke of Somerset raises

---

[93] Scudamore letters, 114, 122.   [94] *APC*, ii. 384–5.
[95] T. Rymer, *Foedera, conventions etc.* (London, 1704–35), xv. 205–7.
[96] *Chronicle of Edward VI*, 19.   [97] Scudamore letters, 116.
[98] Jordan, *The Threshold of Power*, 45–70.

some difficult questions. On 28 March both Somerset and Arundel were among the eight peers whose eldest sons were named as hostages to go to France for the security of the treaty of Boulogne, and a few days later it was rumoured that both would be received at court.[99] In Arundel's case the rumour seems to have been unfounded, but Somerset was readmitted on 31 March. On 8 April he dined with the council at Greenwich, and two days later was restored to the board.[100] On 26 April Richard Scudamore wrote 'My lord of Somerset lyeth at the court and all men seketh upon hym'. Van der Delft was probably not alone in believing that he would recover his former authority.[101]

The reason for this new turn in the wheel of fortune is not clear. It has been alleged that the earl of Warwick was afraid of him, and preferred to have him under close observation rather than nursing his grievances upon his estates. That may have been the case, but Somerset, like Warwick himself, was a 'new man' whose strength was at court and in the central administration rather than in a powerful affinity. It is unlikely that his power 'in his country' would have been as great as that of old peers such as the earls of Derby or Shrewsbury, or even Arundel. Somerset's position had been comprehensively destroyed, first by his defeat in October and second by his unequivocal submission in January. Consequently the decision to rehabilitate him was a positive one rather than negative. Neither Warwick nor Cranmer can have been under any obligation to do more than preserve his life and estate by the terms of his first surrender, so we should conclude that they saw him as a useful ally in the new circumstances of 1550. This must have been in the context of continuing religious reform, because the overt repudiation of his social policy, the abandonment of his cherished schemes in Scotland, and the *rapprochement* with France represented by the treaty of Boulogne can have left him little else to identify with. That religion was a major consideration is also suggested by an interesting letter from Catherine, duchess of Suffolk, to William Cecil, written on 25 March. The duchess was a staunch protestant, and had written to Cecil a number of times over the previous three months, sympathizing with his troubles, and congratulating him when they appeared to be over. In this letter she expressed her satisfaction that 'wicked tongues' had not prevailed against the duke in council, and expressed a willingness to use her own powers of persuasion on his behalf: 'the greatest good I could have done him', she wrote, 'was to have counselled him if he had been impatient at their unkind dealing.'[102] Apart from being a more sympathetic echo of some of Paget's earlier advice, this also indicates the nature of the understanding which Somerset reached with Warwick. He would in future be a member of the team rather than its captain, but he had many talents to contribute to the establishment

---

[99] *Chronicle of Edward VI*, 22; Scudamore letters, 129.   [100] *APC*, ii. 427.
[101] Scudamore letters, 130.   [102] SP10/10, no. 2.

of that 'godly regiment' which they all professed to desire and of which the duchess was such a fervent advocate. It was not only personal friendship which caused her to urge his reinstatement, but his value to the reformed faith. By the time that she concluded her letter word of Somerset's impending rehabilitation had reached her—presumably not from Cecil—and she decided that any intervention on her part would be superfluous. There was, of course, also another dimension to her concern. Within two months she was writing to Somerset as an influential councillor, asking him to promote various of her suits concerning litigation over property.[103] On 3 June Somerset's daughter Anne was married at Sheen in the king's presence to John Dudley, Viscount Lisle, Warwick's eldest surviving son. This marriage must have been intended to seal a reconciliation between the two families, and the restoration of their former friendship. Edward enjoyed himself greatly, and the omens for co-operation seemed good, but they were not to survive the political strains of the next eighteen months.[104]

Meanwhile the normal business of government had to be conducted, and in the autumn of 1549 that meant war with France. Whatever Henry II may have hoped, neither the convulsions of the summer nor the overthrow of the Protector resulted in the collapse of English military power. Nor was there any immediate change in English policy. By the middle of October fresh levies had been ordered for the relief of Boulogne, and although it took nearly two months to get them to their destination, the French were not strong enough to take advantage of the delay.[105] Perhaps because Paget's influence was high in the council at this point, or perhaps because there was no obvious alternative, on 22 October Sir Thomas Cheyney was joined in mission with Sir Philip Hoby to renew the earlier requests to the emperor for permission to recruit troops. Charles was reluctant, standing firmly by his neutrality, but he eventually gave permission for English agents to recruit 5,000 foot and 600 horse in Friesland, provided that they were shipped straight out by sea and did not have to pass through any other part of his dominions.[106] Meanwhile both sides were beginning to feel their way towards a settlement. Warwick had conducted this sort of business with the French before, and particularly with Chatillon, the French commander before Boulogne. Unlike Somerset he had no particular attachment to an imperial alliance, and was unsentimental about Henry VIII's last conquest. With no visible slackening of

[103] SP10/10, no. 8: 18 May 1550.

[104] *Chronicle of Edward VI*, 32. On 9 May the duchess of Suffolk had written to Cecil that the earl of Warwick 'for better show of his friendship' was trying to arrange a marriage betweeen Anne Seymour and her own son, the young duke. However the duchess was insistent that the goodwill of the young people themselves must be obtained, and this, apparently, was not forthcoming. John Dudley had already attained his majority, being about 22 (SP10/10, no. 6).

[105] SP10/9, no. 47: 16 Oct. 1549; Jordan, *The Threshold of Power*, 118–19.

[106] *Cal. Span.*, ix. 478.

military resolve, he nevertheless persuaded the council to put out the first feelers. On 7 November, Van der Delft reported that a Florentine merchant resident in London, named Antonio Guidotti, had been sent to Paris to sound the water. When Chatillon responded, towards the end of the month, the council diliberately made it appear that he had made the first move.[107] The English garrison was being reinforced at this point, and Lord Cobham, the Lieutenant, was talking boldly about recovering the outforts, while the French were being troubled by desertions and financial shortages, so there was a certain plausibility about the misrepresentation. At the end of December Guidotti was back in Paris with firm instructions to negotiate, an advance which may have reflected Warwick's firmer ascendancy and the consequent eclipse of Paget. It was even rumoured that he was authorized to offer a marriage between King Edward and the young French princess Elizabeth, a proposal which would have signalled the final abandonment of the forlorn treaty of Greenwich and a more realistic approach to international relations.[108]

The English and French commissioners were instructed at about the same time, the French commission being drawn up on 8 January, and the English on 10 January. The English negotiators were Lord Russell, Lord Paget, Sir John Mason, and Sir William Petre, while France was principally represented by Chatillon, de la Rochepot, Du Mortier, and de Sacy.[109] It soon transpired that it was the French who were interested in a marriage alliance. Henry had more than one eye on his next struggle with the emperor, and was not anxious to turn England into an imperial ally through the recovery of Boulogne. The English were trying to extricate themselves from the war with the minimum of damage to their honour, which meant obtaining substantial compensation for their willingness to surrender the late king's prize. This at first meant a last-ditch attempt to resurrect the Scottish marriage, a proposal which the French totally rejected. The negotiations did not formally begin until 19 February because of preliminary wranglings over the place of meeting. The English commissioners were instructed to press for the usual venue near Ardres, on the borders of the Calais Pale, but the French insisted on a site close to Boulogne, since that was the main bone of contention. Eventually a special pavilion had to be erected on the French shore of the Liane estuary, and honour was satisfied at the cost of some delay.[110] On 22 February Paget reported to Warwick that the French had

[107] Ibid. 469; BL Harleian MS 284, no. 38, fo. 56.

[108] *Cal. Span.*, ix. 490. At this stage the marriage seems to have been Guidotti's own idea, and it did not appear in serious negotiations for about a year.

[109] BL Cotton MS Caligula E iv, fo. 272; Harleian MS 36, no. 12, fo. 69; Sloane MS 4149, no. 5; PRO E 30 1053, Potter, 'Documents', 74–5.

[110] Another reason for delay may well have been the acute anxiety of the English commissioners about what was happening at home. On 30 Jan. they wrote, 'We do likewise hear bruited here that there have now of very late been many conspiracies attempted in sundry parts of the realm …'. They recommended the dissolution of parliament. This must have

opened their attack by insisting upon the unconditional return of Boulogne, 'they set forth the power of their king and make of ours as little as they list'.[111] English attempts to insist upon the arrears of pensions due under previous treaties were shrugged aside, 'they will no longer be tributaries, as they term it'. However, it is now apparent from the publication of the French side of the subsequent negotiations, that Chatillon and his associates could not afford to be as intransigent as they at first appeared. In spite of his pessimistic dispatches, Paget proved to be a tough negotiator; after all, he was trying to restore his own credit with Warwick, and he had one very strong card in his hand, namely Boulogne itself. Once it became clear that Scotland was a side-issue which could be bypassed, and that the English would be prepared to sell out for what they could get, an agreement was quickly reached, and was concluded on 24 March.[112]

Neither Paget nor Warwick have traditionally been given much credit for this treaty, but in fact the former played his cards well, and succeeded in forcing Henry to pay far more than he had intended, or was happy with: 200,000 crowns (about £80,000) was to be paid at once, and a second instalment of the same size on 5 August. In return the French were to receive Boulogne itself, and most of the military supplies that were in it. Prisoners were to be exchanged and all privateers recalled.[113] Scotland was left for later resolution, except that the English agreed to refrain from unprovoked aggression. The treaty has been described as a shameful abandonment of English interests, and as an unparalleled humiliation,[114] but it was not seen that way at the time. When it was proclaimed on 28 March, bonfires were lit and there was general rejoicing. Even Hayward, who seldom had a good word to say for anything which the earl of Warwick had achieved, did not pretend that the treaty of Boulogne was anything less than satisfactory. He did, however, cast considerable doubt on the earl's tactics. On 21 March Richard Scudamore reported 'My lord of Warrewick lyeth at Greenewhich and is very yll troubled with his syknes ...'.[115] He had been only a sporadic attender at routine council meetings since assuming the presidency on 2 February, perhaps for this reason, but he had been at a meeting at Westminster on 17 March. Hayward clearly suspected him of malingering, and

crossed in the post with a long letter from the council, relating the sequestration of the earl of Southampton, and the arrests of the Arundels and William Honyngs. Also on 1 Feb., the earl of Warwick wrote to inform them of the prorogation of parliament, and of the appointments which had recently been made. His own new diet, he reported 'has eased me thoroughly of my pain', and he was intending to be back at court within the next few days (Cotton MS Caligula E iv, fos. 203, 207, 206).

[111] BL Lansdowne MS 2, fos. 81–3.
[112] D. L. Potter, 'Documents Concerning the Negotiations of the Anglo-French Treaty of March 1550', *Camden Miscellany*, 28 (1984), 59–180.
[113] Rymer, *Foedera*, xv. 212–15.
[114] e.g. Jordan, *The Threshold of Power*, 123: 'His [Warwick's] foreign policy—if indeed he had one—was as weak as it was feckless.'
[115] Scudamore letters, 125.

readily attributed that opinion to certain of his unnamed contemporaries. In connection with the French negotiations, he wrote

These matters advertised into England much troubled the counsaile, and the rather for that the Earle of Warwicke was at that time retired, pretending much infirmity in his health. Hereupon many sinister surmises began to spring up among some of the counsaile, partly probable and parte happely devised, for as they knew not whether hee were more dangerous present or away; so as the nature of all feare is they suspected that which happened to be the worst. From hence divers of the counsaile began in this manner to murmure against him.

What said they is he never sicke, but when affaires of greatest weight are in debating? Or wherefore else doth hee withdraw himselfe from the company of those who are not well assured of his love? Wherefore doth he not now come forth and openly overrule, as in other matters hee is accustomed? Would he have us imagine by his absence that he acteth nothing? Or knowing that all moveth from him, shall wee not thinke that he seeketh to enjoy his owne ends, which bearing blame for every event? Goe to then; let him come forth and declare himselfe, for it is better that [he] should finde fault with all things whilest they are doing, then condemne all thinges when they are done …[116]

Whereupon, hearing of these murmurings, the earl rejoined his colleagues and the peace was rapidly concluded. There is no contemporary evidence for such rumours. Scudamore was sympathetic—'The lyvyng lord send hym amendement'—and the suggestion that the treaty was held up by Warwick's unwillingness to face the responsibilities which power had brought him finds no support in other quarters. At the same time it is worth remembering that Warwick had demolished the Southampton/ Arundel 'plot' from his sickbed. There had been signs of hypochondria in his earlier life, and the fact that these bouts of illness never seem to have been incapacitating suggests that illness had become part of his political style. In normal circumstances the conventional wisdom was that he who was absent from court, for whatever reason, found his influence undermined. But during a minority that did not necessarily apply to the leader of the council. It may be that Warwick chose to distance himself in this way, and let others do his seeing and hearing for him. Whatever the explanation, it does not seem to have impaired his effectiveness; and from the manner in which he was deferred to at the time, it was clearly his leadership which brought the Boulogne negotiations to a successful conclusion.

The emperor had been kept fully informed of these proceedings and could hardly object to so virtuous a conclusion. Guidotti's enthusiasm for an Anglo-French marriage had come to nothing, but the Florentine was in high credit with both sides, and might well try again. Relations between the erstwhile enemies were certainly improving faster than Charles would have wished. The implementation of the first stage of the treaty was carried

---

[116] John Hayward, *The Life and Raigne of King Edward VI*, ed. B. L. Beer (Kent, Ohio, and London), 122–3.

out without a hitch. Lord Clinton handed over the city on 25 April, and the first instalment of the redemption money was paid in Calais on the same day.[117] The so-called 'hostages', the young noblemen who served as pledges for the completion of the treaty, were exchanged in early April, and on 25 May a prestigious French mission arrived to witness Edward's ratification. They were sumptuously entertained, including a 'fair supper' with the duke of Somerset, and departed on 30 May, well satisfied with their reception.[118] Cobham, Petre, and Mason had already performed the same office in France, and on 18 May Henry had staged a ceremonial entry into Boulogne.[119] Sceptics might observe that his next objective would be Calais, but the king could ill afford to pursue such an ambition for the time being. With or without his knowledge, his agents occasionally made their presence felt along the border, but both sides knew that Calais was still guarded by the emperor's protection, and if the king of France was going to fight the emperor, he did not want the king of England as an enemy at the same time, however much he might belittle his military capability.

And now, as Hayward somewhat sardonically observed, 'it remained that the chiefe actors in this peace (whatsoever their aimes were) must be both honoured and enriched with great rewards ...'. Antonio Guidotti received a knighthood, 1,000 crowns in reward, and an annual pension of the same sum, a very reasonable recompense, it would seem, for his skill and application.[120] Sir John Mason became a Privy Councillor on 19 April. Lord Clinton, who had paid no part in the negotiations, but who had acted out his role at Boulogne with credit, took over the Admiralty from Warwick, who was clearly wearing too many hats,[121] and joined the council in that capacity on 4 May. Clinton's promotion probably had nothing to do with the peace, except in so far as the relinquishing of Boulogne freed him for other military work. At the same time, as the intense preoccupation of the last three months began to relax, thought was given to other matters. The Boulogne light horse and 600 infantry from the garrison were sent on to the north of England, to strengthen the border defences, which had been run down disastrously since the previous summer. More significantly, perhaps, on 8 April Warwick decided to return to the north himself as Warden-General of the Marches, an office for which he provided himself with 100 horsemen at the king's expense. On the same day Sir William Herbert 'his chiefe instrument' succeeded him as President of the Council in the Marches of Wales.[122] Each received a substantial grant of land in respect of

[117] *Chronicle of Edward VI*, 27.　　　　[118] Ibid. 22, 25, 31–2.　　　　[119] Ibid. 25, 31.

[120] Hayward, *Life and Raigne*, 124; *Chronicle of Edward VI*, 24. Guidotti's original contact with Henry II went back to 9 Nov. 1549 (Cotton MS Caligula E iii, fos. 69–70; Potter, 'Documents', 170–1).

[121] *APC*, iii. 2, 9, 24.

[122] *Chronicle of Edward VI*, 24, records the decision; the actual appointment, made on 27 May, was to the East and Middle Marches only (*Calendar of the Patent Rolls*, Edward VI, ed. R. H. Brodie (London, 1924–9), iii. 404).

his office—1,000 marks' worth to Warwick and 500 to Herbert. On 9 April the king noted in his journal 'Licenses signed for the whole council and certain of the Privy Chamber to keep among them 2300 retainers'.[123] Warwick had no intention of being taken unaware if there should be another 'camping summer', but in so doing he was resurrecting a security policy against which the Tudors had consistently set their faces since the early days of the reign of Henry VII. Apart from Guidotti's knighthood, most of these appointments and grants should probably be seen in terms of providing for the future rather than rewarding the past. It is perhaps significant that the leading negotiator at Boulogne, Lord Paget, whose role had undoubtedly been important, received nothing. There was, apparently, little future for him in the new regime.

The duke of Somerset, on the other hand, returned to centre stage with his role in the entertainment of the French ambassadors and the marriage of his daughter. During the early summer of 1550 it appears that Warwick made a serious and prolonged attempt to recruit him as an ally, using some of Somerset's former supporters, such as Richard Whalley and William Cecil as intermediaries. Both Whalley and Cecil had been imprisoned for their close association with the Protector, but by June both were on terms of easy familiarity with Warwick, and the latter, particularly, was rising fast in his favour. On 26 June Whalley wrote to Cecil detailing a discussion which he had had with the earl the previous evening.[124] The main thrust of the conversation was an attempt by Warwick to persuade Whalley to use his good offices with his former master. He was, he professed, Somerset's faithful friend, and was anxious to prevent him from ruining his newly restored credit by ill-advised actions. The council was not favourably impressed by his recent attempts to secure the release of Gardiner and the two Arundel brothers, nor by his 'late conference' with the earl of Arundel. The council feared, Warwick continued, that the duke was trying to recover his former authority. The memory of the Protectorate was still disliked, and Somerset's credit with the king was not as high as he appeared to believe. If he could be persuaded to discretion, however, 'he might have the king as his good lord and all he can reasonably desire'. Whalley was convinced of the earl's sincerity, and urged Cecil in the strongest terms to persuade Somerset to see reason;

Never leave him until you persuade him to some better consideration of his proceedings, and to concur with Warwick, who will be very plain with him at his coming to court ...[125]

---

[123] *Chronicle of Edward VI*, 24. Again, this seems to record the decision, which was implemented by the issue of licences to retain, starting on 12 Apr.

[124] SP10/10, no. 9.

[125] Ibid. Whalley was also seeking Lord Paget's support, which suggests that he may not have been reading the political signs very shrewdly.

Whalley's motivation in taking this line may not have been entirely pure, because he was angling for Warwick's patronage, but he seems to have been genuinely convinced of the earl's goodwill. During May and June Somerset attended formal council meetings but seldom, and Warwick, as far as the record shows, not at all. There is no doubt that Warwick was the head of the government; matters were referred to him, and his decision was awaited. Moreover, he was well enough informed to remonstrate indirectly with Somerset over his behaviour. He may have visited the north following his appointment as Warden, or he may have been suffering from real or imagined ailments; but there are no clear references to either of these circumstances. He was, allegedly, too ill to attend the wedding of his son to Anne Seymour, but neither the nature of his illness nor its duration are described. Except at times of crisis the minuted council meetings were seldom of much political significance, and it may well be that Warwick was maintaining a busy, if erratic presence at court without that showing on the register. However, early in July he seems to have changed his tactics and thereafter was a frequent, although not regular, attender.

By comparison with the previous year, the summer of 1550 was tranquil. Relations with the emperor continued to leave a good deal to be desired. One of Van der Delft's last actions before advancing sickness forced his recall was to renew his representations on behalf of the Princess Mary, whose unofficial dispensation to hear mass had been a bone of contention since the previous spring. Her personal relations with the Protector, and even more with the duchess of Somerset, had been amicable, but his fall had spared him from the painful necessity of having to be more rigorous in his enforcement of the law. In fact he had done his best to fudge the issue, which was good for Anglo-Imperial relations in the short term, but stored up trouble for the future.[126] Mary, who was not in any political sense aggressive, or even interested, undoubtedly abused Somerset's tolerance after Whitsun 1549, refusing to allow the authorized Prayer Book to be used in any of her residences.[127] By January 1550 Warwick had been forced to make it clear that this situation could not continue. The princess promptly denounced him to Van der Delft as 'the most unstable man in England', and ascribed his rise to power solely to envy and ambition.[128] Charles, who was not in the least reluctant to undermine a heretical government, instructed his ambassador to demand a full immunity guaranteed by letters patent. The council flatly rejected his demand, and the ambassador immediately began to find fault with the treaty of Boulogne complaining, wrongly, that

---

[126] Somerset clearly gave Van der Delft a verbal undertaking that Mary would continue to be allowed to hear mass in private. Disagreements then arose over what constituted 'private', and the Protector categorically refused to make any undertaking in writing, whereupon the ambassador accused him (repeatedly) of bad faith. The fullest account of these moves is in Loades, *Mary Tudor*, 134–70.

[127] Ibid. 145–6.   [128] *Cal. Span.*, x. 6–7.

it had encompassed Scotland without the emperor's permission.[129] Warwick probably was tougher than Somerset would have been on the subject of Mary's conformity, but in the circumstances he could hardly have given way to such thinly disguised bullying, and it must also be remembered that the young king was beginning to take a personal interest in his sister's intransigence. This was something that Mary could not, and would not, recognize, and she consequently developed an almost hysterical fear and hatred of Warwick, whom she chose to blame exclusively for her troubles over the next three years. In the short term she panicked, and insisted that Van der Delft get her out of the country. The ambassador was more impressed by her fears than his master, but the emperor eventually gave a grudging consent to Van der Delft's scheme to whisk her away from Woodham Walter, a small house which she had near Malden. The ambassador was recalled on 13 May, and was subsequently too ill to play any part, but his secretary, Jehan Dubois, attempted to carry out the operation on 30 June, at considerable personal risk. When it came to the point, however, Mary became suddenly irresolute and the opportunity was allowed to pass.[130] The council quickly learned of her abortive escape and tightened its local security arrangements with, it appears, the full co-operation of the local community.[131] So, intead of being safely deposited in Brussels as an imperial pensioner, the princess remained in England as a thorn in the council's flesh, and an increasingly bitter enemy of the earl of Warwick.

Parliament stood prorogued until the autumn, and by the end of July Somerset had made it clear that he was hoping to use the forthcoming session to reinstate some of the policies which had earlier been reversed. As Protector he had been extraordinarily successful in persuading both Houses to legislate measures which most of the members, as individuals, had no desire to see enforced. Whether he could have exercised similar powers of persuasion in the new situation must remain doubtful, but Warwick was not apparently minded to let him try. At some point between 14 August and 4 September, while Somerset was away from the court, he persuaded the council to defer the recall until January. On his return the duke attempted to get this decision reversed, but Warwick had his way and parliament did not eventually reconvene until January 1552. In view of the way events were to fall out, this has a sinister look about it, but the simple fact seems to have been that Warwick had got what he wanted out of the third session, and saw no need for another. By the end of August he may well have been suspicious of Somerset's motives, but even if he were not, he

---

[129] *Chronicle of Edward VI*, 26; *Cal. Span.*, x. 60–1, 71.

[130] Loades, *Mary Tudor*, 155–7. Dubois's complete report is *Cal. Span.*, x. 124–35.

[131] Dubois's report makes it clear that the watches had been increased, and, although the local people professed the greatest regard for Mary, they were deeply suspicious of the imperial warship which he kept lurking off the coast, and co-operated fully in the council's security precautions (*Cal. Span.*, x. 124–35).

might well have seen parliament as a means of reopening old wounds, and confusing the messages which the council was so concerned to spell out. Relations between the two peers were by this time cool and suspicious, but not overtly hostile. William Cecil, who replaced Nicholas Wotton as Principal Secretary on 5 September, was trusted by both, and formed an invaluable link between them.[132] Committed as he was to the unity and stability of the regime, he seems to have found himself in the role which Paget had occupied two years earlier. Somerset's motives in the autumn of 1550 are not easy to reconstruct. There were naturally those who thought that he was scheming to recover power. One of these was the new Imperial ambassador, Jehan Scheyfve, who reported in November that he was gathering supporters, and trying to revive his popularity with the Commons.[133] A French observer at the same time explained his enthusiasm for a new parliament on the grounds that he was intending to denounce Warwick for misgovernment, and mismanagement of the social and economic situation.[134] This last sounds more like speculation than information, and there is no hard evidence that the duke made any move to challenge Warwick in council. Indeed his lack of standing was spelled out in a manner which no sixteenth-century nobleman could have failed to understand when his mother, who was also the king's grandmother, was refused a state funeral and public mourning when she died in October.[135] Edward himself may well have been responsible for that decision, and Somerset made no recorded protest, but it was a straw in the wind which would not have encouraged any aspirations which he may have been nursing. He seems to have persisted in the delusion that the king was fond of him, and harboured a grudge against those who had supplanted him. In fact the reverse seems to have been the case, but it was a delusion which kept him at court, and kept him involved in public affairs when he could perfectly well have retired to his estates, the management of which would have benefited from more consistent application.

Warwick's motives are easier to assess. Having achieved supreme power, in fact if not in name, he needed above all to retain the confidence of the rapidly maturing king. Edward, now in his fourteenth year, was nobody's fool, and it could never be assumed that he had no independent sources of information. Any repetition of the upheavals of 1549, and above all any backsliding in terms of protestant reformation, and that confidence would be in jeopardy. There was no danger, as yet, of the boy trying to assert himself, but it was only a matter of time. It was important to keep a

[132] APC, iii. 118. Thomas Parry to William Cecil, 8 July 1550 (SP10/10, no. 12).

[133] Cal. Span., x. 186: 4 Nov. 1550.

[134] 'Relation de l'accusation et mort du Duc de Somerset' (Bibliothèque Nationale MS 15888, fos. 205–10); Jordan, Threshhold of Power, 78.

[135] APC, iii. 142–3; J. G. Nichols (ed.), The Literary Remains of King Edward VI (Roxburgh Club, 1857), i, pp. cxlviii–cxlix.

vigilant eye on the Privy Chamber, and the appointment of Henry Neville and Henry Sidney, later the husband of Warwick's daughter Mary, on 18 April, was a step in that direction.[136] It was also important not to allow the religious conservatives any grounds for complacency. Some members of the council had been wanting to come to terms with Gardiner during Warwick's absence from the board in June, a tendency which he quickly reined back when he reappeared. The articles which were eventually presented to the bishop of Winchester on 8 July were unacceptable by intention.[137] So far the aged and extremely conservative bishop of Durham, Cuthbert Tunstall, had avoided drawing attention to himself. He had opposed every step of the reformation since the early 1530s, but had always scupulously obeyed the law, and his experience of administration in the far north of England had appeared to make him indispensable. However, the virtual abandonment of English pretensions in Scotland early in 1550, and the absence of any signs of a Scottish counter-attack, provided a breathing space, and in August 1550 Warwick decided to move against the man who was effectively blocking all attempts to spread evangelical protestantism into the north-east of England. He was also occupying the richest see after Winchester. The occasion provided was trivial: a conspiracy by a shady lowland Scot named Ninian Menville, which the bishop had allegedly failed to bring to the attention of the council. Tunstall was sent for to London, and grilled by Warwick in person. On 16 September the earl wrote to Cecil:

The bishop has been here with me: I am sure he knows perfectly why he was sent for … I could not tell what to make of his reply; he seems full of perplexity and fear. No doubt the matter will touch him wonderfully, and yield the king as good a nest as the bishop of Winchester is like to do if the cards are true …[138]

It is perhaps not surprising that Martin Bucer at about the same time was doubting the sincerity of Warwick's evangelical zeal, but this was a case of killing two birds with one stone. Subsequent developments, although they do not show the earl in a creditable light, suggest that his motives were not quite as cynical as he made them appear.

Unlike Somerset, Warwick could pretend no kinship with the king to underpin his ascendancy in council. He had by this time acquired great wealth, but he was not an 'overmighty subject' in the fifteenth-century sense, with a large retinue at his back. Consequently he had to protect his position until the king came of age by the force of his personality, and by the effectiveness with which he conducted public policy. His personality was reluctantly testified by Van der Delft in March 1550 when he wrote that he was 'absolute master' of the council, who would do nothing without his

---

[136] *Chronicle of Edward VI*, 25.
[137] *APC*, iii. 67–9; G. Redworth, *In Defence of the Church Catholic*, 286–7.
[138] SP10/10, no. 31. The fullest accounts of Tunstall's troubles are given in Charles Sturge, *Cuthbert Tunstall* (London, 1938), 281–96, and D. Loades, 'The Last Years of Cuthbert Tunstall, 1547–1559', *Durham University Journal*, 66 (1973), 10–21.

permission, even when he was away sick or malingering.[139] The ambassador believed that his so-called illnesses were merely tricks designed to disorientate potential opponents and emphasize his own indispensability. The effectiveness of his policies is more a matter of opinion, but should not be judged with hindsight. As early as 3 February he began to address the problems of the coinage, when he had himself joined in commission with Sir William Herbert and Sir Walter Mildmay to take the accounts of the Mint officers 'and to declare how the fineness of the coin has been observed'. A second commission to the same group on the same day empowered them to make whatever changes they deemed to be necessary among the mint officers, and to devise new policies for bringing in bullion supplies.[140] The immediate objective seems to have been less to improve the quality of the coinage than to make sure that the profits of the mint came to the Crown instead of disappearing into the pockets of the officers. Hayward believed that the intention was to produce a profit of £24,000 a year, which would cover the expenses of Ireland and put £10,000 into the treasury.[141] It is very doubtful whether that sort of result was achieved, but the much criticized fiscal policies of the following year probably stemmed from the work of these commissions. Security was provided for partly by redeploying the garrison of Boulogne, partly by retaining the bands of German and Italian mercenaries which had been so effective during the previous summer, and partly by resorting to the old practice of licensed retaining. Between 12 April 1550 and 4 September licences were issued to eighteen separate noblemen and gentlemen to retain bands which varied in size from 24 to 100—a total of about 1,200 men.[142] These retainers were not intended to form a standing army, but to be available in small bands to deal swiftly with any 'stirs' which might arise—a 'rapid response' force, in fact. Sir John Gates, who was not one of those licensed, was sent down into Essex twice in 1550, in March and October, to arrest those responsible for spreading unrest, and a small force was sent down in June to strengthen the local watches after rumours of Mary's abortive escape began to circulate.[143] Towards the end of June there were 'great frays' in and around London, and the mayor increased the watches.[144]

This policy of containment worked extremely well, but the price of security was constant vigilance. The Act of November 1549 for the 'punishment of unlawful assemblies' gave the council a statutory basis for punitive and pre-emptive action. A series of proclamations in May 1550 attempted to clear vagabonds out of the City of London, and offered rewards to anyone whose information led to the arrest of those guilty of having 'conspired

[139] *Cal. Span.*, x. 43–4.
[140] *Cal. Pat.*, iii. 214, 216; C. E. Challis, *The Tudor Coinage* (Manchester, 1978), 103–4.
[141] Hayward, *Life and Raigne*, 126.   [142] *Cal. Pat.*, iii. 326–7.
[143] *Chronicle of Edward VI*, 37; *APC*, ii. 407; Jordan, *Threshold*, 63.
[144] *Chronicle of Edward VI*, 37.

divers and sundry evil facts and enterprises and disorders tending to rebellion …'. In the same month Sir Thomas Manners reported from Nottinghamshire that he had broken up a serious plot amongst the more substantial yeomanry of the county. In June Bartholomew Traheron declared that the country was seething with discontent, and further proclamations ordered all officers and soldiers to depart from London and return to their places of duty. Rumours and alarms were of almost daily occurrence, and magistrates spent a great deal of time and effort disentangling them and tracking down the spreaders of such stories. Individually they were often insignificant, but collectively they created a climate of uncertainty and instability which had to be taken seriously. Both in 1550 and in 1551 the summer months were plagued with such panics, and a number of people were imprisoned for having contributed to them, either by what they had said or by what they had written. Of actual insurrections or serious riots in these years, however, there is very little sign. Whether this was because the reports were exaggerated by apprehensive gentlemen, or because the precautions were actually effective, is not clear. Perhaps some of the rapporteurs were also not above embellishments intended to establish their own credentials, and zeal in the cause of public order. At the same time sheriffs also received instructions to make sure that conciliar and episcopal injunctions ordering the destruction of altars and the removal of images were enforced. However concerned the council may have been about unrest, it did not allow itself to be deflected from confrontational policies. In this, as in all other disciplinary and police work, the officers used their own retinues to overawe, outface, and occasionally defeat, intended resistance. Success, however, depended upon there being no obvious political divisions among the aristocracy themselves. As long as fear of the commons was stronger than personal, factional, or religious antipathies, such a system would continue to work. The danger which was beginning to appear at the end of 1550 was that Somerset's desire to recover his credit and public role might destroy that fragile unity.

Contrary to many expectations, the entente with France survived. Boundary commissioners were appointed by both sides to resolve the perennial disputes concerning the limitations of the Calais Pale, and although that great fortress was repaired, revictualled, and reinforced during the late summer and autumn the French, quite rightly, did not interpret this as indicative of aggressive intentions. In November the boundary commissions were renewed, and attempts were also made to tackle the intractable problem of Channel piracy.[145] By February 1551, however, the council was receiving contradictory advice which indicated a serious difference of opinion. Sir John Mason, the resident ambassador in Paris, was

---

[145] APC, iii. 156; *Calendar of State Papers, Foreign*, Edward VI, ed. W. Turnbull (London, 1861), 61–3.

convinced that Henry and his principal adviser, the Constable Anne de Montmorency, were honest in their professions of friendship, and although they were visibly preparing for war, the emperor was the only object of their aggression.[146] Mason's sympathy may well have been excited by the fact that, although the French king was a notorious persecutor of heretics, Mason was permitted to hold protestant services within his residence without challenge—a very marked contrast to the situation appertaining in Brussels. On the other hand Nicholas Wotton, not actually in France but an equally experienced diplomat, was writing at the same time that the French would prove unreliable friends, because Henry had not given up his desire to recover Calais. He would, in Wotton's opinion, dissemble until an opportunity arose to strike.[147] England's only real hope of international security lay in the friendship of the emperor. Unfortunately, this disagreement struck a sensitive nerve, because friendship with France was Warwick's policy, while Somerset and Paget continued to hanker after the imperial alliance which they had pursued before October 1549. In April Mason was replaced by Sir William Pickering. There was no particular significance in this because Mason was ill and Pickering was equally Warwick's nomination, but the change-over was accompanied by uneasy rumours in France that the English council was divided.[148] Somerset and his friends were in no position to force an issue, but their dissent was clearly known, and may well have been fostered by the imperial ambassador, who had nothing to lose by weakening the English government. On 23 April, however, Warwick scored a notable success. At the chapter of the Order of the Garter held on that day the successful candidates were Lord Clinton and the king of France.[149] Whatever the protocol, both were, in effect, his candidates, and Henry's acceptance of the honour seemed to prove that Mason had been right and Wotton wrong about his attitude to his 'brother of England'.

At the same moment an acrimonious row had broken out with the emperor over Richard Morison's right to use the English form of service. The reformation split was too recent for diplomatic conventions to have addressed this problem. Scheyfve enjoyed his mass in London, although it was contrary to English law, but Charles absolutely refused to extend a reciprocal courtesy to Morison. This was partly the ambassador's own fault. He was relatively inexperienced, and a protestant zealot who insisted on preaching at the emperor about the error of his ways.[150] This may have been

[146] Sir John Mason to the council, 7 Feb. 1551 (*Cal. For.*, 71–3); and 23 Feb. (ibid. 75–6); Wotton to Cecil, 2 Jan. 1551 (*HMC*, Salisbury MSS, i. 82).

[147] Ibid.

[148] *Chronicle of Edward VI*, 59. Pickering's appointment had been mooted in Jan., and his original credentials and instructions were dated 25 Feb. He actually departed on 11 Apr., and it was the end of June when Mason finally came home (*Cal. For.*, 76–7).

[149] *Chronicle of Edward VI*, 59.

[150] Emperor to Van der Delft, 7 Mar. 1551 (*Cal. Span.*, x. 238–41).

just foolishness, but in the circumstances it is hard to avoid a suspicion that he may have been secretly urged or at least tempted in that direction on Warwick's instructions. Morison's actions were formally disavowed by the council, and he was recalled, being replaced by the sympathetic Wotton. Nevertheless his tactlessness had sharply reduced the temperature of Anglo-imperial relations at a critical moment, and taken the wind out of the sails of the pro-Habsburg party. Nor was the issue allowed to go away. Wotton's style was very different from Morison's, and so were his opinions, but he was instructed to press the issue of the English service, and did so. He did not cease to be *persona grata* at the imperial court, but the prospect of a major improvement in relations had become remote by the summer of 1551.[151] Meanwhile the Anglo-French entente was progressing admirably. On 30 April the marquis of Northampton was commissioned, with a lavish entourage, to bear the Garter to France. Ten days later Montmorency expressed his master's gratification to Pickering, and indicated that a reciprocal mission would soon be setting off to deliver the order of St Michael to Edward.[152] Before either of these things actually happened, however, the council decided to capitalize on the warmth of the diplomatic climate by reviving Guidotti's marriage proposal of the previous year. On 21 May this negotiation was therefore added to Northampton's instructions, and he left for France the next day.[153] As a face-saving gesture, the marquis was to start by requiring French assistance to enforce the treaty of Greenwich, which everyone knew would be refused. Once that ritual had been completed, he was to request the hand of the 6-year-old Princess Elizabeth in his master's name, requesting a dot, or portion, of 12,000 marks a year and a dowry of 800,000 crowns.[154] This was, of course, a bargaining position. The French offered 100,000, and the negotiations went on throughout June. By the end of that month the English had come down to 600,000 and the French had gone up to 200,000. Interestingly neither side was seeking a full defensive alliance, and there seems to have been some apprehension on the English side that religious concessions might be demanded. Eventually, on 20 July, agreement was reached. Northampton had failed to get more than 200,000 crowns, but in every other respect he had got the treaty which the English council wanted.[155] It was no mean achievement, and sent shivers of apprehension through the imperial camp.

An immediate corrollary of this successful negotiation was the final resolution of the open-ended situation in Scotland. Warwick was realistic enough to realize that England's priority must be defensive. For the time being there was no challenging French ascendancy, nor any urgent need to

[151] Ibid. 255; Morison to the council, 30 June 1551 (*Cal. For.*, 135–7); council to Wotton and Morison, 15 Aug. 1551 (*Cal. For.*, 161).
[152] Ibid. 102–3; *Chronicle of Edward VI*, 62.   [153] Ibid. 63; *Cal. For.*, 107, 109.
[154] Ibid. For a full description of the negotiation, see Jordan, *The Threshold of Power*, 128–31.
[155] *Chronicle of Edward VI*, 74.

do so. Consequently when the French reinforced their presence in Scotland in February 1551 there was no reaction from the English council. Early in April a Franco-Scottish commission, headed by the sieur de Lansac, arrived to discuss outstanding issues and an English commission headed by Thomas Thirlby, the bishop of Norwich, was appointed to treat with them.[156] As the English council was prepared to surrender the few remaining strong points which were held in Scotland, and accept the neutralization of the debatable ground, there was little to squabble over. The English were under no pressure to lower their guard in the north, or to make any territorial concessions, and agreement was reached on 13 June.[157] Some detailed points of border delineation were left for future resolution, but Warwick had removed any lingering threat of war in the north at virtually no cost beyond the final abandonment of unreal aspirations which had already been defeated. Meanwhile Edward was enjoying himself hugely. It was not the distant prospect of a 6-year-old bride which excited him, but the arrival of the order of St Michael borne by the amiable and entertaining marquis de St André. Nobody was quite sure how the young king would cope. The council, in instructing Sir John Mason to convey Edward's extreme gratification to Henry, wrote

The King's Majesty's young nature being of such modesty that in his most gladness hath not much outward show thereof, and besides that His Majesty's French speech being not natural to him, cannot so abundantly express the joy of his heart as if he should have answered in his natural speech ...[158]

In the event, they need not have worried. St André and Boisdauphin were on a charm offensive, and they succeeded brilliantly. Having landed at Rye on 4 July, they were lavishly escorted across Kent by easy stages, reaching Gravesend on 9 July. Edward noted every step of their advance in his journal, but there was almost a last-minute hitch. The sweating sickness was so severe in London that the king had to make a hasty move to Hampton Court, and the French mission was forced to mark time at Durham Place and Richmond until 14 July, when the court was at last prepared to receive them.[159] The delay did no harm, and the unusual detail in which the king recorded every stage of their entertainment is a sufficient indication of his enthusiasm. Even the tricky question of religious celebrations was not allowed to spoil the fun;

[St André] came to present the Order of Micael; where, after with ceremonies accustomed he had put on the garments, he and Mons. Gye, likewise of the Order, came—one at my right hand, the other at my left—to the chapel where, after the communion celebrated, each of them kissed my cheek. After they dined with me and talked after dinner and saw some pastime ...[160]

[156] *APC*, iii. 252–3; *Chronicle of Edward VI*, 57–8.
[157] Ibid. 65; Rymer, *Foedera*, xv. 265–71.
[158] *Cal. For.*, 129; council to the marquis of Northampton, 16 June 1551.
[159] *Chronicle of Edward VI*, 71–2.   [160] Ibid. 72–3.

Presumably the Prayer Book rite was used as Edward could scarcely have tolerated anything else, especially while Mary was making such a fuss. St André was a big personal success. He dined and hunted with the king almost every day for the remainder of the month. When he left on 29 July, in addition to a generous public reward, Edward gave him 'a diamond from my finger, worth by estimation £150 both for his pains and also for my memory …'.[161] After leaving the court, the French envoys stayed one night with the earl of Warwick at Sheen before leaving for Boulogne. There is no record of what was discussed, but the symbolism of the gesture was appropriate.

One of the great advantages of this ceremonial diplomacy was that it kept everyone busy and out of mischief. At the end of November 1550 the duke of Somerset had been given a substantial sweetener at the expense of the bishop of Bath and Wells, who had been virtually ordered to hand over land to an annual value of £80. 2*s.* 11*d.* in Somerset, including the episcopal palace at Wells.[162] Nevertheless by February 1551 rumours of animosity between the duke and earl of Warwick were again rife. The earl of Shrewsbury reported to an unknown confidant on 17 February that he had been sounded out as to his feelings about the rival peers. He hoped that this did not indicate serious dissension, and observed sensibly that each had too much to lose to quarrel in public.[163] The root of the trouble seems to have lain, not with either of the principals, but with some who believed that they would stand to gain if Somerset were restored to power. One of these was the unstable Richard Whalley who, apparently having been rebuffed in his search for Warwick's patronage, was by early 1551 accused of canvassing support for a renewal of the Protectorate. He denied the charges, but the council was sufficiently concerned to commit him to prison.[164] Another was Sir Ralph Vane who picked a totally unnecessary quarrel with Warwick over pasture rights, and was foolish enough to threaten an affray with two or three hundred men, a disorder for which the council sent him to the Tower.[165] By April the rumours had taken a new twist. Somerset, it was said, would ally with the conservative peers who were increasingly offended with Warwick's continuing programme of protestant reform, and would retire to the north to gather his strength.[166] However, there is no real evidence, or even probability, that he ever had any such intention. The conservatives may not have liked Warwick's religious policies, but another political trial of strength was the worst of all possible options, as the earl of Shrewsbury's reaction demonstrates. Moreover the only evidence for Somerset's supposed conservative sympathies lies in his scepticism towards the charges against Tunstall, and his willingness to deal leniently with the bishop of Winchester. Virtually all these stories come from catholic and

---

[161] Ibid. 75.   [162] BL Royal MS 18 C 24, fo. 16ʳ: 29 Nov. 1550.
[163] BL Cotton MS Titus B II, 23, fo. 48.   [164] *APC*, iii. 215.
[165] Ibid. 244: 27 Mar. 1551.   [166] Jordan, *The Threshold of Power*, 83.

imperialist sources, several from the not very intelligent or well-informed Scheyfve, and these were the same people who had the greatest interest in stirring up trouble in England and destabilizing the regime. The regent of the Netherlands, Mary of Hungary, who had had many brushes with the English council over commercial disputes, was to write to Granvelle in October 1551:

We must, therefore, have a port in that country [England] at our disposal, either by force or through friendship. Many people are of the opinion that the kingdom ... would not be impossible to conquer, especially now that it is a prey to discord and poverty ...[167]

There is no reason to suppose that the emperor, sick and facing another war with France, would have wished to commit resources to such an enterprise. However, if the English began to fight among themselves, then Mary's safety, to which Charles had a strong commitment, might provide a pretext for some appropriate gallant to do the emperor's work for him.

It seems that there are three persons who might try their fortune, conquer the country, and marry our cousin ... under colour of taking the king out of the hands of his pernicious governors ... If they had already got rid of the king we could intervene with the pretext of avenging him, or some other excuse easily to be devised.

Jealousy and mutual antagonism between Somerset and Warwick was therefore ideal grist to the imperial mill, as Scheyfve's dispatches make clear.

If Somerset ever entertained serious ambitions of recovering his lost power, he had certainly abandoned them by the summer of 1551, although not necessarily with a good grace. However popular he may have been with the Commons, and however busy agents like Whalley may have been on his behalf, he had no serious political following. By the autumn of 1551 the danger which he represented was rather different. As John Hayward was to put it:

the Duke of Somerset was thought fit to be taken away, whose credit was so great with the common people, that although it sufficed not to beare out any bad attempt of his owne, yet it was of force to crosse the evill purposes of others ...[168]

An opinionated and extremely obstinate man, he was prepared to go on campaigning against the French alliance, and against other aspects of Warwick's policies, even though there was no prospect of reviving the Protectorate. In other words, his challenge was negative rather than positive. If he could not exercise supreme power himself, he could inhibit its effective use by anyone else. This was a challenge which Warwick could not afford to tolerate. His government was already perceived to be weak wherever

---

[167] *Cal. Span.*, x. 378–9: 8 Oct. 1551. Mary was very much the active partner in the Habsburg team at this time, but she did not control sufficient resources to have pursued a policy of this kind independently.

[168] Hayward, *Life and Raigne*, 137.

imperial propaganda had currency, and if England was to avoid becoming a mere punchbag in the impending Franco-Imperial conflict, then he had to avoid divisions and disputes within the council. Ironically, he was caught in rather a similar dilemma to that which had afflicted Somerset over his brother. Seymour had not been a serious rival for the Protectorate, but he had represented a challenge which could not be ignored. Leniency would have invited contempt; severity attracted charges of fratricide. Unlike Seymour, however, Somerset had not acted with the kind of irresponsibility which would have presented his enemies with an opportunity. In August relations were apparently harmonious, and in September Somerset spent much time at home on his sickbed. By the end of that month Warwick had clearly decided that his former friend had become too serious a threat to be tolerated. The only option was to remove him at the first plausible opportunity, and such an opportunity lay ready to hand in the bizarre stories which were beginning to circulate at court during Somerset's absence. Ostensibly the source of these stories was an unreliable adventurer called Sir Thomas Palmer, who was a client of Warwick's.[169] In fact they may well have originated with Warwick himself, who subsequently confessed to having framed his victim. Rightly or wrongly, Warwick had concluded that England's security, both international and domestic, depended upon having a single, unchallenged source of power. On 11 October 1551 he was elevated to the dukedom of Northumberland, and on 16 October the duke of Somerset was arrested upon a charge of high treason.

One of the reasons why it had been necessary to remove Somerset from the Protectorate had been that the country could not afford him. Between 1542 and 1547 Henry VIII had spent some £2,100,000 on warfare. This enormous expenditure he had attempted to cover in a number of ways. Unusually generous parliaments had contributed some £656,000 in lay and clerical subsidies; about £700,000 had come from the sale of former monastic property, and £270,000 through the unpopular device of the forced loan. The remaining half-million or so had come partly from commercial loans raised in Antwerp and partly from the debasement of the coinage, which contributed £363,000 to the Exchequer in rather less than two years.[170] When he died, Henry's actual debts had not been enormous: £100,000 in Antwerp and about half as much at home, but the political price had been heavy. Another subsidy in the immediate future was out of the question, as was a fresh loan. The Exchequer had lost £75,000 a year in income from monastic lands, and debasement had caused a rapid surge in inflation, which contributed significantly to the social tensions of the following years. Consequently Somerset's decision to press ahead with the war in Scotland had serious implications. Between 1547 and 1549 military expenditure ran

---

[169] See above, for Palmer's misadventure in Scotland, which seems to have been the root of his animus against Somerset (*Chronicle of Edward VI*, 86–8, and above, pp. 110–11).

[170] D. Loades, *Lectures on the Reign of Edward VI* (Bangor, 1994), 130–1.

at about £580,000, not counting £30,000 a year for the defence of Boulogne, and rather more on the navy. The extraordinary expenditure for each of those years was thus in the region of £350,000, against an ordinary income of £150,000. The Protector's ingenious but unpopular tax on sheep, which was designed to circumvent opposition by taxing new wealth, produced less than £100,000, and the main expedients were once again the sale of Crown lands and the mint. Somerset extracted about £280,000 from further debasement, with the result that by 1550 the pound sterling had collapsed from 26s. Flemish on the exchanges, to 13s. Flemish.[171] A protracted war with France was therefore out of the question, and it is not surprising that Warwick took immediate steps to cut his losses over Boulogne. The withdrawal of that garrison not only effected a substantial saving, but the French redemption payments provided an extremely useful cash float which could be used to cover some of the debt. It is probably no coincidence that on 18 May the council was able to bring forward the repayment of £20,000 out of the £54,000 which was owed to the Fuggers, and thus secure the continuance of the balance at no more than 12 per cent.[172] Faced with the need to find about £26,000 a year in order to service existing debts, Warwick naturally turned to the City of London for expert advice. Unfortunately the first person he went to was his friend John York. In early October 1550 York proposed an ingenious and obscure scheme, which seems to have involved speculating on the Antwerp exchange, using debased English coin which had been specially minted for the purpose. This device may have been similar to that which was to be successfully employed by Thomas Gresham a little later. Gresham fed small amounts of sterling on to the market on a daily basis, thus creating a controlled shortage, and hence a demand. However, Gresham used coin of good quality, and York's project probably foundered upon the over-clever device of unloading base metal. The syndicate of which York was the head also had the misfortune to be caught trying to make an illegal export of £4,000 worth of bullion in April 1551.[173] Diplomatic embarrassment was thus added to a financial loss which eventually amounted to almost £10,000.

Somerset had carried out a major issue of base coin in July 1549, and Warwick's advisers in the City had left him in no doubt about the detrimental effects of such a course. However their own short-term remedy had failed, and by April 1551 he was looking around for alternative expedients. To restore confidence and to curb the activities of forgers, both at home and abroad, a new issue of sound weight and content was required, but that

---

[171] H. Buckley, 'Sir Thomas Gresham and the Foreign Exchanges', *Economic Journal*, 34 (1924), 595–6; Loades, *Edward VI*, 134.

[172] *APC*, iii. 33.

[173] *Chronicle of Edward VI*, 48–9; SP10/10, no. 45: 6 Oct. 1550; *Cal. Span.*, x. 264; Challis, *Tudor Coinage*, 104–5. Some parts of these transactions also appear in Cotton MS Caligula E IV, fo. 292 ff.

would only be effective if it could be accompanied by the redemption of all base coin, a process which the council believed it could not afford. Instead a complex manœuvre was attempted, whereby a further base issue, designed to yield a profit of £160,000, would be immediately followed by a proclamation 'crying down' the value of all base coin. Thus it was intended to pay some of the king's debts and to restore confidence at the same time. The result was a fiasco. The fresh coinage went ahead at an unprecedented level of baseness: a silver content of no more than 30 per cent.[174] At the same time, on 30 April, a proclamation was issued reducing the value of the base teston, or shilling, from 12*d.* to 9*d.*, and of the groat from 4*d.* to 3*d.*[175] Since, however, this devaluation was not due to take place until 30 August, prices immediately began to rise as tradesmen sought to protect themselves. On 10 May the Lord Mayor of London and a selection of aldermen were summoned to the council and given a dressing-down for this inevitable reaction:

tooching the misdemeanour of the merchantes within the same [City], who even nowe upon a kinde of mallice or gredinesse of gayne, in contempt of the Proclamation made for the reformeng of the coyne … have sodainely raysed the prises of all thinges to a mervaylouse rekening …[176]

Such admonition was worse than useless, and the confusion continued until, on 1 July, in an attempt to stabilize the situation, the sheriffs were issued with sealed instructions to bring forward the date of devaluation to 8 July, that is, with immediate effect.[177] Finally, on 16 August the shilling was 'cried down' to 6*d.*, and inflationary pressure eased. Warwick and his advisers knew what had to be done, but they did not know how to go about it, and made the mistake of trying to extract one final profit from a policy which they knew to be discredited, and which they had every intention of abandoning.

As a result they were given little credit, either at the time or subsequently, for ending the exploitation of the English coinage. On 5 October a new issue of coin was authorized with the silver content at 11 oz. 1 dwt. fine, a quality not seen since 1544.[178] When the problem of redemption was approached by seeking to persuade people to surrender two base shillings for one fine one, however, confidence was so low that they preferred to cling to the base issue. As a result, by the end of the year the bad coin had driven the good out of circulation, and the issue remained unresolved. There was, however,

---

[174] This move is particularly surprising in view of the fact that York was already experimenting with an issue of 11 oz. fine. In fact this base issue was aborted after only about half the planned issue had been made. Whether this reflected divided councils or a sudden change of circumstance is not clear (Challis, *Tudor Coinage*, 104–7).

[175] Hughes and Larkin, *Tudor Royal Proclamations*, i. 518–19.   [176] *APC*, iii. 272.

[177] SP10/13, no. 29.

[178] *Chronicle of Edward VI*, 80–1; Challis, *Tudor Coinage*, 109–10; Hughes and Larkin, *Tudor Royal Proclamations*, i. 535–6.

no return to debasement, and the foundations of recovery had been laid. The necessary recoinage did not finally take place until Elizabeth's reign, but the policy of the council in 1551 was inept and misguided rather than 'utterly irresponsible', as it has been recently described. Warwick's declared financial strategy was unexceptionable. Regular income must cover regular expenditure, and the king's debts must be liquidated. However, it was too optimistic to assume that there was a short cut to such a goal.

By the end of 1551 the most pressing problem was the adverse exchange rate. The general financial situation, although not healthy, was by no means as adverse as has sometimes been represented. A survey taken in December declared a net ordinary income of £168,000 a year, and an ordinary expenditure of £131,000. This gives a misleading impression of solvency, because extraordinary expenditure was running at £200,000 a year, and income at a mere £130,000, leaving a total deficit of nearly £40,000.[179] The Crown debt, both at home and abroad, stood at about £250,000. However, such sums were trivial, both in absolute and relative terms, when compared to the indebtedness of Henry II or the emperor, and Edward could still borrow in Antwerp at 12 per cent, despite the lamentations of his merchants. Apart from his final flirtation with debasement, Warwick seems to have approached a very difficult financial situation with an honest determination to get it under control, although no very good idea of how to set about it. He also had to balance the economic imperative against the need to maintain England's defences in a hostile world. The continuing extraordinary expenditure was almost entirely military. The navy, for example, once supposed to have been left to 'rot at its moorings' after the treaty of Boulogne, was in fact maintained in full working order at a cost of over £20,000 a year.[180] When the last of Somerset's Scottish garrisons was abandoned in 1550, the whole border was thoroughly surveyed by Sir Robert Bowes, and the main English defences at Berwick and Carlisle strengthened. There were serious doubts about the competence and reliability of the northern levies, raised through 'border tenure' to carry out this work, and the garrison troops were brought up from the south, with a stiffening of German and Italian mercenaries. All this imposed a great strain upon the Exchequer, but nothing like as great as that of waging war, and when Franco-Imperial hostilities were renewed in September 1551, the English council could reasonably congratulate itself on its degree of detachment from the combatants. Having failed to obtain an extension of the Anglo-Imperial treaty of 1543 to cover Boulogne, after that city had been surrendered, Edward made it clear that he did not consider himself to be bound by the

---

[179] Loades, *Edward VI*, 132. The assessment of debt in Dec. 1551 is contained in Lansdowne MS 2, fo. 125. A report of Mar. 1552 was to estimate ordinary income at £272,000 and expenditure at £235,000. See also below, pp. 212–13.

[180] D. Loades, *The Tudor Navy* (Aldershot, 1992), 154–6.

treaty, although he professed his willingness to negotiate a new one.[181] Nor, in spite of the marriage treaty, was there any military alliance with France. Consequently, in the autumn of 1551 the council could concentrate upon domestic affairs in the secure knowledge that England's defences were adequate to deter any opportunist aggression, and that there was no need to prepare for involvement in any continental adventures.

All this, however, depended upon the preservation of domestic order and stability, and that in turn depended upon strong leadership. By deliberately taking the office of Lord President of the council, rather than Protector or Lord Treasurer, Dudley imposed an additional strain on himself. He did this, it seems clear, in order to bring the young king forward as he began to approach his majority, so that no sudden changes would be needed when Edward assumed personal responsibility for his government. This, of course, would work to Warwick's personal advantage, and that of his clients, but it would also benefit the realm if a power struggle following the king's eighteenth birthday could be avoided. In order to achieve this, he needed two things, a good personal relationship with Edward, which could adapt to the boy's developing personality, and effective control over the patronage network. During the Protectorate he had benefited considerably from Somerset's patronage, and so had several other peers who eventually turned against him. After January 1550 Warwick could reward himself, his family, and his supporters at will, but that in itself would not be sufficient. The indiscriminate distribution of largesse could not purchase loyalty, but ruthlessness could deter opposition. Part of Somerset's problem had been that his personality offended, but did not intimidate. He excited annoyance and distress rather than fear. Warwick's outburst to the council in December 1549 had caused consternation. In January 1551 he launched a fierce missive at Lord Paget, concerning some threat to the king's security which cannot now be identified:

God preserve our Master. If he should fail there is watchers enough that would bring it in question, and would burden you and other (who will not understand the danger) to be destroyers of the whole body of the realm. With one instrument forged to execute your malicious meanings …[182]

Since the 'other' are named as the Lord Treasurer, the Lord Chancellor, and the Lord Privy Seal, Jordan deduced a serious split in the council.[183] However, that cannot be demonstrated. Paget never enjoyed Warwick's confidence after December 1549, and eventually fell from grace for his continued association with Somerset; but the earls of Wiltshire and Bedford are otherwise known as allies of Warwick, both before and after this outburst. Consequently, too much should not be read into these fits of irascibility; they may even have been a technique designed to keep his

---

[181] *Chronicle of Edward VI*, 134–5.   [182] BL Cotton MS Titus B II, fo. 38.
[183] Jordan, *The Threshold of Power*, 51.

colleagues on their toes. Former opponents who had withdrawn from the fray were treated without malice. The chagrin which apparently tormented Southampton's last months was self-induced, and not the result of any further action by the council. The earl of Arundel had £8,000 of his fine remitted in January 1551, and there was no protracted campaign of terror in Norfolk following the defeat of Kett.[184] On the other hand individuals arrested on suspicion of attempting to provoke 'stirs' were sometimes treated with great severity. In September 1551 Lord Clinton wrote to Cecil about the need for extreme vigilance and sharp measures of correction, while in Northamptonshire at about the same time a man named Appleyard was executed when the Solicitor-General, Sir Edward Griffin, threatened to take the jury before Star Chamber if they failed to convict, an action which greatly offended Sir Robert Stafford, who seems to have been Appleyard's patron.[185]

Warwick undoubtedly set out to be a hard man, on the grounds that trouble was better deterred or prevented than allowed to develop. Commissions of Lieutenancy, issued for the first time in April 1551, contained provision for the use of martial law against the civilian population.[186] As far as I know those clauses were never invoked, but they were a fair reflection of the council's determination not to allow dissension to escalate for lack of vigilance. He also recruited a clientage of soldiers with reputations for tough and unscrupulous action. One such was Sir John Gates, who became Vice-Chamberlain on 8 April 1551, and was sworn of the council two days later; another was Sir Thomas Palmer, who had narrowly escaped punishment for his foolhardiness in Scotland, and who was to play a shady part in the final fall of Somerset. The French mercenary captains, Berteville and Ribaut, should also be placed in this category. At the same time it would be a serious mistake to overemphasize this aspect of Warwick's personality. He was not running a clientage of bully-boys, in the manner of the Beauforts or the Bonviles in the previous century, and was never accused of maintaining wrongdoers to the detriment of the king's justice. Nor did he attempt to conduct the processes of government through a private council, as the Protector was accused of doing. Of the eight appointments to the council for which he was responsible between May 1550 and September 1551, four were established peers—the earls of Huntingdon and Westmorland and Lords Clinton and Cobham—while three of the others were diplomats and administrators of undoubted ability—Sir William Cecil, Sir Philip Hoby, and Sir Robert Bowes. Only Sir John Gates could be regarded as a personal follower. Cecil's appointment as Principal Secretary was of par-

---

[184] *Chronicle of Edward VI*, 51.   [185] Jordan, *The Threshold of Power*, 68–9.
[186] *APC*, iii. 258–60. The military functions of these Lieutenancies gave them the right to invoke the martial law *ex officio* (G. S. Thompson, *Lords Lieutenant in the Sixteenth Century* (London, 1923), 149–50; BL Add. Charter 981, relating to the county of Warwick).

ticular significance, because he had to overcome the handicap of having been equally close to the Protector.[187]

The one characteristic which all those advanced by the earl of Warwick appeared to share was protestantism. When he was appointed Lord Great Master of the household in February 1550, his patent specifically referred to his 'constancy in the Christian religion, bravery in war, sedition and tumult, and fidelity towards the king …',[188] and the radical preacher John Hooper, in the euphoria of realizing that the mass was not going to be restored in the winter of 1549–50, described him as 'that intrepid soldier of Christ'. As we have seen, Warwick's theological understanding was un-sophisticated, and during 1550 there began to be signs that he was getting out of step with his erstwhile partner, Cranmer. There were three episcopal appointments in that year, the orthodox Nicholas Ridley to London in place of the deprived Bonner, John Ponet to Rochester in place of Ridley, and the diplomat Thomas Thirlby to Norwich. None of these was contro-versial, but on 15 May the council decided to offer the vacant see of Gloucester to John Hooper.[189] Hooper was a mighty preacher, and for that reason found favour with the king, but it was Warwick who promoted his case in council. The offer was declined. Hooper, who was a cross-grained, cantankerous man, found fault with the recently issued *Ordinal*, com-plained about the 'shameful and impious' form of oath which he would be required to take, and objected to the 'Aaronic habits' which he would be required to wear.[190] Cranmer, whose credentials as a reformer were thus being challenged, was not amused, but the council, influenced by War-wick, went out of its way to reassure him that they would not require him to do anything burdensome to his conscience, and on 5 August the king wrote personally to the archbishop, asking him to waive the offensive requirements.[191] Given his Erastian principles, Cranmer could hardly have resisted, but fortunately for him Hooper had no political sense. Convinced that he had the backing of the king and council he decided to undermine the archbishop's 'prelatical' authority still further. As concessions were made, his scruples became more numerous and more profound. In the dis-pute which followed Cranmer's main support came from Nicholas Ridley, and he seems to have had little backing in the council, because the logic of the royal supremacy left no room for the Church to insist upon what the king had dispensed. However, Hooper made the mistake of becoming a nuisance. His railing against the *Ordinal* was provoking scandal, and the council imposed silence on both parties. That injunction Hooper ignored, seeking to recruit the support of the most respected continental divines working in England, Peter Martyr and Martin Bucer, and publishing his

[187] Hoak, *King's Council*, 61–71.   [188] *Cal. Pat.*, iii. 189.   [189] *APC*, iii. 31.

[190] Hooper to Bullinger, 29 June 1550, *Original Letters Relative to the English Reformation 1531–1558*, ed. Hastings Robinson (Parker Society, 1846–7), i. 87.

[191] Jordan, *The Threshold of Power*, 294.

Confession of Faith in January 1551.[192] As his principal backer, Warwick had already warned him that his behaviour was becoming intolerable, and on 27 January he was committed to the Fleet. Hooper submitted, and was consecrated in due form in March 1551, so the honours were eventually even, but the episode did not improve relations between Warwick and Cranmer.

For whatever reason, and theological convictions do not appear to have been among them, the earl was steadily moving into a more radical religious position than that of the establishment which he had helped to create. Part of the explanation for this probably lay in the increasingly clear views of the young king himself. With all an adolescent's capacity for running to extremes, by 1551 he was thoroughly intolerant of anything which he chose to regard as 'popery'. In December 1550 he began to take a personal interest in the continued recalcitrance of his sister Mary, and the letter which the council wrote to her on the 25th of that month was more than half protestant sermon. A month later the king followed this up with a second letter, partly in his own hand, upbraiding her for her behaviour, an epistle which caused her great distress, but did nothing to weaken her resolution.[193] However, a more important consideration in determining Warwick's attitude was probably disagreement over the nature of the episcopate. Cranmer and Ridley believed that a suitably endowed bench was necessary for the proper functioning of the Church. This was not a matter of preserving status and authority, but of having adequate resources to support scholarship, poor candidates for the priesthood, and charitable enterprises of all kinds. Cranmer had admonished Henry VIII of this need after the dissolution of the monasteries, not entirely without success. Since 1547, however, he had seen the chantries go the same way, most of their revenues ending up in the hands of royal stewards, or of the king's lay servants. By 1551 the bishops themselves were under pressure to exchange lands for spiritual revenues, and to grant out rich properties on long leases to favoured courtiers. The radicals regarded this process with equanimity. Bishops, they argued, if they were necessary at all, should be 'unlorded'. Like any other pastor, a bishop should have no more resources than were necessary to support his ministry of teaching and preaching. This was an attitude which strongly appealed to a man who was not only keenly aware of the pressures upon the Exchequer, but also acquisitive by nature, and surrounded by equally acquisitive supporters. The Docquet Book tells its own story:

13 November (1550)	Confirmation to Sir Thomas Speke in fee simple of the manor and burgage of Paynton in Devon, sold to him by John, bishop of Exeter by indenture dated 21 December 3

---

[192] *APC*, iii. 136, 191; Micronius to Bullinger, 13 Oct. 1550, *Original Letters*, ii. 571–3.
[193] J. Foxe, *The Acts and Monuments of the English Martyrs*, ed. S. R. Cattley and George Townsend (London, 1837–41), vi. 11–12; *Cal. Span.*, x. 209–12.

	Edward VI, with the assent of the Dean and Chapter and release of the king's rights.
29 November	A licence to the bishop of Bath and Wells to give, grant and alienate to Edward, Duke of Somerset in fee simple all the site, circuit and precinct of the chief mansion called the palace of the bishops at Wells in Somerset, with divers other lands to the value of £80 2s. 11d. to be held by fealty only.
7 January (1551)	A letter to the bishop of Bristol all excuses setting apart that he will send one up to the council to give order on his behalf for his sufficient recompense of the manor of Tye, who hath with vain excuses (as the Kinges Majestie was enformed) abused his highness.[194]

Both the substance and the tone of these representative entries is self-explanatory. Similarly when John Ponet accepted the see of Winchester in March 1551, he was allocated a salary of 2,000 marks, and surrendered lands to the value of £3,000 a year to the Crown. As we have seen, Warwick's pursuit of the bishop of Durham was motivated by a similar ambition. There is no reason to suppose that he had undergone a Zwinglian conversion. His interests, and those of his secular supporters, corresponded with those of Hooper, Knox, and Ponet over this issue, and an alliance of convenience was formed.

Warwick never attempted to pay himself the enormous salary which Somerset had received. The office of Lord President of the council does not seem to have carried any traditional fee, and the Great Mastership of the Household only £100 per annum, in addition to bouge of court and suitable accommodation.[195] While he was Lord Admiral he received 200 marks a year, together with various perquisites and allowances. On 27 May 1550 a patent was issued to Warwick for the offices of 'governor' of the county of Northumberland, and Warden of the East and Middle Marches, with the very substantial fee of £1,000 a year. However, it appears that this appointment never took effect, because upon 19 July the council noted

forasmuch as it was not thought convenient that the Earl of Warwick should, according to the former order, go into the north, but rather for many urgent considerations attend upon the king's person ...[196]

Therefore it was resolved that Sir Robert Bowes should remain at his post. The reason for this change of mind can easily be deduced, because it coincides with a renewal of tension between Warwick and the duke of Somerset, and the former probably decided that it was not an appropriate time to undergo a period of voluntary exile from the court. So he forfeited his £1,000 a year, at least for the time being. Significantly, Warwick's renewed

---

[194] BL Royal MS 18 C 24, fos. 7ʳ, 16ʳ, 29ʳ.   [195] PRO LC5/182.
[196] *Cal. Pat.*, 404; *APC*, iii. 88.

interest in the north coincided almost exactly with the final fall of his rival. Somerset was arrested on 16 October, and on 20 October a patent was issued to the duke of Northumberland as Warden-General of the Marches, with a yearly fee of 2,000 marks.[197] This time the appointment did take effect, and the fee was paid, but he did not reside continuously upon his cure. During the two years from the autumn of 1549 to the autumn of 1551 the earl of Warwick enjoyed the income from a large number of small fees attached to a variety of offices, but they formed only a minor part of his income. Unlike his predecessor he was not rewarding himself in cash from fees and annuities, but in land.

Warwick's transactions in land during this period were large-scale, and not always easy to interpret. For example in January 1550 he sold the castle, lordship, manor, and town of Warwick, by which he had earlier set such store, to the king—only to receive them back on 25 July as part of an exchange package worth £473. 5s. 7d. a year.[198] He sold lands, not only to the king, but also to Somerset, Sir John York, and others, often in small parcels. The augmentations records show a very substantial exchange by request in January 1550, involving mainly lands in Oxfordshire, Berkshire, and Hertfordshire; a second in March 1551 exchanging the manor and park of Esher for the manor of Chelsea; and a third in May 1551 by which he surrendered the manors of Langley and Burford in Oxfordshire, and obtained that of Otford in Kent.[199] Two undated grants in Warwickshire and Staffordshire may also belong to this period. By far the greatest acquisition, however, and the most significant, came in connection with his abortive appointment to the East and Middle Marches. As early as 8 April the king had noted 'My Lord of Warwick made General Warden of the North [sic] … and had granted to him a thousand marks of land …'. This was duly honoured on 20 May with a very extensive grant covering Prudhoe, Warkworth, and Rothbury in Northumberland, to a total value of £693. 6s. 10d.[200] This does not appear to have been cancelled, nor the lands subsequently surrendered in spite of the non-implementation of the appointment. This important extension of his holdings into the far north-east seems to have been the only shift of focus of any importance. By 1550 Warwick held land in about half the English counties, as well as some in Wales, and although he still regarded the West Midlands as in some sense his 'country', he made no particular effort to build up a power base there, either for himself or his clients.

Many of Warwick's minor acquisitions similarly seem to make no particular sense in terms of a power strategy. For example, he received the offices of keeper of the park at Esher and lieutenant of the chase at Hampton Court,

[197] *Cal. Pat.*, iv. 195.   [198] Ibid., iii. 71; ibid. 364.
[199] PRO E318/2046; 2050; 2043. See also the summary and particulars of a gift from the king on 20 May 1550, and a further substantial grant of lands in Northumberland on 14 Feb. 1551; E318/2049, 1819.
[200] Edward VI, *Chronicle*, 24; *Cal. Pat.*, iii. 371.

just a few months before he exchanged Esher for Chelsea.[201] In a fairly typical award he picked up seven minor local offices, none of them paying more than ten pounds a year, but collectively useful, especially as he received them in survivorship with his elder son. For the subsidy of the third year of Edward VI he was assessed on goods worth £400, while the duke of Somerset was assessed on £1,500,[202] but that should not be taken as an indication of their relative wealth. After Somerset's fall, Warwick was probably the richest, as well as the most powerful, man in England. The search for 'worship', however, still drove him as it had done earlier in his career. On 17 April 1551 he was created Earl Marshall of England, an office of no political significance, and no great profit, but of immense prestige.[203] Having married his eldest son to Anne Seymour in June 1550, it must have been with a sense of frustration that he allowed his fifth son, Robert, to wed Sir John Robsart's daughter, Amy, a few days later.[204] Sir John Robsart was a Norfolk gentleman of reasonable substance but no court connections, and his family was not of the kind that one would have expected to find picking up the younger Dudleys. A love match is the obvious explanation, but Warwick may also have been not unwilling to acquire a kinsman in a county where, otherwise, he had little influence. He certainly did not enrich his family unduly at the expense of the Crown. His brother Andrew, having held a number of minor court and military appointments, was appointed Keeper of the Jewels in the Palace of Westminster in January 1551, an office which carried a fee of 100 marks.[205] Andrew also received a single gift of land, worth £180 a year, on 25 September 1551.[206] Lord Lisle had a survivorship interest in some of his father's minor offices, but apart from that the Dudley family fortunes were very much concentrated in its head. The charges later made that he enriched his friends are more substantial, as we shall see. In this period the marquises of Dorset and Northampton, and Lord Clinton, were particular beneficiaries, and apart from Clinton their services seem to have been fairly notional. Household appointments, annuities, and minor grants to useful men, like William Cecil and Jean Ribaut, were frequently used to build up and retain his clientage. Some knighthoods were used for the same purpose, and when Sir Thomas Darcy became Lord Chamberlain in April 1551 he was created Lord Darcy of Chiche.[207] However, until the autumn of 1551 considerable restraint was exercised, after the crop of creations which had followed the defeat of Arundel and Southampton in January 1550. Then, in the few days preceding the arrest of the duke of Somerset, there was a fresh round, headed by Warwick's own elevation to the dukedom of Northumberland. The last successful *coup* of the reign was taking place.

---

[201] BL Royal MS 18 C 24, fo. 26ᵛ.   [202] PRO E179/69/75.   [203] *Cal. Pat.*, iv. 126.
[204] *Chronicle of Edward VI*, 33. This was to be a marriage of great significance a few years later.
[205] BL Royal MS 18 C 24, fo. 27ʳ.   [206] SP10/19; Beer, *Northumberland*, 186.
[207] *Cal. Pat.*, iv. 138.

5

Duke of Northumberland, 1551–1553

THE Tudors commonly signalled important shifts in policy, or in the structure of power, with clusters of peerage creations or promotions. Henry VIII had done it in 1514, 1525, and again in 1529. The earl of Hertford had done it on securing the Protectorate in February 1549, and the earl of Warwick after disposing of his rivals in January 1550. In October 1551 the second and final fall of the duke of Somerset was immediately preceded by three promotions and one new creation of the greatest significance. The creation was that of Sir William Herbert, Master of the Horse and President of the Council in the Marches of Wales, as earl of Pembroke, a title which his grandfather had held until his death in 1469.[1] The promotions were William Paulet, earl of Wiltshire and Lord Treasurer, to be marquis of Winchester, Henry Grey, marquis of Dorset, to be duke of Suffolk, a title made available by the tragic deaths of the two young Brandons in July,[2] and John Dudley, earl of Warwick, to be duke of Northumberland. The king's journal also records 'Mr. Sidney, Mr. Neville, Mr. Cheke, all three of the Privy Chamber, made knights. Also Mr. Cecil, one of the two chief secretaries.'[3] The ceremonial was splendid and traditional. Suffolk was created first, followed by Northumberland, the same order being followed in each case:

First proceeded the officers of Arms in their robes of arms. Then Garter brought the patent upright in his hand. Then Sir George Brooke, Knight of the Order, Lord Cobham, bearing upright in his hand a verge of gold [placed the mantle and girdle on the candidate] … then his hood turned down again about his neck, and the label plucked out over his mantle, then his mantle open on the right side, with his hand put forth [the] same side, and over that his collar of the Garter. Then followed Sir Henry Manners, Earl of Rutland, in his robes bearing the caps crowned or coronets, and after him Sir John Russell, Earl of Bedford, Lord Privy Seal in like manner bearing the sword, the pomell upwards in the sheath. The Sir Henry Grey, Knight of the Order, Lord Marquis of Dorset in his robes of estate, led between Sir Edward Seymour, Knight of the Order, Duke of Somerset, on the right hand, and Sir William

---

[1] William Herbert was the son and heir of Richard Herbert of Ewyas, Hereford, an illegitimate son of the first earl of Pembroke.

[2] Henry Brandon died of the sweating sickness in Cambridge on 14 July 1551, aged about 16. His brother Charles, two years his junior, died the same day. Their half-sister, Frances, the daughter of Mary Tudor, was Henry Grey's wife.

[3] W. K. Jordan (ed.), *The Chronicle and Political Papers of King Edward VI* (London, 1970), 86.

Parr, Knight of the Order, Marquis of Northampton and Great Chamberlain of England on his left hand, and so proceeded forward until they came afore the King's Majesty into the Chamber of Presence, and after three reverent obeisances done, the said lords standing and the said Marquis kneeling, Garter delivered the Letters Patent to the Lord Chamberlain, Lord Darcy, who delivered them unto the king, and he gave them to Mr. Secretary Cecil to read, who read them openly ...[4]

At the appropriate words in the text, the sword, orb, and coronet were given to the new duke, followed by the copy of his patent and the grant of his £40 fee. Warwick was supported in the same way by Somerset and Northampton, while Paulet and Herbert were supported by Northampton and Bedford. Once the ceremonies were completed:

all the said lords after obeisance done returned in like manner as afore all together to the Queen's Great Chamber, and there, the trumpets sounding before them, put off their robes and so went to dinner. But the lords that were newly created sat in their surcoats without mantle or coronet ... and they sat at dinner as followeth. First on the bench sat the Duke of Suffolk, next to him the Duke of Northumberland, then the Marquis of Winchester and last the Earl of Pembroke. And then on the other side a little lower sat the Duke of Somerset, the Lord Privy Seal, the Marquis of Northampton, the Earl of Rutland, the Lord Cobham, the Lord FitzWalter and the Lord Thomas Howard ...

As a spectacle it could hardly be improved upon, and apparently a demonstration of loyal solidarity. In fact it was the triumph of John Dudley and his friends, and one in which the former Protector featured rather in the manner of a captive king to a Roman emperor.

Edward Seymour had elevated himself to a dukedom as an integral part of the campaign which had given him the Protectorship. John Dudley had been head of the regency council for nearly two years before he took a similar step. As we have seen, he was very much concerned with status and prestige, so the long delay calls for some explanation. Possibly he took some time to convince himself that such a step was feasible. Henry VIII had created only two dukes, apart from his bastard son, and Somerset was a member of the royal kindred.[5] It was a very rare distinction, and not to be conferred lightly, especially in a situation where dangerous divisions were liable to open up at any moment within a nobility which desperately needed to remain united. Just as Dudley had no desire to assume the risky and discredited dignity of Protector, so he may have had no desire to provoke unnecessary hostility and jealousy by seeking his own aggrandizment. If that was the case, then it becomes necessary to explain his change of mind in the autumn of 1551. He was no more, and no less, ambitious then than he had been before, but his relations with the king were improving month by month, and the theatre of power in which he was operating required some grand gestures. Wolsey had understood the importance of

---

[4] BL Add. MS 6113, fo. 129.
[5] Thomas Howard, earl of Surrey, as duke of Norfolk (a restoration) and Charles Brandon as duke of Suffolk, both in 1514.

magnificence, and if Thomas Cromwell had not, that was because he was not given the chance by a king who decided that it was in his interest to claim a monopoly. Like Wolsey, and like Somerset, Dudley could claim that his own magnificence was for the king's honour; and that would not have been a hypocritical pretence.[6] As earl of Warwick, Dudley had discharged his political debts to Paulet, Russell, Ferrers, and Darcy, but his position remained insecure. Both Van der Delft and Scheyfve had commented that Dudley did not attempt to exercise power autocratically, as Somerset had. He was the leader, but his style was oligarchic and the continued support of his team was crucial.[7] It was the lack of such support which had proved fatal to the Protector. The rehabilitated Somerset had, as we have seen, proved to be a difficult and unrewarding colleague. His destruction would not only be a demonstration of political strength and resolve, it would also bring the enormous Seymour wealth back into the pool for redistribution. Deserving friends could thus be rewarded at no further cost to the Exchequer, and the lingering possibility of a *rapprochement* between Edward and his uncle banished for ever. As long as Somerset was alive, there could be no certainty that, in the long run, blood would not prove to be thicker than water.

There were, therefore, a number of reasons why Warwick should have carried out his second *coup* in October 1551. The fact that Somerset had virtually given up his political ambitions was not really relevant. He had undoubtedly entertained hopes of a comeback in 1550, and he might do so again. He had also received a number of small rewards and some marks of confidence since his return to the council,[8] but they do not seem to have produced the desired result, and by September Warwick had decided to stage the double drama which was to follow in the first half of October. The curtain was raised in council on 4 October, at a meeting attended by both Somerset and Warwick. It was then announced that the king was persuaded that the marquis of Dorset should not be sent to the north as Warden-General, but that Warwick should go in his place. This was an appointment which had nearly come to fruition in the previous summer, and indicates that either Warwick himself, or possibly the king, had changed his mind about the need for the Warden-General to be resident.[9] The record then proceeded,

his Highnes ... hath further determined aswell to thend that the sayd Earle of War-

---

[6] S. J. Gunn and P. G. Lindley, *Cardinal Wolsey: Church, State and Art* (Cambridge, 1991), 1–54.

[7] *Calendar of State Papers, Spanish*, ed. Royall Tyler *et al.* (London, 1862–1954), x. 47–8: 17 Mar. 1550; ibid. 568–9: 10 Oct. 1552.

[8] e.g. a commission to hear all treasons etc. in the counties of Buckingham and Berkshire, dated 4 May 1551 (BL MS Royal 18C 24, fo. 88). Also the grant of the former bishop's palace at Wells in November 1550 (ibid., fo. 16ʳ).

[9] Dorset had been appointed as a man of 'honour and subtance', rather than for his competence, on 25 Feb.. In spite of the long delay, he seems never to have taken up the post (*Acts of the Privy Council*, ed. J. Dasent *et al.* (London, 1890–1907), iii. 223, 379).

wicke may the rather be had in thestimacion he deserveth for his dignities sake, as for that allso his Majestie thinketh necessarie, the noble houses of this his realme being of late much decayed, to erect other in theyr stead by rewarding suche as have allredy well served and may be thereby the rather encoraged to contynnewe the same …

The intended creations were then listed as they were to happen a few days later.[10] Somerset's endorsement of this move had clearly been planned, because he had been politely summoned to return to the court on 30 September, along with certain other absent councillors, such as Clinton, Bedford, and Huntingdon. The creation of two new dukes required the maximum possible attendance of other senior peers, and Somerset seems to have had no suspicion of any other intention. However, the outcome makes it clear that the ceremonies were also a trap to ensure that the intended victim did not take fright. If Somerset was unsuspecting, others may not have been so innocent. Warwick was not popular outside the court, and extravagant rumours of his ambitions had already begun to circulate. On the second of October an anonymous yeoman of the guard was summoned before the council, charged with spreading reports that coins were being minted bearing the badge of the bear and ragged staff, in other words that the earl had some sinister but undefined designs either upon the crown or upon the integrity of the realm.[11] Similar rumours were to be numerous over the next two years. This one was unintentional, but no sooner were the new creations completed than the court began to buzz with reports of a different kind. The duke of Somerset was being defamed of conspiracy.

According to the story later recorded in the king's journal, on 7 October Sir Thomas Palmer, visiting the earl of Warwick on routine business connected with the honorific mission of the Baron de Jarnac which was then at court, 'declared a conspiracy'.[12] The first part related that Somerset had been sounding out opinion during the spring, to find out how much support he could count on, and in April had with difficulty been dissuaded from retiring to the north to 'raise the people'. The second part was a wild tale about his intention to invite Warwick and Northampton to a banquet 'to cut off their heads', and about seizing the Tower and raising the population of London. Warwick apparently kept quiet about these revelations until 12 or 13 October, when he went and reported what he had been told to the king. As he no doubt intended, this immediately leaked out, and on 14 October Somerset confided to Sir William Cecil that he 'suspected some ill'.[13] Cecil may have been privy to the plot, but even if he was not he had no intention of risking his political credit in a lost cause. So he gave the correct, if not very encouraging answer, that if the duke was innocent then he had

[10] *APC*, iii. 379–80.   [11] Ibid. 377.
[12] The purpose of Jarnac's brief visit, which lasted only two days, was to announce the birth of Henry II's third son (*APC*, iii. 379; *Chronicle of Edward VI*, 86–7).
[13] Ibid. 88.

nothing to fear, but if not 'he had nothing to say but to lament him'.[14] Somerset then sent for Palmer, who apparently denied that he had made any accusations. On 16 October Somerset attended the council as usual, but after dinner was arrested and consigned to the Tower, along with his kinsmen John and David Seymour and two of his servants named Hammond and Newdigate.[15] In what looks like a carefully planned operation his alleged accomplice Lord Grey was arrested on the same day 'coming out of the country', Palmer and Sir Thomas Arundel were arrested at court, and Sir Ralph Vane was picked up in Lambeth.[16] By 18 October the duchess of Somerset, Sir Michael Stanhope, Sir Thomas Holcroft, and a few others had joined the duke in the Tower, when servants were appointed for them and the security of the fortress strengthened.[17] A very brief announcement of the duke's arrest, with conventional expressions of regret, was sent out to all Justices of the Peace, with strict injunctions to prevent any 'stirs' or demonstrations.[18] At the same time the council released an official version of events for the benefit of the ambassadors. This played down the possibility of trouble in the north, and concentrated upon the assassination plot (the scope of which seems to have been vaguely widened) and the seizure of London. When asked for an explanation of this extraordinary conduct on the part of the former Protector, Northumberland professed blandly that he was as baffled as anyone, because Somerset enjoyed the highest reputation, and a personal fortune worth between £15,000 and £20,000.[19] Scheyfve was understandably sceptical of what he was told, and reported that the *coup* was being very badly received in the country as a whole, most people being quite unpersuaded of Somerset's guilt.

There is little doubt that the sceptics were right. The manner in which the charges were subsequently scaled down, and Northumberland's own eventual confession of fraud, are sufficient proof that the assassination plot was a fabrication. It is even possible that Palmer never made the original confession which Dudley attributed to him, because he not only denied it to Somerset, but produced a rather different and inconsistent statement a few days later.[20] The former Protector was no more guilty of treason than the marquis of Exeter had been in 1538, the duke of Norfolk in 1546, or the duke of Buckingham in 1521. Each of these men had committed indiscretions which enabled their enemies to destroy them, and each had been perceived to offer a political threat which could not be resolved by mere rustication.

---

[14] According to the king, Somerset's response was to send him 'a letter of defiance' (ibid.).

[15] John Seymour was Somerset's son by his first marriage; David Seymour was an unidentified kinsman; Lawrence Hammond was probably a yeoman servant; and Francis Newdigate was the Steward of the duke's household (ibid. 88–9).

[16] Ibid. There is no reference at this stage to Somerset resisting arrest, which was later one of the charges against him.

[17] BL MS Harley 284, fo. 97; *Chronicle of Edward VI*, 89.   [18] SP10/13, no. 57.

[19] Scheyfve to the emperor, 18 Oct. 1551 (*Cal. Span.*, x. 384–6).

[20] SP10/13, no. 65; *Chronicle of Edward VI*, 89.

Anne Boleyn had suffered for the same reason. Northumberland followed up his first strike in two ways. Propaganda, both written and verbal, was stimulated, alleging, among other wild claims, that Somerset had been plotting to murder the king and seize the crown himself. Secondly, the prisoners in the Tower were subjected to rigorous examination, some of it under torture according to the council's instructions. This immediately began to produce results, particularly from one William Crane.[21] Parts of Crane's confession are inherently improbable, particularly the statement that the mass assassination of councillors was supposed to have taken place at Paget's London house, and that he, Crane, was still trying to whip up support for it on the duke's orders during August. On the other hand, the picture which he sketched of discussions going back over many months for the arrest of Warwick and Northampton on charges of misgovernment, and of the use of parliament to confirm such proceedings, carries much more conviction. Not surprisingly, the earl of Arundel's name was mentioned in this connection, and also that of Lord Strange, the son of the earl of Derby. Warwick had gone out of his way during the summer to repair his relations with the powerful earls of Derby and Shrewsbury, and both had come to London out of the north with 'goodly companies' for the courtly celebrations in June and July.[22] Strange was consequently handled with kid gloves, and his testimony, which he repeated at the subsequent trial, was probably authentic. Arundel was less gently dealt with. He was arrested, and questioned in the Tower by Northumberland himself.

Between them Strange and Arundel probably provided the most authentic account of Somerset's 'conspiracy'. They did not support, or even mention, the wilder charges which had been made. Strange testified that Somerset had solicited his good offices with the king to arrange a marriage between Edward and the duke's younger daughter, Anne, then aged about 10.[23] Strange, who was about 20, enjoyed the king's personal favour, and had been one of the hostages for the treaty of Boulogne, so Somerset may well have felt that he was closer to their young master than his somewhat estranged uncle. There would have been nothing treasonable about such a suggestion, but it was indicative of the duke's continuing ambitions. Arundel's testimony was altogether more serious in its implications. Talking with Northumberland

after some protestations, with much difficulty, as though loath to say anything that might touch himself, he said: I cannot deny I once talked with the Duke of Somerset and determined to arrest, but not harm, you in the council ...[24]

Under pressure he then admitted that there had been several such

---

[21] *APC*, iii. 407: 5 Nov. 1551; *Chronicle of Edward VI*, 92.
[22] *The Diary of Henry Machyn*, ed. J. G. Nichols, Camden Society, 42 (1848), 6.
[23] *Chronicle of Edward VI*, 93.
[24] SP10/13, no. 67.

conversations, both at Syon and at Somerset House. Asked whether he had
sent a message to the duke and duchess via Sir Michael Stanhope, warning
them to desist from their practices because too much was becoming known,
he at first denied it, and then confessed that he had sent to the duke, but not
by Stanhope.[25] No dates were ascribed to any of these events, but they seem
to have occurred during the winter of 1550–1, when there was certainly
some pressure for the recall of parliament. Somerset had clearly hoped to
overthrow Warwick as leader of the council, and had solicited others for
that purpose. Finding inadequate support, and failing in his attempts to
have parliament reconvened, he had desisted. Thereafter he had been
nervous, and aware of his vulnerability, an awareness which had probably
caused him to overprovide for his own security, and thus provoke further
rumours of his hostile intentions. There was, and is, no evidence that he
conspired to murder Warwick, or anybody else, but, in spite of Arundel's
protestation, it must be questioned whether he could really have hoped to
remove the earl from power without also removing him from this world.
Somerset's own survival after losing power should have warned him not to
leave himself open to a second counter-attack.

   Warwick did not intend to allow him to escape a second time. On this
occasion there were no undertakings, and Cranmer, who had not attended
the council since 9 August, reappeared on 1 October and played a full part
in the activity attending Somerset's arrest and interrogation.[26] The duke's
goods were inventoried on 19 October, and on 30 October his wife followed
him into captivity. By the end of November the council had assembled as
good a case as it was ever going to get, and the indictment of treason was
found true bill by the High Steward's court on 30 November. The charges
were five in number: conspiring to raise men in the north, gathering men at
his house for the purpose of killing the earl of Warwick, resisting arrest,
plotting to raise London and attack the royal guard, and conspiring to
attack and murder the council.[27] On 1 December Somerset was brought to
trial in Westminster hall, the marquis of Winchester presiding as High
Steward, and twenty-six other peers assisting. He pleaded not guilty, and
conducted his own defence with skill and resolution. The principal witnesses against him were Sir Thomas Palmer, William Crane, and Richard
Whalley, who had been arrested a few days after the others. Somerset took
the obvious line of attacking Palmer's integrity as a witness, and when the
three witnesses were described as being fit instruments for his nefarious
purposes, he responded 'fit instruments indeed, but not for me'.[28] Strange's
testimony was also taken, and denied, although it did not bear upon any of

   [25] SP10/13, no. 67.
   [26] *APC*, iii. 375, 389, etc. Cranmer was an irregular attender, but was clearly not absenting
himself.
   [27] *APC*, iii. 392; *Chronicle of Edward VI*, 97–9; BL Harley MS 1294, fos. 19–20.
   [28] Ibid., fo. 20.

the charges. Somerset denied any conspiracy in the north, and, because that accusation rested upon Palmer's unsupported testimony, it was not pressed. What actually happened at the trial is in some doubt. According to one account, which is very sympathetic to Somerset, he challenged the propriety of Northumberland, Northampton, and Pembroke sitting among his judges, but was overruled.[29] The king's journal makes no mention of this, and since he was charged with designs on the whole council, there would not seem to have been much point. Having made that statement, the first narrative then becomes mainly vilification of Northumberland, and is of little use as a source. The king's journal, on the other hand, provides circumstantial details.

The lawyers rehearsed how to raise men at his house for an ill intent, as to kill the Duke of Northumberland, was treason by an act 3 anno of my reign against unlawful assemblies: for to devise the death of the Lords was felony; to mind resisting his attachment was felony; to raise London was treason; and to assault the Lords was felony ...[30]

This makes it clear that the duke was being tried under the statute 3 & 4 Edward VI, c. 5, although by the terms of that act his alleged intention to murder 'the Lords' would have been treason, not felony. Somerset categorically denied any intention of raising London, and seems to have declared that the alleged witnesses were not even present when they claimed to have been.[31] He admitted assembling men, but claimed that it was only for his own protection. In response to the main charge, of plotting to kill Warwick and his colleagues:

He answered ... He did not determine to kill the Duke of Northumberland, the Marquis etc., etc., but spoke of it and after determined the contrary; and yet seemed to confess that he went about their deaths ...[32]

If this is a fair representation of his words, it is not inconsistent with the testimony of the earl of Arundel. There had been a plot to overthrow Warwick, which had been abandoned without coming anywhere near fruition, and there may well have been some talk of having him executed. That was the substance of the case, and the spectacular embellishments were pieces of judicial theatre, very characteristic of the state trials of the period.

When the evidence had been completed, and the lords consulted over their verdict, a problem arose. Although it was treason by the statute to assemble twelve or more persons for the purpose of killing or imprisoning any member of the Privy Council—whether any action followed or not—the penalties only became enforceable if the guilty parties had ignored a

[29] Ibid., fo. 19.   [30] *Chronicle of Edward VI*, 99.
[31] Ibid. As to his alleged intention of attacking the gendarmery 'it were but a mad matter for him to enterpise, with his hundred against 900'. This amounted to a confession of having assembled 100 men under arms, and would not have been so mad if he had been expecting a sympathetic rising in London.
[32] *Chronicle of Edward VI*, 99.

lawful order to disperse.[33] No such order had been given to Somerset and his associates, and therefore he could not be convicted. The alternative treason charge of seeking to raise London was clearly a non-starter, so only charges of felony remained. The observation in the king's journal, that 'the Duke of Northumberland would not agree that any searching of his death should be treason', is an irrelevance, although the words may well have been spoken for effect.[34] It was not Northumberland's wish which frustrated a conviction for treason, but the words of the act. On the other hand to call such an assembly of twelve or more together for the same nefarious purpose, was in itself felony, irrespective of the outcome, and irrespective of any order to disperse. It was on that charge that Somerset was convicted, and he may very well have been guilty. In spite of the elaborate fabrications of Palmer and others, the only effective 'framing' of the duke was the insistence that his plot to overthrow Warwick also involved killing him, which may, or may not, have been true. It was probably to substantiate this crucial point that the French mercenary Berteville, earlier known as an associate of Warwick's, was imprisoned on a charge of having been the assassin hired by Somerset to carry out the 'banquet massacre'.[35] He confessed, and the king was told that Somerset had also confessed to the arrangement, but that seems extremely unlikely as neither statement was used at the trial. Shortly after, Berteville was not only released but rewarded, and that seems to tell its own story. In the event his evidence was not needed, or could not be used, but his role confirms how thoroughly the duke of Northumberland had prepared the ground for his decisive blow.

When Somerset emerged from Westminster hall with the blade of the axe turned away from him, the rejoicing could be heard at Charing Cross.[36] Only gradually was the truth understood. If Northumberland had been under any illusions about the state of popular feeling, he must have been disabused by that experience, but the commons were his enemies anyway, and the more clearly that was revealed the more the self-interest of the aristocracy would rally them behind him. Much more important was how the king felt about it all. His journal account of the trial is fairly detailed, but cool and dispassionate, and it has been correctly observed that he never showed any signs of doubting the horror stories about his uncle's treason which had been fed to him, and which the ambassadors treated with such scepticism.[37] His eventual record of Somerset's execution on 22 January is brief and dismissive. On the other hand it was noticed at the time how hard

---

[33] Statute 3 & 4 Edward VI, c. 5 §2; *Statutes of the Realm*, ed. A. Luder *et al.* (London, 1810–28), IV. i. 105.

[34] *Chronicle of Edward VI*, 99.

[35] Ibid. 100. Berteville was an adventurer. He had been knighted by Warwick on the battlefield at Pinkie but was also a regular paid informant of the French ambassador.

[36] *Diary of Machyn*, 12; *Chronicle of Edward VI*, 100.

[37] W. K. Jordan, *Edward VI: The Threshold of Power* (London, 1970), 87–8.

his minders worked to keep him amused over the Christmas season, and some concluded that he was not as indifferent as he appeared to be. Among these was the anonymous author of the account of Somerset's trial, already noticed, who wrote:

albeit the king gave noe token of any ill discomposed passions, as taking it not agreeable to Majestie openly to declare himself, and albeit the lords had laboured with much variety of sport to dispel any dumpy thoughts which the remembrance of his uncle might raise, yet upon speech of him he would often sigh and let fall tears. Sometimes holding opinion that his uncle had done nothing; or if he had it was very small and proceeded from his wife rather than himself, and where then, said he, was the good nature of a Nephew, where was the clemency of a Prince? Ah, how unfortunate have I been to those of my blood. My mother I slew at my birth and since have made away with two of her brothers …[38]

Who the observers were who reported these sighs and tears is not revealed. Nobody else noticed them, and it seems that the king was fully cognisant of the council order, when it was given on 19 January for the execution of the duke and his associates two days hence 'as appertaineth to our surety and the quietness of our realm, that by their punishment example may be showed to others'.[39] Somerset's alleged accomplices had not even been tried at this point, let alone condemned, but the fall of their principal made such a reservation unnecessary. It is unlikely that Edward felt any remorse for his uncle's execution, being convinced of his guilt. The words attributed to him by the anonymous author 'how falsely have I been abused, how weakly carried, how little was I master of mine own judgement, that both his death and the envy thereof must be laid upon me', simply do not carry conviction, although they certainly represent what many people at the time thought he should have felt.

It is not surprising that the council wished to see Somerset dispatched before the parliament reconvened. The demonstrations in London on 1 December had been a revelation, and soon after reports began to come in of similar scenes from as far away as Bath, where bells had been rung and bonfires lit in celebration of the duke's supposed acquittal.[40] The man responsible, Thomas Holland, was arrested shortly after for spreading the familiar tale about coins bearing the Warwick badge, and for claiming 'thow shalt see another worlde er Candlemas; the Duke of Somerset shall cumme forth of the Tower, and the Duke of Northumberland shall goo in'.[41] Security around London was tightened, and on 7 December 'a great muster' of men at arms was held in Hyde Park to overawe the City. Over 1,000 men were involved, headed by the Gentlemen Pensioners and including the retinues of Northumberland and nine other peers of his party.[42] These precautions

---

[38] BL Harley MS 1294, fos. 19–20.   [39] BL Cotton MS Vespasian F xiii, fo. 171.

[40] *APC*, iii. 462. For an account of Somerset's execution, citing several sources, see Jordan, *The Threshold of Power*, 100–1.

[41] *APC*, iii. 462: 24 Jan. 1552.   [42] *Chronicle of Edward VI*, 100.

were successful in the sense that there were no riots or other manifestations of discontent, but the actual execution, early in the morning of 22 January, was potentially a dangerous occasion. According to Henry Machyn, who was probably an eyewitness, 'as great a company as have been seen' turned up, together with the king's guard with their halberds, and about 1,000 of the London trained bands, drawn from all the eastern wards of the City. Amid rumours of a pardon, and general public confusion, Somerset made a dignified and correct speech, not admitting any guilt, but submitting to the judgment of the law.[43] He was buried on the north side of the quire in the chapel of St Peter ad Vincula. On 27 and 28 January Sir Ralph Vane, Sir Thomas Arundel, Sir Miles Partridge, and Sir Michael Stanhope were all arraigned of treason. In view of what had happened to Somerset it is not surprising, or particularly significant, that they were all acquitted, and then found guilty of felony and sentenced to be hanged. Only in the case of Thomas Arundel does it seem to have been necessary to pressurize the jury.[44] A month later, on 26 February, Stanhope and Arundel were beheaded, and Vane and Partridge hanged, the reason for the distinction not being explained. The duchess of Somerset, although much vilified, suffered no further punishment. She was released from the Tower on 30 May 1553, to pick up the pieces of her life as best she could.[45]

At the beginning of 1552, in spite of having attracted deep and widespread unpopularity, the duke of Northumberland was in an unassailable political position. Henceforth his peril would come, not from rivals but from the tricks of fate. Lord Paget, who might have been an influential voice in Somerset's defence, and certainly owed Northumberland no favours, was incriminated by Palmer's confession and arrested on 21 October.[46] On 8 November he was removed from the Fleet and taken, along with the earl of Aundel, to the Tower. Unlike Arundel, however, he does not seem to have been examined about Somerset's plot, probably because he knew nothing about it, and nothing was to be gained by listening to him say so. He was eventually charged with peculation in his office as Chancellor of the duchy of Lancaster, dismissed, and heavily fined.[47] Although he admitted

---

[43] *Diary of Machyn*, 14; John Stow, *The Annales of England* (London, 1592), 607; John Foxe, *The Acts and Monuments of the English Martyrs*, ed. S. R. Cattley and George Townsend (London, 1837–41), vi. 294.

[44] 'at noon the quest went together; they sat shut up together in a house, without meat or drink, because they could not agree, all that day and all night; this 29 day in the morning they did cast him' (*Chronicle of Edward VI*, 108).

[45] The reason for the long incarceration of the duchess is not clear, as she was not charged with any offence. Her servants were occasionally harrassed, and it may have been hoped that she would make some public admission of her husband's guilt.

[46] *Diary of Machyn*, 12. There never seems to have been any intention of charging Paget with complicity in the supposed conspiracy, and his disgrace was purely political (S. R. Gammon, *Statesmen and Schemer* (Newton Abbot, 1973), 180–1).

[47] He was dealt with at the same time as John Beaumont, although it was never claimed that there was any connection between the cases (SP10/14, nos. 33, 34; *APC*, iv. 65, 72). For a further discussion of Beaumont's case, see below, pp. 228–9.

the offence, there is no trace of irregularity in the accounts of the duchy, and the probability is that both the accusation and the confession were bogus. He remained in prison until the following summer, and was gratuitously and insultingly stripped of his Garter on 23 April.[48] By the autumn of 1552 he was apparently a toothless tiger, but the duke of Northumberland had acquired an implacable and bitter enemy. Arundel was not charged, although he was certainly open to indictment for misprision, and it is unlikely that his already poor relations with the duke deteriorated any further. Nor was Lord Strange accused of any offence, so the shaky entente with the Stanleys and the Talbots emerged undamaged. Lord Grey, who had been Somerset's most stalwart and outspoken defender among the military establishment, received a free pardon in June 1552, and his feelings towards Northumberland in the last year of the reign can only be conjectured.[49] By December 1551 the only senior officer who had not been either appointed by Dudley or entered an alliance with him was the Chancellor, Lord Rich, and Rich had been in serious trouble since the beginning of October. On 30 September the king had signed a commission 'for hearing and determining the causes and contempts of the bishops of Worcester and Chichester', which had then been sent to Rich for the Great Seal. Rich duly sealed the commission, but returned the royal letter of instruction on the grounds that the eight signatures which supported it were insufficient.[50] As Professor Hoak has pointed out, this was not quite the technical quibble which it appears to be. Rather it represented a protest on Rich's part against what he saw as the manipulation of the procedures of the council on progress by the earl of Warwick.[51] Whether his suspicion was justified or not is dubious, because there had certainly been no abuse, and he was extremely unwise to take a stand over such a questionable point. The king responded to his gesture in a signet letter which contains more than a touch of recognizable Tudor spirit.

We think our authority is such that whatever we do by the advice of our council attendant, although much fewer than eight, has more strength than to be put into question. You are not ignorant that the number of our councillors does not make our authority ...[52]

Edward was 14 at this point, and although it is reasonable to suppose that his letter was to some extent dictated by Warwick it almost certainly represented his own opinion as well. Rich began to consider his position. By 26

---

[48] *Chronicle of Edward VI*, 119.

[49] Grey had been unwise enough to object to the clause in Northumberland's patent of creation which gave him the credit for the victory in Scotland in 1547. There was an intention to appoint him Lord Deputy of Calais in Sept. 1552, but he was actually appointed to the captaincy of Guisnes a month later (*Chronicle of Edward VI*, 130, 144, 147).

[50] BL MS Royal 18 C, fo. 137a; *Chronicle of Edward VI*, 84; D. E. Hoak, *The King's Council in the Reign of Edward VI* (Cambridge, 1976), 140–1.

[51] Hoak, *King's Council*, pp. 139–41.   [52] SP10/13, no. 55; Hoak, *King's Council*, 319 n. 138.

October he had declared himself too ill to act, and had put his functions into commission.[53] Dudley, however, seems to have recognized a tactic of which he was himself a master, and the council continued to send instructions directly to Rich. On 10 November, at a meeting attended by thirteen councillors, a change of procedure was announced, whereby letters passing under the king's signet were no longer to require conciliar endorsement in order to be valid, and three days later they wrote to Rich, instructing that 'if anything signed by his Majesty alone do come to his Lordship's hands to pass the seal, that he stay not thereat, but cause it to be passed, as was accustomed in the King's Majesty's time late deceased'.[54] In other words, in this important respect the king was to be treated as though he was of full age. If Rich's earlier protest had been designed to ensure that the whole council would be consulted about important issues, then this decision signalled the total defeat of his efforts. On 21 December he resigned his office rather than become a party to what he must have seen as a dictatorial style of government.

As the king became older, the question of his personal involvement in government became critical. Rich resigned rather than face it, and it has divided historians ever since. The Elizabethan view was straightforward, but unhelpful. If they approved of what had been done—such as the advancement of protestantism—then it was credited to the 'young Josias', that paragon of godly learning. If they disapproved, as they generally did of the execution of Somerset or the attempt to divert the succession, then it was the work of the wicked duke of Northumberland. The prevailing view from the seventeenth century to the nineteenth, was that Edward was little more than a puppet in the hands of his powerful and unscrupulous servant.[55] More recently Professor Jordan tried, with impressive learning but rather less impressive judgement, to argue that the young king was making important decisions himself in the last year of his life, and that by the beginning of 1553 the duke of Northumberland was seriously contemplating retirement from public life.[56] This thesis Professor Hoak and others have subjected to critical investigation, pointing out that some of the contributions to policy debate which ostensibly came from the king had in fact been fed to him in prepared documents.[57] A clear-cut answer will not be found, and should not be expected, because we are dealing with a complex human relationship. John Dudley knew, far better than Edward Seymour had done, how to deal with the clever, obstinate and vulnerable adolescent which Edward had become by the age of 14. The Protector had seen the king as a child, and had made no serious attempt to get to know him, relying

---

[53] *Calendar of the Patent Rolls*, Edward VI, ed. R. H. Brodie (London, 1824–9), iv. 113–14.

[54] *APC*, iii. 411, 416.

[55] e.g. John Hayward, *The Life and Raigne of Edward VI*, ed. B. L. Beer (Kent, Ohio, and London, 1993), 20; J. A. Froude, *The Reign of King Edward VI* (London, 1909), 265–312.

[56] Jordan, *The Threshold of Power*, 494–535.   [57] Hoak, *King's Council*, 118–24.

instead upon the constitutional powers bestowed by his letters patent. Dudley had no patent, and no defined constitutional position. He clearly wanted the king to grow into his monarchy gradually. As early as August 1550 the council had decreed 'For divers good considerations' that the words 'by the advice of the council' should no longer be included in warrants which passed in the king's name;[58] and then in November 1551 the endorsement of council signatures on commissions was also withdrawn. Henry VIII's will had defined his son's minority as extending until his eighteenth birthday, and that had been confirmed by Somerset's original patent in March 1547.[59] However, when that patent was reissued in December of the same year, it had removed all reference to a time limit, being issued for the duration of the king's pleasure.[60] That pleasure was deemed to have come to an end in October 1549, but after the deposition of the Protector there was no formal definition of the king's minority. Custom would still suggest his eighteenth birthday, but by 1551 that had no legal force, and there was no regency government to displace.

Edward's formal education continued through the troubles of 1549–50 without a break, largely because there was no change of ideological direction. He was still producing Latin and Greek exercises for his tutors in the spring of 1551, and his journal, which should probably be seen as a tutorial exercise, was to continue until November 1552. Nevertheless by 1551 a change can be discerned. Physical exercise began to play a much larger part in the curriculum, a development which may be attributed to the military and largely unintellectual influence of the earl of Warwick, but could equally have been an automatic result of advancing puberty. According to a Venetian observer the young king 'soon commenced arming and tilting, managing horses, and delighting in every sort of exercise, drawing the bow, playing rackets, hunting and so forth, indefatigably, although he never neglected his studies …'.[61] At this stage he was not the pale, sickly child of romantic imagination, but a thoroughly healthy and normal boy. On 31 March 1551 he noted in his journal:

A challenge made by me that I, with sixteen of my chamber, should run at base, shoot and run at ring with any seventeen of my servants, gentlemen in the court …

On 1 April, the first day of the challenge, the king won at base, or running; and on 6 April 'I lost the challenge of shooting at rounds, but won at rovers …'.[62] Such references are not common, and perhaps Barbaro was overenthusiastic, but Edward certainly enjoyed hunting, and watching jousts. He did not take part in the latter, partly because of the danger involved, and partly because of his age. At 14 he was still running at the ring. Edward was

---

[58] *APC*, iii. 110–11.   [59] See above, p. 94.   [60] Ibid., p. 102.

[61] *Calendar of State Papers, Venetian*, ed. Rawdon Brown *et al.* (London, 1864–98), v. 535.

[62] *Chronicle of Edward VI*, 57–8.

fond of music, and kept up his father's court orchestra in some style. He also loved spectacles and pageants of all kinds, describing in loving detail the river tournament with which Lord Clinton entertained him at Deptford in June 1550.[63] Like his father, he was interested in ships and guns, noting the comings and goings of the former in his journal, and attending the launching of the *Mary Willoughby* and the *Primrose* in July 1551.[64] By 1552 all observers, including some critical Italians, were impressed by his classical learning, and, although his sympathetic tutor John Cheke was forced by ill health to give up his duties in the summer of that year, Edward's enthusiasm for study seems to have continued under its own momentum. Another, and very well-documented taste was for sermons. His courtiers occasionally had to be coerced into attending these lengthy and improving experiences, but the king himself was indefatigable, and as preaching was the corner-stone of protestant evangelism, he won golden opinions from the divines concerned. This can make it difficult to separate fact from later protestant hagiography, but Richard Grafton tells a story which has an authentic ring about it. In the spring of 1552 Nicholas Ridley, the bishop of London, preached before the king at Westminster, choosing as his subject the woes of the London poor, which was certainly not a 'politically correct' subject. Much moved by what he had heard, Edward

did sodeinly and of himselfe send to the sayd Bishop assoone as his Sermon was ended ... and accordyng to the kinges commaundement, he gave his attendaunce ... [and] the kinges Majestie much commended him for his exhortation for the reliefe of the poore, but my Lorde sayth he, ye willed such as are in aucthoritie to be carefull thereof, wherein I thinke you meant me, for I am in highest place, and therefore am the first that must make answer unto God for my negligence ...[65]

Whereupon he sent for the Lord Mayor of London to initiate a programme of poor relief, and made over the royal palace of Bridewell to house one of the resulting institutions.

This type of social conscientiousness was much more in keeping with the 'commonwealth' priorities of the Protectorate than it was with the policies of the council since early 1550, and raises the whole question of the authorship and purpose of the king's political papers. There are five of these, or six if a rather scrappy exercise on the end of the Hundred Years War is included.[66] They vary in length, subject-matter, and degree of polish, but all are written in the king's own hand. As Jordan pointed out when he edited them in conjunction with the journal, they show a knowledgeable, and sometimes sophisticated understanding of affairs of state, but they do not

[63] *Chronicle of Edward VI*, 36–7.   [64] Ibid. 70
[65] Richard Grafton, *A Chronicle at large* ... (London, 1568), ed. H. Ellis (London, 1809), 529.
[66] 'The governance of this realm ...' (BL Cotton MS Nero C x, fos. 113 ff.); 'Reasons for establishing a mart in England' (Cotton MS Nero C x, fos. 85 ff.); 'Payments of debts beyond seas ...' (BL Lansdowne MS 1236, fo. 21); 'A summary of matters to be concluded' (MS Lansdowne 1236, fos. 19–20); 'Certain Articles Devised and Delivered ...' (Cotton MS Nero C x, fos. 86–9); 'Notes on the English occupation of France ...' (Cotton MS Nero C, x, fos. 94–7).

bear any consistent relationship to policies which were actually being pursued. Similarly there is a memorandum in the king's hand of 'Actes for this (coming) parliament' drawn up in December 1551, and described in the journal as 'certain devices for laws delivered to my learned Council', none of which found expression in actual legislation.[67] If these papers were intended to convey the king's wishes to his council, then they did not make a great deal of impression; but they were probably never intended for that purpose. Like the journal itself, they were academic exercises, albeit of an applied nature. This is particularly evident with the first 'discourse on the reform of abuses ...', tentatively dated to April 1551, which is full of good common-weal doctrine, taken straight from Latimer's sermons or the pages of Robert Crowley.

But this is sure: this commonwealth may not bear one man to have more than two farms, than one benefice, than 2000 sheep, and one kind of art to live by ...[68]

Edward loved making lists, and systematizing information, as he did in 'reasons for establishing a mart' (9 March 1552) and 'memorandum for the council' (13 October 1552). None of these papers prove in themselves that he was an active participant in the decision-making process; if anything they indicate the opposite. Like the political briefings which he received, and his attendance at council meetings, they formed a part of the second stage of his education, his training in kingcraft. At the same time they are vastly more important than the essays of the average schoolboy, because they suggest a degree of commitment and a sense of duty which would very soon have to be taken seriously. Anyone who wanted to influence Edward in the long term would have to earn his confidence by paying attention to those convictions and concerns, which were beginning to turn from adolescent ideals into mature principles. The secret of the duke of Northumberland's power over the last two years of the reign was that he took the king seriously, and thus established a partnership which could work without any proper constitutional basis, and was completely impervious to the hatred and suspicion which the duke provoked in almost every section of English society.

Ecclesiastical affairs provide some very good examples of this. The Prayer Book of 1549 was unsatisfactory in many respects. It represented what the council, and particularly Cranmer, had believed that they would be able to enforce at that time, rather than what they really wanted. Almost before it had come into use steps were being taken to reform it, which involved consulting the two most prominent foreign theologians working in England, Martin Bucer and Peter Martyr, as well as a variety of English

---

[67] SP10/14, no. 4; *Chronicle of Edward VI*, 100. The king also drew up in his own hand a sumptuary bill which received one reading (Inner Temple, Petyt MS 538, 47, fo. 318; J. G. Nichols (ed.), *The Literary Remains of Edward VI* (Roxburghe Club, 1857), ii. 495–8).

[68] *Chronicle of Edward VI*, 161–2.

protestant opinion.[69] A draft had been completed by about February 1551, when it was circulated for comment, and the archbishop seems to have found this a congenial task by comparison with attempting to defend his episcopal colleagues against plunder, both principled and unprincipled. The work was probably completed by the end of the year, but it was never submitted to convocation for approval. Like the first Prayer Book, the second made its public appearance as an appendix to a parliamentary bill, and was officially adopted by the second uniformity act of April 1552.[70] It was very much more austere than its predecessor, although not all the suggestions of Bucer's *Censura* had been adopted, and its theological implications were distinctly Zwinglian. An introduction explained that many familiar ceremonies, which had been retained in 1549, had now been abolished because they had grown up spontaneously, without proper thought for their meaning, until they had overlaid the word of God with distracting human preoccupations. The English Church, it was implied, had now grown up sufficiently to be able to discard such unworthy props. The printing of the new book, which was a very large task, was entrusted to Richard Grafton, and by October the work was well in hand, for scheduled completion by the end of the year. However there then occurred a very significant hitch. John Hooper had already made representations against the inclusion of a rubric requiring the Holy Communion to be received in a kneeling position, but he had not prevailed. During the summer the fiery Scottish preacher John Knox, then practising his art around Newcastle upon Tyne, added his voice to Hooper's, and the campaign against the rubric began to make headway. Knox attracted the duke of Northumberland's attention while the latter was in the north during July, and was given the opportunity to exercise his ministry in London.[71] He preached at court, and was favourably heard by the king. Northumberland's patronage of Knox is consistent with his earlier favour to Hooper, and should be seen in the context of his plans for the future of the Church. The decision to bring him to court was calculated on the premiss that the king, whose evangelical zeal was waxing by the day, would find him congenial. This produced a consequence which the Duke may not have foreseen, because about the beginning of October it appears that Knox's rhetoric against the kneeling rubric persuaded Edward to intervene personally. The council wrote somewhat apprehensively to Cranmer that the king wished the book of common service to be 'diligently perused' on the grounds that 'some were

---

[69] E. C. Whitaker, *Martin Bucer and the Book of Common Prayer* (London, 1974). Bucer had produced a long critique of the 1549 Prayer Book, called the *Censura*. He had used a Latin version, having very little English.

[70] 5 & 6 Edward VI, c. 1; *Statutes of the Realm*, iv. i. 130–1.

[71] He was appointed a royal chaplain at some point before the end of Oct. 1552, in which capacity he signed the articles of religion (SP10/15, no. 28; Jordan, *The Threshold of Power*, 373–4).

offended'.[72] Cranmer, who had not attended the council for some time, responded indignantly that of course the king's wishes would be respected, but the book was in an advanced state of preparation, and had already been approved both by Peter Martyr and by the parliament. 'I trust', he wrote, 'you will not be moved by these glorious and unquiet spirits, which can like nothing not after their own fancy, and cease not to make trouble when things are in good order ...'.[73] The council's intervention was a direct infringement of his own authority, and an encouragement to anabaptists and other sectaries who claimed that everything not directly commanded by the scriptures was unlawful. Cranmer understandably blamed Northumberland for the council's attitude, and relations between them, which had been noticeably chilled by the advancement of Hooper, became still more distant. Whether the archbishop's prolonged absences from the court were a cause or an effect of the king's increasingly extreme views is not clear, but there was certainly a connection. By the autumn of 1552 Northumberland had discovered that the most certain way to preserve his influence over Edward was to humour and encourage his religious prejudices.

At first this worked very well, and down to the later part of 1552 he was winning golden opinions, not only from Hooper but also from disciples of Bullinger, such as John and Conrad ab Ulmis, and from Hooper's theological ally, John a Lasco. However, by November doubts were beginning to assail even the most zealous minds, and his patronage of Knox backfired spectacularly. This estrangement arose originally from the long-running saga of Bishop Tunstall. Tunstall had been committed to the Tower in December 1551, having been unable to clear himself of the suspicions arising from Ninian Menville's 'conspiracy'.[74] Rather than bring him to trial, Northumberland then attempted to have him condemned and deprived by Act of Parliament—a variant of attainder—and failed. The motive for this attack was not personal antipathy to Tunstall, but a desire to bring what was left of the palatinate jurisdiction of the diocese of Durham under the direct control of the Crown: 'it is thought it should be used as that of Chester is', Northumberland wrote to Cecil on 7 April 1552; that is, not abolished but annexed to the royal domain in perpetuity.[75] The fact that the bishopric was in the king's hands by virtue of Tunstall's imprisonment was not in itself sufficient to enable that to be done. The bishop had to be formally removed before any such change could be affected. After making further unsuccessful attempts to obtain conclusive

---

[72] The contents of the council's letter, which does not survive, can be reconstructed from Cranmer's reply (SP10/15, no. 15).

[73] Ibid.

[74] *APC*, iii. 348–9; Charles Sturge, *Cuthbert Tunstall* (London, 1938), 281–96; D. Loades 'The Last Years of Cuthbert Tunstall, 1547–59', *Durham University Journal*, 66 (1973), 10–21.

[75] SP10/14, no. 18.

evidence against Tunstall during the summer, on 21 September the council set up a commission to investigate the case, with power to deprive the
bishop if it so found.[76] On or about 15 October sentence of deprivation was
pronounced, and Tunstall was returned to imprisonment. By this time the
duke had sketched out a plan. The palatinate jurisdiction would remain in
the hands of the king, with himself as 'chancellor and steward of the same',
an appointment which would fit very well with his Wardenship of the
Marches.[77] The old see would then be divided into two, with a new bishopric erected at Newcastle on Tyne. The lands of the bishopric, worth
some £2,800 a year by the *Valor Ecclesiasticus*, would be taken by the king.
The Deanery, augmented by 1,000 marks per annum, would be used to create a new endowment for the bishop: 'the chancellor's living converted to
the Deanery ...', and so on. The revenues of the suffragan bishop of
Berwick, with a small addition, would then be used to support the new see
of Newcastle. 'Thus the king may place godly ministers in these offices and
receive £2,000 a year of the best lands in the north; it will be 4,000 marks of
as good revenue as any in the realm ...'.[78] The next session of parliament,
in March 1553, duly abolished the bishopric of Durham, and empowered
the king to establish two successor sees by letters patent. The patents
passed the privy seal in May 1553, but were aborted by the king's death in
July.

There were, however, several major hitches in this apparently successful
story of expropriation. In the first place, Northumberland did not understand the financial structure of Durham at all. The suffragan see of Berwick
had no revenues to speak of, and the Deanery was part of the cathedral
endowment, which was nothing to do with the bishopric.[79] Secondly, the
patents which were eventually issued lend no support to the obvious conclusion, drawn both at the time and since, that Northumberland's primary
objective was to create a vastly wealthy palatinate in the north for himself.
Over 80 per cent of the revenue of the old see was to be transferred to the
successor sees, the remainder being mainly used to support the garrison of
Norham castle.[80] The episcopal palatinate was converted into the 'King's
County Palatine' by patent in May 1553, and Northumberland was duly
appointed Steward, with the leadership of the king's men.[81] But of land or
revenue he obtained not a jot. What did happen was that he fell out with
several of his evangelical allies. At some point during November he offered
the see of Rochester to John Knox 'to be a whetstone to sharpen the archbishop of Canterbury', as he put it, and the reconstituted see of Durham,
when the formalities should be completed, to the incumbent dean, Robert

[76] *APC*, iv. 127–8.   [77] SP10/14, no. 18.   [78] SP10/15, no. 35.
[79] D. Loades, 'The Dissolution of the Diocese of Durham, 1553–4', in *Politics, Censorship and the English Reformation* (London, 1991), 167–79.
[80] PRO Parliament Roll, 7 Edward VI, C65/161, item 12.
[81] *Cal. Pat.*, v. 177, PRO C66/858 m. 20; *Cal. Pat.*, v. 175, PRO C66/858, m. 17.

Horne.[82] On what terms these offers were made we do not know. Presumably Durham was offered in the form suggested in Northumberland's letter, but we can only guess whether Knox was offered a salary rather than an endowment. For whatever reason, both refused in what must have been fairly blunt terms. By 3 December Horne had become 'This peevish dean … [who] lets not to talk on his ale bench that if he may not have it after his own he will refuse it', and Northumberland was lamenting that he had been 'much mistaken' in him.[83] For a couple of months the duke went on agitating about a nomination, but none was made, and that may have been one factor in forcing a complete rethink of strategy in the north-east. Knox had been even more outspoken. In a letter which Northumberland sent on to Cecil, he questioned the duke's religious sincerity, 'he cannot tell whether I am a dissembler in religion', a blow which seems to have struck its target on a raw nerve. 'I love not to deal with men neither grateful nor pleasable. I mind to have no more to do with him … because under colour of conscience, he can malign others.'[84] Northumberland clearly saw himself at this time as a well-intentioned man, much misunderstood and maligned. 'Had I sought the people's favour without respect to his highness's surety I needed not so much obloquy from some kinds of men.'

This mood continued into January 1553. On 3 January he wrote to Cecil excusing his long absence from the court.

It is time for me to live of that which God and the king have given me, and keep the multitude of crawlers from his court that hang daily at my gate for money … What comfort may I have after my long and troublesome life? So long as health gave me leave I as seldom failed my attendance as any others. When they went to their suppers and pastimes after their travail I went to bed careful and weary. Yet no man scarcely had any good opinion of me. Now by extreme sickness and otherwise constrained to seek health and quiet, I am not without a new eveil imagination of men.[85]

Such moods of self-pity had assailed him before, and need not be taken at their face value, but his confrontation with Knox and Horne seems to have shaken him badly. Whether he was persuaded by these experiences to change his mind over the bishoprics, or whether he was no longer in control of that aspect of policy, must remain in some doubt. There are no signs that other councillors were challenging him, so if he was overruled it must have been by the king himself. On the other hand, it is quite possible that his real concern was to serve the interests of the king and the realm as he saw them, and that he was genuinely distressed to realize that others believed he was only interested in helping himself. Having taken a calculated political risk in promoting protestant evangelism, he now found himself being cold-shouldered by the majority of the bishops, and denounced as a hypocrite by

---

[82] SP10/15, no. 35; MS Royal 18C 24, fo. 275ᵛ.   [83] SP10/15, no. 62.

[84] SP10/15, no. 66. Two days before this letter was written, Knox had been granted an annuity of £40 'until presented to some benefice' (BL Royal MS 18C 24, fo. 279ᵛ).

[85] SP10/18, no. 2.

those very radicals whose ideals he had embraced and promoted. He could, however, take comfort from one very important fact; however unpopular he may have been, he retained the confidence of his young master, who increasingly needed personal support as his health declined.

Part of Northumberland's difficulty in providing that support, however, was his own lack of intellectual sophistication. His education had been patchy, and he never committed to writing anything which could be regarded as a coherent theory of government. On the other hand, he does seem to have found a congenial man of ideas in the person of William Thomas, an Oxford graduate of Welsh gentry background, whose hitherto undistinguished career was interrupted in 1545 by a period of exile in Italy.[86] This experience may have been the result of his having picked up some radical protestant ideas, and consequently fallen out with Sir Anthony Browne, who until then had been his patron. Unlike many exiles, Thomas had made good use of his time in Italy, writing an Italian panegyric on the death of Henry VIII, a substantial Italian–English dictionary, and a history of Italy in English. This last, with a dedication to the earl of Warwick, was published in London after his return, in September 1549.[87] Such a dedication probably indicates a hopeful search for new patronage rather than a pre-existing contact, and if so it was singularly well timed. Within six months Warwick was Lord President of the council, and in April Thomas was appointed to one of the clerkships. Although the clerks were normally excluded when the council was discussing sensitive political issues because of Warwick's style of control, statements were occasionally made in the registers about controversial matters, when it was considered desirable to record an 'official' version, so Thomas was something more than a sixteenth-century stenographer. Indeed, the day after his appointment, it was decreed that no warrant to the Exchequer or any other treasury should be honoured, although it bore the signatures of councillors 'onless it be also subscribed with the hande of the said William Thomas'.[88] He was entrusted with a number of specific tasks, including that of supporting the marquis of Northampton's embassy to France in May 1551, and received a number of rewards, including the large payment of £248 in January 1551. Thomas, in short, was a minor but not insignificant figure in the court and administration. He did not, however, have the kind of standing which would have given him direct access to the king, and his adoption, in the autumn of 1551, of what was ostensibly a self-appointed role as Edward's political tutor calls for some explanation.

On 14 August 1551 the king recorded in his journal 'appointed that I should come to, and sit at, Council, when great matters were in debating, or

---

[86] E. R. Adair, 'William Thomas', in R. W. Seton Watson (ed.), *Tudor Studies* (London, 1924), 133–8.

[87] William Thomas, *The History of Italy*, ed. G. B. Parks (New York, 1963), pp. ix–xi.

[88] *APC*, iii. 3–4: 19 and 20 Apr. 1550.

when I would', and by October he was attending what Professor Hoak has called 'specially staged' council meetings.[89] Thomas's apparently spontaneous suggestion in September that he should send Edward weekly essays on political topics was clearly a part of this new educational strategy. The idea was ostensibly brought to the king's attention by Sir Nicholas Throgmorton, a favoured gentleman of the Privy Chamber, and presented in a mildly conspiratorial manner, designed to appeal to a 14-year-old. Thomas, who does not seem to have met the king, wrote that he would send the topics secretly 'that no creature living is or shall be privy either to this or to any of the rest through me, which I do keep so secret to this end, that your majesty may utter these matters as of your own study; whereby it shall have greater credit with your council'.[90] Thomas started by drawing up a list of eighty-five questions or propositions, mostly of a very general or philosophical nature, such as 'what is virtue?' Many of these questions were about the conduct of war, and they assume a high degree of royal and aristocratic authority—quite different from the common-weal ideas to which Edward was naturally prone. This authority, Thomas implied, was already the king's to use 'since your highness is by the providence of God ... grown to the administration of that great and famous charge that hath bene left unto you by your right noble progenitours'.[91] Only six of these topics were actually addressed in the papers which followed, and of those only two were of much significance. The first of these was on the restoration of the coinage, a subject under active consideration in September and October 1551, and the second on foreign policy. Thomas denounced the evils of debasement in eloquent but unsubtle prose, advocating a full recoinage as the only sensible target to restore the credibility of the currency both at home and abroad.[92] The ideal foreign policy, he argued, would be a firm alliance with another major protestant power; but since there was no other protestant power of any significance the best course was to play off the emperor against the French, avoiding the overt hostility of the former by threatening a firm alliance with the latter, but never actually entering into such a commitment. The king certainly read the former of these memoranda with care, and it is heavily reflected in a number of entries in his journal. It was also not very different from the policy which Warwick was struggling to bring into effect. In fact both the style and the content of Thomas's papers are consistent with a strategy on Dudley's part to get Edward thinking about real issues, and persuading himself that he was making a full contribution to decisions. A young Tudor would not respond to pressure, and would resent being lectured, but he could be led, and it

---

[89] *Chronicle of Edward VI*, 76; Hoak, *King's Council*, 121.
[90] BL Cotton MS Vespasian D, xviii, fos. 2–45.
[91] BL Cotton MS Titus B ii, fos. 84–90; John Strype, *Ecclesiastical Memorials* (London, 1721), II. i. 157–61.
[92] His thoughts are reflected in the entries in the king's journal during Sept. 1551 (pp. 80–6).

seems that Thomas was Dudley's agent for that purpose. It worked up to a point, but there was no way in which the king could be prevented from listening to other voices when their owners had the right of access. Dudley may well have been responsible for appointing such men as Knox and Bill as royal chaplains, but when their paths began to diverge, as they did over Church property, he found that he sometimes had powerful rivals for the king's ear.

Because of Dudley's method of dealing with him, it is extremely difficult to tell whether Edward's reaction to the information which was fed to him made any difference to council policy or not. By January 1553 the secretaries were required to keep memoranda of council business for the king's information, whether he was attending meetings or not, and it is known that he sometimes annotated these, or made relevant entries in his journal, but evidence of his actual intervention is conjectural even when, as in the case of the diocese of Durham, it seems a reasonable conclusion to draw.[93] Edward's political acumen, like his religious convictions and his prowess at sports, were a part of the theatre of the court, just as his father had used his own personal qualities, real and imagined, as aspects of his *maiestas*. An Italian visitor, Petruccio Ubaldini, described the English court in this period as bound by extremely rigid etiquette and permeated by a 'contrived adulation' of the young king.[94] Every ambassador and visitor was expected to comment on the boy's precocity in learning and godly zeal, and most did so. He seems to have had a genuine taste for fine clothes, and to have been affable and gracious by nature, as well as possessing real qualities of faith and intellect, so it is impossible to know with any certainty where the image ended and the reality began. Even Edward's letters to his boyhood friend and favourite Barnaby Fitzpatrick have a contrived air about them, although there is every reason to believe that their mutual affection was strong and genuine.[95] So strong, indeed, that the council thought it prudent to send the young Irishman to France in December 1551, where he remained for the best part of a year. The king's portraits tell the same story—a very youthful body clad in the carapace of royalty and striking unconvincing imitations of his father's regal pose. In January 1552 he was encouraged to draw up some detailed proposals for legislation in the forthcoming parliament, which are revealing of his obsessive concern with detail, as well as reflecting his interest in economic regulation, the protection of Church livings, and social hierarchy.[96] As we have seen, very little came of the exercise; but a few months later he had more success. The

---

[93] Hoak, *King's Council*, 120–3. A servant of the French ambassador left a highly circumstantial account of the way in which the duke of Northumberland influenced the king, using Sir John Gates as an intermediary (ibid. 123; see also below, p. 234).

[94] BL Add. MS 10169, fos. 1–125; Jordan, *The Threshold of Power*, 420.

[95] Nichols, *Literary Remains*, i. 63–89. Nine of these letters survive. Four of Fitzpatrick's letters to the king are in BL Cotton MS Caligula E IV, fos. 296–301.

[96] SP10/14, no. 4; Jordan, *The Threshold of Power*, 421–2.

Garter ceremonies, in which he took great pleasure and interest, had been designed for the faith of an earlier generation, and in April 1552 he personally redrafted the statutes to eliminate all traces of catholic ritual, and to ensure that the Order's surplus revenues should be devoted to charitable and education work rather than 'unprofitable superstitions'.[97] This was useful and politically harmless work which went through a number of versions before being finalized by Cecil, as Chancellor of the Order, early in the following year. It was given to Northumberland for comment in December 1552, and he wrote to Lord Darcy soon after, complaining somewhat disingenuously, 'as it is all in latin, I can but guess at it'. However, since he then went on to make some very specific suggestions, either he had an English version or his Latin was better than he would admit.[98] Also, by 1553 the situation was changing. The king was ill, but he was also 15H, and possessed of all his father's autocratic temper. The balance between appearance and reality in his relations with the council was changing all the time, and even if we conclude that he had very little influence upon public affairs in the six months following his uncle's execution, that was not necessarily still true by the time his last parliament was convened.

The policies which were pursued between the autumn of 1551 and the beginning of 1553 were, therefore, the policies of the council under the effective leadership of the duke of Northumberland, and, in spite of what is sometimes alleged, this was a period of considerable achievement. Hostilities had recommenced between France and the empire in September 1551, and the main thrust of Northumberland's foreign policy was to avoid becoming involved. This inevitably has an unheroic appearance, but it is hard to see how England's interests could have been better served. Professor Jordan's scathing criticisms are largely unjustified, because they are based on the a priori assumption that a stance of determined neutrality was both negative and supine.[99] Sir Richard Morison, who remained with the emperor in spite of the embarrassment caused by his religious zeal, was not a particularly intelligent ambassador, but he was actually quite a suitable representative at a court with which it was desired to maintain formal, and fairly cool, communication. The council relied for its real information on German affairs on the diligent and perceptive Christopher Mont in Strasburg, and on occasional envoys, such as John Brigandyne.[100] Sir Thomas Chamberlain, accredited to the regent of the Netherlands, performed his difficult and sometimes thankless task with considerable efficiency. Sir William Pickering in Paris had a rather easier ride, although he was not

[97] BL Cotton MS Nero C x, 13, fos. 93–101; *Chronicle of Edward VI*, 120.

[98] SP10/18, no. 4.

[99] Jordan, *The Threshold of Power*, 131, and elsewhere.

[100] *APC*, iv. 89, etc. Mont's dispatches are fully calendared in the *Calendar of State Papers, Foreign, 1547–1553*, ed. W.Turnbull (London, 1861). He was German-born, and his proper name was Christoff Mundt. Brigandyne sent three dispatches from Hamburg between Sept. and Nov. 1551 (*Cal. For.*, 174, 190–1).

immune from scares and panics, while Italian news came mostly from Peter Vannes in Venice. No diplomatic representation was maintained in Rome, for obvious reasons, nor at the court of the regent of Spain. Officially this was because Spain was a part of the emperor's dominions, but in reality because the Inquisition made the position of any non-catholic untenable. All these envoys complained repeatedly, and sometimes strenuously, of being kept short of money—in October 1552 Sir William Pickering informed Cecil that 'he had not 20 crowns left'—but such lamentations were common to all sixteenth-century diplomats, and mild by comparison with those of Elizabeth's representatives later in the century.[101] There are long gaps between Vannes's dispatches in 1552, and he complained after a long silence in October of being kept short of reliable tidings from England. However, that was in a specific context, and some of his letters seem to have been lost. Morison, Pickering, and Chamberlain were all diligent correspondents, Morison sometimes too much so, and there is little reason to argue that the English diplomatic network was run down and neglected by the council.[102]

What is true is that English policy was reactive rather than proactive: another characteristic which Edward's council was to share with Elizabeth. Four hundred English mercenaries served under the duke of Aumale in the autumn of 1551, to the emperor's great annoyance, but that was no more than a tiny gesture, and neither the French themselves nor their German Lutheran allies were able to obtain anything more than rather opaque expressions of goodwill.[103] The Anglo-French treaty of July 1551 was sealed in December with an exchange of ceremonial envoys and gifts, but the recent outbreak of war was blandly ignored. When the envoys of Maurice of Saxony revealed their secret treaty with Henry in March 1552, the council simply reaffirmed English neutrality, and rejected a French request to move troops through the Calais Pale as being contrary to their 'league' with the emperor.[104] In spite of Edward's personal liking for the Frenchmen who came to his court, the council was aware that Henry was subjected to conflicting pressures from his own advisers, and unwilling to believe that he had finally abandoned his design to recover Calais. In September 1552 this lurking fear was reawakened by a soldier of fortune named Thomas Stuckley. Stuckley was an Englishman who had served in the French campaign of the summer, and claimed a confidential relationship with the king. The only evidence to support that claim was a testimonial from Henry in warm but formal terms. On his return to England he immediately contacted the council to warn them that the French king had every intention, not only of

---

[101] *Cal. For.*, iv., 223; Garrett Mattingly, *Renaissance Diplomacy* (London, 1955), 222–4.

[102] Jordan, *The Threshold of Power*, 157–9.

[103] *Chronicle of Edward VI*, 95–6. François de Rabutin, *Commentaires des guerres en la Gaule Belgique, 1551–59*, ed. C. G. de Taurines (Paris, 1932), i. 52.

[104] *Chronicle of Edward VI*, 119–20.

overrunning the Pale, but of invading the south of England, and that when he did so the duke of Guise would look to come in from the north with Scottish backing.[105] The reaction was a mixture of alarm and incredulity. Pickering was immediately informed, and the ambassador responded that Stuckley had never enjoyed the kind of credit with Henry or the Constable that would have led either to confide in him. Northumberland, with sound common sense, consigned Stuckley to the Tower, and instructed Pickering to declare the whole matter to the French king.[106] Meanwhile an apology was offered to the French ambassador in London. Whether or not there was any substance in the report, Northumberland had adroitly secured the high ground, and the only tangible consequence was that Edward's friend Barnaby Fitzpatrick was recalled.

It may well be that Stuckley had exaggerated rather than invented his story, because in November 1552 there was a genuine diplomatic incident, arising from the seizure of French dispatches from Scotland by the imperial authorities at Gravelines. These did not directly disclose any nefarious intentions on the part of the French king, but they did reveal that the Guise interest in Scotland remained implacably anti-English, and quite prepared to take hostile action.[107] If the duke of Guise ever gained the upper hand in the councils of France, then the days of the entente would certainly be numbered. At the same time there were many in England who regarded any understanding with France as contrary to the law of nature, and some, like Thomas Burnaby, entrusted their views to paper.[108] Northumberland, however, stuck to his guns, not because he was particularly fond of the French, but because he judged such an understanding to be in the best interest of the country: 'he never desired [it] in all his life but for the service of his master', as he confided to Cecil. Nor did he believe that a benign neutrality towards France was necessarily incompatible with a better understanding with the Habsburgs, unless Charles chose to make it so. Apart from religion, the main bone of contention in the Low Countries was trade. The trade in unfinished English cloth was equally vital to the well-being of London and Antwerp, but the independent attitude of the Merchant Adventurers based in Antwerp, and their increasingly obvious protestantism, made them unwelcome guests to the Flemish authorities. The outbreak of war in 1551 disrupted commerce, even though England was not a belligerent, and there was a sharp decline in the quantity of cloth passing through the mart at the same time, for purely economic reasons.[109] By November Sir Thomas Chamberlain believed that the regent was deliberately strangling

---

[105] Ibid. 143–4; Nichols, *Literary Remains*, ii. 455.   [106] *Cal. For.*, 221.
[107] Jordan, *The Threshold of Power*, 171.   [108] BL Lansdowne MS 285, fos. 187–91.
[109] The debasement of the English coinage after 1545 caused a sharp fall in the price of English cloth abroad. This stimulated overproduction, and a decline in quality. When the coinage was 'cried down' in 1551, the price went up again, leaving large quantities of inferior cloth on the market. There was consequently a collapse of demand.

the trade, and urged reprisals although his diagnosis was only partly correct. Piracy and overproduction in England were as much to blame as deliberate political action, and by early 1552 it was clear that an agreed strategy would be in the interest of both parties. In February Sir Philip Hoby was sent across to exercise his famous charm on Mary of Hungary. This, and a determined attempt by the English fleet to tackle the problem of piracy, brought about a noticeable relaxation of tension.[110] By June a reciprocal mission sent by the regent had produced an agreed strategy for dealing with subsequent grievances and complaints. By this time, however, the emperor was in extreme military difficulties, under the combined attack of Henry II and Maurice of Saxony. A French army invaded Luxemburg and threatened Flanders, prompting the regent to invoke the Anglo-Imperial treaty of 1542. On 5 July she demanded 5,000 infantry, financial assistance, and an early declaration of war, as provided in that treaty.[111] No more embarrassing or impossible request could have been made. Although Northumberland had been careful to sign no incompatible treaty with France, a war with Henry II was out of the question for a variety of reasons. The English council stalled, pleading the king's progress as an excuse for delay, and eventually, on 31 July, refused.[112] A number of excuses were presented, of which the most relevant was that the treaty had not been confirmed since Henry VIII's death, but a clear obligation had been dishonoured. The rebuff was expected, and was received with no more than conventional protests, but the recent improvement in Anglo-Imperial relations was sharply checked.

Depressed and ill as he was in the summer of 1552, Charles had neither the energy nor the resources to spare to punish England in any way for her breach of faith. He was prepared to wait for the self-interest, if not the guilty consciences, of Edward's councillors to prompt a reappraisal of their attitude. This began with a memorandum in Cecil's hand, which can probably be dated to late September, and set out, in the *pro* and *contra* style so much favoured by both the Secretary and the king, the issue of the French alliance.[113] In that debate the *contra* was clearly the favoured side, and the king's annotations suggest that he shared that view, but it would be rash to conclude that Edward was intervening effectively in favour of an imperial alliance. The only foreign diplomat who ever made a real impression on the king was St André, and the emperor's continued support of his recalcitrant sister Mary was a thorn in his conscience by this time. The most probable explanation for the shift of tone and emphasis which can be discerned in the autumn of 1552 is the influence of the City of London, and particularly of the powerful financial manipulator, Thomas Gresham. Gresham, like Sir

[110]	*APC*, iv. 19, 22, 26, 30, etc; *Chronicle of Edward VI*, 116.	[111]	*Cal. Span.*, x. 549.
[112]	*Chronicle of Edward VI*, 135–6, 137; *Cal. Span.*, x. 558.
[113]	BL Cotton MS Nero C x, fo. 69; Nicholas, *Literary Remains*, ii. 539–43.

John York, was a friend and supporter of Northumberland, and had probably been advising him on financial policy since the spring of 1551. In April 1552 he had been appointed the king's agent in Antwerp, and had commenced those subtle and eventually successful manœuvres which rescued the sterling exchange rate, and made considerable progress in discharging the royal debt.[114] Access to the Bourse was absolutely essential for Gresham's operations, and he was strongly in favour of the best possible relations with the authorities in Brabant. By October 1552 the cloth trade was flowing normally, although not in its pre-1550 quantities, and in late November some informal hints were dropped from the Flemish side that a Habsburg marriage link might replace Edward's existing undertaking to Elizabeth Valois.[115] These seeds fell on stony ground, because the main objects of English policy had already been secured with the improvement in commercial and financial relations. There were also good reasons not to antagonize the French gratuitously. Troop movements were observed around Calais, which were almost certainly part of the preparations for another campaign in the Low Countries, but the council were taking no chances, and sent Henry Dudley across with reinforcements for the fortress of Guisnes.[116] Moreover, the commercial quarrels which had earlier troubled relations with the regent were now disturbing the peace of the Channel. In August 1552 the French took an initiative, ostensibly to ease these tensions, but, according to the astute Hoby, in the hope that they would be able to bypass genuine English grievances by moving first. The council responded by drawing up a somewhat inflated list of claims, totalling more than £50,000, which they knew it would exceed the authority of the French commissioners to concede.[117] The wrangle went on, throughout October and November, the English being somewhat more aggressive in their approach, possibly because they did not believe that the French really wanted to settle. In the words of the knowledgeable Pickering, nothing was on offer except fair words. By the end of December, however, it transpired that he was wrong. Worried by the improvement in Anglo-Imperial relations, the French suddenly gave way, and conceded the bulk of the English demands. At the end of 1552 Northumberland's standing with the merchant community was high, and by playing a weak hand with skill he had achieved amicable relations with both sides without commitment to either, and at no further cost to England in either money or pride.

As long as the cloth continued to flow to Antwerp, Gresham would be able to keep the king's debts under control, but his operations also needed the co-operation of his colleagues in the company of Merchant Adventurers. Not only must they be willing to allow their cloth to be used as

---

[114] He is first specifically referred to as agent on 9 May, but he had been functioning as such since at least the beginning of Apr. (*APC*, iv. 23, 27, 33, 40).

[115] Jordan, *The Threshold of Power*, 171.   [116] *Chronicle of Edward VI*, 139; *APC*, iv. 111.

[117] *Chronicle of Edward VI*, 145.

short-term security, they must also be prepared to underwrite the repayment bonds to banking houses such as the Fuggers and the Schetz, which passed in the king's name.[118] That degree of co-operation carried a political price tag which went beyond diplomatic support in dealing with the regent. On 24 February 1552 the council issued an adjudication in the dispute between the Merchant Adventurers and the Hanseatic League, which had been rumbling on since the last years of the previous century.[119]

The Hanse had been given extensive privileges by King Edward IV in the treaty of Utrecht of 1475, which gave the Germans a monopoly in the export of English cloth to the Baltic, and preferential treatment in bringing their own goods into England. In return the Hanseatic merchants were supposed to respect the Adventurers' monopoly in the export of cloth to the Low Countries, and extend reciprocal privileges to English merchants trading to Hanseatic ports. Long before the end of Henry VIII's reign, the Englishmen were complaining, first, that the agreed reciprocal privileges were not being granted; secondly that the Germans were taking cloth out, ostensibly for their own ports, and then selling it in the Netherlands; and thirdly that they were abusing their import privileges by 'colouring' the goods of other alien merchants, who should have paid at much higher rates.[120] Each of these complaints seems to have been justified, up to point, but that was not the real issue. The Merchant Adventurers were determined to use their indispensability to the council to get rid of their foreign rivals completely, and although the council investigated with a show of impartiality, and waded through a considerable body of evidence and expert opinion, the outcome was really a foregone conclusion: 'notwithstanding', the decree ran, 'That divers requestes hath been made, aswell by the Kinges Majesties father as by his Majestie, for the present redresse of suche wronges as hath been doone to thenglishe merchauntes contrary to the said Treaty, yet no reformatcion hath hitherto ensued …'. In consequence whereof

the pryvelege liberties and fraucheses claymed by the foresaid Merchauntes of the Stillyard shall from hensforth be and remayne seased and resumed into the Kinges Majesties handes untill the said Merchauntes of the Stillyarde shall declare and prove better and more sufficient matter for their clayme in the premises …[121]

The Hanseatic League was not the power which it had once been, and it was not under the direct protection of the emperor, but most of the merchants involved were his subjects, and the decision did not please him. It was,

---

[118] The City of London underwrote the government's borrowing, using the capital provided by the Merchant Adventurers' trade in woollen cloth. When the king's bonds were discharged, the City's obligations were cancelled at the same time. See e.g. *APC*, iv. 269: 11 May 1553.

[119] *APC*, iii. 487–9; Jordan, *The Threshold of Power*, 482–8. The council was supplied with massive documentation in support of the Adventurers' case, much of which survives. See e.g. Harley MS 306, 16, fos. 94b ff.; Cotton MS Claudius E vii, fo. 99, SP10/14, nos. 10, 11.

[120] SP10/14, no. 11 §4.   [121] *APC*, iii. 489.

however, of a piece with the remainder of Dudley's policy, designed to protect English interests without reference to traditional attitudes or previously accepted obligations. International relations, whether political or economic, were strictly pragmatic. Unlike Somerset, Northumberland had neither grand strategies nor principles, nor even preferences. He was concerned only to protect the territorial integrity of the king's dominions, the commercial prosperity of English merchants, and his own freedom of action in domestic affairs.

These priorities can also be demonstrated in a number of other connections. Military expenditure remained extremely high for peacetime—almost £200,000 a year. The garrisons of the Calais Pale, and of the Scottish borders, were brought back to strength during the summer of 1550. The navy was carefully maintained, and used in limited but effective ways. A survey of the fleet was carried out on 26 August 1552, showing fifty-five vessels with a combined displacement of over 10,000 tons.[122] Since the last survey in 1548 only one ship had been disposed of, the ageing *Mary of Danzig*, sold for £400 in December 1551. Four had been added, including the *Primrose* and the *Mary Willoughby*, each of about 300 tons, whose launching the king had attended in July 1551. This survey also provides evidence of good husbandry. Twenty-four ships were listed as 'in good case to serve', seven needed to be 'docked and new dubbed', three other were already in dock, four 'thought meet to be sold', and so on. A council decision was needed as to whether the galleys should be kept or scrapped. The Council for Marine Causes, which was the body responsible for administering the navy, had come into existence in 1545, and its structure was completed in the summer of 1550 when Edward Baeshe was appointed Surveyor-General of the victuals.[123] The accounts for the years 1550–3 do not survive in a complete form, but it appears that well in excess of £20,000 a year was being spent on the king's ships. Substantial dockyards existed at Deptford, which was the main base, Gillingham, Woolwich, and Portsmouth, each with a small permanent staff, and large numbers of casual labourers who were employed on a job by job basis.[124] Regular patrols seem to have operated in the summer, a custom which had been established before the outbreak of Henry VIII's last French war. On 11 March 1552 Benjamin Gonson, the treasurer of the navy, was paid £3,000 for the equipping and fitting out of four ships, and in June of the same year Baeshe was instructed to provide victuals for the ships at Gillingham 'appointed for the narrow seas'.[125] Each year warships were provided to convoy the Merchant Adventurers' fleet to Antwerp. Piracy was a besetting problem, as we have seen, which could provoke incidents of international significance, and successes were

[122] BL Harley MS 354, fo. 9; PRO E351/2194.
[123] D. Loades, *The Tudor Navy* (Aldershot, 1992), 81–4, 150.
[124] E351/2194; Loades, *Tudor Navy*, 153–6.   [125] *APC*, iii. 503; iv. 79.

only occasional. However, there is enough evidence to show that efforts were made. On 26 March 1552 the king recorded in his diary

Harry Dudley was sent to the sea with four ships and two barques for the defence of the merchants, which were daily before robbed, who, as soon as he came to the sea, took two pirates ships and brought them to Dover.[126]

Perhaps these were the same ships which Gonson had fitted out earlier in the month. On 27 August 1552 William Thomas was given a special commission to try piracy cases within the liberty of the Cinq Ports, where the regular franchisal courts, which had normal admiralty jurisdiction, were suspected of being too sympathetic to offenders.[127] John Dudley handed over the office of Admiral to Lord Clinton in May 1550, but he retained a deep interest in maritime affairs, and an enlightened understanding of the role of the navy in English policy. The alleged neglect of the king's ships during the period of his political ascendancy is merely another aspect of the 'black legend', without any justification in the surviving records. Before his fall in 1553 he was to play a key part in initiating the search for the northeast passage, a voyage which was eventually to reorientate the whole direction of English commerce, but we do not know whether he had any share in the event which was to make that possible, the return to England of Sebastian Cabot.

As a very young man, Cabot had sailed with his father from Bristol in 1497, and had shared in the discovery of Newfoundland. He seems to have liked England, but subsequent attempts to obtain patronage from Henry VII and Henry VIII had failed, and the Bristol merchants had begun to lose interest. Cabot had consequently taken himself off to Spain, where he had made a successful and lucrative career in the royal service, eventually becoming Charles V's Pilot Major. In 1548, for some unexplained reason, he returned to England. The emperor was extremely angry, and refused to believe that the old man had moved voluntarily, but there is no doubt that he had.[128] He could hardly have been induced by the modest pension of 100 marks which the English council found for him, and, if any invitation was issued, we have no record of it. The most likely explanation is that the Inquisition had begun to show an interest in him, and he decided to leave while the going was good. If that was the case, England would have been an obvious refuge, even without his earlier contacts. However, someone in authority was quick to spot his importance, and to deflect the emperor's indignant protests. The obvious source of that knowledge was London, but both Somerset and Warwick had strong links with the City, as did Paget and several other councillors. Subsequent events seem to indicate Warwick as the most likely candidate, but the evidence is purely circumstantial.

The creation of new wealth by trade was the most positive way to tackle

---

[126] *Chronicle of Edward VI*, 116.   [127] SP10/14, no. 69.
[128] Van der Delft to the emperor, 19 July 1549 (*Cal. Span.*, ix. 408–9).

the social problems which it was so fashionable to lament, and hence the Crown's high level of indebtedness. By the end of 1551 the exchange rate had 'bottomed out', and mint operations had been returned to their earlier integrity. Nevertheless the first half of 1552 was extremely difficult, and the most important contribution which Northumberland made to solving the problems was to recognize his own limitations. As early as the summer of 1551 he had admitted that he found finance a baffling and uncongenial subject, and his letter to the council on 16 June proves that he did not exaggerate.[129] He knew that there was no alternative to expert advice, but unfortunately he could not even chose that correctly, as his unwise endorsement of John York's speculations had demonstrated. It seems that early in 1552 he stood back and allowed the Lord Treasurer, the marquis of Winchester, to assume his proper responsibility for the direction of financial policy. Winchester, rather than Northumberland, was probably responsible for the decision to rely on Gresham and Mildmay rather than York, and for Gresham's appointment to Antwerp. The new agent could hardly have begun his task in more difficult circumstances. As much as £106,000 was due to be repaid between March and July, because of the way in which the obligations had been allowed to 'bunch', and nothing like that sum was available to discharge them.[130] On 15 March Sir Philip Hoby returned to the council the bonds for about £65,000 which had just been repaid to the Fuggers, but that had been achieved by recycling most of the debt on disadvantageous terms. Gresham was forced to reborrow over £90,000 of the £106,000 due, using accumulated credits for the balance, but he did manage to stagger the repayment dates, so that a similar crisis would not arise again.[131] After that, it could only get easier. By the autumn Gresham had complete control of the cloth credits, which in a good year could have been as much as £300,000; 1552 was a bad year, but they still placed about £60,000 at his disposal, and enabled him to discharge about £36,000 without reborrowing. By August the debt in Antwerp was down to £108,000, and was probably below £100,000 by the end of the year. The more valuable England's trade with Antwerp, the stronger Gresham's position became.

Having restored a measure of credibility to English financial operations, Gresham then decided to try his own variation on York's speculation, and it says a good deal for his standing with the council that they were prepared to back him in spite of having burnt their fingers once. He was supplied with about £1,200 weekly, which he fed on to the market at the rate of about £200–300 a day, accumulating Flemish pounds and creating a shortage of bills on London on the Antwerp market.[132] This was perfectly legal in that it did not involve the illicit export of bullion, and had the effect of forcing up

[129] *Historical Manuscripts Commission*, Salisbury MSS, i. 86–7.
[130] Cotton MS Otho E x, fo. 43; *APC*, iv. 27; Jordan, *The Threshold of Power*, 464.
[131] Cotton MS Galba B xii, 46, fos. 186–7; Jordan, *The Threshold of Power*, 464–6.
[132] Cotton MS Galba B xii, 54, fos. 205–6; Galba B xii, 46, fos. 186–7.

the sterling exchange rate from its low point of 0.65, where it had been in late 1551, to 0.95 against the pound Flemish. By April 1553 it had returned to 1.2, which was where it had stood before 1550. The money was provided from the sale of Crown lands, including property recently acquired from the chantries, to a capital value of almost £145,000.[133] This meant sacrificing about £8,000 a year in recurrent income, but the improvement in the exchange rate and the reduction of interest charges more than compensated for that loss. However, that was not the only price which the Crown had to pay. The council fully realized that the customs rates were hopelessly out of date, not having been revised since the reign of Henry VII, and various schemes were floated to remedy that situation, but they all foundered on the adamant opposition of the London merchants. When Mary's council eventually grasped that nettle in 1558, the revenue shot up from £25,000 a year to £80,000, so London was charging a substantial price for its co-operation with Northumberland's regime.[134] On balance it was probably a price worth paying, because in addition to financial services, the council also enjoyed the wholehearted co-operation of the City authorities in maintaining order on its own doorstep, which could otherwise have been both an expense and an embarrassment. In spite of these notable successes, financial anxiety remained endemic. Every few months fresh investigation of the accounts produced new summaries of the position, all more or less misleading, and on 23 March 1552 a commission was established with the most ambitious brief to date: 'for the survey and examination of all his majesties courts of revenue'. When this commission reported in December, it purported to have discovered an income of £272,000 against expenditure of £235,000.[135] It also made a number of draconian recommendations for economies, which do not seem to have reached the council, let alone been implemented.[136] But since its main purpose seems to have been to identify and put pressure on Crown debtors, it may be unfair to judge it by any other criteria. The English government at this time was short of money, so short that even modest demands for £300 or 400 could appear to cause cash-flow problems, and in August 1552 the council postponed a payment to Anne of Cleves's servants 'for that his Highnes is presently in Progresse and resolved not to be trobled with paymentes untill his returne ...'. But it never suspended payments in general, and the crisis was consistently exaggerated by interested contemporaries for their own purposes.[137] Scheyfve,

[133] W. K. Jordan, *Edward VI: The Young King* (London, 1968), 118.

[134] D. Loades, *The Reign of Mary Tudor* (London, 1991), 353; SP10/13, no. 82, 'Arguments against raising customs on cloths'.

[135] BL Add. MS 30, 198, fos. 5–52; Harley MS 7383, no. 1; W. C. Richardson, *The Report of the Royal Commission of 1552* (Morganstown, W. Va., 1974), 393 ff.

[136] J. D. Alsop, 'The Revenue Commission of 1552', *Historical Journal*, 22 (1979), 511–33.

[137] Jordan (*The Threshold of Power*, 462) reports this as though it were a virtual declaration of bankruptcy, but it is clear from the entry in the council register that it was a very specific case, and that other warrants for payment continued to be passed, both before and after (*APC*, iv. 109).

in particular, before relations began to improve in late 1552, was anxious to present England as on the verge of bankruptcy and civil war. These partisan statements have often been accepted by historians as objective assessments, just as the wild denunciations of the 'commonwealth men' appealed to the social consciences of the early twentieth century.[138] In fact the financial problems which followed the overthrow of the Protectorate, although severe, and made worse by inept meddling with the currency in 1551, were well under control by the end of 1552. It was not even necessary to run the political risk of asking the 1552 parliament for a subsidy, although that had been indicated in the king's original memorandum. Northumberland may have been financially illiterate, but he had the good sense to hand the management of that aspect of affairs over to men who, by the standards of the time, knew what they were doing, and did it effectively.

A parliamentary session was always a good test of a government's management skills, and that which convened on 23 January 1552 was no exception. Stress is always laid on the fact that the duke of Somerset had been executed on the previous day, but it is very unlikely that the members would have made any attempt to protect him. It was customary in cases of treason for attainders to be confirmed by statute, but an attempt to have Somerset's condemnation ratified was either abandoned or defeated. This probably had less to do with sympathy for Somerset than with the fact that it was not customary to ratify convictions for felony, no matter how exalted the victim.[139] The main bill, of which this was a subsidiary clause, was concerned with the settlement of the late Protector's estate. In 1541 the then earl of Hertford had procured a private act entailing the whole of his estate upon the children of his second marriage, thus disinheriting his existing son, John Seymour. Not surprisingly, this was represented as having been due to the machinations of his unpopular second wife, Anne Stanhope. The purpose of the 1552 bill, which had received the royal assent before it was introduced, was to repeal the 1541 entail, and to restore to John Seymour the right of inheritance to all that his father had possessed before that act was passed.[140] This bill had a troubled passage, not, it would seem, because anyone objected to its main purpose, but because of the clause confirming Somerset's attainder, and because an unsuccessful attempt was also made to introduce an amendment annulling the marriage contract between Edward, his son by his second marriage, and a daughter of the earl of Oxford.[141] It eventually passed at the very end of the session, and the bulk

---

[138] See particularly R. H. Tawney, *The Agrarian Problem in the Sixteenth Century* (London, 1912).

[139] The attainders were declared to be 'good and effectual in law', but not repeated by the act (SP10/14, no. 20).

[140] Ibid.; HLRO Original Act 5 & 6 Edward VI, no. 37.

[141] *Journals of the House of Commons* (London, 1803–52), i. 19, 20; Jordan, *The Threshold of Power*, 337.

of Somerset's estate, acquired since 1541, was seized to the king's use. It took some time to work out exactly what John Seymour was entitled to by the terms of this act, because Somerset had sold some of his earlier holdings between the making of the entail and his attainder.[142] As early as 18 December 1551 Winchester had written to Sir John Thynne to obtain the necessary information, and had concluded his letter 'in all which matters I pray you show yourself the child's good friend ...'. There seems to have been no ulterior motive for this action, which righted an undoubted wrong, but the continued vilification of the duchess is interesting.[143] She remained in prison, although not charged with any offence, until the following year. The remaining work of the session looked to the future rather than the past. An act 'for the maintenance and increase of tillage and corn' looks at first sight like a return to the days of 'commonwealth' legislation, but it did not reverse the policy laid down in the previous parliament, and, having been altered a number of times in passage, emerged both vague and toothless. It has been fairly described as a 'pious gesture'.[144] Much more significant was the statute 5 & 6 Edward VI, c. 2, 'For the Provisyon and Relief of the Poore', which decreed the election of Collectors of Alms in every borough and parish during Whitsun week in each year, for the purpose not only of collecting but also of administering the funds for poor relief. There was as yet no compulsion to contribute, but another step had been taken which was to lead to the Elizabethan Poor Law. A number of other measures of economic regulation and control also stemmed from council initiatives: 5 & 6 Edward VI, c. 6, was an attempt to restore the international demand for English cloth by laying down higher and more strictly enforced standards of manufacture; c. 7 sought to control the storage, buying, and selling of wool; while c. 8 forbade the weaving of broadcloths by anyone who had not served the standard seven-year apprenticeship.[145] None of these acts showed a progressive or imaginative approach to the problems of the cloth trade, but they were responsible measures according to the best economic thinking of the time, and show a government properly concerned with, and listening to, the agencies of the trade. Many other acts of a similar nature can probably be attributed to specific lobbies: an act for resisting the regrating of tanned leather, an act for putting down gig mills, an act for the making of hats in Norfolk, and many others.[146] It should not be concluded that Northumberland, or any other senior councillor, was deeply interested in the licensing of pedlars, or the repeal of an old statute against bringing in wine in foreign ships, but the fact that these issues were being addressed indicates a conscientious stewardship.

---

[142] Longleat, Thynne Papers, II, fo. 178 (microfilm in the Institute of Historical Research).
[143] John Seymour gained little by his restoration, as he died on 19 Dec. 1552 (*Diary of Machyn*, 27).
[144] Jordan, *The Threshold of Power*, 338; 5 & 6 Edward VI, c. 5; *Statutes of the Realm*, IV. i. 134–6.
[145] Ibid. 136–42.   [146] Jordan, *The Threshold of Power*, 339–40.

The same might also be said of measures of a moral or religious nature. The most important of these was the second act of uniformity, not repealing the first, but 'amplifying' it and introducing the second *Book of Common Prayer*.[147] In spite of having been carefully prepared, this bill clearly encountered some difficulties. Three attempts were made before an acceptable format was discovered, and even then there was opposition in the Lords. That three lay peers dissented on the final vote is not surprising, but every effort had been made to secure a compliant bench of bishops by that time, and the opposition of two of them, Thirlby of Norwich and Aldrich of Carlisle, is therefore somewhat remarkable.[148] The Commons do not seem to have been difficult, although four readings were needed before the measure eventually passed on 14 April. This major act was accompanied by a number of minor ones designed to clarify the existing situation rather than to introduce innovations. One imposed severe penalties for quarrelling and brawling on ecclesiastical premises; another regulated the observance of holy days and fast days, pointing out that these were intended for the honour of God, and not to encourage devotion to saints, or any other members of the heavenly hierarchy.[149] Neither of these was contentious, but there was fierce debate in the Lords over another measure of a similar nature. This was a bill affirming the legitimacy of the children of married priests. Since the marriage of priests had been declared lawful in 1549, this was merely intended to plug legal loopholes, and to protect such children from defamation. It seems to have met with no objections either from the bishops or the Commons, but a number of lay peers resisted its passage with determination, and ten of them voted against it on the final reading.[150] This was not enough to defeat it, but is a reminder of how fierce the prejudice against married clergy could be, and helps to explain the tenacity with which the Marian authorities later pursued them. A rather similar prejudice from quite a different angle was, however, specifically upheld. Usury, that *bête noir* of biblical theologians, had been sensibly defined in 1545 as any interest rate over 10 per cent. This parliament, however, catering for the moral fervour of the advanced protestants, repealed that act, and totally forbade 'any manner of usury, increase ... gain or interest to be had ... or hoped for over and above the sum or sums so lent'.[151] That such a measure should have passed without significant opposition in either House is likewise a comment on the mores of the period. The powerful banking interests of the

[147] 5 & 6 Edward VI, c. 1.
[148] *Journals of the House of Lords* (London, 1846), i. 421: 6 Apr. 1552. Their opposition may have been occasioned, not by the content of the book, but by the fact that it had not first been submitted to convocation. John ab Ulmis, the only person to give any account of that convocation, makes no mention of it. Ab Ulmis to Bullinger, 10 Jan. 1552 (*Original Letters Relative to the English Reformation 1531–1558*, ed. Hastings Robinson (Parker Society, 1846–7), ii. 443–6).
[149] 5 & 6 Edward VI, c. 3; *Statutes of the Realm*, iv. i. 132–3.
[150] 5 & 6 Edward VI, c. 12; *Statutes of the Realm*, iv. i. 146–7.
[151] 5 & 6 Edward VI, c. 20; *Statutes of the Realm*, iv. i. 155.

City of London would have been ruined by the enforcement of such a law, and the City had plenty of ways of making its views known, both inside parliament and outside. But it did not bother to voice any dissent. As one contemporary had written on a different matter 'it boots not how many laws be made, for men see few or none put in execution', and we have to conclude that there was a type of legislation which really belonged to the confessional rather than the law courts. The council was prepared to defer to radical protestant opinion in such innocuous matters, but on more immediately practical issues such as social discipline and poor relief, it followed a much less ideological programme. Northumberland had no intention of burning his fingers with the fire of pure commonwealth doctrine when enforcement was seriously intended.

Apart from the vexed question of the Black Rubric, the second Prayer Book was not particularly a triumph for the protestant radicals; it was a development of mainstream Anglicanism, led by Cranmer and his colleagues. The same was equally true of the remaining doctrinal statements to be made by the English Church during Edward's reign, the *Catechismus Brevis*, or *Shorte Catechism*, and the forty-two articles. Cranmer had not been enthusiastic about issuing a confession of faith, because it would inevitably be profoundly contentious. He preferred liturgical statements which permitted a degree of interpretation. Nevertheless, after Hooper's appointment to Gloucester, it became clear that he would have to act unless he wanted to see a different catechism being issued in each diocese.[152] Towards the end of 1551 he circulated a draft set of articles to some, at least, of his episcopal colleagues for comment. Having signalled his intention, however, he did not take any steps to promulgate his confession, and on 2 May the council wrote asking him to submit it for their scrutiny.[153] This he eventually did in September, and on 20 October the council sent a set of forty-five articles, which were presumably the same, to the king's chaplains for their comments. Since this coincided very closely with the row over the kneeling rubric, the archbishop cannot have been very pleased by this move. We do not know what alterations, if any, were suggested, or how they were responded to, but on 24 November Cranmer submitted his final revised draft, with the request that the council take appropriate steps to give it the necessary authority, and the code by then consisted of forty-two articles.[154] The council, however, took no action. Whether the chaplains were still not satisfied, or some other doctrinal dispute had arisen by then which made the issue of an official doctrinal statement undesirable, we do

[152] John Hooper, 'Articles Concerning Christian Religion … within the Diocese of Gloucester', in W. H. Frere and W. M. Kennedy, *Visitation Articles and Injunctions* (Alcuin Club, 1910), ii. 269–70.

[153] *APC*, iv. 33.

[154] SP10/15, no. 28; the date is approximate. Thomas Cranmer, *Works*, ed. J. E. Cox (Parker Society, 1844–6), ii. 441.

not know, but the articles were not to be promulgated until the following June, shortly before the king's death, and too late to make any impact on the Church.[155] If Northumberland played any significant part in this process, it has escaped the record, but we can be reasonably sure that he was not eager to see the articles given public authority, because no one else had any known interest in delaying them. His attitude, on the other hand, may have been similar to that which he displayed towards the revision of the canon law.

This was a project with a long history, because as far back as 1532 convocation had agreed to submit all its canons to the king for his scrutiny and approval. The subsequent establishment of the royal supremacy had inevitably shot large holes in the existing canon law, but parliament had also decided that the remaining law should remain in force until it could be properly revised.[156] The king was then authorized to establish a commission of thirty-two members, clergy and lawyers, to produce a new code appropriate to the English Church. By 1545 Cranmer, working largely on his own, had produced a revised code, but it was never submitted for approval, and Henry's commission expired with his death.[157] The circumstances of the new reign appeared to be propitious, but when Cranmer was urged to press on with his work on the canon law, he responded in a manner which is very informative of his whole attitude in the early days of the Protectorate:

if the king's father had set forth anything for the reformation of abuses, who was he that durst gainsay it. Marry! we are now in doubt how men will take the change or alternation of abuses in the church...[158]

It was not until the third session of Edward's first parliament, after the Protector's fall, that the project was revived, and it is not at all clear that Cranmer was responsible for reviving it. In January 1550 a bill was introduced to authorize a new commission of sixteen, but in the course of debate this was amended to the old figure of thirty-two, and passed eventually in that form against the opposition of almost all the bishops, including Cranmer.[159] Whether the archbishop was opposed to the increase in the size of the commission, or whether he was opposed to the whole idea of a new commission is not clear. His enthusiasm for the reform of the law was undiminished,

---

[155] BL MS Royal 18C 24, fo. 357ᵛ.

[156] The fullest account of this process is given in James C. Spalding, *The Reformation of the Ecclesiastical Laws of England, 1552*, Sixteenth Century Essays and Studies, 19 (Kirksville, Miss., 1992), 14–32.

[157] Authority to appoint a commission was renewed in 1544, by 35 Henry VIII, c. 16. From a letter written by Cranmer to the king in Jan. 1546, it seems that this commission was actually appointed, but it is not clear that it ever met (Cranmer, *Works*, ii. 415). Cranmer's draft code survives in Corpus Christi College, Cambridge, MS CCCXI, and was printed by G. Burnet, *The Historie of the Reformation of the Church of England* (London, 1694), iv. 520 ff.

[158] Foxe, *Acts and Monuments*, v. 563.

[159] 3 & 4 Edward VI, c. 11; *Statutes of the Realm*, iv. 111–12.

but a new commission would have meant abandoning the work which he had already done, and starting again. The king was as keen as anyone on the reform of abuses, but he was more interested in the appointment of good bishops than he was in the redrafting of the law, and in that he probably reflected the views of his evangelical chaplains. Consequently it was not until October 1551 that the council finally got round to naming the new commissioners, and February 1552 before the commission was issued.[160] The working of this commission does not concern us here, but it would appear that a draft code was completed by October, which strongly suggests that it was largely based on Cranmer's earlier work. One of the king's memoranda, headed 'Matters for the council, October 13 1552' contains the item 'th'abrogating of the old canon law and th'establishment of the new'.[161] However, no document was submitted to the council at that time, perhaps because the archbishop, whose recent experience of council intrusions into his jurisdiction had not been happy, preferred to take it straight to the parliament which was called for March 1553. If such was the case, it was an error of judgement, because neither Northumberland nor any other leader of the council had any sympathy with what he was trying to achieve. There is no official record of what happened, but on 10 April Scheyfve drew up notes for a dispatch, which contain circumstantial and convincing detail.[162] When Cranmer attempted to introduce his work on behalf of the commission, the duke declared 'openly and before all ... that it should come to nothing, and warned him and his brother bishops to beware what they were about'. Scheyfve does not make it clear where this exchange took place. It could hardly have been on the floor of the House of Lords, because speeches there could only be directed to issues which were before the House, and no bill to give effect to the revised canon law was introduced; nor could it have been without the approval of the Lord Chancellor, who controlled the agenda. 'Openly and before all' does not suggest the restricted company of the council, but nobody else seems to have recorded the clash, which would be surprising if it had been public in the ordinary sense. We should probably conclude therefore that the dressing down to which the archbishop was subjected took place at one of the meetings which were convened to prepare matters for the parliament, which may not have been confined to Privy Councillors. The duke's oration, as recorded, was explicit and irate. The commissioners had exceeded their powers. The business of the clergy was to preach and teach, and the business of the bishops was to ensure that they did it, and not to meddle in matters of state. Certain bishops, motivated by pride and greed, were opposing the king's worthy plans for the reorganization of bishoprics and the redistribution of Church property. Cranmer and his colleague should in future 'take care

---

[160] *Chronicle of Edward VI*, 110–11.   [161] Nichols, *Literary Remains*, i. 547.
[162] *Cal. Span.*, xi. 33. The whole document is printed from Rymer's transcript by James Gairdner in *Lollardy and the Reformation in England* (London, 1908–13), Appendix III, 400–1.

that the like should not occur again, and let them forbear calling into question in their sermons the acts of the prince and his ministers, else they should suffer with the evil preachers ...'[163]

Whether or not Northumberland used the words quoted, the sentiment is consistent with what we already know of his attitude. Nor was his anti-clericalism a personal eccentricity. The common lawyers had done very well in recent years by encroaching upon the uncertain territory of the Church. The last thing they wanted was to see the Church again administering a clearly defined and autonomous code of law. Cranmer was as devoted to the royal supremacy as any man living, and had not the slightest desire to encroach upon the prerogatives of the king, but he believed that the king's ecclesiastical servants had their own proper jurisdiction, with which the laity should not meddle. Northumberland, on the other hand, believed that the Church should be substantially disendowed, and was already by the spring of 1553 feeling frustrated by his lack of progress in that direction. The council had indeed just issued instruction for the confiscation of 'superfluous' Church goods, but nobody knew better than the duke that this was merely scratching the surface.[164] A survey carried out in 1552 had valued the wealth of all the bishoprics of England and Wales at £30,325 per annum, and of other ecclesiastical benefices in excess of £50 a year at £24,073.[165] If those surveys were accurate, it means that the capital value of the endowments of the upper level of the Church alone was approximately £1,088,000. As there were in addition some 10,000 parochial livings and other preferments with an average annual value of about £12, and a total capital worth of some £2,400,000, the whole valuation of the Church's remaining assets would have come to about three and a half million pounds.[166] How far Northumberland and his secular allies would have carried the policy of disendowment if they had been given a free hand, we cannot know, but by 1553 the opposition was becoming formidable. The radicals, happy enough to cut down bishoprics and cathedrals, wished to build up the parishes rather than to diminish them, and to provide better stipends for good preachers. As we have seen, the duke's plans for Durham were frustrated, and the 'Winchester experiment' was not repeated. On this matter at least it seems that the king was listening to other advisers, and there was little to be hoped for in his mature years. The preferment of John Harley to Hereford in May 1553 and of John Bale to Ossory in Ireland both appear to have been by Edward's personal initiative.[167] Northumberland may well have believed that his schemes would have vastly benefited the

---

[163] Ibid.

[164] *APC*, iii. 467. Inventories of these goods had been ordered as long ago as 1548, and this move surprised no one.

[165] SP10/15, no. 78; Jordan, *The Threshold of Power*, 377–8. [166] Ibid. 378.

[167] *Chronicle of Edward VI*, 179; John Bale, *The vocacyon of Johan Bale ...* (London, 1553), fo. 17: Bale's own account of his 'calling'.

Crown, and it should not be assumed that he was motivated chiefly by personal greed, nor even by the desire to build up his clientage; but he was not making enough progress, and he was failing to carry the king with him. It is not surprising that he lashed out at Cranmer when he was confronted by what he saw as another example of clerical ambition and intransigence. The archbishop, on the other hand, who accepted without demur the idea that bishops exercised their jurisdiction by commission from the Crown, also had to accept that he required a specific commission to investigate heresy and other purely ecclesiastical offences.[168] Certain aspects of the royal supremacy were beginning to show an unacceptable face.

Northumberland's strategy of government depended increasingly upon his personal and informal ascendancy over the king, because it was upon that influence, and its presumed implications for the future, that his control of the council depended. Cranmer's bid for increased ecclesiastical autonomy had to be defeated, and the archbishop himself humbled, because he was the only man who could challenge the duke in Edward's confidence. The tactics which supported that strategy are usually assumed to have consisted mainly in the advancement and enrichment of himself, his family, and his friends, a view typified in the next generation by Stow's opinion that the dissolution of the see of Durham was mainly designed 'to add another title to the ambitious Duke of Northumberland, viz. Earl of Durham …'.[169] As we have seen, he did not achieve that aim, if he ever held it, but his activity in the north provides a good illustration of his style and methods. In October 1551 he was granted the office of Warden-General of the Marches against Scotland, with a yearly fee of 2,000 marks. On 26 November he surrendered an annuity of 500 marks drawn on the revenues of North Wales, and received in return lands in Northumberland to the annual value of £233. 6s. 8d., consisting mainly of the lordships of Alnwick and Warkworth.[170] At the same time he sold other lands in the south of England to the king, and on 5 January 1552 was granted lands in Tynemouth and other adjacent lordships to the same annual value, £695. 9s. 9d.[171] On 13 April he was granted for life the office of Chief Steward of the East Riding of Yorkshire, with the leading of all the king's tenants there, and on 7 May he received a commission as King's Justice, 'to enquire of all Treasons, misprisions, insurrections, rebellions … and all other ill doings within the counties of Northumberland, Cumberland, Newcastle and Berwick, and to appoint certain days and places and to do all other things in as large a man-

---

    [168] e.g. 'A commission to the archbishop of Canterbury, the bishop of London and others for the examination and punishment of erroneous opinions in religion' (BL MS Royal 18C 24, fo. 260ᵛ: 9 Oct. 1552).

    [169] Loades, 'Dissolution of the diocese of Durham', 169.

    [170] MS Royal 18C 24, fo. 141ᵛ: 18 Oct. 1551; *Cal. Pat.*, iv. 195: 20 Oct.; MS Royal 18C 24, fo. 159ᵛ: 26 Nov. 1551; *Cal. Pat.*, iv. 185: 2 Jan. 1552.

    [171] MS Royal 18C 24, fo. 159ᵛ; *Cal. Pat.*, iv. 117: 5 Jan. 1552.

ner as the council (of the north) might do by their commission made the last year …'.[172] This was part of a scheme which covered the whole country, and showed no particular favour to the duke. The earl of Westmorland held the commission for County Durham, while Northumberland also held that for Warwickshire. On 4 June he was also granted letters of Lieutenancy for the same counties, also as part of a national scheme, and two weeks later became Steward of the former lands of Holm Cultram abbey, in the hands of the Crown, with leadership of the king's tenants, a post previously held by Lord Wharton.[173] Finally, on 30 April 1553, at the same time as the new royal palatinate of Durham was created, he was appointed Steward of all the former bishopric lands, with a fee of £50. 13s. 4d. a year, and granted the lordship of Barnard castle, which was a duchy of York property worth £229 per annum.[174] Taken together these grants increased the duke's wealth by nearly £2,000 a year, and appear to have given him an unchallengeable political position in the north-east of England. His presence there, however, was confined to one diligent tour of inspection, which lasted from mid-June to late August 1552. In spite of the apparent sufficiency of his own powers, a renewed acquaintance with the region convinced him that the resident deputy wardens who had been appointed for each march in the wake of his own appointment were insufficient to protect the order and security of their charges. Writing to the council in London early in August, he recommended new fortification work to be undertaken at Berwick, and the appointment of Lord Wharton as Deputy Warden General, both suggestions which were immediately acted upon.[175] In November 1552, while still gathering offices in the north, he sold Tynemouth and other lands in Northumberland back to the king, purchasing in their place lands in Wiltshire and Yorkshire.[176] In spite of appearances, Northumberland was not attempting to create a power base for himself in the north. He could not have hoped to re-establish the manred of the old earldom, it would have taken generations to do that, and in any case his power had to be at court. He certainly derived a large income from his northern lands and offices, and a considerable amount of patronage, but neither Wharton nor any of the deputy wardens who served under him were particularly Northumberland's men; Eure, Conyers, Dacre, and Musgrave were all local men of standing and reputation.[177] What he seems to have been looking for was a position which would give him the right and authority to intervene in the king's name if he was not satisfied with the conduct of border affairs. As Warden-General he could supersede the authority of any of his deputies whenever he chose, and his various stewardships gave him the right to

---

[172] *Cal. Pat.*, iv. 344; MS Royal 18C 24, fo. 209ᵛ.   [173] Ibid., fo. 214ᵛ; ibid., fo. 223ʳ.

[174] Ibid., fo. 339ᵛ; *Cal. Pat.*, v. 174.   [175] PRO SP15/4, no. 8; MS Royal 18C 24, fo. 246ᵛ.

[176] *Cal. Pat.*, iv. 368.

[177] The only exception may have been Sir Nicholas Strelly, appointed Deputy Warden of the East March on 23 Dec. 1551 (*Cal. Pat.*, iv. 128–9).

raise men in the north to back him. In other words his tactics were designed to bring the north under more effective central control without having to intrude outsiders into the area in normal circumstances.

Outside the north, Dudley served on commissions of the peace in Staffordshire and Warwickshire, and on a number of other commissions, as any major nobleman would have expected to do.[178] He also continued to collect land. In addition to the grants and exchanges in the north, on 19 May 1551 he had received the manor of Otford in Kent, worth £40 a year, apparently as a gift, and then in March 1553 exchanged it with the king for other lands to the value of £104.[179] Other exchanges in the same month brought him an income of 1,000 marks, but the value of what was surrendered is not clear.[180] At some unspecified date, but after his elevation to the dukedom, he received the manor and hundred of West Coker, and other manors in Somerset, jointly with his wife, but whether as gift or purchase is not clear.[181] In June 1553 he carried out another substantial exchange, and finally, on 26 June received a valedictory gift of further land to the value of £400 a year 'for the better support of his great charges in attendance upon the king's person, and upon the business of the realm and commonwealth...'.[182] Dudley's transactions in land were numerous and complex; he received dozens of licences to alienate, which in most cases indicate sales, and made a large number of purchases, which can be glimpsed but not accurately quantified in the absence of the appropriate accounts. On 10 May 1552 he created an enfeofment to use when he granted the manors of Knole, Sevenoaks, and Tonbridge, together with other lands in Kent, to his son-in-law Henry Sidney, Francis Jobson, and others to hold on behalf of his wife Jane 'for life, in augmentation of her jointure ...'.[183] Two years earlier he had settled Coxford priory in Norfolk upon his son Robert and Amy Robsart in anticipation of their marriage, and in 1553 added the manor of Hemsby in the same county. After his attainder in 1553 his lands were valued at £4,300 a year, which was great wealth, but not disproportionate to his status.[184] Making due allowance for inflation, it was no more than the £3,900 which the fifth earl of Northumberland had received in 1523, and significantly less than the £5,000 which the duke of Buckingham was judged to be worth at the time of his fall in 1521. In 1580 the earl of Hertford recorded that his father's income at the time of his fall had been £7,500 a year, but there is no contemporary evidence to support that estimate.[185]

Land formed the major part of Dudley's income, but by no means the whole of it. His office of Warden-General was extremely lucrative at

[178] *Cal. Pat.*, iv. 391, 394–5; ibid., v. 414–15.

[179] Ibid., iv. 180; *HMC*, 80, Sackville (Knole) MSS, i. 316; Beer, *Northumberland*, 185.

[180] Ibid. [181] PRO E318/58. [182] *Cal. Pat.*, v. 171. [183] Ibid., iv. 431.

[184] PRO LR2/118, fo. 12^{v}, etc.; *HMC*, MSS of the marquis of Bath, IV, Seymour Papers, 187; Beer, *Northumberland*, 191.

[185] Ibid.

£1,333. 13s. 4d, and nothing else that he held approached it in value, but he collected lesser positions, like that of constable to Beaumaris castle at 40 marks a year, and the keeperships of numerous forests and chases.[186] Altogether his receipts from fees and annuities probably approached £2,000 a year at their maximum: a lot of money but not approaching the 8,000 marks which Somerset had been paid as an official salary. There were in addition other ways by which a man in power could improve his financial position, but even his worst enemies never accused the duke of Northumberland of corruption in the ordinary sense. On 15 June 1552 the council released him, and a group of men who had probably been among his sureties, from debts to the Crown going back to 1541. The total release was for £2,094. 17s. 3d., the great majority of which was owed by Northumberland himself.[187] Earlier in his career he had sold lead and leather, obtained at preferential rates, to his substantial profit, but by 1552 his only known commercial activities involved the management of a coal-mine at Wrexham and of an iron foundry at Southfrith in Kent.[188] He does not seem to have made any personal profit out of the coinage debasement of 1551, or Gresham's intricate operations in Antwerp. He must have been investing in London, but, in the absence of any personal accounts, we have no means of knowing how deeply.

Other members of the Dudley family profited from his ascendancy, but not to an extravagant extent. His loyal brother Andrew, already one of the four knights of the Privy Chamber, received the Garter in 1552, but obtained only two grants of land with a total annual value of £234. 16s. 9d.[189] When he fell from grace at the beginning of Mary's reign, his lands were valued at £555. He served in a number of military and naval commands, culminating in the captaincy of Guisnes in 1551, but when he became involved in a strident jurisdictional dispute with Lord Wentworth, the Lord Deputy of Calais, Northumberland showed no partiality. Both parties were summoned before the council in January 1552, and both were eventually relieved of their commands in October of the same year.[190] As far as can be discovered, Andrew made only two preferential purchases, the farm of the manor of Witney 'late of the bishop of Winchester', in June 1551, and that of the lordship of Minster Lovell in January 1553. Northumberland's oldest surviving son, John, styled earl of Warick after his father's promotion, does not seem to have shared the military precocity of his elder brother. He was a courtier rather than a soldier, and his first appointment was as Master of the Buckhounds in April 1551.[191] By then he was a familiar figure in the jousts and entertainments of the court, and had married Anne Seymour in June of the previous year. Presumably some lands must have

---

[186] BL MS Royal 18C 24, fo. 26ᵛ; ibid., fo. 172ᵛ, etc.   [187] *Cal. Pat.*, iv. 347.
[188] Beer, *Northumberland*, 193.
[189] *Cal. Pat.*, iv. 153: 23 Sept. 1551; ibid., v. 194: 3 Feb. 1553; PRO E318/1586.
[190] *Chronicle of Edward VI*, 106, 147.   [191] *Cal. Pat.*, iv. 104.

been settled on the young couple, because John was of full age, being about 22 at the time of his wedding, but there is no record of their location or value.[192] In May 1551 he accompanied the marquis of Northampton to France, but not with any serious diplomatic role. To judge from some of the goods found in his possession after his attainder he was a young man of some education and culture, but nothing is known about his upbringing. He was too old to have shared the king's schooling, and it is possible that he may have been placed with the earl of Hertford while their fathers were still friends and allies. In January 1552 Northumberland gave him the leading of half of his own retinue of 100 men at arms, and on 28 April he received the important preferment of Master of the Horse.[193] This was a position normally occupied by men of much greater service and experience, and must be seen as one of the few examples of clear Dudley nepotism. At about the same time he was also elected to the Order of the Garter in the place of the disgraced Lord Paget. On 30 March 1553 he received the wardship of his young brother-in-law, Edward Seymour, and custody of the land which had been allocated for his support, to the value of £510. 9s. 6d.[194] On 17 June he was licensed to retain 100 men in his own right, and at the beginning of July, just days before Edward's death, received a joint grant with his other brother-in-law, Henry Sidney, of land to the value of £158.[195] If the Dudley family was running a campaign of plunder, not very much of it came the way of the younger John, who never emerged from his father's shadow, and is hard to identify as a person in his own right. His lack of an adequate independent living and the high cost of life at court seem to have troubled him, and at some point, probably during 1552, the duke wrote to him what was no doubt intended to be a reassuring letter.

I had thought you had more discretion than to hurt yourself through phantasies or care, especially for such things as may be remedied and holpen. Well enough you must understand that I know you cannot live under great charges. And therefore you should not hide from me your debts whatsoever they be, for I would be loathe but you should keep your credit still with all men. And therefore send me word in any wise of the whole sum of your debts, for I and your mother will forthwith see them paid …[196]

He then proceeded with some Polonius-like warnings on the subject of honest service, and the need to avoid 'wild and wanton men', concluding 'and so with my blessing I commit you to (God's) tuition …'. The duchess then added a one-line postscript in her own hand 'Your loving mother that wishes you health daily'. Many a young courtier, forced to live beyond his means, would have given a great deal for such sympathetic parents, but the earl of Warwick at the age of 24 would probably have preferred a proper

---

[192] *Chronicle of Edward VI*, 32. The settlement would presumably have been similar to that later made for Robert q.v.
[193] Ibid. 107; *Cal. Pat.*, iv. 325.   [194] Ibid., v. 4.   [195] Ibid. 78, 242; PRO E318/2052.
[196] HMC, 70, Pepys MS, Magdalene College, Cambridge, 2.

income under his own control; which may be why he was given the custody of young Seymour's lands a few months later.

Ambrose, about three years younger than John, was also a man about the court, noted mainly as a jouster. He served with his father in the Norfolk campaign of 1549, but seems to have received no office or other reward. From the perspective of his later life, it seems that he was a rather pious and colourless young man. As with John, we know virtually nothing of his upbringing, but he was married before 1552 to a young woman named Anne, who died in May of that year, probably of the sweating sickness. The duke wrote a graphic description of his daughter-in-law's death, but very little else in known about her.[197] She appears to have been the widow of one Whorwood, perhaps the son of William Whorwood, sometime Attorney-General, a follower of Dudley's, who had been killed at the battle of Pinkie. She was an heiress, whose husband had held her land by 'courtesy of England' before his death, and the whole inheritance now passed to her child by Whorwood, who was the duke's ward.[198] Ambrose thus received no part of his wife's inheritance, because she had borne him no surviving child, and he married again before the year was out, his second wife being Elizabeth, the daughter of Lord Talbot.[199] Like John, Ambrose seems to have had no independent living; nor was he licensed to retain, or given the leading of any men. His father clearly did not trust him in any military capacity. Northumberland's favourite son, after John, was the dashing Robert. Robert, born in 1533, was only four years older than the king, and shared at least some part of his schooling as a member of the band of henchmen. He was the only Dudley of the right age and aptitude for such a promising role. Robert married at the early age of 17, in June 1550, just a few days after Lord Lisle, a ceremony which was followed by the gruesome entertainment of decapitating a live goose.[200] His bride was the ill-fated Amy Robsart, daughter of Sir John Robsart. In this case the marriage settlement survives, and we know that Warwick settled on the young couple the extensive lands of Coxford priory, and an annuity of £50 a year.[201] Sir John Robsart contributed another £20 a year, and Robert became an important Norfolk gentleman in his own right. He did not give up his career at court. On 15 August 1551 he was appointed an ordinary gentleman of the Privy Chamber, along with the king's favourite, Barnaby Fitzpatrick, and in February 1553 received the office of Chief Carver, a virtual sinecure worth £50 a year.[202] In June 1553, when

[197] SP10/14, no. 38.

[198] Ibid., no. 37. The child's name was Margaret (BL MS Royal 18C 24, fo. 225ʳ).

[199] Anne had borne him one child, but it had lived only a few months (D. Wilson, *Sweet Robin: A Biography of Robert Dudley, Earl of Leicester* (London, 1981), 2–3).

[200] *Chronicle of Edward VI*, 33.

[201] Wilson, *Sweet Robin*, 43–4; Dudley Papers at Longleat, Box II, no. 1; Beer, *Northumberland*, 104.

[202] *Chronicle of Edward VI*, 77; *Cal. Pat.*, v. 49. He also followed his brother as Master of the Buckhounds in Nov. 1552 (*Cal. Pat.*, iv. 104).

Edward was already dying, he was licensed to retain 50 men in his own livery, and a few days later purchased extensive further estates in Norfolk, probably at preferential rates.[203] Thanks, perhaps, to the accidental survival of his marriage settlement, we have a much clearer impression of the young Robert than of his two elder brothers, but he also seems to have been much more his own man.

By contrast his younger brothers Guildford and Henry are mere shadows. Guildford would have been about 18 when his father was raised to the dukedom, and Henry a year or two younger. All we know about either of them concerns their marriages. On 4 July 1552 the council wrote both to the duke of Northumberland and to the earl of Cumberland 'to grow to some good end concerning the marriage between the Lord Guildford and his daughter …'.[204] The letters were couched in pressing terms, as though this was something which the king greatly desired, although the truth probably is that Northumberland was trying hard to strengthen his links with the 'old' nobility, although Clifford himself was only a second-generation peer. For whatever reason, the union never took place, and Guildford was reserved for his fateful match with Jane Grey, the daughter of the duke of Suffolk, in May 1553, a matter to which we shall be returning in due course. Henry's marriage, about the circumstance of which nothing is known, was to Margaret Audley, daughter and heiress of the former Chancellor, Lord Audley of Walden.[205] Margaret seems to have brought to her husband lands to the value of about £1,000 a year in London and the home counties, but as he would not have achieved his majority until 1555, his degree of independence is uncertain. Of the Dudley daughters, Mary was married to Henry Sidney in 1551, and Catherine was still a child. Northumberland certainly did not neglect the fortunes of his children, but it would be a great exaggeration to claim that he practised extensive nepotism on their behalf.

Apart from Northumberland himself, the people who did best out of his political ascendancy were his noble friends and his gentle dependants. The most conspicuous collector of offices, leases and grants of land, preferential purchases and exchanges was, rather surprisingly, Edward, Lord Clinton. Clinton was also pardoned debts to the Crown amounting to £2,265 in December 1551.[206] He was allowed, indeed encouraged, to build up a powerful base in Lincolnshire, receiving altogether sixteen grants of one sort or another. The next most favoured was the marquis of Northampton, who received nine grants, and had his tangled matrimonial affairs resolved by parliament in February 1552.[207] Sir John Gates received six grants of modest scope; Lord Darcy and the duke of Suffolk four each; Sir William Cecil, Sir Henry Seymour, Lord Cobham, and a number of other men associated with

---

[203] *Cal. Pat.*, v. 79; ibid. 221; PRO E318/1588.   [204] BL MS Royal 18C 24, fos. 235–6.
[205] Beer, *Northumberland*, 194–5.   [206] MS Royal 18C 24, fo. 168ᵛ.
[207] 5 & 6 Edward VI, c. 30; *Statutes of the Realm*, IV. i, p. xii (statute not printed); MS Royal 18C 24, fo. 183ʳ: 23 Feb. 1552.

the regime received two or three each, and there were several individual grants of interest. Ninian Menville, the Scot who had ensnared Cuthbert Tunstall, received a 'reward' of £100;[208] Jean Ribault, Northumberland's French mercenary captain, was granted the manor of Northey in Gloucestershire, worth £24 a year;[209] and the Princess Elizabeth was given 'for fealty only' the estates of Missenden abbey in Buckinghamshire, worth £3,084 a year. This last was not as generous as it sounds, because it appears to have been a confirmation of the settlement made for her under the terms of her father's will, but she also received two other, much smaller, grants which confirm the impression that, unlike Mary, she was *persona grata* at her brother's court.[210] Northumberland was reasonably generous with rewards in the king's name, but a much more cautious and thorough examination of the Augmentations records is really needed before he can be convicted of plundering the resources of the Crown, as distinct from those of the Church. Grants were more often purchases or exchanges than outright gifts, and even 'gifts' sometimes turn out to have been made in consideration of the surrender of some other land or benefit. In spite of the sale of Crown lands, which undoubtedly accelerated in the last year of the reign, there was no serious decline in the income of the court of Augmentations, and we should probably conclude that attainders and continuous pressure upon the bishops were bringing almost as much land into the pool as grants and sales were taking away.[211] The property of the duke of Somerset was worth at least £5,000 a year, and that of the bishopric of Winchester another £3,000. When Miles Coverdale was collated to the see of Exeter in March 1551, it was declared to be 'of the yearly value of £500, which was £1565. 13s. 6d.'.[212] The distribution of patronage by the council during Northumberland's ascendancy was not out of line with that of the Protectorate, or of the reign of Henry VIII, although it was generous by comparison with that of Henry VII or Elizabeth.

There was, consequently, nothing hypocritical about the duke's campaign against corruption. Sir William Sharrington had eventually been pardoned for his malfeasance at the Bristol mint, probably in return for his help in bringing Lord Thomas Seymour to book. In January 1551 an even bigger fish was swept into the net, when Warwick and Herbert reported to the council that they had taken the accounts of Sir Martin Bowes, the undertreasurer of the Tower mint, and found him in deficit to an extent which could not be calculated because of the incompleteness of his records.[213] Whether this was the result of incompetence or dishonesty is not clear, and

[208] Ibid., fo. 320ᵛ: 25 Mar. 1553.   [209] Ibid., fo. 98ᵛ: 19 May 1551.
[210] Ibid., fo. 80ᵛ: 17 Apr. 1551; *Cal. Pat.*, iv. 91.
[211] Between Michaelmas 1552 and Michaelmas 1553 sales amounted to just over £170,000, which at 20 years' purchase would have diminished income by about £8,500 per annum (PRO E351/2080).
[212] MS Royal 18C 24, fo. 121ʳ: 28 July 1551.   [213] *APC*, iii. 188.

probably was not clear at the time. Warwick and Herbert gave him the benefit of the doubt on criminal intent, and 'entered into a communicacion with him what he wolde give unto the Kinges Majestie, besides his reckening, to be clear of all demaundes etc.'. They settled for a fine of £10,000—£3,000 down and the rest in annual instalments.[214] At the same time Sir Martin was pardoned for any criminal offence which he might have committed. In view of some of the dubious operations which had been going on at the mint over the last few years, there may even have been a degree of inadvertence about his deficit, but the absence of proper accounts inevitably created suspicion. Bowes was in other respects a successful and reasonably honest merchant, but the same cannot be said of John Beaumont, whose sins eventually caught up with him in June 1552. From early 1545 to December 1550 Beaumont had been Receiver-General of the court of Wards and Liveries. He then resigned to become Master of the Rolls. Throughout his tenure at the court of Wards the Master had been William Paulet, now Lord Treasurer, who seems to have entertained no suspicion of his subordinate's activities. However, in the course of a survey of all the king's revenue courts towards the end of 1551, his suspicions were aroused, probably because Beaumont's successor could not make any sense of his accounts.[215] On 11 February 1552 Beaumont was committed to the Fleet and a thorough investigation began, carried out largely by Cecil, but motivated by Northumberland himself. The reason for the latter's zeal had less to do with deficiencies in the Wards' accounts than with a more recent offence. Sitting as a judge in Chancery, Beaumont had entered into a corrupt understanding with Anne Grey, Lady Powis, whereby she had obtained lands through a forged instrument of her late father, Charles Brandon, duke of Suffolk, and had then immediately conveyed them to Beaumont.[216] Perversion of justice in this manner was peculiarly abhorrent to a landed aristocracy, and, to make matters worse, the victim of Beaumont's fraud in this case was Northumberland's friend and close ally, Henry Grey, then marquis of Dorset. In the wake of this discovery, Beaumont's accounts were given a thorough going-over, and in spite of the cleverness with which he had covered his tracks, he was forced to confess a debt totalling £20,871. 18s. 8d.[217] To make matters even worse, he had concealed a felonious theft by one of his servants. Unlike Sharrington or Bowes, Beaumont was destroyed. On 28 May he conveyed all his lands and goods to the king. The following month he was brought before the Star Chamber, attempted to

---

[214] *APC*, iii. 188. In consideration of his fine, he was pardoned a few days later (MS Royal 18C 24, fo. 34ᵛ).

[215] Jordan, *The Threshold of Power*, 442–3; J. Hurstfield, *The Queen's Wards* (London, 1958), 199–204.

[216] *APC*, iii. 478; *Chronicle of Edward VI*, 109; SP10/14, no. 34: Northumberland to Sir William Cecil, 31 May 1552. Beaumont was tried in Star Chamber in June (E. Lodge, *Illustrations of British History* (London, 1838), 170–5).

[217] BL Lansdowne MS 2, fos. 178–9; Nichols, *Literary Remains*, ii. 427.

retract his confession, and was condemned to the forfeiture which he had already made.[218] There are some odd features of the way in which his case was handled, but there does not seem to be any doubt about his substantive guilt, or the justice of his expropriation. At a time when the council was straining every nerve to improve financial administration, peculation on this scale was very worrying, and the case for a radical reform of the revenue courts was greatly strengthened.

For this, and a number of other reasons, it was decided in December 1552 to call a new parliament to meet on 1 March. By Christmas, the king was unwell, but his ailment seemed to be nothing worse than a bad cold. He had thrown off a mild attack of smallpox in April with great resilience, and had been adequately protected from the sweat, which had killed so many of his subjects in 1551 and 1552.[219] There was nothing to give rise to any particular anxiety, but there was much to be done to remedy the affairs of the realm, and Edward was anxious to play his part. At some point during the Christmas holidays, out of a general sense of responsibility rather than prompted by any immediate concern, he started to think about the succession. Neither he nor the duke of Northumberland realized how important that was to become over the succeeding months.

[218] E. Lodge, *Illustrations of British History* (London, 1838), 175.
[219] *Chronicle of Edward VI*, 117. On the destructiveness of the sweat in general, see Jordan, *The Threshold of Power*, 468–70.

6

1553: Crisis and Catastrophe

THE year 1553 opened without any premonition of the dramatic events which it was to contain. A parliament had been convened for 1 March, and preparations for the session were already in hand.[1] The chief need was for money, and a subsidy bill, only the second of the reign, was proposed. The whole council approached this necessity with some trepidation. Not only had the last subsidy been imperfectly collected, thanks to the troubles of 1549, but there were problems about demanding direct taxation in peacetime. There were precedents. Thomas Cromwell had succeeded in 1534, arguing the king's general need to defend and govern his realm, and the subsidy of 1540 had also been voted when there were no formal hostilities to justify it.[2] On the other hand, Henry VIII had been an imperious king, whom it had been hard to gainsay, and there was an understandable reluctance to test the limits of his son's authority in the same way. Northumberland was so concerned about the possible effect of such a demand that he even suggested putting the session off until the autumn.[3] A subsidy voted in the spring would have to be collected during the summer, when the popular mood was always at its most volatile, whilst one voted after the harvest had been gathered would be collected during the winter. However, either the Lord President did not press his point, or the council did not accept it, because the session went ahead as planned. There could be no question of the reality of the need, nor of Dudley's awareness of it. Writing to the council on 28 December, he observed, fairly enough:

These things are now so onerous, having been all this time put off as best we could, that without your speedy help dishonour and peril may follow. Sale of lands must be the most honourable means; you have tried calling in debts and seeking every man's doing in office—yet you perceive this cannot salve the sore so long suffered to fester ...[4]

---

[1] The decision to summon a parliament had been taken in Dec. 1552; the date of convening was probably fixed on 6 Jan. 1553 (SP10/15, no. 73; *Acts of the Privy Council*, ed. J. Dasent *et al.* (London, 1890–1907), iv. 200).

[2] G. R. Elton, 'Taxation for War and Peace in Early Tudor England', in J. M. Winter (ed.), *War and Economic Development* (Cambridge, 1975), 33 ff.; G. L. Harriss, 'Thomas Cromwell's "New Principle" of Taxation', *English Historical Review*, 93 (1978), 721–38; J. D. Alsop, 'Innovation in Tudor Taxation', *English Historical Review*, 99 (1984), 83–93.

[3] SP10/15, no. 73.

[4] Ibid.

This situation he went on, rather less fairly, to blame mainly on the late Protector 'who took up the protectorate and government of his own authority ... and by [his] unskilful protectorship and less expertise in government, plunged into wars'. At the end of the day, Northumberland's anxiety to get the credit for solving the problems which his predecessor had allegedly created, proved to be greater than his reluctance to meet parliament. There was also the related matter of the reform of the revenue courts to be attended to, in response to an initiative from the Lord Treasurer, and the planned dissolution of the diocese of Durham to be formalized.

The succession did not feature in these plans, any more than it had done in the previous year. The fact that the king had already begun to toy with the subject merely reflected his own sense of responsibility, and not any perceived need. With the benefit of hindsight it seems immensely significant that Edward had a bad cold at Christmas, and that his journal suddenly ended on 30 November 1552. At the time the cold seemed no worse than several others he had suffered from, and he may simply have decided that the journal, which had probably begun as a school exercise, was no longer a worthy occupation for a sovereign prince in his sixteenth year. The real responsibilities of government, for which he had been consciously preparing for the last two years, had almost arrived. Whether his thoughts on the succession were prompted or spontaneous, we do not know, but the extraordinarily messy document which now survives in the Petyt MS was certainly not the work of a mature political mind.[5] The handwriting is the king's own, and is firm and legible, indicating, as Jordan argued, a date not later than February, and possibly an intention to take the issue to parliament.[6] Edward knew perfectly well that if he married and had issue of his own there would be no problem to address, so the fact that he does not allude to that situation does not prove that he already realized it to be impossible. He was only concerned with the eventuality of his death without issue, and the fact that he provided for the possibility of his heir having already achieved his majority indicates that he was not thinking in the short term. Two things are immediately noticeable about his plan, and they may be connected. One is the exclusive preoccupation with 'heires masles', and the other is the absence of any reference to his father's will, or to the statute which had authorized it. In January 1553 the lawful heir, in the event of Edward's death without issue, was his half-sister Mary, unless she should have been foolish enough to marry without the consent of the council.[7] If she should have died, or excluded herself, then the next heir was Elizabeth. Only if both these princesses were deceased, or married without consent,

---

[5] Inner Temple, Petyt MS xlvii, fo. 316, printed and edited in J. G. Nichols (ed.), *Literary Remains of King Edward VI* (Roxburgh Club, 1857), ii. 571–2.

[6] W. K. Jordan, *Edward VI: The Threshold of Power* (London, 1970), 515 and n.

[7] 35 Henry VIII, c. 1; *Statutes of the Realm*, ed. A. Luder *et al.* (London, 1810–28), III. 955–8.

would the crown have descended to Henry's niece, Lady Frances Brandon, and the heirs of her body. If there was an alternative to this order, it was that of 'divine right'. It could be argued, and the catholic Church did argue, that Henry's succession act was *ultra vires*, and that his only true heir, even in preference to Edward himself, was his legitimate daughter Mary. After her, in default of offspring, the crown should pass to the oldest descendant of Henry's elder sister, Margaret. In 1553 that person was the 11-year-old queen of Scots, betrothed to the Dauphin and living at the French court.

The king completely ignored his half-sisters, and the queen of Scots, starting his scheme with 'the L. Frauncese'. The reasons for this need to be unravelled, for they are crucial to an understanding of the relationship between Northumberland and Edward during the last six months of the latter's life. Mary's exclusion has always been explained in terms of religious incompatibility, and of the threat which she was perceived to offer to the Edwardian settlement.[8] That is valid, but is by no means the whole story. Whoever was responsible for the king's 'Device' also seems to have believed that her illegitimacy was more important than her statutory rehabilitation. Moreover Elizabeth's religion was by no means incompatible, and her relations with her half-brother had always appeared to be good. Consequently her exclusion has been explained in terms of Northumberland's influence, on the grounds that he preferred his biddable daughter-in-law to the enigmatic and tough-minded princess. However, an acute aversion to the state of illegitimacy, and a willingness to believe all that was said to the detriment of both Henry VIII's first two marriages, could be sufficient explanation for both exclusions. By no stretch of imagination could the queen of Scots be described as illegitimate, but she was an alien born and reared, and at this stage no one in England seems to have given her a second thought as a claimant. Perhaps the most important consideration of all was that all the visible candidates, even into the next generation, were female, and Edward shared, to an extreme degree, his father's aversion to a female succession.[9] This was not as irrational as it might appear to a late twentieth-century mind, because of the perceived inevitability of marriage and the ill-defined powers of the crown matrimonial. The main reason why Henry had moved heaven and earth to get a male heir was to preserve his realm from foreign domination or domestic faction. In 1553 that danger was acute in that both the king's half-sisters were unmarried, and if either of them should succeed the Tudor dynasty might well come to an end. These considerations seem to have weighed heavily with the young man as he jotted down his not very coherent thoughts:

[8] Jordan, *The Threshold of Power*, 515.
[9] The nearest male to the succession was Henry, Lord Darnley, the son of Matthew Stuart, earl of Lennox, and his wife Margaret, the daughter of Margaret Tudor's second marriage to Archibald, earl of Angus. Darnley was considered to be an alien, and like his cousin Mary (whom he subsequently married) he was never mentioned in this connection.

For lakke of issu of my body ... to the issue masle...To the Lady Fraunceses heires masles if she have any such issue befor my death to the Lady Janes heires masles, To the Lady Katerins heires masles, To the Lady Maries heires masles, To the heires masles of the daughters wich she shal have hereafter. Then to the Lady Margets heires masles. For lakke of such issue, To th 'eires masles of the L. Janes daughters. To th'eires masles of the L. Katerins daughters, and so forth til you come to the L. Margets daughters heires masles.[10]

This extraordinary genealogical wild-goose chase through three genera-tions could have lasted upwards of twenty years, as sons were envisaged to daughters who had not yet been born. As if this was not sufficiently eccen-tric, after some rational suggestions for the organization of another royal minority, in clause 5 the king returned to his besetting problem.

If I died w^t out issu, and there was none heire masle, then the L. Fraunces to be govvernres. For lakke of her ... her eldest daughters, and for lakke of them the L. Marget to be govvernres after as is aforsaid, til summe heire masle be borne, and then the mother of that child to be govvernres.

These are not the thoughts of a practical politician, but of a person pursuing an obsession. Should Edward die before either he or any of his multitude of female kinsfolk can either beget or bear a son, the monarchy is to be placed in abeyance until the magic feat is performed! Such a proposal lacked any kind of sense. The only rational way to exclude a female succession was to follow France and adopt the Salic law. However, that was scarcely an option, given the extraordinary dearth of royal kindred. Not only were there no cadet branches of the Tudor family, none of the lines stemming from the sons of the prolific Edward III ran in an unbroken male line to the mid-sixteenth century.[11] It is hardly surprising that the 'Device' was not presented to parliament, nor apparently discussed in council. It amounted to little more than ingenious and rather far-fetched speculation. It is hard to believe that Northumberland, or any other responsible adviser, had any share in the preparation of this document. The question is whether anyone knew about it at all until the king's fluctuating health suddenly made the issue not only real but urgent.

Careful consideration of the 'Device' should therefore prompt a cautious reappraisal of the view that the Lord President exercised a Svengali-like domination over his young master. Edward was growing up fast, and extremely conscious of his royal dignity. Nearly twenty years ago, Pro-fessor Hoak drew our attention to a fascinating French account of the

---

[10] Petyt MS xlvii, fo. 316. Catherine and Mary were Jane's younger sisters. Margaret was the daughter of Frances's younger sister, Eleanor, and Henry Clifford, earl of Cumberland.

[11] The senior male line had ended with Henry VI; the second male line, via Richard Planta-genet, earl of Cambridge, had ended with Edward, earl of Warwick, in 1499. The royal houses of Castile and Portugal were descended through the female line, as were the Tudors them-selves, and Reginald Pole. The Staffords, the Neville earls of Westmorland, and the earls of Huntingdon came twice or more through the female line.

inwardness of the king's relationship with his chief councillor. According to this observer, probably a servant of the French ambassador, Edward

> revered him as if he were himself one of his subjects—so much so that the things which he knew to be desired by Northumberland he himself decreed in order to please the Duke and also to prevent the envy which would have been produced had it been known that it was he who had suggested these things to the king ...[12]

This ascendancy the duke preserved, partly by planting his loyal familiar, Sir John Gates, as Vice-Chamberlain of the Household, and partly by private nocturnal visits to the royal bedchamber.

> When there was anything of importance which he wanted to be done or said by the king without it being known that it had proceeded by his motion, he visited the king secretly at night in the king's chamber, unseen by anyone, after all were asleep ...

This account is not dated, but cannot be earlier than the beginning of Boisdauphin's mission in July 1551. It sounds very convincing, but should probably be classed as servants' gossip. Northumberland may well have paid private visits to the king, but the kind of total secrecy implied would have been impossible given the strict organization of the Privy Chamber watch.[13] Moreover he would have been wasting his time, since Edward's decisions were popularly attributed to him anyway. What is being reported here is a somewhat distorted version of the king's political education, which we know Northumberland was controlling in the latter part of 1551 and well into 1552. We should not assume that the boyish desire to please, even if it existed in the form described in the summer of 1551, was necessarily present to the same degree by the end of the following year. The award of an annuity to John Knox, pending a more substantial preferment, just a few days after Northumberland had declared that he would have nothing more to do with him;[14] the substantial re-endowment of the north-eastern bishoprics, contrary to his clearly expressed intention; and the continuing failure to appoint to Durham in spite of his persistent representations, all suggest that the duke's will was not law by the beginning of 1553.[15] The young king was beginning to develop a will of his own, and the appearances which Northumberland had been promoting for two years for his own purposes were now beginning to acquire substance. If he wanted to retain his authority, he would have to adjust to the changing circumstances.

    [12] Bibliothèque Nationale MS Ancien Saint-Germain Français, 15888, fos. 214*b*–215*b*; D. E. Hoak, *The King's Council in the Reign of Edward VI* (Cambridge, 1976), 123.
    [13] 'Order taken for the Chamber that three of the outer Privy Chamber gentlemen should always be here, and two lie in the palat, and fill the room of one of the four knights, that the esquires should be diligent in their office, and five grooms should always be present, of which one to watch the bedchamber' (W. K. Jordan (ed.), *The Chronicle and Political Papers of King Edward VI* (London, 1970), 26).
    [14] MS Royal 18C 24, fo. 279ᵛ: 4 Dec. 1552.
    [15] SP10/18, no. 1: Northumberland to Cecil, 2 Jan. 1553.

Behind an intermittent smokescreen of sickness and self-pity, he embarked upon this essential task. He had known that it would happen, and had prepared for it as best he could, but he could not have foreseen the combination of stubborn wilfulness and increasing physical debility which Edward began to exhibit as the year advanced. His own health may well have been fragile, but, as before, it did not inhibit his political energy: 'bear with my infirmity', he wrote to the council on 28 December, 'for I mean as well to master and country as the fittest.'[16] For the time being, business continued much as usual, but with a number of indications of the king's developing role. On or about 15 January Sir William Petre, one of the Principal Secretaries, drew up a memorandum for the conduct of council business which appears to represent an important advance.

5. A memorial to be delivered to his majesty on Saturday night by a secretary, and thereupon the matters to be appointed to several days.
6. On Friday afternoon a collection to be made of things done the week past, with a note of the principal reasons for any conclusions.
7. This collection to be presented on Saturday morning and his majesty's pleasure to be known on things concluded, and suits of importance to be moved that time.
8. On Sunday his majesty hearing by a secretary such more matters as are arisen, will appoint days for their consideration ...[17]

Edward annotated and endorsed this paper, which does not in itself prove anything, because as we have seen he had been drawing up 'political papers' for some time, but in this case the agenda suggested does not appear to be cosmetic. When the king wishes to hear 'the debating of any matter' he will give the council due notice. One of his own notes suggested that if fewer than four councillors were present at a meeting and an urgent matter arose 'they shall declare it to the King's Majesty and before him debate it', but not reach a decision 'without it require wonderful haste'.[18] The reality of these procedural changes seems to be confirmed by a number of memoranda of 'matters to be moved to the king', in the hands of Petre, Cecil, or one of the council clerks, which are variously dated between January and June 1553,[19] and remain among the domestic state papers. There is no suggestion here that the king was controlling the agenda, an impression which could be given by some of his earlier exercises. Nor did he intend to be present at regular council meetings. He would receive summaries of the council's proceedings, and deal with matters which had been referred to him for decision. The notice to be given of debates in the king's presence was a warning for them to attend upon him, not the other way round.

---

[16] SP10/15, no. 73.
[17] SP10/1, no. 15; F. G. Emmison, 'A Plan of Edward VI and Secretary Petre for reorganising the Privy Council's Work, 1552–3', *Bulletin of the Institute of Historical Research*, 31 (1958), 203–7.
[18] *Chronicle of Edward VI*, 184. [19] SP10/18, nos. 33, 34, 16, 27, 28, 32.

Whether these policy discussions should be called 'councils of state' or not is hardly an issue. Edward intended to do what his adult predecessors had always done, summon his councillors, or such of them as he chose, to advise him on 'matters of state'. Such meetings would not, and never had in the past, constitute minuted sessions of the Privy Council.

Although it meant the occasional frustration of his wishes, the duke of Northumberland had everything to gain from this situation if he handled it correctly. If he was to convert dominance over a boy into influence over a mature man, and retain the king's confidence for the foreseeable future, he had to nurture these fledgling aspirations, not suppress or divert them. Consequently, although the preparations for parliament were largely in his own hands, he carefully wrote to Lord Darcy to know the king's pleasure over the appointment of a Speaker for the House of Commons, the naming of a preacher, and the nature of the service which should accompany the opening.[20] Cecil had sent him a memorandum of business, which he returned with the comment that he thought it too defensive and apologetic: 'I believe we need not imagine the objections of every froward person, but burden their minds and hearts with the king's undeniable extreme debts and necessity.'[21] Nor should any apology be offered for the king's liberality to his servants, a subject which the Secretary clearly believed was likely to attract criticism. As usual councillors and officers of the household deployed their influence and patronage in pursuit of a tractable House of Commons, and as usual they were only partially successful. Perhaps a couple of dozen placemen were deployed to assist the council's management tactics, but not by any stretch of imagination could the parliament be described as packed.[22] Rather unusually, the king himself seems to have instructed his council to secure the return of one or two favoured servants, and he interested himself busily in the preparation of the agenda, although there is no sign that he contributed anything distinctive to the process. In the event it was probably Cecil, with Northumberland breathing down his neck, who drafted the subsidy bill. The duke considered strengthening his hand in the House of Lords by summoning those eldest sons of peers who held courtesy titles of nobility, most notably his own son the earl of Warwick, but the plan was not realized.[23] A number of licences were issued to peers to absent themselves from parliament, but there is no reason to suppose that this was a device to keep away potential troublemakers. The earl of Cumberland might have come into that category, and so might Lords Mordaunt and Vaux, but hardly such important office-holders as Lords Wharton and Darcy, to say nothing of the bishops of Peterborough, Salis-

---

[20] SP10/18, no. 6: 14 Jan. 1553.   [21] Ibid.
[22] BL Lansdowne MS 523, no. 21, fo. 31; Lansdowne MS 3, no. 19, fo. 36; Jordan, *The Threshold of Power*, 505–6.
[23] SP10/18, no. 8, 19 Jan. 1553. Although the plan was not carried out as proposed, the earl of Warwick did attend. Whether he was allowed to participate is not clear.

bury, and Coventry.[24] In the event the session was organized with exemplary efficiency, and lasted exactly a month, the shortest of the entire century. The subsidy bill required an initial shove by the council when it was introduced in the Commons on 6 March, but went through all readings in both Houses in less than a fortnight without any recorded opposition. Bills authorizing the king to reorganize his revenue courts by letters patent, and dissolving the ancient see of Durham, were also pushed through, the latter receiving three readings in a single day in the House of Lords, but other legislation was extremely meagre.[25] William Cecil must have looked back on this achievement with nostalgia in later years.

However, if the conduct of business gave grounds for satisfaction, the king's health did not. He was well enough to open the session, but only just. The ceremony was held in the royal residence at Whitehall, rather than in the palace of Westminster nearby, and the speech from the throne was delivered by the Lord Chancellor. He was somewhat better by the end of the month, when he seems to have closed the session in the normal way, but the usual Easter move to Greenwich was cancelled and the king remained at Westminster.[26] There is no reason to doubt the conventional diagnosis of pulmonary tuberculosis, but it is important to remember that contemporary diagnostics were not able to identify it, or to give any informed opinion of the seriousness of Edward's condition until very late in the day. The nature of the illness is that it progresses by rallies and relapses. There was a panic as early as the beginning of February, and the Princess Mary was sent for, being met on the outskirts of London and conducted to court with full honours by Lord William Howard and the earl of Warwick.[27] On that day, 6 February, the king was too ill to see her, but a few days later the fever had subsided, and they had a cordial meeting. The question which must have been in the minds of the council was not even alluded to. By the end of February he was conducting business with an appearance of normality, and in spite of the curtailed opening of parliament there was cheerful and relieved talk of his recovery. Throughout March he remained weak, and stayed indoors, but only the pessimistic Scheyfve thought that he was in any serious danger. Northumberland, the ambassador reported, was keeping Mary carefully informed of any change in her brother's condition. During April the tension was further relaxed. The king was allowed to take the air in the mild spring sunshine, and on 11 April to make his delayed journey to Greenwich.[28] At the end of the month he may have suffered some relapse,

---

[24] MS Royal 18C 24, fos. 299, 306, etc.

[25] D. Loades, 'The Dissolution of the Diocese of Durham, 1553–4', in *Politics, Censorship and the English Reformation* (London, 1991), Statute 7 Edward VI c. 12, PRO C65/161.

[26] *Calendar of State Papers, Spanish*, ed. Royall Tyler *et al.* (London, 1862–1954), xi. 16–19: 17 Mar. 1553.

[27] J. G. Nichols (ed.), *The Diary of Henry Machyn*, Camden Society, 42 (1848), 30–1.

[28] *Cal. Span.*, xi. 32: 10 Apr. 1553.

because the new French ambassador, Antoine de Noailles, was unable to present his credentials, and reported a general gloom when he dined with the council. However, the black mood did not persist, and by 7 May Petre could write to Cecil that the king was much amended, and expected soon to be able to 'take the air' again.[29] Cecil himself was absent from the court at this point, suffering from some unidentified malady. The suggestion that he was malingering is probably misplaced, because although there was intense intermittent anxiety at court, there was no sense of an impending political crisis. As far as anyone knew at that time, if Edward should die his father's succession act would apply, and Mary would succeed. That would certainly mean major changes, and the power structure would change, but there was no reason to suppose that heads would roll. In fact Cecil was absent during the calm before the storm, and walked straight into it on his return.

Throughout most of May the appearance of 'business as usual' was sustained. On the same day that Petre wrote to Cecil, Northumberland also wrote, announcing cheerfully that 'our sovereign lord doth begin very joyfully to increase and amend, they [the royal physicians] having no doubt of the thorough recovery of his highness …'.[30] A few days later the king sat at a window to watch Hugh Willoughby's ships drop down river on their way to seek the north-east passage, and on 17 May he briefly received the French ambassador.[31] No one doubted that he was still sick, but the threat to his life appeared to have receded. It was at this juncture, on 21 May, that Northumberland brought to fruition a series of matrimonial negotiations upon which he had been engaged for many months. His efforts to match his fourth son Guildford with Margaret Clifford, the daughter of the earl of Cumberland, having finally come to nothing in spite of the king's support, he turned his attention to his ally and friend, the duke of Suffolk. The fact that he had preferred the Cliffords to the Greys demonstrates that his plans were unconnected with the succession issue. The duchess of Suffolk and the countess of Cumberland had been sisters—both daughters of Mary Tudor, Henry's sister—but the countess had died in 1547. The duchess of Suffolk was the same 'Lady Fraunces' who featured in the king's 'Device', but it seems that no one except Edward knew that at this point. Both Jane Grey, Frances's daughter, and Margaret Clifford were members of the royal kindred, and Jane was slightly closer to the throne because her mother was the elder, but neither were thought of as serious claimants. At the end of April, when Scheyfve was already convinced that Northumberland was hatching some nefarious plot, he had no idea what it might be,

---

[29] R. A. de Vertot, *Ambassades des Messieurs de Noailles* (Leyden, 1763), ii. 3–4; *Historical Manuscripts Commission*, Salisbury MSS, i. 121.

[30] Lansdowne MS 3, no. 23.

[31] De Vertot, *Ambassades*, ii. 26–7; Richard Hakluyt, *The principall navigations*, ed. W. Raleigh (Glasgow, 1903–5), ii. 217.

and did not connect it with the intended wedding, merely commenting that Guildford was to marry 'the duke of Suffolk's eldest daughter, whose mother is third heiress to the crown by the testamentary disposition of the late king ...'. At the same time Guildford's sister Catherine was married to Henry Hastings, the heir to the earl of Huntingdon, and Jane's sister, also Catherine, to Henry Herbert, son of the earl of Pembroke.[32] With hindsight these marriages seem to have been very significant, but in fact they were routine actions of dynastic politics; less significant when they took place than the wedding of Lord Lisle to Anne Seymour three years before. Jane was something of a matrimonial prize, not because of her royal blood but because she was well known to Edward, being much of an age, and a great favourite of his. There had even been talk of him marrying her himself at one point. Unfortunately she had no desire to marry Guildford, and, although hard evidence of their relationship is lacking, it was certainly believed afterwards that she was constrained by her unsympathetic parents. Guildford may have needed little urging, but it seems that he was not indulged in the way his brother Robert had been. The weddings took place at Durham Place, and although the king was not present, the arrangements had his full approval.

However, within a few days Edward's hopeful remission came to an end, and his condition began to deteriorate alarmingly. Scheyfve had a reliable informant within the Privy Chamber, and by 11 June was able to give a circumstantial account of the king's condition which left little to the imagination.[33] There was now recognized to be a serious possibility that the king would die, and the ambassador's prognostications, which had been gloomy for months, were now generally shared. Northumberland, and Edward himself, now faced for the first time the conviction that a crisis was imminent, and the duke the probability that he had been building his political house upon the sand. His whole strategy had been geared to the power structure of Edward's court as it would be in 1555, and suddenly all his efforts seemed to have been in vain. It was probably at this juncture that the king produced his 'Device'. Even on 12 June, when Scheyfve repeated his conviction that Northumberland had formed a mighty conspiracy against the princess, 'and feels confident that he will prevail', he still had no idea of what was intended. In other words he was repeating popular rumours, with no specific information. Given the precision of his sickroom reports, it seems certain that Jane's claim could not have been unveiled any earlier. This must have been improvised at the last minute to remedy the defects of the 'Device' as it then stood. The duchess of Suffolk had not conceived for several years, and there was no chance of her bearing a son before the king's death. Jane was newly wed, but

---

[32] Jordan, *The Threshold of Power*, 513–14; *Cal. Span.*, xi. 46.
[33] *Cal. Span.*, xi. 50: 'the sputum which he brings up is livid, black, fetid, and full of carbon; it smells beyond measure.'

even the promptest conception could not have produced a son in less than nine months, and there was little chance that Edward could last that long. None of the other ladies mentioned were even wed. So either the contingency plan had to be put in operation, and the duchess made regent for the unborn heir, or the 'Device' had to be abandoned and the statutory order followed, or the wording had to be altered. The first option was a political impossibility which could not be seriously considered, and the second was unacceptable to the king. So the wording had to be altered. This was accomplished very simply by inserting the words 'and her' between 'Lady Jane' and 'heires masles', thus making the 17-year-old Jane Dudley queen, with remainder to any son she might bear. Such a solution had no logic to commend it, since Jane's mother, through whom she derived her claim, was still alive. There may well have been serious doubts about the suitability of the duke of Suffolk for the crown matrimonial but that scarcely strengthens the case. We do not know who actually made the alteration. It may well have been Northumberland, but Edward must have accepted it despite his dislike of a female succession, because he liked and trusted Jane. However, in the circumstances it is hardly surprising that when the news of this development was released it served to confirm the existence of Scheyfve's 'mighty plot', and to exacerbate the fear and suspicion with which the duke was already regarded. Should Edward convert his 'Device' into a will it would inevitably be subjected to legal challenge. Could the king, as a minor, make a lawful will at all? Could any king demise the crown by will *mere moto suo*, without the consent of parliament? Recent precedent suggested that the answer to both these questions should be in the negative. Nevertheless on 12 June Edward sent for his chief justices and other law officers, and instructed them to draw up a formal will on the basis of his 'Device'.[34]

Northumberland's initial reaction to the king's resolution can only be guessed. He had taken some care to repair his relations with the Princess Mary, as though he expected the statutory succession to be followed, if it should come to that. She had carried out a big exchange of lands with the king in April, and although that was not necessarily a sign of favour, she also received a substantial grant of lands in Hertfordshire on 6 June, barely a week before Edward dropped his bombshell.[35] There is no substantial evi-

---

[34] Jordan, *The Threshold of Power*, 516. Robert Wingfield, writing soon after the event, put a long speech into the mouth of the dying king, adding cautiously 'Hic fere, et non absimilia, perinde absurda, ac vana Northumbri ex suggestu, et aliorum ex coniuratis (qui debita quasi opera circa principem collati erant, ad eius dementandum puerile caput huiusmodi deliriis) in proprii generis, et regni perpetuam ignominiam non multum ante mortem ingruentem protulit minus felix princeps'. In this speech he made the illegitimacy of both the king's half-sisters the cause of their exclusion, and then described in some detail the reactions of the law officers. The source of Wingfield's information is not known, but is thought to have been John Gosnold, 'Vita Mariae Reginae', ed. D. MacCulloch, *Camden Miscellany*, 28 (1984), 198–200/247–9.

[35] MS Royal 18C 24, fo. 356ʳ.

dence to suggest that the duke had been plotting for months to deprive her of the succession. It was rather that the king's obsessive determination presented him with a gambler's opportunity. In the short term there was nothing to be gained from opposing Edward's will. If he should recover, he would not quickly forget those who had moved to thwart him, and if he should die, that would be the moment to decide what to do. So Northumberland would have no truck with those who tried to claim that altering the succession was high treason. It could not be treason to obey the king's express command, so when Sir Edward Montague and his colleagues tried to claim that they could not draw up a will to the king's specifications because of the Henrician succession act, the duke flew into a rage and threatened them with physical violence.[36] His loss of temper was probably due to the fact that he knew exactly how strong an argument they were deploying, but could not afford to acknowledge the fact. On 15 June Edward sent for the judges again, and commanded them on their allegiance to do his bidding, whereupon the lords of the council correctly advised them that it would be manifest treason to refuse.[37] However divided the council may have become later, at this stage they were unanimous in accepting the king's action, and Montague, comforting himself with the thought that 'the making of the book without the execution of it was no treason', proceeded to draft the letters patent. He solemnly warned the council that the king could not abrogate a statute by letters patent, but even so some of his colleagues refused to support his action.[38] On 21 June a specially convened gathering of notables, including the whole Privy Council, the officers of the household, the civic dignitaries of London, and twenty-two peers other than the council, signed the document and swore an oath to observe its provisions.[39] In spite of this, it never became a legally binding instrument, for it never passed the seals, and no official record of it now survives. It would seem that the officers of the chancery were also anxious to protect themselves against the possible consequences of an ill-considered action; or perhaps the law officers had a second line of defence. How much these signatures and oaths would actually be worth once Edward's fervent and inflexible will was removed also remained to be seen.

By June the succession crisis occupied the whole political horizon, and it is not surprising that other business should have been relegated to the sidelines, but earlier in the year the work of government had proceeded much as before. Although it was normally in England's interest to promote hostilities between the emperor and the French, by the end of 1552

---

[36] *HMC*, MSS of Lord Montague of Beaulieu, 4.

[37] Ibid. 5; Jordan, *The Threshold of Power*, 516.

[38] 'Vita Mariae', 249. Montague also argued that parliament should be summoned for Sept. to ratify the new order, but he probably realized that such advice was academic. It seems to have been mainly intended to salve his own conscience.

[39] Nichols, *Literary Remains*, ii. 572–3.

Northumberland's balancing act made peace a preferable option. Too close a friendship with the emperor might provoke the French to attack Calais—always a lurking fear, in spite of the recent treaty. On the other hand 'amity' with Henry II could easily mean difficulties in Antwerp, and, with both sides quick to take offence, it would be better if there was no war to provide a pretext for hostile actions. Consequently, towards the end of December the council decided to send out special envoys to each of the belligerents, indicating Edward's willingness to arbitrate their quarrel.[40] The two men chosen for these potentially sensitive missions were Northumberland's brother, Sir Andrew, and his son-in-law Sir Henry Sidney. Neither had any diplomatic experience, and Sidney was very young, so their selection has been taken as further evidence of how completely English policy was driven by Dudley priorities at this time. However, it appears from a letter written to Cecil by the duke on 28 December that he had not been personally responsible for their selection.[41] This would suggest that they were chosen, not for their skill but for their status as known intimates of both the king and the Lord President. Henry VIII, and other kings before him, had used their personal servants, and Gentlemen of the Privy Chamber, in the same way. If their initial soundings were successful, they could be followed up by professional diplomats; if not, they could be written off without any serious loss of face. Dudley, chosen to visit the emperor, called first on Scheyfve in London, considerably to the ambassador's surprise. On 8 January he was received by Mary of Hungary in Brussels, and then set out, in defiance of all the best advice, to intercept Charles as he journeyed towards Flanders. Sir Richard Morison, the accredited ambassador, who was travelling with the emperor, was unaware of Dudley's mission until he met him at Treves. Whether the council had neglected to write to him, or had deliberately kept him in the dark in case he should hinder the mission, is not clear. Once they had met, Morison did his best to further Dudley's efforts, but the latter's impatience was a serious handicap. Eventually he saw the emperor twice, and Charles told him that, while he was well disposed to peace, he was not at all disposed to trust French assurances, and would make no move until he knew Henry's mind more fully.[42] On 4 February Dudley was recalled, and Morison instructed to keep the matter fresh in the emperor's mind. Sidney certainly visited the French court at about the same time, but it is not certain that he ever saw the king, or delivered his message in person. On 15 February Sir William Pickering, the resident ambassador, reported that he

---

[40] According to Jordan (*The Threshold of Power*, 174), Northumberland did this without consulting the council, but it is clear from his letter to Cecil on 28 Dec. that the council had discussed the initiative, whether it came from the king (as is implied) or from Northumberland himself (SP10/15, no. 74).

[41] Ibid.

[42] Dudley and Morison to the council, 25 Jan. 1553; *Calendar of State Papers, Foreign, 1547–1550*, ed. W. Turnbull (London, 1861), 239–40.

had delivered a letter from Edward, and Henry's response had been that he would willingly negotiate, provided that the emperor declared his position first.[43] What part Sidney played is not clear, except that Pickering solicited his good offices in an attempt to persuade the council to recall him.[44]

Scheyfve was pleased with these inconclusive exchanges, because he believed that Northumberland's desire to cajole the emperor into negotiations was responsible for the marked improvement in Mary's position which he noted at the same time. He also believed that Northumberland was becoming increasingly autocratic and insecure, although the duke's surviving correspondence from January and February does not suggest either of those things. The fact that he was hated by the religious conservatives no doubt seemed important to the ambassador, who sympathized strongly with their position, but was actually of little significance as long as the king lived. Northumberland went out of his way to persuade Scheyfve of his sympathy with the emperor's position, and of his distance from the French, but in the circumstances such statements are no reliable guide to his true thinking.[45] His real priority in early March seems to have been to bring the European war to an end, and perhaps even to recreate the situation of 1518, with himself in the role of Wolsey. Throughout that month the resident ambassadors sought to keep the English initiative alive. Both sides were still bidding too high for serious negotiations to begin, but no one questioned Edward's earnestness in a good cause, and the papacy also entered the arena as a rival mediator, which caused the English efforts to be redoubled. On 1 April the council approved the instructions to two sets of commissioners, sent to the hostile courts to endeavour to break through the barriers of mutual suspicion and distrust.[46] Nicholas Wotton and Sir Thomas Chaloner were added to Pickering's existing presence in France, Chaloner also being designated as the ambassador's successor. At the same time Thomas Thirlby and Sir Philip Hoby were sent to join Morison in Brussels, with a similar intention that Hoby should replace the latter at the end of the negotiations.[47] The whole exercise quickly proved to be futile. Henry was not interested in ending a war which was going rather well for him. Although his resources were badly stretched, his ally Maurice of Saxony was scoring striking successes against the imperial armies, and even if he had wanted to he might not have been able to call him off. In Brussels the problem was different. The emperor's health was so poor that all negotiations were referred to the regent, indeed there were persistent rumours of Charles's death. Mary had no desire to negotiate at a disadvantage believing, rightly, that the military situation would improve in time. At the same time the English council had the ingenious idea of making both sides more amenable by doing a deal with the German protestants, and called up the

---

[43] Ibid. 245–6.   [44] Ibid. 246.   [45] *Cal. Span.*, xi. 17–19: 17 Mar. 1553.
[46] *APC*, iv. 46.   [47] *Cal. For.* 260.

experienced Christopher Mont for consultations.[48] This idea was not as wild as it might appear. If the English commissioners could broker an agreement between the emperor and his German enemies, it would not only make Charles more amenable to a general peace, it would also cut the ground from under the French war effort. However, all such hopes, reasonable or unreasonable, were soon to be dashed. On 4 June Wotton and Chaloner reported that Henry would make no concessions, and would respond only to a direct approach from the emperor.[49] Four days later Thirlby and Hoby had been dismissed by the regent with the verdict that there was no possible grounds for mediation. The best that could be said for six months of diplomatic effort was that it had done no harm, and had not actually damaged English relations with either side. Indeed relations with the regent had probably improved, in spite of her negative final conclusion. A few days later the envoys were able to take their leave of Charles, who was bedridden and weak, but in full possession of his faculties. Consequently the crisis of Edward's health arrived at a moment when English foreign policy was not going anywhere in particular, but at which all options were open. Neither war nor the threat of war was forcing the council's hand in June 1553.

If Northumberland's foreign policy was unproductive during the first half of 1553, the same cannot be said of other activities. In spite of the efforts of Thomas Gresham, the cloth trade to Antwerp remained slack after the slump of 1551. In addition to the economic circumstances, the emperor's decision in that year to let the Inquisition loose on the city did not help, and even the ultra cautious Merchant Adventurers were beginning to think that the time had come to broaden their horizons, especially as their victory over the Hanse had gone some way towards opening the Baltic. Individual English merchants had been probing far afield as early as 1470, when the first Bristol ship was recorded in the Azores, but the collective enterprise which supported the Cabots' voyages in the 1490s had not been sustained. William Hawkins had taken a ship as far as Brazil in the 1530s, but nothing much had come of his adventure, which had not shown an immediate profit. This was partly because, in spite of urging, Henry VIII had shown no interest in commercial expansion. The royal navy had made enormous strides under his eager patronage, but his concern had been almost entirely military.[50] As long as there were French galleys to be fought in the Channel, he was not prepared to invest money in developing the maritime base. Nor were the Londoners, who could derive a secure and increasing profit from the Low Countries trade, prepared to take unnecessary risks, or to press the king for a change of priorities. These attitudes had begun to change in the wake of the 'Reneger incident' in 1545, when a Southampton merchant,

[48] *Cal. For.* 283–4: 26 May 1553.   [49] BL Harley MS 523, no. 65, fo. 100*b*.
[50] D. Loades, *The Tudor Navy* (Aldershot, 1992), 74–102.

exasperated by the religiously motivated harassment from which he was suffering in Spain, took the law into his own hands and seized an inward bound West Indiaman with a rich cargo.[51] The imperial ambassador complained bitterly, and the Privy Council slapped Reneger gently on the wrist, giving him the command of a royal ship. The Lord Admiral at the time had been John Dudley, then Viscount Lisle. If Anglo-Spanish relations had become strained after the establishment of the royal supremacy, they became glacial with the advance of England into fully fledged protestantism, and the willingness of individual English merchants to defy the Spanish authorities was consequently enhanced. Some sort of an organized voyage was made to Morocco in 1551, but very little is known about it. In 1552 three ships out of London visited the Barbary coast, trading cloth and ironmongery for sugar and saltpetre. The Barbary corsairs were the implacable enemies of Spain, and many of the Jewish middlemen used by the English traders came of families expelled from Spain some sixty years before. Early 1553 saw a further escalation of this process when another expedition traded as far south as the Guinea coast, in what is now known as Sierra Leone. This voyage was commanded by Sir Thomas Wyndham, the Master of Naval Ordnance, and accompanied by two royal warships which had been leased to Wyndham for the occasion.[52] Although the voyage was not a success, and Wyndham died in the course of it, it signalled an important move in the direction of royal involvement. The capital had been privately raised, and we do not know the identity of the investors, but in view of Wyndham's position, it is quite likely that courtiers and councillors were among them. Angry Spanish protests were ignored, and, since the council was endeavouring to improve relations with the emperor at the time, this indicates that the adventurers must have had protection at the highest level.

The most significant venture, however, and the one in which the ailing king was particularly interested, was the search for a new route to China. China had existed on the fringes of European consciousness for a long time, and by the middle of the sixteenth century the Portuguese had established direct contact. However, they had hardly begun to tap what was correctly identified as a vast market, and one which lay very largely within temperate latitudes. This made it an extremely attractive outlet for woollen cloth, which tended not to sell well in the tropics. In order to exploit this market, and avoid tangling with the Portuguese, who had a powerful commercial and political presence in the far east, it was very desirable to find a new, and if possible shorter, route. Sebastian Cabot almost certainly had his own ideas about that, and was listened to with respect in the City. He played a leading part in the consortium which was established to fund and direct

---

[51] G. Connell-Smith, *The Forerunners of Drake* (London, 1954), 137–42.
[52] MS Royal 18C 24, fos. 278ʳ, 313ᵛ; Jordan, *The Threshold of Power*, 489.

such an exploration, but was persuaded that his advancing years made it impracticable for him to take part in person. The other inspirer, with similar ideas although less practical experience, was the English cosmographer John Dee. Dee had been introduced to the Dudley family via John Cheke and William Cecil, and became a close friend both of the young earl of Warwick and of Sir Henry Sidney.[53] Towards the end of 1552 it was decided to invite subscriptions towards a commercial enterprise designed to open up a new route to China around the north of the Eurasian land mass—what would later be known as the north-east passage. Some 240 shares were sold, at £25 each, mostly to London merchants, but also to a significant number of aristocrats and councillors, including Winchester, Bedford, Arundel, Pembroke, and Cecil.[54] It is not known that Northumberland or any of his family were shareholders, and the extent of his direct commitment is in doubt, but his relations with both Dee and Cecil were sufficiently close to be evidence of at least a general support. The three ships commissioned for the voyage were the *Edward Bonaventure* of 160 tons, the *Bona Esperanza* of 120 tons, and the *Bona Confidentia* of 90 tons, all belonging to members of the Merchant Adventurers company. On 10 May were issued 'Three several letters of commendation or safe conduct and passports for the three ships going to the new found lands, written ... to all kings, princes and other states ...', in Latin, Hebrew, and Chaldean.[55] This assumption that the rulers of the far north (to say nothing of the emperor of China) would be familiar with one of the languages of the ancient near east, is a forceful reminder of what an extraordinary feat of optimism and confidence the whole enterprise represented. Other letters were also carried, of a more fulsome and less formal nature, in which Edward addressed all his fellow sovereigns in the name of God and of trade. The expedition was commanded by Sir Hugh Willoughby, under licence from the Lord Admiral, with the experienced Richard Chancellor as Pilot Major. The ships were victualled for eighteen months and carried a total complement of 110 men. The ordinances and regulations for the fleet were drawn up in the name of Sebastian Cabot, but the use of English, and the insistence on the Prayer Book for onboard worship, suggests that he can only have been partly responsible. In spite of the brave start which the king witnessed, the fleet did not clear the Thames estuary until 24 May, and thereafter made such slow progress that Edward was already dead before they reached the Lofoten Islands, about 14 July.[56]

The eventual fate of Willoughby and Chancellor, and the nature of their achievement, are not part of this story, but the first half of 1553 marks a

[53] *Dictionary of National Biography*, *sub* Dee.
[54] *Cal. Span.*, xi. 14; Hakluyt, *Voyages*, iii. 331.
[55] MS Royal 18C 24, fo. 345ᵛ. Greek was also used for the letters of introduction, which may have been more useful in Moscow, where they were eventually presented.
[56] Sir William Foster, *England's Quest of Eastern Trade* (London, 1933), 9–10.

turning-point in the maritime history of England, the importance of which can hardly be overemphasized. For the first time royal authority, in the form of the council, was substantially involved in the promotion of long-distance trade. This was quite different from the small-scale direct patronage which Henry VII had given John Cabot, and represented a shift in government policy which the long reign of Elizabeth was to render permanent. By investing directly in the voyages of John Hawkins Elizabeth was to carry the process a stage further. Edward did not, as far as we can tell, contribute ships to any enterprise as a form of investment, although the terms upon which the *Primrose* and the *Moon* were made available to Sir Thomas Wyndham do not suggest a straightforward lease. The council book records:

A letter to the Admiraltie to deliver to George Bowes, mayor of London, William Garnet, one of the Sheriffs, John York and Thomas Windham or their assigns the ship called the Primrose and the pinnace called the Moon with all the tackle and apparel in them belonging, taking sufficient bond of them for the delivery to his Majesties use by midsummer 1554 one other ship and pinnace of like goodness and burden and as well apparrelled and trimmed ...[57]

Nothing is said about any share of the profit, and in the event there was none, but this seems to represent a half-way house between the traditional commercial lease and the new system developed in the 1560s. There is no direct evidence of who was responsible for this shift in policy, and it may have resulted from force of circumstances rather than personal initiative. But it certainly occurred between 1550 and 1553 when, by general consent, John Dudley was the leader of the council and the principal manager of affairs. If we also take into account the fact that the navy was well and carefully maintained during these years, that Clinton, the Lord Admiral, was a close ally of Dudley's, and that several others known to have been in his confidence—Wyndham, York, Dee, and Cecil—played leading parts, the circumstantial evidence certainly points to him. Whether this sprang from an enlightened perception of England's long-term needs, or from the urgent necessity to raise more revenue from the commercial wealth of London, must remain an open question, but in truth there was no great distance between the two factors. In Henry VIII's reign England had been a formidable naval power, but a negligible force in the great navigational and commercial expansion which was then going on. By the end of Elizabeth's reign English navigators, cartographers, and explorers were second to none. Northumberland presided over the beginnings of a maritime revolution about which, as far as I am aware, he never made any recorded comment.

As we have seen, the idea that the duke's financial policy was an unmitigated disaster has long since been revised. Bonds to Anthony

[57] MS Royal 18C 24, fo. 307^v: 4 Mar. 1553.

Fugger, Caspar Schetz, and other bankers were discharged at regular inter-
vals, the cancelled obligations being returned to the council by Gresham,
and thence passed on either to the Lord Treasurer or to the City, as appropriate.[58] On 5 May 1553 the officers of both the Staplers and the Merchant
Adventurers came before the council and agreed to discharge Crown debts
in Antwerp to the considerable sum of £36,371, due on five different obligations: 'in consideracion whereof the Lordes have promised that the seyd
Merchauntes, aswell Staplers as Adventurers, shalbe answered here of the
sayd sumes that they shall disburse beyonde the sees after such rate as here
after shalbe agreed uppon.'[59] Inevitably a lot of this debt was recycled but
the overall burden was gradually reduced. By the time of the king's death it
stood at no more than £110,000, and was costing about £1,200 a month to
service. Thanks to Gresham's successful manipulations the interest rate
averaged no more than 13 per cent, which represented a better 'credit rat-
ing' than either the Valois or the Habsburg could achieve. Throughout the
spring the king's agent continued to struggle with the exchange rate. In
February he suffered a setback when it fell from 19s. 9d. to 19s., but by the
end of April he was able to report that it had risen to 20s., and that he was
able to buy bullion.[60] He urged the council to persuade or force the merchants with whom they were negotiating for loan repayments to accept an
exchange rate of 23s. 4d., in which case 'the exchange will doubtless rise,
and never likely fall again …'.[61] In this manœuvre it would appear that he
was largely successful. No new coin seems to have been issued during this
period to assist his efforts, and, although some base coin was recycled, this
did not result in any significant improvement.[62] Parliament, as we have
seen, voted a standard subsidy plus a tenth and fifteenth, the first instalment of which was due in June. In spite of the grumbling this was paid with
reasonable promptness, but none of it reached the Exchequer in time to
make any difference to Northumberland. The government's principal
source of supplementary income continued to be the sale of lands, which
brought in about £145,000 between Michaelmas 1552 and the end of the
reign.[63] Financial reform occupied an important place on the parliamentary
agenda in March. Not only was the king empowered to merge or abolish
the independent revenue courts by letters patent, procedures for the collection of both lay and clerical taxation were tightened up, and another act
augmented the powers of the Crown to control the export of bullion, also
giving the council greater discretion to act.[64] Although the economies recommended by the 1552 commission were largely ignored, and the house-

[58] e.g. on 12 May 1553; *APC*, iv. 269.   [59] Ibid. 267.
[60] Gresham to the council, 28 Apr. 1553 (*Cal. For.* 273).   [61] Ibid.
[62] C. E. Challis, *The Tudor Coinage* (Manchester, 1978), 318; *Calendar of the Patent Rolls,*
Edward VI, ed. R. H. Brodie (London, 1924–9), iv. 186.
[63] Jordan, *The Threshold of Power*, 463; PRO E351/2080.
[64] 7 Edward VI, c. 2, c. 6; *Statutes of the Realm*, iv. i. 164–5, 170.

hold expenditure in the last full year of the reign amounted to nearly £56,000, the overall financial situation was improving rather than deteriorating.

The marquis of Winchester may well have wanted to reduce the revenue courts in order to simplify administration and revitalize the Exchequer. However, he may also have wished to revive the type of Chamber finance which had flourished under Henry VII and Wolsey, and which had been effectively ended by Cromwell's development of the independent courts. This would have been entirely consistent with Northumberland's desire to strengthen the personal authority of a monarch with whom he expected to be on exceptionally good terms. A means of doing this lay ready to hand in what was usually known as the King's Coffers. This was not a spending department in the ordinary sense, but rather a glorified expansion of the Privy Purse.[65] Between 1542 and 1547 Sir Anthony Denny, as Chief Gentleman of the Privy Chamber and Keeper of the Palace of Westminster, had held four separate accounts, and had been responsible for the custody of a great deal of money. When his account was taken in February 1548 he was held responsible for £246,404, the great bulk of which (over £200,000) had been spent on the king's building projects, on furnishings, jewellery, plate, and private rewards.[66] One of these accounts was the Privy Purse proper— 'Thordinary paymentes made by vertue of thoffice ef the Grome of the Stole'. This amounted to a little more than £3,000, the remainder being held and dispensed by virtue of his custody of the Palace, although it was no accident that so sensitive a position was in the hands of one of the king's most intimate servants. On Henry VIII's death the coffers, allegedly then containing some £11,500, were removed from Westminster to the Tower of London on the orders of the earl of Hertford, who was later accused of having purloined it.[67] There is no evidence to substantiate such a charge, but Denny's functions at Westminster were greatly reduced during the remaining months of his charge. The main expenditure for which he had been responsible seems to have been carried by the court of Augmentations. It certainly did not revert to the Treasury of the Chamber, from which Cromwell had removed it. That account continued to be almost entirely concerned with the wages of the Chamber staff. In August 1547 Sir Michael Stanhope became Chief Gentleman of the Privy Chamber, and, over the remaining months of his accounting period, Denny was issuing money to Stanhope for the Privy Purse expenses, but had lost the custody of the main coffers, which remained at the Tower.[68]

Denny died in August 1549, and Stanhope was removed in the wake of the Protector's fall. The Privy Purse then passed to the four Principal

[65] D. E. Hoak, 'The Secret History of the Tudor Court: the King's Coffers and the King's Purse, 1542-1553', *Journal of British Studies*, 26 (1987), 208–31.
[66] BL Lansdowne Charter 14.   [67] Library of the Society of Antiquaries, MS 129A.
[68] BL Lansdowne Charter 14; *APC*, ii. 121, 128, 130.

Gentlemen in commission, while their clerk, Peter Osborne, kept the account.[69] At first it seems that Osborne handled only the small-scale payments which had previously been made by Stanhope, while Sir John Williams as Master of the Jewel House took over responsibility for the coffers proper. The Privy Purse account from 10 January 1550 to 1 January 1552 shows expenditure of a little under £4,000.[70] However, in January 1552 a significant reorganization took place. Osborne took over from Williams £16,687. 7s. 11d., including arrearages of £826. 11s. 10d., which was presumably the balance remaining in the coffers, and when he accounted himself for the period from January 1552 to May 1553, the total which he answered for was £39,948, exclusive of £600 which had been stolen, and for which he was allowed.[71] Osborne's 'file' shows him to have been acting in very much the same way that Denny had acted in the last years of the previous reign. The king's 'secret affairs' included the wages of soldiers, payments for goldsmith's work, part of the ordinary charges of the household, repayments in Antwerp, and several payments to the treasurer of the navy. On 15 May 1553, when he rendered his account, Osborne handed over a balance of £1,647 to Sir Andrew Dudley, who seems to have been handling the Privy Purse proper at least since the reorganization.[72] Professor Hoak has traced the origin of this arrangement to a memorandum written by the earl of Warwick to Cecil in June 1551, urging the need for a special account which should be outside the control of the normal revenue courts.[73] The fact that Osborne was also appointed King's Remembrancer of the Exchequer on 7 September 1552 no doubt facilitated understanding between the two financial systems, but was not designed to bring the coffers under Exchequer control.[74]

Exactly why Mildmay and Berners were commissioned to take Osborne's account on 15 May is not clear. There may have been no particular significance in the date, and the account may have been no more than a routine check. However, the fact that Osborne surrendered his cash balance suggests that he was not intended to continue in post. We do not know whether he was replaced, or whether the coffers were discontinued at that point. There is no further reference to them in the last two months of Edward's reign, and Mary does not seem to have inherited such a system. Her own use of Sir Edmund Peckham in 1553/4 was analogous, but not the same, and the Privy Coffers, as such, were never resurrected. We are therefore left with some unanswered questions about Peter Osborne and his activities. The coffers were established to be a flexible revenue department under the direct control of the Privy Chamber, which was in turn closely monitored by the council, Dudley and his friends having the ascendancy in

---

[69]   *APC*, iv. 28; PRO E101/546/19.   [70]   PRO E101/426/8.
[71]   MS Royal 18C 24, fo. 348v: 17 May 1553; ibid., fo. 360r: 17 June 1553; PRO E101/546/19.
[72]   *HMC*, Salisbury MSS, i. 127.
[73]   Ibid. 86–7; Hatfield House, Cecil Papers, 151, fos. 7–8.   [74]   MS Royal 18C 24, fo. 253v.

both. This could well have been a part of Northumberland's strategy for retaining political control, but Osborne's accounts do not suggest that the money was in any way misappropriated. It was probably intended that the coffers would be supplied with monies received from the collection of debts due to the Crown, upon which great emphasis was being placed in 1552. On 8 February the treasurers of all the revenue courts, including the Exchequer, were instructed to pay weekly to Osborne all 'sommes of monye … which … hath byn levyid of the dettes and Arrerages dew unto his majestie within his said courte(s)'.[75] However, it seems unlikely that almost £40,000 would have been recovered in this way in about fifteen months and the coffers were almost certainly replenished from other sources as well. It is possible that the discontinuance of the coffers was never intended, and that Osborne was simply moved aside in order to make way for an officer who would be appointed by the king personally, in which case the move could be seen as an attempt to increase Edward's direct control, in the manner of his father and grandfather. His rapidly worsening illness and early death would obviously have prevented that from happening, and leaves the whole matter in the realm of conjecture. What is clear is that the king's coffers constituted a major spending department, adapted by Dudley from earlier practices, and largely controlled by his agents. It stood outside the normal accounting procedures, and therefore needed a special commission to assess it. In spite of these circumstances Osborne clearly felt that he had nothing to hide, and he was almost certainly right. In spite of the criticisms heaped upon Northumberland's financial administration by the Marian council, Osborne was never mentioned, and his subsequent career is best known for his membership of several Elizabethan parliaments.

The relative success of the financial administration over the last two years of the reign was obtained partly by ruthless economies in certain directions. Officials, like diplomats, constantly complained of lack of money, and too much attention should not be paid to cries of despair like that uttered by Sir Philip Hoby in August 1552: 'For God's sake', he wrote to Cecil, 'Help the miseries of the ordnance office for lack of money.'[76] Hoby's lament was detailed and circumstantial, and no doubt reflected a genuine crisis, but it should not be taken to mean that the whole military establishment was in terminal decline. Very broadly the strategy seems to have been to maintain the navy and the garrison of Calais, but to run down or discontinue the garrisons of the elaborate coastal fortifications which Henry VIII had built between 1539 and 1544. This was perfectly justifiable on the grounds that a full-scale war was extremely unlikely after March 1550, and that Calais was the only piece of English territory which could not be defended by the fleet. In May 1552 some of the coastal forts in Devon and Cornwall were placed on a care and maintenance basis, and the blockhouses in Kent were

---

[75] *APC*, iii. 475.   [76] SP10/14, no. 56.

surveyed, although it is not clear that any further reductions were made there.[77] After the surrender of Boulogne the garrison was not disbanded but redeployed within England, part on the Scottish borders, and part to those counties where disaffection was particularly feared, or which were felt to be vulnerable to attack. In July 1550 mobile bands of 100 or 200 men were sent to Suffolk, Essex, Sussex, Kent, Hampshire, and Dorset, perhaps because such bands were felt to be more useful than garrisons tied down to particular forts.[78] In June 1553, at the very end of the reign, a few more garrisons were stood down, and the ordnance recalled to the Tower. About half of the foreign mercenaries which had played such a key role in suppressing the disorders of 1549 were paid off in the summer of the following year. The remainder, about 800 in number, were gradually phased out over the next two years, except for a few bands who remained on the Scottish border, where the local levies were thought to be particularly unreliable.

In spite of the persistent anxiety about disaffection, which continued to absorb a disproportionate amount of council time, and the ale bench attacks upon Northumberland, reports of which came in almost daily, there were no serious disorders after the end of 1549. This was no doubt partly due to the debilitating affect of the sweating sickness, particularly in 1551, but it was quite reasonable of the council to conclude by the summer of 1552 that the expensive professional gendarmerie set up in December 1550 was no longer required. No doubt saving £20,000 a year was a major consideration, but money had been, if anything, even shorter when they had been established. What had changed was not the ability to pay such men, but the priority which they represented. The existing security provision had been substantially enhanced in December 1551, at the time of the duke of Somerset's trial, but had never, in fact, been called upon. On the other hand, the system of licensed retaining continued to be expanded. On 3 May Sir Henry Neville and Sir William Fitzwilliam were each licensed for 20 men, Sir Henry Gate and Sir Nicholas Throgmorton for 25, and Sir Henry Sidney for 50.[79] The last licences were issued on the very eve of the crisis, 24 June 1553, to the Kentish quartet of Sir George Harper, Sir Henry Isley, Sir John Guildford, and Cuthbert Vaughn.[80] Northumberland accepted, in substance if not in form, the plan for a select militia which Sir Thomas Wyatt had presented to the council in the wake of the 1549 disturbances:

to streanghten the kings part with apower of the choise of his most able and trusty subjectes, which might be upon a very short warninge in a reddines, wel armed and ordered against al suddin attemptes either at home or abrode.[81]

---

[77] SP10/14, no. 26: 13 May 1552; *APC*, iv. 34: 4 May 1552.
[78] *Chronicle of Edward VI*, 39–41; Jordan, *The Threshold of Power*, 59–61.
[79] MS Royal 18C 24, fo. 341ᵛ.   [80] Ibid., fo. 366ʳ.
[81] BL Wyatt MS 23, fo. 1; *The Papers of George Wyatt*, ed. D. Loades, Camden Society, 4th series, 5 (1967), 165.

However, Wyatt's intention had been to defend the council against popular insurrection, not to win a civil war in which the aristocracy was divided: 'on the one side', he wrote, 'is the king his aucthority all the nobilyty and gentlemen of any credit ...'. That had been true in 1549, but what might happen in the different circumstances of 1553 was another matter. Even in the last days of Edward's life, Northumberland was making no attempt to prepare the kind of private army upon which a fifteenth-century magnate of similar status would have relied. Apart from paying off the German and Italian mercenaries, the run-down of the extraordinary security precautions of 1550 and 1551 did not weaken his position as much as might be imagined. Licensed retaining was quite a good way of protecting civil authority against rebellion, but it was no protection at all against a disaffected noble faction, and we must conclude that right up to the king's death Northumberland was concerned with social discipline in the ordinary sense rather than preparing to fight for a crown.

As we have already seen, the protestant establishment was in a certain disarray by the spring of 1553. The council was at odds with the most senior and responsible bishops over the codification of the canon law, and the long-threatened expropriation of Church plate and other 'surplus' goods had at last been ordered in January.[82] Inventories had already been prepared and commissions appointed, but the latter dated back to 1549 and needed replenishing. The commissioners were now instructed to complete their work by the end of May, but many complications had arisen to make that unrealistic. Goods inventoried in 1552 had since disappeared. Inventories had been lost, or were challenged as inaccurate. Illicit sales had taken place. There was no overt resistance, but it was uphill work, and even those protestant zealots who in theory applauded the action, found it distasteful in practice: 'they took the spoil of that which King Henry could not take for shortness of life', as one of them later wrote.[83] At the same time the council's intervention in ecclesiastical affairs was by no means always negative. In June 1552 a letter was sent to the Dean and Chapter of Exeter 'to continue the Divinitie lectureship in the cathedral as the king's visitors have appointed it'. John Hooper, newly appointed to the combined sees of Gloucester and Worcester, was discharged of all first fruits and, contrary to the normal trend, given the lordship and manor of Alchurch in Worcestershire, worth a thousand marks a year.[84] In October 1552 Peter Martyr Vermigli and his wife were granted free denizenship, and on 10 May Philip

[82] There had been many reasons for delay. In Dec. 1552 fresh commissions had been issued for monastic plate and chantry goods still unaccounted for, and it was not until Feb. 1553 that the out-of-date commissions for Church goods were filled up. At the same time argument still raged about the propriety of such confiscations (SP10/15, no. 76; *APC*, iv. 219; SP10/15, no. 77; Jordan, *The Threshold of Power*, 390–1).

[83] A. G. Dickens (ed.), *Tudor Treatises*, Yorkshire Archaeological Society Record Series, 125 (1958), 140.

[84] MS Royal 18C 24, fo. 278ᵛ: 29th Nov. 1552.

Melanchthon was offered the chair at Cambridge formerly held by Martin Bucer.[85] Cranmer had been trying to induce Melanchthon to come to England for several years, and it looks as though he was on the point of success. The German must have responded favourably, because on 6 June the treasurer of Augmentations was instructed 'to deliver to the Archbishop of Canterbury £100 to be sent overseas by him for the expenses of Philip Melanchthon coming to his majesties presence'.[86] This was too practical to have been mere wishful thinking, and it looks as though it was Edward's death rather than the superior attractions of his homeland which prevented Luther's greatest disciple from crossing the North Sea. How Cranmer had managed to persuade a council allegedly dominated by radical and hostile influences to import this great but relatively conservative reformer must remain an unanswered question. Did the king give the order himself? Was Northumberland trying to back off from his radical allies? Or was the archbishop not quite as powerless as we have been led to suppose? The latter seems unlikely, because pressure upon ecclesiastical property, to which he was strongly opposed, continued. In October 1552 the bishop of Hereford was virtually ordered to hand over his London house to Lord Clinton, and the following month the bishop of Carlisle was pressed into selling his lordship of Horncastle in Lincolnshire to the same man. In April 1553 the Dean and Chapter of Chester were licensed to grant to Sir Richard Cotton land to the large annual value of £603. 18s. 10d., which must have constituted the bulk of its landed estate.[87] The forty-two articles were finally issued with a council letter on 9 June enforcing their use, but even that was not without controversy. The printed version bore upon its title-page the legend *Articles agreed on by the Bishops and other learned and Godly men*, clearly implying that it had been authorized by convocation, which in fact had never seen it. Cranmer, much as he wanted the articles promulgated, could not refrain from protest against this misrepresentation, but was merely told that it had been intended to issue them in the time of convocation.[88] Why it had not been done was not explained, and it seems that as the crisis over the king's will approached, relations between Edward's secular advisers and his chief spiritual counsel, who should have had a powerful voice on such an issue, had never been worse.

By the middle of June it was generally known that the king was dying, and widely rumoured that there was a plot to deprive Mary of the succession. This was inevitably attributed to Northumberland rather than Edward. The people who were most interested in this impending crisis were the French. Boisdauphin had been replaced as ambassador at the end

---

[85] MS Royal 18C 24, fo. 263ᵛ: 26 Oct. 1552; fo. 343ᵛ, 'A letter in latin to Philip Melanchthon signifying that the king hath elected him to that place that Martin Bucer had in Cambridge'.

[86] Ibid., fo. 356ʳ.   [87] Ibid., fo. 336ᵛ.

[88] John Foxe, *The Acts and Monuments of the English Martyrs*, ed. S. R. Cattley and George Townsend (London, 1837–41), vi. 468.

of April by the acute Antoine de Noailles, but the king was too ill to receive his credentials until 17 May. Conversations with the council, particularly the duke of Northumberland, and the evidence of his own eyes, convinced Noailles that there were great possibilities for a French *coup* in Edward's febrile determination.[89] Mary, as everyone understood, had been the emperor's protégée for many years. The prospect of England's friendship, or even neutrality, under her rule was remote. It was therefore very much in Henry's interest to support the plotters, whoever they were. Noailles discreetly communicated this to Northumberland before the end of May, without committing his master to anything specific.[90] Since the beginning of the year, the duke had been anxious to improve his relations with the emperor, but Noailles's arrival, and a special mission from Claude de l'Aubespine, the First Secretary of the French council, at the end of May seem to have convinced him that he should invest in a different bank. Inevitably Scheyfve picked up rumours of these developments, and reported them to Brussels with some alarm. He had heard that l'Aubespine had made 'offers of service, going so far as to say in so many words that the duke's cause should also be the king's'.[91] In fact there seems to have been no clear understanding, because beyond the exclusion of Mary the two parties had no common aim. Northumberland intended to honour Edward's wishes and in the process to strengthen both the protestant religion and his own power base. Henry had no interest in promoting either the Dudleys or the heretics, and had his own candidate in the background in the person of Mary Stuart. Nevertheless it is quite probable that Noailles gave Northumberland a broad diplomatic hint that French support would be available if he should persevere in the course which was being set. How much this may have weighed with the duke is uncertain. He knew perfectly well that an unpopular regime propped up by the French would have no serious chance of survival. On the other hand, he may have calculated that Mary would depend for success upon Imperial support, if she decided to press her claim at all, and that the French would be needed to neutralize that threat. Until the beginning of June neither the emperor nor the regent had been much disturbed by Scheyfve's warnings; perhaps they underestimated the accuracy of his information as he had not always been correct in the past. However, l'Aubespine's mission seems to have galvanized Charles into action. He began to take seriously the imminence of Edward's death, and of a disputed succession in which he would have a vital interest. On 23 June he dispatched a high-powered special mission, ostensibly to commiserate with Edward on his illness, but in reality to keep a close eye on events after his death. The leader of this embassy, the Sieur de Thoulouse, was high

---

[89] Noailles to Henry II, 28 June 1553, Archives du Ministère des Affaires Etrangères, Correspondance Politique, Angleterre, IX, fo. 34; E. H. Harbison, *Rival Ambassadors at the Court of Queen Mary* (Princeton, 1940), 43.
[90] Harbison, *Rival Ambassadors*, 36.   [91] *Cal. Span.*, xi. 51.

powered only in rank, but Jean de Montmorency, Sieur de Courrières, was a man of some ability, and Simon Renard was one of the best diplomatic brains of his generation.[92] They arrived in London only hours before Edward's death on 6 July—too late for their ostensible mission, but in the nick of time for the real one.

By the beginning of July the end was expected almost hourly, and Scheyfve's dispatches read like sickroom bulletins. However he got his information it was swift, and substantially accurate. At the same time he reported that the Tower of London was being reinforced, that troops were gathering in proximity to London, and that the king's ships in the Thames were being mobilized.[93] The king died in the evening, surrounded by his closest friends and servants, and the decisive moment had arrived. Edward's wishes now counted for nothing, and Northumberland was free to act as his own interests and conscience dictated. It is important to realize that, up to this point no one had acted treasonably, in spite of the accusations which had flown backwards and forwards, and that when legal proceedings were eventually initiated against the losing side, no offence was alleged to have taken place before 6 July. If, as seems likely, the driving force behind the alteration of the succession was Edward himself, it then has to be explained why the council, and particularly Northumberland, did not simply abandon his rather ridiculous 'will' and take refuge in safer courses. Some of them certainly felt that they were bound by an oath which could not be lightly disregarded. Archbishop Cranmer subsequently explained his conduct in that way, and, although his conscience may have been unusually sensitive on that score, he was certainly not alone. At the same time, virtually every contemporary observer who had any knowledge of the circumstances thought that the plot would succeed. Reporting an interview with Northumberland just before Edward's death, Noailles wrote:

I sounded him out so far on the illness and exhaustion of [the king] and also on the proposal which your Majesty had M. de l'Aubespine make to him that he finally disclosed much to me. He told me that they had provided so well against the Lady Mary's ever attaining the succession, and that all the lords of the council were so well united, that there is no need for you, Sire, to enter into any doubt on this score ...[94]

The ambassador went on to conclude that he believed that the crown would pass first to a regent, until the fury of the people had been pacified. Although recently arrived, he knew how unpopular the *coup* would be, but did not consider that to be a decisive factor, and seems to have had some

[92] The instructions for this embassy are set out at length in *Cal. Span.*, xi. 60–5. On Renard, see Harbison, *Rival Ambassadors*, and Mathieu Tridon, 'Simon Renard, ses ambassades, ses negociations, sa lutte avec le cardinal de Granvelle', *Mémoires de la société d'émulation du Doubs*, 5th series, 6 (1881); *Cal. Span.*, xi. 67.

[93] Scheyfve to the emperor, 27 June 1553 (*Cal. Span.*, xi. 67).

[94] Noailles to Henry II, 28 June 1553 (Aff. Etr., IX, fo. 34; Harbison, *Rival Ambassadors*, 43).

knowledge of the 'Device' in its penultimate form, before the succession was settled on Jane. Simon Renard, who was the brains of the imperial mission, rapidly came to a similar conclusion. Although his sympathies were entirely with Mary, and he believed that three-quarters of the population supported her, he still believed that Jane Grey would secure the crown. 'The actual possession of power', he wrote along with his colleagues, 'is a matter of great importance, especially among barbarians like the English',[95] so that, in any contest between justice and force, force would win every time. The emperor shared this view, and made a pessimistic prognosis of Mary's chances. Noailles believed that the imperial ambassadors were briefed to assist the princess's cause in every way possible, but he was wrong. In fact Charles's instructions were that they should only assist Mary's cause if she appeared to have a realistic chance of success. Otherwise they were to do business with the new government as though it was legitimate, his priority being to avoid giving the French any pretext to interfere.[96] Consequently in the first few days after Edward's death both the major European powers were sitting on their hands assuming that Northumberland would win. It is therefore not surprising that he came to the same conclusion himself, and embarked upon the course which was to have such fatal consequences.

The king's death was concealed for two days, which was a routine precaution, but in this case allowed time for the council to decide whether to persevere with Edward's plan or not. Rumours had been flying around the country for weeks, and were constant during the first week of July. Mary, knowing how imminent her brother's death was, and knowing perfectly well what the council might do, left her house at Hunsdon on 5 July and travelled by way of Sawston to Kenninghall in Norfolk. She may have been specifically warned, as tradition has it, but she could equally well have heeded the persistent rumours.[97] Meanwhile the general opinion was that the young king was being poisoned by the duke of Northumberland. Just about every contemporary chronicle and diary refers to the same charge, which is a good example of the worthlessness of public opinion. Not only is there no scrap of evidence which would suggest such a crime, but the duke was the man who had gambled most heavily on Edward's life, and had the most to lose by his death.[98] Although they tell us nothing about the king's

[95] Ambassadors to the emperor, 13 July 1553 (*Cal. Span.*, xi. 72–80). They also believed that religion would be a major factor telling against Mary.

[96] *Cal. Span.*, xi. 60–5; Harbison, *Rival Ambassadors*, 44–50.

[97] *Cal. Span.*, xi. 72–6. The tradition that she was warned by Sir Nicholas Throgmorton stems from his own poetical autobiography, printed in the *Chronicle of Queen Jane*, Camden Society, 48 (1850), 2.

[98] Ironically, it may have been Northumberland's desperate attempts to keep the king alive which gave rise to these rumours. When the royal physicians had given up hope, he seems to have resorted to quacks, and news of their ministrations may soon have spread (Jordan, *The Threshold of Power*, 520).

fatal illness, such reports say a great deal about how the duke was regarded. Some of them may have been concocted afterwards, when failure had made him fair game, but his reputation seems to have been that of a ruthless man who would stick at nothing to gain his ends. On 7 July, before the king's death was announced, Sir James Croft was replaced as Constable of the Tower by Lord Clinton, and a rather half-hearted attempt was made to ensnare Mary by pretending that her brother wanted to see her. However, it soon transpired that Northumberland was much less well prepared for a crisis than he was reputed to be. He did not have a large private army, and the mercenaries who might have responded to his call as their paymaster were far away on the Scottish borders. His own retinue, and those of his brother and sons, numbered only a few hundred men. The retinues of his allies and associates, upon whom the council had relied so heavily for domestic security, were only as reliable for his purposes as those allies and associates themselves. At the same time what might be described as the public forces of the realm—the gentlemen and yeomen of the household and the crews of the king's ships—owed their allegiance to the Crown, and not to the house of Dudley. In a similar situation in 1483 the duke of Gloucester had overawed London with a large army of loyal northerners in his own livery. Northumberland had no such resource. The outcome of his gamble therefore depended entirely upon what Mary was able and willing to attempt.

Her past record did not promise much. Pressured by her father in 1536, she had surrendered. Confronted with similar pressure from the council in 1550 she had attempted to run away, and had then panicked and stayed where she was. When they found that she had left Hunsden for Norfolk, the council assumed that she was again attempting to flee to the continent, and alerted the fleet to intercept her. In fact nothing was further from her mind, and the rapid sequence of events which then followed demonstrate that she (or someone on her behalf) had laid careful and thorough plans. Following her endowment in accordance with the terms of her father's will, Mary had become the greatest landholder in East Anglia, with an income approaching £4,000 a year.[99] Most of these manors came from the former Howard estates, and the princess inherited much of the Norfolk clientage along with them. Although she had had only a short time in which to establish herself in that specific context, she had been a popular figure for many years, and rapidly built up a loyal following among the East Anglian gentry, a number of whom entered her service. She therefore enjoyed the service of a small but extremely loyal affinity, and was much less dependent upon the support of other peers than was her chief rival. On 7 July she reached Euston Hall, near Thetford, and was there overtaken by a messenger described as 'her goldsmith', who was probably a man named Robert Reynes. This mes-

[99] *Cal. Pat.*, Edward VI, ii. 20; D. Loades, *Mary Tudor; A Life* (Oxford, 1989), 137–8.

senger told her of her brother's death the previous day, but she suppressed the news, fearing that it was a snare.[100] Her doubt was well founded, for, however the news was obtained, it was unofficial, and if she had moved to claim the crown while Edward was still alive, she would have been guilty of treason. It was not until the following day, when she had arrived at Kenninghall, that Mary received confirmation that her brother was no more, and that the time to act had come. Given the agonies of hesitation which she had endured in 1550, her speed and resolution on this occasion were remarkable. It was as though she had become a different person. The main reason for this is probably that her conscience spoke clearly. With her brother dead, she was the lawful queen, both by God's decree and parliament's, and she had a clear duty to claim her inheritance. To have done anything else would have been to betray her trust. Not only had she reached this decision before the event, it seems clear that letters and proclamations announcing her accession had already been drafted, and that her affinity had been warned to be ready to ride to her at an hour's notice. Having disclosed the situation to her household, and received their loyal acclamation, the next day, 9 July, she sent out the prepared letters, probably dozens if not scores in number, calling upon her loyal subjects to proclaim her, and to dispatch forces to her immediate aid.[101] At the same time, a carefully worded missive was sent to the council in London, commanding their allegiance. Within twenty-four hours her followers, headed by Sir Henry Bedingfield and Sir John Shelton, had begun to arrive at Kenninghall, accompanied by bands of men, not large but well armed and provisioned for action.

This was the last reaction which Northumberland had expected, and demonstrates the weakness of his intelligence system. He had been prepared for panic-stricken flight, or for a desperate appeal to the emperor, but this instant and extremely practical response took him completely by surprise. Having decided to stand by Edward's disposition, the council made their own arrangements, promptly but without any sense of emergency. The Lord Mayor and aldermen of London were sworn to Queen Jane, and letters were sent out to sheriffs and justices of the peace, announcing her accession, and ordering them to repress any stirs or disorders—very much the sort of letter which would be sent out at the beginning of any new reign.[102] The only distinctive feature was that Mary was declared to be in flight towards the coast, either to pass overseas or to wait for military support from abroad. On 9 July Bishop Ridley preached to an unreceptive audience in the City, declaring that both Mary and Elizabeth were bastards incapable of succeeding, who by their marriages might have brought the

---

[100] 'Vita Mariae Reginae', 203/251 and notes.
[101] Loades, *Mary Tudor*, 175–6; Foxe, *Acts and Monuments*, vi. 385; J. G. Nichols (ed.), *The Chronicle of Queen Jane and of the First Two Years of Mary*, Camden Society, 48 (1850) 5; Raphael Holinshed, *Chronicles etc*. (London, 1577), ed. H. Ellis (London, 1807–8), iii. 1069–70.
[102] HMC, Molyneux MSS, 609; *Chronicle of Queen Jane*, 2–3.

realm into subjection to a foreign power.[103] This sermon was a mistake. By
offering explanations it appeared to apologize for a situation which in
theory had come about by applying the natural and divine law of the succession. It also drew attention to the claims of the two princesses. In spite of
their protestantism the Londoners needed no reminding of Mary's claim,
and Jane's entry to the Tower on the following day was greeted with omi-
nous silence and a few hardy protests. However, those with long memories
might have recalled that Anne Boleyn had been similarly greeted twenty
years before, without it making any significant difference to her position.
The yeomen of the guard were sworn to the new queen, and the protesters
set on the pillory.[104] Also on 10 July Mary's letter reached the council out of
Norfolk, and they knew that Jane was not going to succeed by default.
However, the seriousness of Mary's challenge remained to be tested,
because the council had no reliable information about what was happening. If they had, they might have replied with something more substantial
than words, because although the princess's support was growing by the
hour, the progress of her cause, even in her centre of greatest support, was
not unchallenged. The first reaction of most of the major towns in East
Anglia was to accept Jane. Norwich, Ipswich, King's Lynn, and Great
Yarmouth all started to go down that road, although it appears that in each
case the ruling group was divided.[105] Moreover, Northumberland's son,
Lord Robert Dudley, from his base in Norfolk, was making his presence
felt. If the council had moved immediately to support him, and sent a force
north at once, Mary's power might have been strangled in its cradle, for she
had as yet no captain with military experience and prestige, and only a few
thousand men.

For two or three days the issue hung in the balance, and it seems to have
been the resolution of Mary's still comparatively small following which
tipped the balance. According to the enthusiastic Robert Wingfield, who
wrote an eyewitness account a few months later, it was the spontaneous
action of ordinary people which forced the issue.[106] The crews of six of the
king's ships, forced into the Orwell by bad weather, mutinied against their
officers, and declared for Mary. The earl of Oxford was won over by his
'menial servants' against the wishes of his gentlemen retainers. However,
Wingfield also makes it clear that the initial momentum was sustained by
local gentlemen who were not part of the princess's immediate affinity,
men such as Sir John Mordaunt, Sir William Drury, Sir Richard Southwell,
and Thomas, Lord Wentworth.[107] It seems clear that Mary's cause was promoted by committed and effective agents, such as Henry Jerningham, who

---

[103] Foxe, *Acts and Monuments*, vi. 389.   [104] *Chronicle of Queen Jane*, 3–4.
[105] R. Tittler and S. L. Battley, 'The Local Community and the Crown in 1553: The Accession
of Mary Tudor Re-visited', *Bulletin of the Institute of Historical Research*, 136 (1984), 131–40.
[106] 'Vita Mariae Angliae', 209/258.   [107] Ibid. 206/255.

made it their business to tackle community leaders and to spell out the merits of Mary's case, not omitting to stir up that hostility to the Dudleys which was never very far below the surface. By 13 July it was already clear that a military operation would have to be mounted swiftly if the growing but still leaderless army at Kenninghall was to be defeated. This created other problems which reveal the inadequate state of Northumberland's preparations. He had no network in East Anglia which could raise a comparable force—Lord Robert's modest following being far too small. This meant that he would have to commit the councillors' retainers and the household troops which were gathered near London. That in turn meant relying on the Tower garrison to cover the City, and bringing in additional forces from further afield, if they could be found. It would also take at least three days to get an army up into Norfolk, and in that time Mary's following might have doubled in size. The longer she was unchallenged the more her confidence grew, and that confidence was infectious. Moreover there was a problem of leadership. Northumberland himself was the most accomplished, and the most feared soldier in the realm, particularly in Norfolk. On the other hand he did not trust the resolution of some of his colleagues, and wished to remain in London to preserve the common front. Jane herself refused to contemplate sending her father, the duke of Suffolk, who was reliable, if not very competent. By 13 July Dudley had decided that he would have to go himself, and rely on Suffolk to hold the council together.[108] On the morning of 14 July he set out with about 1,500 men and a small artillery train. The citizens solemnly watched him depart, but, as the duke himself is alleged to have remarked, 'no man saith Godspeed'. It was not a good omen.

Before he left, Northumberland harangued the council; not, as he hastened to point out, because he did not trust them, but in order to 'put them in remembrance' of the cause they were defending 'what chance of variance soever might grow amongst you in my absence …'.[109] He had good cause to be concerned for a number of reasons. On 12 July Lord Cobham and Sir John Mason had waited upon the imperial ambassadors to inform them that as their credentials were to King Edward, they should consider their mission discharged and go home. The councillors also made it clear that the envoys were suspected of being behind Mary's unexpected resolution, and warned of dire consequences should they endeavour to communicate with her.[110] Renard responded with pained surprise. They had come, he assured his visitors, simply to express their master's goodwill towards England. They had no instructions to support Mary, or to communicate with her in any way. At the same time they thought that the English council should know that the apparent French willingness to support Jane was

[108] *Chronicle of Queen Jane*, 5–6; Jordan, *The Threshold of Power*, 526.
[109] John Stow, *The Annales of England* (London, 1592), 611; *Chronicle of Queen Jane*, 7–8.
[110] Ambassadors to the emperor, 12 July 1553 (*Cal. Span.*, xi. 84–6).

insincere. The French wanted Mary excluded, not in order to help Northumberland and his friends, but in order to stir up civil strife. Once that had been achieved they would intrude their own candidate, Mary Stuart. His words struck a responsive note. Cobham and Mason, who were not part of Northumberland's affinity, withdrew their request that the ambassadors should leave, and instead arranged a meeting for them with a larger group of councillors on the following day. Northumberland, who was still in London, was not informed.[111] Just a week after Edward's death, the unity of the council was beginning to break down.

This happened partly because Dudley had made some serious tactical errors. The earl of Arundel had been severely harassed for his part in the supposed conspiracy of Somerset, and had been held in the Tower until December 1552. On 2 December he had made his submission before the council, and his fine had been set at 6,000 marks, covered by a recognizance for 10,000.[112] As late as 10 May 1553 the fine had been revised to £3,221, to be paid in yearly instalments of £303. 6s. 8d.[113] Yet a month later he was recalled to the council and his fine remitted. He signed the instrument recognizing Jane's right to the succession, but so rapid a rehabilitation cannot have represented a real change of heart. Northumberland no doubt believed that he had secured his acquiescence, if not his support, but it was a transparent gesture, and Arundel was one of the first to break ranks. The others who met the imperial ambassadors on 13 July were Shrewsbury, Pembroke, Bedford, and Petre. They did not give any immediate assurances, but merely requested that Renard and his colleagues should remain in London for the time being, while their message was communicated to the rest of the council. Lord Paget did not, apparently, attend this meeting, but his rehabilitation had followed a similar course to that of Arundel, and for the same reason. Originally fined £5,000 for his supposed offences, his penalty had been reduced to £4,000 in October 1552, and then in December he had received a full pardon for everything except his debt.[114] By the end of February 1553 he had paid his debt in full, and his coat of arms had been restored to him.[115] In March he had again been received at court, and at about the time of Edward's death he had been summoned to rejoin the council. Like Arundel, he had made a gesture of accepting Jane, but he had no loyalty to Northumberland, and every incentive to betray him.

The duke did not know of these clandestine moves, but he did know that his gamble was hanging by a thread, and before he left London he dis-

[111] *Cal. Span.*, xi. 84–6; Harbison, *Rival Ambassadors*, 49–50: At the second meeting Renard pretended to have intercepted letters from Northumberland to France, proving that he knew of the French intention (*Cal. Span.*, xi, p. xvii and n.).

[112] *APC*, iv. 185.　　[113] MS Royal 18C 24, fo. 343ʳ.

[114] He arranged to pay the debt in Nov. by surrendering to the crown lands to the annual value of £200 (*APC*, iv. 176; MS Royal 18C 24, fo. 280ʳ: 6 Dec. 1552).

[115] Ibid., fo. 299ʳ, fo. 318ᵛ: 21 Mar. 1553.

patched his soldier kinsman Henry Dudley on a secret mission to France. Dudley's brief was to follow up Noailles's hints, and to secure from the king himself a positive undertaking of support.[116] It was later alleged that Dudley was authorized to offer the surrender of Calais, and even Ireland, in return for such assistance, but there is no real evidence to support such a charge, and it is intrinsically improbable because his mission was not intended to achieve a formal diplomatic result. He reached the French court at Compiègne about 18 July, and was received by the king, who seems to have given the required undertaking, but informally and with no timetable attached.[117] By the time that Dudley reached Calais on his way back, it was already too late. On 26 July he was arrested there by the Governor, Lord William Howard, on the orders of Queen Mary's council. Northumberland's position had collapsed with a speed which astonished everyone, including those most directly involved. On 14 July it was still expected that Lord Clinton and the earl of Oxford would reinforce the duke as he moved north, isolating Mary's East Anglian stronghold from the rest of the country. Clinton did indeed arrive at Cambridge, although with less force than expected, but Oxford defected to the princess, and the loss of his power base in the home counties may well have been crucial. On 15 July Mary moved her swelling but still rather undisciplined army from Kenninghall to Framlingham. Her advisers were still expecting a serious conflict, and Kenninghall was not easily defensible. Men of substance were joining her every day with their followings—Lord Windsor, Sir Edward Hastings, Sir Edmund Peckham, Sir John Williams, and a number of others—but the great lords were not moving. Only the earls of Oxford and Bath represented the highest rank of the peerage in her camp, and Bath lacked the power commensurate with his rank. On the other hand the protestants, who were expected to rally to Jane's standard, were doing no such thing. Reformed strongholds such as Coventry proclaimed Mary and sent men to her assistance, while Northumberland's favourite bishop, John Hooper of Worcester and Gloucester, did the same.[118] Had the council remained substantially united in support of Jane, there would almost certainly have been serious fighting, and no predictable outcome. In those circumstances the majority of the non-conciliar peers would probably have supported their colleagues, and given Northumberland sufficient critical mass to make his superior military talent effective. But the best general can do nothing without soldiers, and the defection of most of the council between 16 and 19 July was crucial. On 16 July, in spite of his success in sowing the seeds of doubt, Renard remained convinced that Jane's party would stay together, and he ignored an appeal from Mary for imperial assistance. In so doing he

---

[116] Harbison, *Rival Ambassadors* 50–1. The imperial ambassadors made many references to this mission.

[117] *Cal. Span.*, xi. 173.

[118] HMC, Records of the Corporation of Gloucester, 466; Jordan, *The Threshold of Power*, 527.

promoted her cause better than he knew, for had it become known that the princess was proposing to invite foreign intervention her popularity might have suffered a severe setback. On 18 July, with rumours flying that Mary's force had now reached 30,000, a number of councillors met at the earl of Pembroke's residence at Baynard's castle to consider their position. The lead was taken by Pembroke himself and the earl of Arundel.[119] The latter apparently denounced Northumberland as a bloodthirsty tyrant, and declared that Mary had the best title to the crown. Those present endorsed his views, and the council effectively divided at that point. On the following day, 19 July, the defectors proclaimed Mary in London, amid universal rejoicings, and Suffolk, who still held the Tower along with Northampton, Cranmer, and a few others, was effectively defeated. As late as 17 July fresh supplies of arms had been sent to the Tower, but there was to be no fighting. Suffolk surrendered, and himself informed his daughter that she was no longer queen.

Meanwhile Northumberland had reached Cambridge, where Clinton joined him, but reports of Mary's strength, followed by news of what was happening in London, undermined his position: 'alle was agayns ym-selff, for ys men forsok hym', as Henry Machyn wrote.[120] In fact he was not totally deserted, for a number of the household troops, perhaps as many as half, remained loyal to him, or possibly to the memory of their late master, but there were not enough of them to fight a campaign.[121] Flight does not seem to have been an option which occurred to him. Faced with the *coup* in London, he proclaimed Queen Mary in his turn, and awaited events. The sentiments of London are well authenticated. One eyewitness reported:

I saw myself money thrown out at windows for joy. The bonfires were without number, and what with shouting and crying of the people, and ringing of bells, there could no man hear what another said ...[122]

However, in relation to Mary, Northumberland got what might be described as the 'loser's press', just as Mary herself was to do in relation to Elizabeth. Within a few weeks everyone was remembering how much they had hated and mistrusted the ambitions of the fallen duke, but the absence of actual fighting tends to conceal what a close run thing it was. Mary certainly had more popular support all over the country, but probably no

---

[119] Francis Godwin, *Rerum Anglicarum Henrico VIII, Edwardo VI* (London 1653), 366–8.

[120] *Diary of Machyn*, 36. Northumberland seems in fact to have advanced to Bury St Edmunds before being forced to abandon his intentions. According to indictments later found against several of his followers, he had as many as 3,000 men with him there. Renard believed that he had 3,000 foot and 1,000 horse. Mary's force by that time was at least twice that size, although nowhere near the 30,000 it was reported to be. It is not clear how many men remained with the duke when he retreated to Cambridge (*Cal. Span.*, xi. 93–6).

[121] R. C. Braddock, 'The Character and Composition of the Duke of Northumberland's Army', *Albion*, 8 (1976), 342–56; W. J. Tighe, 'The Gentlemen Pensioners, the Duke of Northumberland and the attempted Coup of 1553', *Albion*, 19 (1987), 1–11.

[122] BL Harley MS 353, no. 44, fo. 139; *Diary of Machyn*, 37.

more than her mother had had in 1533. We do not know what would have happened if Catherine had attempted to lead an insurrection against her husband, but Henry feared the possibility. Nor do we know what would have followed if Mary had led the Pilgrimage of Grace with the resolution which she showed in 1553. Such speculations, however, should warn us not to explain Mary's triumph over Jane simply in terms of overwhelming spontaneous support. Northumberland was no Henry VIII, but more to the point he was completely unprepared for the crisis which actually overtook him. He was already losing his grip upon the situation before the council defected, and that was why they did it. Neither Noailles nor Renard played any significant part. The latter encouraged a split which would probably have happened anyway, but as late as 19 July he was still convinced that Northumberland would win, and flabbergasted when he was told later the same day that the council had proclaimed Mary in London.[123] At the same time Noailles wrote, 'I have witnessed the most sudden change believable in men, and I believe that God alone has worked it.'[124]

The fact is that the plan to exclude Mary and Elizabeth in favour of Jane was formulated by Edward only a short time before his death, and with a feverish disregard for advice, constitutional and otherwise. Northumberland's decision to implement it once Edward was dead was a gamble based upon a complete misjudgement of Mary. He feared imperial intervention, and took steps to frustrate it, but he did not expect resolute action from the princess herself. He had troops, but not enough for serious fighting. Once they had failed to deter Mary's mobilization, they had failed of their whole purpose. The aristocracy was totally divided, except upon one crucial point; a civil war was the worst of all possible evils, and would open the floodgates to popular insurrection in the manner which had so nearly happened four years before. Better a usurpation than that; but better still a Tudor princess who was prepared to show the traditional spirit of her lineage. Northumberland lost the war of nerves, and his own affinity was too small to enable him to fight his way out of a corner. He had relied upon controlling the machinery of state, and had fallen into Somerset's error of forgetting that he was not the king. Unfortunately we do not know how the battle within the council was resolved. The defectors had almost certainly made up their minds to act by the evening of 18 July, and yet as late as the morning of 19 July they signed, along with Suffolk, Cranmer, Goodrich, and others, a letter to Lord Rich in Essex, informing him of the treachery of the earl of Oxford, and requiring his continued loyalty to Jane.[125] Before the end of the same day the same men signed a letter to Northumberland,

---

[123] *Cal. Span.*, xi. 79–1, 92–3, 95–6, 105. Renard constantly returned to the theme of miracle in discussing Mary's success.

[124] Noailles to Montmorency, 3 Aug. 1553 (Aff. Etr., IX, fo. 47); Harbison, *Rival Ambassadors*, 53 and n.

[125] BL Lansdowne MS 3, fo. 25.

instructing him to disband his forces and await the pleasure of Queen Mary.[126] The following morning, 20 July, Lord Paget and the earl of Arundel were dispatched to Framlingham bearing a letter of extraordinary abasement, even by the standards of the mid-sixteenth century.

we your most humble, faithful and obedient subjects, having always (God we take to witness) remained your highness's true and humble subjects in our hearts ever since the death of our late sovereign lord and master your highness' brother, whom God pardon, and seeing hitherto no possibility to utter our determination therein without great destruction and bloodshed both to ourselves and others till this time, have this day proclaimed in your city of London your majesty to be our true natural sovereign liege lady and queen ...[127]

The writers then went on to beseech pardon by the (relatively) unspotted hands of their messengers. It is difficult not to dismiss this as sheer hypocrisy, at least on the part of some of the signatories, but a genuine dilemma can be read between the lines. Had Mary not moved resolutely, her cause would not have been worth fighting for, and until the situation actually arose, no one had known what would happen. By the time that Paget and Arundel reached Framlingham, the only real issue was how the new queen would deal with her erstwhile opponents. Everyone ran for cover, and those who had begun to move in the wrong direction hastened to cover their tracks. But the problems were not all on one side. Those who had joined Mary at Kenninghall and Framlingham had perforce provided her initial council, but they were not a very promising collection in terms of political experience.[128] She had little option but to pretend to believe the professions of the councillors if she wanted to avail herself of their services, and most of them were received, even if they were not at once readmitted to office.

For Dudley and his affinity, however, there could be no instant rehabilitation. After a bloodless victory, Mary was inclined to clemency, but she could not afford to be too easy. Northumberland surrendered to the earl of Arundel on 24 July at Cambridge, and it is reasonable to suppose that those who accompanied him to the Tower on 25 July were arrested with him; Sir Thomas Palmer, Sir Henry Gates, Sir John Gates, Lord Hastings, the earl of Huntingdon, and most of his family, Andrew, Ambrose, Henry, and John.[129] On 26 July they were joined by the marquis of Northampton, Lord Robert Dudley, Sir Edward Montague, Sir Roger Cholmley, and Sir Richard Corbet.[130] On the following day the duke of Suffolk, Sir John Cheke, Sir John York, and Richard Cox were added to the tally. Jane and Guildford

---

[126] Stowe, *Annales*, 612   [127] BL Lansdowne MS 3, fo. 26.

[128] D. E. Hoak, 'Two Revolutions in Tudor Government: The Formation and Organisation of Mary I's Privy Council', in C. Coleman and D. Starkey (eds.), *Revolution Reassessed* (London, 1986); A. Weikel, 'The Marian Council Revisited', in J. Loach and R. T. Tittler (eds.), *The Mid-Tudor Polity, 1540–1560* (London, 1980); D. Loades, *The Reign of Mary Tudor* (London, 1991), 18–57.

[129] *Diary of Machyn*, 37–8.   [130] Ibid. 38.

may never have left the Tower, and if they did they did not get far, because, according to one report, they were brought in with the duchess of Northumberland as early as 23 July.[131] The earl of Rutland and Lord Russell, the earl of Bedford's son, were sent to the Fleet, and finally, on 6 August, the other Henry Dudley, Northumberland's messenger to France, arrived under arrest from Calais.[132] There were other arrests, including some of the gentlemen pensioners who had remained with Northumberland, and Nicholas Ridley, the bishop of London, whose sermon had singled him out for retribution, but, rather surprisingly, not Lord Clinton, nor Cranmer, nor Sir William Cecil. Considering the nature of what had happened it was a very modest tally, and consisted mostly of Northumberland's affinity. Only Suffolk, Northampton, Rutland, and Huntingdon could really be classed as allies rather than followers. This was to some extent dictated by Mary's own needs, as we have seen, but it also reflects her particular animosity against the Dudleys.[133] It was both convenient and congenial to her to place the weight of blame on the duke, and also fitted comfortably with popular prejudice. Not only was Northumberland held entirely responsible for the plan to place Jane on the throne, Mary also seems to have chosen to blame him for her brother's regrettable religious policies. In short he became the scapegoat for what the new queen regarded as the disgraceful aberrations of the previous four years.

All the prisoners were questioned by the new council in the early days of August, and the duke of Norfolk, newly released from the Tower himself, was appointed High Steward for the trial of the noble defendants, which was held on 18 August. Warwick and Northampton offered no defence, but Northumberland argued two points, firstly that all his actions had been approved under the broad seal of England, and secondly that many of his judges were as guilty as himself, and no fit persons to be members of the court.[134] The first point had no substance in law, because the seal of a usurper has no validity, and the second, which was a political point, was a waste of breath in the circumstances. He comported himself with dignity, and, being condemned, requested the privilege of a nobleman's death, which was granted. He also asked to speak with four of the council concerning the secrets of state which were his particular knowledge, and to 'confess to a learned divine'. This was to be a more significant matter than anyone at the time realized, because the divine with whom he spoke was his old enemy Stephen Gardiner.[135] The former bishop of Winchester,

---

[131] *The Chronicle of Queen Jane*, 8.   [132] *Diary of Machyn*, 38, 39.

[133] There seems to be no evidence to support the contention that Mary was disposed to pardon Northumberland, but was dissuaded by her council. She had not been placated or deceived by conciliatory gestures earlier in the year, and held him primarily responsible for the harassment to which she had been subjected.

[134] BL Harley MS 2194, fos. 22[r-v]; Antonio di Guaras, *The Accession of Queen Mary*, trans. R. Garnett (London, 1892), 102–3.

[135] B. L. Beer, *Northumberland* (Kent, Ohio, 1973), 158.

newly released from imprisonment, was about to be restored to his see and already named as Lord Chancellor. Exactly what transpired between them we do not know. Gardiner may have offered to use his influence in return for a public recantation, or the offer may have come from the duke. Whichever way it was, Northumberland let it be known that he was prepared to renounce the protestant faith which he had proclaimed strongly, and with every sign of sincerity, for at least five years. His execution, already ordered for the morning of 21 August, was stayed after the crowd had already assembled and the executioner was in place.[136] Instead he was paraded to mass in the chapel of the Tower, in front of a distinguished audience of dignitaries and citizens of London. At the end of the service he addressed the assembled congregation, saying:

Truly, I profess here before you all that I have received the sacrament according to the true Catholic faith; and the plagues that is upon the realm and upon us now is that we have erred from the faith these sixteen years. And this I profess unto you all from the bottom of my heart ...[137]

The twentieth century has witnessed so many show trials, and protestations of a similar nature, that we have no right to be surprised or incredulous at such a performance. Perhaps Northumberland expected to buy his life with such a submission, or perhaps he genuinely believed that the death of the young king and the failure of his own plans were a divine judgement upon a heretical people. In spite of his status he was a simple man in such matters, not intellectual, or even particularly thoughtful. Nor did his faith have any strong theological roots. He seems to have drifted into reform, and from reform into protestantism, on the tide of political opportunism: saying the right things, but perhaps hardly knowing himself what he believed. Faced with the imminence of eternity, the certainties of the new faith may well have broken in his hand, and driven him back to the unchallenged Church with which he had grown up. Equally his professed conversion may have been no more genuine than his earlier professions of piety. We cannot get beyond his words, which were clear enough, and gave great gratification to the queen, and to Renard, who declared that they had edified the people more than a month of sermons. The protestants were equally dismayed. 'Woe worth him!', his daughter-in-law is alleged to have said on hearing the news, 'who would have thought he would have done so?'[138] Four of his colleagues appeared with him in the chapel, and made similar statements, Northampton, Palmer, Henry Gates, and his brother Andrew. None of his sons offered, or could be persuaded, to make a similar gesture. But in spite of the stir which it made at the time, his apostasy

---

[136] *Diary of Machyn*, 42. Machyn, curiously, does not record the actual execution, which took place on the following day.

[137] BL Harley MS 284, fo. 128ᵛ; J. G. Nichols (ed.), *The Chronicle of the Greyfriars of London*, Camden Society (1852), 83.

[138] *The Chronicle of Queen Jane*, 20.

changed little. As it transpired, the protestants were well rid of a man who had acquired such an evil reputation, and could concentrate instead upon the godly virtues of the late king. Nor did it serve to secure his own pardon. Before the end of the same day the Lieutenant of the Tower warned him to prepare for death the following morning, and in a sudden agony of mind he sat down and wrote to the earl of Arundel—of all people—a letter reminiscent of one of the speeches which Shakespeare was later to put in the mouth of Claudio in *Measure for Measure*:

Honourable lord, and in this my distress my especial refuge; most woful was the news I received this evening by Mr. Lieutenant, that I must prepare myself against tomorrow to receive my deadly stroke. Alas my good lord, is my crime so heynous as no redemption but my blood can wash away the spots therof? An old proverb there is and that most true that a living dog is better than a dead lion. O that it would please her good grace to give me life, yea, the life of a dog, that I might live and kiss her feet, and spend both life and all I have in her honourable service, as I have the best part already under her worthy brother and her most glorious father. O that her mercy were such as she would consider how little profit my dead and dismembered body can bring her, but how great and glorious an honour it will be in all posterity when the report shall be that so gracious and mighty a queen had granted life to so miserable and penitent an object. Your honourable usage and promises to me since these my troubles have made me bold to challenge this kindness at your hands. Pardon me if I have done amiss therein and spare not I pray your bended knee for me in this distress, ye God of heaven it may be will requite it one day on you and yours. And if my life be lengthened by your mediacion and my good Lord Chancellor's (to whom I have also sent my blurred letters) I will vow it to be spent at your honourable feet. O my good lord remember how sweet life is, and how bitter ye contrary. Spare not your speech and pains for God I hope hath not shut out all hope of comfort from me in that gracious, Princely and womanlike heart; but that as the doleful news of death hath wounded to death both my soul and body, so that comfortable news of life shall be as a new resurrection to my woeful heart. But if no remedy can be found, either by imprisonment or confiscation, Banishment and the like, I can say no more but God give me patience to endure and a heart to forgive the whole world.

> Once your fellow and loving companion, but now
> worthy of no name but wretchedness and misery,
>
> JD[139]

If this letter is authentic, and there must be some doubt since it survives only in transcript, it can only be described as the triumph of optimism over both dignity and common sense. Both Arundel and Gardiner had suffered at his hands in the days of his prosperity, and it is hard to see why he expected either of them to put themselves out for him when fortune had deserted him. Perhaps after his co-operation over the mass he had expected reward, and sudden devastating disappointment had deprived him of his normal sense of reality. He had also devoted his whole adult life to the service of the Crown, and had considered it his duty to accommodate every

---

[139] BL Harley MS 787, fo. 61ᵛ.

change of the royal mood. That was why he had striven so hard to make Edward's will effective at the end of his life. He was equally willing to serve Mary in the same uncritical spirit, and it was her rejection of that service, as much as the imminence of death, which drove him to such eloquent despair. Such a position had an integrity of its own which needs to be taken into account, and which reflected a common contemporary morality, but it does not show up too well in the spotlight which John Foxe was shortly to turn on the victims of Mary's government.

On the morning of 22 August Northumberland, together with his two faithful henchmen, Sir Thomas Palmer and Sir John Gates, was handed over by the Lieutenant to the sheriff of London. According to one contemporary account, Gates took a dignified farewell of his former patron, and the two men exchanged forgiveness.[140] Palmer spoke briefly, acknowledging his faults, and admitting that his zeal for the reformed faith had been a sham. The duke, as was expected of the principal actor in the drama, made a longer and more elaborate oration, several reports of which survive. His sentiments were extremely correct, in the best tradition of scaffold speeches, where the victim was expected to confess his (or her) fault, to acknowledge the justice of the sentence, and to beg for the forgiveness of the onlookers:

Indeed I confess unto you that I have been an evil liver and have done wickedly all the days of my life … Do you think, good people, that we … be wiser than all the world besides, even since Christ? No, I assure you, you are far deceived. I do not say so for any learning that I have, for God knows I have little or none, but for the experience which I have had …[141]

Fortune had spoken with the voice of God. He went on to confess his specific offences against the queen, and to beg her forgiveness, but even in this extremity he refused to admit sole responsibility for the plot in favour of Jane, 'not I alone the original doer thereof I assure you, for there were several other which procured the same …'.[142] In the circumstances this is unlikely to have been mere rhetoric, but he would name no names, and the late king was nowhere alluded to. In conclusion he reaffirmed, as he was bound to do, his loyalty to 'the true catholic faith', which he urged all his hearers to embrace. He was attended on the scaffold by Nicholas Heath, whose deprivation from the see of Worcester he had secured, and who was now in the process of restoration. But whatever consolation Heath may have been able to offer him, it could not have included reconciliation to the catholic Church. Heath, like all the rest of Mary's bishops, was a schismatic, out of communion with Rome, as was the queen herself. What Northumberland and his colleagues meant by the 'true catholic faith' was pre-

---

[140] BL Harley MS 2194, fo. 23.   [141] BL Harley MS 284, no. 79, fo. 127.
[142] Ibid. There are numerous versions of this last speech, which vary only slightly (BL Cotton MS Titus B II, fo. 144; BL Harley MS 2194 etc.).

sumably the faith of the Henrician Church, although neither Renard nor any other foreign observer was disposed to quibble in such a way. Antonio Di Guaras, who was an eyewitness, recorded his last moments: 'he again stretched himself out, as one who constrained himself, and willed to consent patiently without saying anything, in the act of laying himself out inactively and afraid, he smote his hands together, as one who should say this must be, and cast himself upon the said beam.'[143]

An authorized version of his speech was immediately published by the queen's printer, John Cawood, and translated into Latin, Italian, and German over the next few months.[144] As John Foxe was later to put it:

he denied in word that true religion, which before time, as well in King Henry the Eighth's days as in King Edward's, he had oft evidently declared himself both to favour and further; exhorting also the people to return to the Catholic faith, as he termed it; whose recantations the Papists did forthwith publish and set abroad, rejoicing not a little at his conversion, or rather subversion, as it then appeared.[145]

Northumberland died a martyr to no cause, and respected by neither side in the developing ideological conflict. He lost his life, like many noblemen in earlier generations, and some after, for having taken a political gamble and lost. At the end he cut an extraordinarily unheroic figure: less dignified than his father, who had had far better cause to protest against the injustice of fate. An unreflective man, who had lived on his wits, in his prosperity he had commanded service, but little loyalty or affection, and in adversity he was abandoned by most of those who owed him gratitude. Whatever he might profess, the queen held him uniquely responsible for the attempt upon her crown, and the three who died on 22 August were the only direct victims of the failed *coup*. Northampton, Andrew, Ambrose, John, Henry, and Robert all escaped the axe, although all were indicted, tried, and condemned. John fell mortally sick and died a few days after his release from prison, on 21 October 1554.[146] Guildford and Jane were executed under the sentences passed against them in August, but as a direct result of Wyatt's insurrection in January and February 1554.[147] The duke of Suffolk, who was probably the most guilty man after Northumberland, was inexplicably released a few days after his arrest, and never even charged. If it had not been for his foolish involvement with Wyatt, he might have escaped altogether. As it was he was arraigned at Westminster on 17 February 1554, and executed on February 23.[148]

---

[143] Guaras, *Accession*, 109.
[144] *Short Title Catalogue*, 7283. For a modern edition of this work, and a full discussion of its provenance, see W. K. Jordan and M. R. Gleason, 'The Saying of John, late Duke of Northumberland upon the Scaffold, 1553', *Harvard Library Bulletin*, 23 (1975), 324–55.
[145] Foxe, *Acts and Monuments*, vi. 402.
[146] He died in Sir Henry Sidney's house at Penshurst (*Diary of Machyn*, 72).
[147] D. Loades, *Two Tudor Conspiracies* (Cambridge, 1965), 115. There are many accounts of Jane's execution. See particularly Foxe, *Acts and Monuments*, vi. 423–4.
[148] *Diary of Machyn*, 56–7.

The rehabilitation of the Dudleys was slow, because Mary had no intention of allowing them to recover even a shadow of their former strength and coherence. Moreover none of the duke's sons had followed his example in renouncing their protestantism. Whether the duchess was imprisoned, and if so for how long, is not clear. She was not charged with any offence, and seems to have retained control of her jointure lands. She was pardoned on 2 May 1554, and on 19 June executed an exchange of lands with the Crown, surrendering manors at Knole and Sevenoaks in Kent in return for others in Warwickshire and Staffordshire.[149] At the same time she successfully petitioned the Exchequer to be admitted to her lands at Fecknam and Henly in Arden. Jane was by no means left penniless by her husband's execution, but she seems nevertheless to have been devastated by the catastrophe to her family. She spent the summer of 1554 haunting the court with petitions in favour of her sons, and seems to have met with kindness and favour, particularly from some of Philip's servants after his arrival in July. Her eldest son, the earl of Warwick, was released in early October, already seriously ill, and died on 21 October, without ever securing his pardon. Jane herself died at her house in Chelsea on 15 January 1555, at the age of 46.[150] It may have been because of her deteriorating health that Ambrose, Robert, and Henry were released from the Tower shortly before that time, and received their pardons a week after her death. She must have been aware that this was impending before she died, because she made her will knowing that Ambrose, who was now the heir, had been pardoned for life only, and not restored in blood. As he was thus incapable of inheriting, she left all her lands in trust to her son-in-law Sir Henry Sidney and three others 'in consideration that they should have special regard to aiding her sons and daughters'. She also remembered 'my lord, my dear husband' with more than dutiful affection. If John had died unloved by the world, he had left a grieving widow, who did not long survive him.

Within a few days of their release, and almost immediately after their mother's funeral, Ambrose and Robert Dudley were back at court. This was not because the queen had suddenly developed a soft spot for the Dudleys, but because Philip was trying to improve his relations with the English aristocracy. In January 1555 he decided to stage a joust of the kind which had been so much favoured by Henry VIII—'a grett ronnyng at the tylt at Westmynster with spayrers, boyth Englys men and Spaneards' as Henry Machyn noted.[152] Ambrose and Robert appeared among the defenders, although their skills can hardly have been sharp after nearly eighteen

[149] *Cal. Pat.*, Philip and Mary, i. 418; ibid. 128.

[150] G. E. Cockayne *Complete Peerage*, rev. V. Gibbs (London, 1910–49), ix. 726. Her will survives as PRO PROB 11/37, fos. 194–5. The date of her death is variously given as 15 Jan. (IPM) and 22 Jan. (funeral monument). I have followed the former.

[151] *Cal. Pat.*, Philip and Mary, ii. 121–2.

[152] *Diary of Machyn*, 80. On the Dudleys' role in this , see R. C. McCoy, 'From the Tower to the Tiltyard: Robert Dudley's Return to Glory', *Historical Journal*, 27 (1984), 425–35.

months, incarceration. Andrew, who was not required for this public relations exercise, may have been released at the same time, but he was not pardoned until 5 April. Just over a fortnight later he was granted an annuity of £100 a year, and on 30 May his goods were returned to him. His lands at the time of his attainder had been valued at no more than £160, so although there is no sign of those lands being returned by the summer of 1555 he had more or less recovered his earlier modest prosperity.[153] Ambrose was restored in blood and his lands returned to him on 17 July 1556.[154] Henry had been pardoned at the same time as his brothers, and was restored in blood on 5 July 1556, but received only an indirect restitution. His young wife Margaret, the daughter of Lord Audley, had been under 14 at the time of their marriage. By the time of Henry's attainder she must have attained the age of 16 and obtained her inheritance, because it was forfeited to the Crown. When he was restored, his wife's lands were returned to her, to the value of £1,080 a year, but he seems to have received nothing himself.[155] Finally, on 30 January 1557, Robert was similarly restored, being granted his goods and the manor of Hemsby, a portion of his former lands.[156] All three of the younger Dudleys served in the expeditionary force which the earl of Pembroke led across the Channel in the summer of 1557 as a contribution to Philip's war effort against the French. This was not necessarily a mark of favour, as a deliberate effort seems to have been made to send potential troublemakers and malcontents to earn their keep abroad. Henry was killed at the seige of St Quentin on 27 August, but Ambrose and Robert returned to the modest lifestyle which was all that Queen Mary was prepared to allow them.

The queen's health, however, was poor, and after the spring of 1557 Philip assiduously stayed away from her. It was during these months, after his return from France, that Robert renewed his acquaintance with his one-time fellow prisoner, Princess Elizabeth. We know very little about how this came about, just as we know little of Sir William Cecil's developing relationship with her at the same time. Although it was dangerous to do so, by the summer of 1558 ambitious men were cautiously gravitating towards the heir to the throne, and Robert Dudley, from his base in Norfolk, was one of them. On 11 November 1558 Queen Mary died, and the following day he became Master of the Horse to the new queen.

---

[153] *Cal. Pat.*, Philip and Mary, ii. 42–3, 71, 98; PRO LR2 118. At the time of his attainder he also held lands belonging to the bishopric of Winchester worth £426. 2*s*. 1*d*. a year. These were listed separately, and were not returned. They may have been held on lease as there is no record of him being granted them.

[154] *Cal. Pat.*, Philip and Mary, iii. 533. This restoration, along with that of Robert, was confirmed by statute in Mary's last parliament.

[155] *Cal. Pat.*, Philip and Mary, iii. 11–12.

[156] Ibid. 251. He had already obtained Halesowen from his mother's executors by a family compact (Birmingham Reference Library, Hagley Hall MS 351613; S. Adams, 'The Dudley Clientele, 1553–1563', in G. W. Bernard (ed.), *The Tudor Nobility* (Manchester, 1992), 241–65).

Epilogue

Eclipse and Recovery

THE fall of the duke of Northumberland disbanded his household, and scattered his family-based affinity. On 28 August 1553 Lord Rich was appointed to head a commission for the purpose of inventorying and disposing of the goods of all the attainted parties, and taking stock of their assets and liabilities.[1] His report, delivered on 13 September, included a complete list of Dudley's household servants at the time of his arrest, showing that his provision had been on a truly regal scale. His Chamber staff consisted of seven gentlewomen, forty-one gentlemen, ten grooms, four footmen, twenty-six yeomen ushers, an apothecary, and a bookkeeper. In addition to her gentlewomen, the duchess retained seven grooms and three wardrobe keepers. Below stairs eighteen separate departments employed a total of sixty-five persons; the stables counted another forty, and there were several individuals—an armourer, a drummer, a piper, and a couple of gardeners—making a grand total of 200. This list did not include the men of business who would have made up his council, such as his controller, Sir Thomas Blount, or his auditor, William Kynyat, presumably because they were not paid wages (which was Rich's concern), but were rewarded in other ways. The commissioners' list is plainly incomplete.[2] In addition to Blount and Kynyat, John Holmes, the duke's secretary, and Henry Brooke, his receiver-general, are also missing, while Charles Tirrell, his master of the horse, appears only as the chief gentleman of the Chamber. Virtually all Northumberland's household gentlemen disappeared into total obscurity during Mary's reign, the only notable exception being Henry Killigrew, who joined his brother Peter in a career of piracy from a base in France.[3] Blount and Kynyat later served Robert Dudley, but he was scarcely in a position to employ such substantial men until the accession of Elizabeth brought a dramatic improvement in his fortunes. Only one of the duke's forty-one gentlemen later featured in the earl of Leicester's service, and that

[1] PRO LR2/118. See also SP46/163, fos. 53–74. Some additional information can be derived from a surviving wardrobe inventory of John, Lord Lisle and earl of Warwick, covering the years 1545–50 (Bodleian Library MS Add. C. 94).

[2] For a partial reconstruction of John Dudley's affinity at the time of his fall, see Simon Adams, 'The Dudley Clientele, 1553–1563' in G.W. Bernard (ed.), *The Tudor Nobility* (Manchester, 1992), 241–65, particularly pp. 243–4.

[3] PRO SP11/7, no. 59; D. Loades, *Two Tudor Conspiracies* (Cambridge, 1965), 259–62; Nicholas Wotton to the queen, 30 Nov. 1556 (*Calendar of State Papers, Foreign, 1553–58*, ed. W. B. Turnbull (London, 1861), 277).

was his kinsman Thomas Dudley.[4] There was no great continuity between the households, to suggest a loyal and established Dudley clientele, of the sort which had earlier served the Percies or the Staffords. The evidence of continuity relates rather to that much looser penumbra of associates who in an earlier generation would have been known as his 'well willers'.

Northumberland's brother and sons all paid a heavy price for their loyalty, but his sons-in-law were scarcely inconvenienced. Sir Henry Sidney made no secret of his continuing relationship with the family. He was the chief executor of the duchess's will, and played a leading part in negotiating the settlement in favour of Robert in March 1556.[5] By contrast Catherine's husband, Lord Hastings, and his father, the earl of Huntingdon, distanced themselves from their tainted kinsfolk. Huntingdon, in particular, seized the opportunity presented by the duke of Suffolk's folly in February 1554 to establish his credit with the new regime.[6] Sir Francis Jobson, who was married to the duke's half-sister, Elizabeth, was arrested early in August, having apparently attempted to hold the palace of Westminster for Jane while Northumberland went to Cambridge.[7] He was indicted on 14 August, but never tried. Released at some point during November, he was pardoned on 22 December, and thereafter kept a very low profile until he reappeared as a leading member of Leicester's affinity in the 1560s.[8] Henry, John, and Thomas Dudley were cousins, who were imprisoned in the summer of 1553, but released without charge. Late in 1555 Henry became deeply embroiled in a conspiracy of English exiles to invade with French support. He was for a time in French service, and was even described as being of Francis II's Privy Chamber, but his restless intrigues achieved no positive results.[9] He seems to have remained in France until 1563, when he returned to enter the earl of Leicester's service. Sir James Croft was another cousin, who was somewhat mysteriously discharged from his office as Constable of the Tower on 7 July, and thereafter seems to have played no part in the usurpation.[10] However, he became a leading member of Sir Thomas Wyatt's conspiracy in the winter of 1553–4, and was tried on 28 April 1554 for his alleged attempt to raise Herefordshire against the queen.

---

[4] LR2/118 and Dudley MS Box V, fo. 282. He also served the duchess of Northumberland in the time between the duke's execution and her death (Adams, 'Dudley Clientele', 245 and n.).

[5] PRO PROB 11/63, fos. 117–18; Birmingham Reference Library, Hagley Hall MS 351613, 351614, 346500; Adams, 'Dudley Clientele', 250 and nn.

[6] Loades, *Two Tudor Conspiracies*, 30–1.

[7] On 16 July it was reported to Mary that a force moving to her aid out of Oxfordshire intended ' this day to mershe forth towards the Palaice of Westminster, wher there purpose ys to apprehende Mr. Jobson …' (*Acts of the Privy Council*, ed. J. Dasent *et al.* (London, 1890–1907), iv. 293. On the other hand his indictment declares that on 16 and 17 July he was at Cambridge (*Calendar of the Patent Rolls*, Philip and Mary (London, 1936–9), i. 224)).

[8] Ibid.; Adams, 'Dudley Clientele', 245.

[9] Nicholas Throgmorton to Cecil, 26 Nov. 1561 (*Calendar of State Papers, Foreign, 1558–1565*, ed. Joseph Stevenson (London, 1863), iii. 418); Loades, *Two Tudor Conspiracies*, 202.

[10] J. G. Nichols (ed.), *The Diary of Henry Machyn*, Camden Society, 42 (1848), 35.

He was condemned, but pardoned in February 1556, and later became a prominent associate of Leicester.[11] Outside his family, Northumberland's following consisted chiefly of soldiers who had served with him, either in Scotland or Boulogne, although some of them, such as Sir Thomas Palmer, may well have had links going back before that. Apart from Palmer, the most prominent of these associates were the Gates brothers, Sir John and Sir Henry. Sir John was probably the closest and most trusted of all the duke's men, which was why he became Vice-Chamberlain of the king's household, and captain of the guard.[12]

Because of the position which he occupied in the last three years of his life, there are no clearly defined limits to the duke of Northumberland's 'affinity'. All sorts of men and women looked to him for patronage and protection who did not enjoy any special relationship with him, or his family. The most conspicuous beneficiary of patronage during Dudley's ascendancy was Edward Fiennes, Lord Clinton, who received no fewer than twenty-two recorded grants, offices, and favours between October 1550 and July 1553, more than any individual member of the Dudley family and about 60 per cent of the tally of the whole kindred.[13] But Clinton had no links with the Dudleys, and cannot in any sense be described as the duke's servant. He was a companion in arms. Sir William Cecil was promoted by Northumberland, who relied on him, confided in him, and rewarded him in various ways, but Cecil was in the king's service, not the duke's, and it is questionable whether he should be regarded as a member of the 'affinity'. At the same time men like Sir Thomas Wyatt and Sir Nicholas Arnold, who served at Boulogne and were on friendly terms with Northumberland, received little or nothing at his hand and, in spite of his later rebellion, Wyatt was one of the first in Kent to declare for Mary in July 1553.[14] Sir George Harper, Cuthbert Vaughn, and Alexander Brett were also former Boulogne officers who became embroiled in Wyatt's rebellion. Harper and Vaughn had been among those who had received licences of retainer in Edward's last days, but none of them made any move to assist Jane's cause during the succession crisis.[15] Among his peers Northumberland's closest allies were Henry Grey, marquis of Dorset and duke of Suffolk, and William Parr, marquis of Northampton. Both featured significantly in the distribution of patronage between 1550 and 1553, and both remained loyal to him after Edward's death, but both were weak personalities and proved

[11]   PRO KB8/29, r. 2; J. G. Nichols (ed.), *The Chronicle of Queen Jane*, Camden Society, 48 (1850), 76; *Cal. Pat.*, Philip and Mary, ii. 124.

[12]   See above, for his alleged role in conveying Northumberland's ideas to the king.

[13]   BL Royal MS 18C 24, *passim*.

[14]   Loades, *Two Tudor Conspiracies*, 16.

[15]   BL Royal MS 18C 24, fo. 366ʳ. Harper, Culpepper, and Isley had also been parties to a settlement in May 1553, with Northumberland, for the covenanting of lands in Kent to Sir Henry and Mary Sidney (*Historical Manuscripts Commission*, 77, De Lisle and Dudley MSS, i. 15).

ineffectual when put to the test. Among the barons, Lords Wentworth, Darcy, and Brooke should probably be classed as Dudley supporters, and Darcy owed his title to Northumberland.[16] Wentworth had been sufficiently trusted to be given a commission of Lieutenancy in May 1553, but before the end of August he had been recruited on to Mary's council.[17] Lord Darcy was placed under house arrest on 30 July, but his restraint does not seem to have been prolonged, and no further action was taken against him. Among those who were trusted with office and commissions, and regularly rewarded during the Dudley ascendancy, the most conspicuous, apart from the Gates brothers, were Sir Philip Hoby, Sir Henry Seymour, and Sir Robert Bowes. Bowes lost his offices, but was sufficiently trusted to be serving on commissions in the north before the end of 1553.[18] Hoby, whom Renard described as 'the craftiest heretic in England', obtained a licence to go abroad in June 1554, and travelled in Germany and Italy.[19] Seymour disappeared from public life, and may have died.

It is natural and very tempting to look for a consistent pattern in the politics of these years, and to see a continuity between the benefits of patronage and office while Northumberland was in power, disfavour, and possibly punishment in the immediate aftermath of the *coup*, retirement from public life during the remainder of Mary's reign, and rehabilitation after Elizabeth's accession. Such a pattern would establish the rise, fall, and resurgence of a Dudley affinity, but, outside the ramifications of the family itself, it can be only very patchily traced. Many of those most conspicuously employed and rewarded by Northumberland deserted him in July 1553, and were quickly employed by the new regime. At the same time several of those indicted or arrested for their part in the usurpation do not appear to have been close to the duke, or particularly his followers—the earl of Rutland, Sir Edward Montague, Sir Roger Cholmley, Richard Cox, Nicholas Ridley, and, most conspicuously, Thomas Cranmer.[20] Some of those who later made themselves noticeable by their opposition to Mary's policies, such as Sir Ralph Bagenal, Henry Killigrew, Sir Nicholas Throgmorton, Sir George Harper, and Henry Dudley himself, had traceable connections with Northumberland, but most did not. Apart from service at Boulogne, there is nothing to connect Sir Thomas Wyatt with a Dudley affinity, nor do such men as Sir Anthony Kingston, Sir William Courtenay, or Christopher

---

[16] He was created baron of Chiche on 7 Apr. 1551 (BL MS Royal 18C 24, fo. 72ᵛ).

[17] *APC*, iv. 277; ibid. 323, etc.   [18] Ibid. 367.

[19] S. E. Brigden (ed.), 'The letters of Richard Scudamore to Sir Philip Hoby', *Camden Miscellany*, 30 (1990), 85.447; *Cal. Span.*, xii. 265.

[20] Rutland appears to have been with Northumberland at Cambridge; Ridley preached a notorious sermon against Mary; Cholmley and Montague seem to have been arrested for their role in accepting the king's settlement rather than for anything which they did to implement it. Cranmer played no part in the duke's campaign, and was arrested later. Rather surprisingly, his armoury at Lambeth was far larger and better stocked than that of the duke at Durham Place, but that was possibly because he had not used it (PRO E154/12/39, 63).

Ashton feature in any list of known Dudley supporters. There were con-
tinuities, but they were seldom clear-cut, and should not be overemphasized. Many men held offices on the huge and ramifying Northumberland
estates in the early 1550s who did not have particularly close links with the
duke, and it is not surprising that they did not rally to his defence in 1553. A
number of those who had sought Northumberland's patronage when he
was in power looked to his rapidly rising son, Lord Robert, earl of Leicester, in the 1560s and beyond. Simon Adams, in his recent studies of the Dudley connection, has identified a number of these: Sir John Throckmorton,
Clement Throckmorton, Simon Musgrave, and Thomas Wilson, for example.[21] There were members of Robert Dudley's affinity who had been in
trouble under Mary, such as Thomas Leighton and Edward Horsey, who
had no known connection with his father, and there were others seeking the
help of Robert or Ambrose in Elizabeth's reign who claimed former Dudley
service on very dubious grounds.

There clearly was a Dudley affinity, but it did not much resemble the
indentured retinues of the fifteenth century, and it was not held together by
generations of family loyalty. It was much closer in spirit to the networks of
the later seventeenth and eighteenth centuries. This can be clearly seen in
the earl of Leicester's parliamentary patronage, so similar in nature and
effect to that of the duke of Newcastle.[22] The attitude of Ambrose and
Robert Dudley towards their father and his career also leaves the question
of continuity in some doubt. John Dudley had few defenders in the generation after his execution, and his fate was cast in the earl of Leicester's face as
a reproach. This was less because of his treason than because of his apostasy. A protestant culture, increasingly influenced by John Foxe, expected
its heroes and heroines to be godly. Foxe himself was noncommittal on
Northumberland, lamenting his fall but without explicit condemnation. A
reference to the duke as a 'carnal gospeller', which had appeared in the 1559
Latin version, was removed from the first English edition in 1563.[23] Nevertheless Leicester did not advertise his origins. When a certain Thomas Trol-
lope wrote to him at some point before his elevation to the earldom,
offering to write in defence of his father and grandfather, and adding 'these
spread abroad will win the hearts of all the nobility and commons ...', his
offer was not taken up.[24] Such hints as there are of appeals to family feeling
usually have some visibly ulterior motive. As early as April 1559, Sir James
Croft was writing to him, commending 'a gentlewoman widow, whom my
lorde your father (whose soule God pardon) favoured well ...'.[25] In July of

---

[21] Adams, 'Dudley Clientele'; also 'The Dudley Clientele in the House of Commons,
1559–1586', *Parliamentary History*, 8 (1989), 217–39.

[22] Ibid.

[23] I am indebted to Professor Tom Freeman of Rutgers University for this observation.

[24] *HMC*, 58, MSS of the marquis of Bath at Longleat, V, Talbot Dudley and Devereux MSS,
1533–1659 (Dudley Papers. I. D. 207).

[25] Ibid. 139.

the same year Dominico Conncino appealed for the reinstatement of his Edwardian pension of £200 a year on the grounds of his services to his 'noble father'.[26] Such appeals became numerous as Robert's favour increased. Even his brother Ambrose appealed for his help in placing 'an old chaplain' of their father's in the Deanery of Lincoln.[27] Sir Thomas Chaloner, writing to him as an established favourite in June 1564, thanked him for an earlier letter 'in which I have imprinted the image of that noble Duke your father's favour …'.[28] Robert himself probably felt some obligation to those who had been cast adrift by Northumberland's fall, and it is not surprising that those who felt that they had a claim on the duke's gratitude should have drawn themselves to his attention. It would, however, be unwise to go much beyond that. Robert built up his own affinity to suit his own purposes, and apart from his kindred this was only to a small extent the reconstruction of the earlier Dudley connection.

Similarly it would be a mistake to see the Dudleys and their friends behind the opposition to Mary. It was the government, not Sir Thomas Wyatt, who claimed that the conspiracy of January and February 1554 was designed to restore Jane and Guildford to the throne. If there was a positive, as distinct from a negative, purpose behind that movement, it was almost certainly the replacement of Mary with Elizabeth.[29] There was protestant involvement, but the recognized protestant leaders disowned it. Moreover, most of the surviving Dudleys were in prison, several under sentence of death, and, if the rebellion was designed to rescue them, it went a very strange way about it. The original plan was for a pattern of revolts in Devon, the Midlands, and the Welsh borders as well as Kent, which, if it had matured, would have given the council plenty of time to have executed the prisoners even if their friends had ultimately been successful. Some of Northumberland's friends and clients were undoubtedly involved, but as general opponents of what Mary was coming to stand for rather than as protagonists of a renewed Dudley ascendancy. Sensitive as they were to opposition, Mary's council did not really fear the Dudley affinity as a political force, actual or potential, which is why they were so lenient with the remaining members of the family. Similarly, although the conspiracy of 1555–6 bears Henry Dudley's name, and he was probably its originator, hardly any of those arrested and interrogated had former connections with the family, although some were later employed by the earl of Leicester.[30] The Dudleys were not sufficiently popular to be usable as a lever against the Spanish connection, and what was left of the affinity by that time showed every sign of reconciling itself to the new situation. The most implacable, although mainly non-violent, enemies of Mary and her

---

[26] Ibid. 52. [27] Ibid. 70.
[28] *HMC*, 70, Pepys MSS at Magdalene College, Cambridge, 24.
[29] Loades, *Two Tudor Conspiracies*, 19.
[30] Ibid., Appendix IV, 265–7; Adams, 'Dudley Clientele'.

government continued to be the protestants, but, as we have seen, Northumberland had spectacularly distanced himself from the reformers before his death, and they no longer had time or use for his friends. When Jean Ribault, a French mercenary formerly conspicuous in the duke's service, helped to convey Thomas Stafford's small force to Scarborough in April 1557, he was probably acting as a double agent, and no member of the affinity was foolish enough to get involved in that desperate adventure.[31] Philip also liked English soldiers, if they were not too obviously heretical, and recruited them into his service. Cuthbert Vaughn became a colonel of infantry, and Robert Dudley was Master of the Ordnance on the St Quentin campaign. If Mary had not died in November 1558 the Dudley connection would simply have disappeared, because it had no territorial roots, and represented no particular ideological tradition.

However, Mary did die, and with Elizabeth's accession the surviving Edwardians rapidly came back into favour. This did not happen a moment too soon for Robert Dudley, who was beleaguered with debts. He had sold £500 worth of his wife's marriage portion in order to follow the earl of Pembroke with a respectable band.[32] At about the same time he also pledged the Halesowen estates, which he had acquired in the previous year, to his father's former steward Anthony Foster for £1,928.[33] What he did with this money is not quite clear. In spite of his strenuous efforts to curry favour with Philip, he was not welcome at court when the king was not there. He was thus excluded from the milieu in which his good looks and natural charm would have given him the biggest advantage. He was also saved a great deal of expense, and it is possible that he was casting his bread in a different direction altogether. In 1561, when he was commenting upon the hostility of the English to the prospect of a marriage between the queen and Lord Robert, the Saxon diplomat Hubert Languet wrote:

The queen replied … that she had never thought of contracting a marriage with my Lord Robert, but she was more attached to him than to any of the others, because when she was deserted by everybody in the reign of her sister not only did he never lessen in any degree his kindness and humble attention to her, but he even sold his possessions that he might assist her with money, and therefore she thought it just that she should make some return for his good faith and constancy …[34]

Such a story raises inevitable doubts. Far from being 'deserted by everyone', Elizabeth had had a large, if discreet, following during the last two years of her sister's life; and why a princess with an estate worth over £3,000 a year should have been dependent upon hand-outs from a relatively impe-

---

[31] For a discussion of Jean Ribault's role in this episode, see D. Loades, *The Reign of Mary Tudor* (London, 1991), 307 and nn.

[32] PRO CP26/1, r. 94; Derek Wilson, *Sweet Robin: A Biography of Robert Dudley, Earl of Leicester* (London, 1981), 72.

[33] PRO C54/546, m. 16; Society of Antiquaries MS 139, fos. 129, 131.

[34] Quoted by Wilson, *Sweet Robin*, 73, from F. Chamberlain, *Elizabeth and Leicester* (London, 1939), Appendix IX, 92–3.

cunious Norfolk squire was never explained. In 1561 the queen was inventing excuses for her favour to Lord Robert, but he may well have sent her
expensive presents which he could not afford, or advanced modest sums in
cash for immediate purposes. It was part of a courtier's skill to cast his
bread upon the waters before the fish began to rise. Robert may have made
a profit on his military adventure, but it is unlikely that he came back from
the brief and strenuous St Quentin campaign with much in the way of
booty. No sooner was he back in England than he sold the Halesowen property to a Shropshire neighbour, John Littleton, and it was probably out of
the first instalment of the sale price that he repaid Foster.[35] He was not to
receive the final instalment until 1561. Syderstone, which should have been
his principal seat in Norfolk, was unsuitable, and may have been empty for
some time. While his agents looked for a smaller and more commodious
residence in the summer of 1558, Robert and Amy were living in London,
probably in rented or borrowed accommodation. His efforts to re-establish
himself had so far brought no success, except in one respect. In spite of the
fact that his uncle was still alive, and that Ambrose was his elder brother, by
the autumn of 1558 Robert had been accepted as the leader of the family. It
was he who inherited his father's energy and political ambition, and perhaps also his unscrupulousness. Time was to prove that Ambrose was the
better soldier, but he was to live the rest of his life under the shadow of his
more dashing and magnificent brother. Within hours of receiving the news
of Mary's death Robert was summoned to the court of his new sovereign,
and named Master of the Horse.

This was an office of great significance, in that it involved constant attendance upon the monarch, but it was not in itself very profitable. Nor did it
occur to anyone at first that Elizabeth had any special regard for Robert. He
was one of a number of her brother's former servants who were recalled to
office, and the appointments of Sir William Cecil and Nicholas Bacon probably seemed more important at the time. There was speculation that Sir
William Pickering or Lord Grey of Wilton would occupy the role of personal favourite.[36] Consequently Lord Robert was not immediately cata-
pulted from debt into affluence. At first, with new and expensive
commitments, he may have found it even more difficult to make ends meet.
However, by the summer of 1559 he had begun to purchase land on a
modest scale, and in 1561 he received the first of a series of major grants
from the Crown.[37] By that time it must have seemed in some ways as
though the reign of Mary had never been. If John Dudley had died in his

---

[35] Technically Dudley sold the land to Thomas Blount and George Tuckey, and they sold to
Littleton, but it seems almost certain that Blount and Tuckey were Dudley's agents, and that
he arranged the sale in this way in order to make a capital gain (BRL Hagley Hall MSS 351493,
351494, 351621; *Cal. Pat.*, Philip and Mary, iv. 345, 440–1). For a discussion of this transaction,
see Adams, 'Dudley Clientele', 251 and nn.

[36] Wilson, *Sweet Robin*, 100.

[37] *Cal. Pat.*, Elizabeth, i. 86, 288; ii. 189–90, 291–3, 534–43; iii. 59.

bed, his son Ambrose would have been duke of Northumberland, but Elizabeth was allergic to dukes and on 26 December 1561 the oldest surviving Dudley was restored to the earldom of Warwick. He had already served as Chief Pantler at the coronation, and been appointed Master of the Ordnance.[38] Robert's office of Master of the Horse had previously been held by his elder brother, and might well have come to him in due course if Edward had lived. Mary Sidney became one of the queen's ladies, and in due course perhaps the most intimate and trusted member of the Privy Chamber. As the oldest remaining female Dudley she carried the family's standard on the distaff side, and would probably have played the same part had either Edward married or Jane succeeded. Elizabeth seems to have made a policy of granting to Mary's brothers lands which had formerly belonged to their father, so the estates which they began to assemble after 1561 were not only closely intermeshed, but were also in areas where Dudley influence was already strongly established.[39] The special nature of Lord Robert's relationship with the queen began to be noticed in the early part of 1559, and when she created him a knight of the Garter on 23 April it was, as William Camden commented, 'the wonder of all men'.[40]

For the next three years England's domestic politics were to be dominated by this relationship, which has fascinated contemporaries and historians alike. However, in this context it is not the fluctuations of Elizabeth's emotions which are significant, but the effect which her love had upon his fortunes and influence. It has been said that he felt overshadowed by his father, and was always seeking to emulate John's political and military achievements. There does not seem to be much evidence for this, however, and although suitors might invoke his father's memory, he never replied in kind. Given the choice, Robert might well have chosen to shine upon the battlefield rather than in the boudoir, but he was a courtier to his fingertips, something which his father had never been, and he must have realized that clearly enough. Like his father in ambition and in political ability, he was unlike in almost every other respect. We know very little about how John chose to relax, except that he liked to give the impression that he never did anything of the kind. He did have a company of players in his livery, who were granted a special licence in 1552, but I do not know of any reference to his witnessing one of their performances.[41] He was not a significant patron of artists, writers, or scholars, although he was Chancellor of Cambridge University for about two years, and his memory was respected there.[42] By contrast, Robert was a

[38] Feria to Philip, 21 Nov. 1558 (*Calendar of State Papers, Spanish, Elizabeth*, ed. M. A. S. Home (London, 1892–9), i. 1; Wilson, *Sweet Robin*, 82–3).

[39] Adams, 'Dudley Clientele', 254.

[40] Wilson, *Sweet Robin*, 96. It had been only five years earlier that John Dudley's hatchments had been taken down and ceremoniously hurled into the ditch (BL Add. MS 38140, fo. 194).

[41] BL Royal MS 18C 24, fo. 191ʳ: 18 Mar. 1552.

[42] *HMC*, 58, Dudley Papers, i. 179, University of Cambridge to Lord Robert Dudley, 19 Aug. 1563.

cultivated gentleman with many intellectual interests, an organizer of revels and entertainments, and a man with an insatiable appetite for the good things of life. He was alleged to carry the price of several manors upon his back, and, as he ruefully admitted in later life, always lived beyond his means. John had built his political career by many years of hard graft in the service of Henry VIII, and real success had come late in life. Robert rebuilt the Dudley fortunes by captivating a susceptible young woman who also happened to be his queen. It was only after that relationship changed, and it became clear that the ultimate prize of the crown matrimonial was beyond his grasp, that he was created earl of Leicester in September 1564, and settled down to the long-term roles of councillor and confidant, which were his solid contributions to the politics of a remarkable reign.

Different generations require different tactics, and the court of the 1560s was quite different from that of the 1520s, dominated by Wolsey, or the 1530s, dominated by Cromwell. Elizabeth's accession was above all an Edwardian restoration, but the queen had no need of a new duke of Northumberland. It took a long time for Ambrose and Robert to reassemble their father's wealth, and they never acquired anything like his political ascendancy. Whatever her personal feelings, the queen balanced her favours to the Dudleys with those to other in-favour families, particularly those of Cecil, Howard, and Radcliffe. Elizabeth had hated her half-sister and all she stood for, and the council memoranda of the first few weeks of the reign are full of disparaging asides about the mismanagement of the previous regime, just as those of Mary's early council had been. Mary's Church was overthrown, and her confidants banished into obscurity, but there were no attainders, and no encouragement to settle old scores. It was believed abroad that one of the reasons why the English nobility was opposed to the idea of the queen marrying Lord Robert was because 'they fear that if he becomes king he will want to avenge the death of his father, and extirpate the nobility of that kingdom'.[43] However, it seems that nothing was further from Robert's mind. Even the obvious feud with the earl of Arundel produced no more than a chilly detachment. When the question was raised in Elizabeth's presence, she is reported to have said 'in commendation of my Lord Robert ... that he was of a very good disposition and nature, not given by any means to seek revenge of former matters past, wherein she seemed much to allow him ...'.[44] There was a happy-go-lucky streak in the future earl's disposition, but whether his eirenicism in 1560 was really due to the sweetness of his nature, or to clear warnings from the queen as to what would happen to him if he stepped out of line, is not clear.

---

[43] Pope Pius IV to the Cardinal of Ferrara, July 1561 (J. H. Pollen (ed.), *Papal Negotiations with Mary, Queen of Scots*, Scottish Historical Society, 37 (1901), 60–1).

[44] BL Cotton MS Titus B XIII, fo. 28. This did not, of course, prevent many people from hating Lord Robert. The duke of Norfolk's hostility was frequently referred to, but Dudley does not seem to have taken the initiative in such feuds.

Elizabeth was quite rightly concerned to rally a united aristocracy behind her, and succeeded to a remarkable extent. Only the earls of Northumberland and Westmorland were so alienated from the court that their loyalty was called in question before the end of the decade. Paradoxically, the quarrel which did develop was not between the duke's sons and those who had deserted their father in 1553, but between Robert and John's former right-hand man, Sir William Cecil. Cecil was adamantly opposed to Dudley's pretensions to the crown matrimonial. His reasons were cogent, and almost certainly justified. Whatever loyalty he may have felt to his old patron, after November 1558 his allegiance was entirely to the queen, and whatever he may initially have felt about the Dudleys, by 1560 he saw Robert's ambition as a menace to the Crown and to the state.

The earl of Leicester is much the best-documented, and consequently the most studied member of his family. He remained a leading figure in council and in court until his death in 1588, and his career provides an excellent case-study in the realities of Tudor politics, but only for about three years, from 1559 to 1562, did it seem likely that he would hold the destiny of the kingdom in his hands. In August 1562, when it was already clear that the queen would not marry him, she fell desperately ill of smallpox, and informed her council that, in the event of her death her beloved Robert Dudley was to be appointed Protector of the Realm, with a salary of £20,000 a year.[45] Such a disposition was almost as unrealistic as Edward VI's original 'Device', and if Elizabeth had died a protracted political crisis, perhaps culminating in civil war, would have followed. Similarly, if the queen had insisted on marrying him, against the advice of her council, there would have been a real possibility of armed insurrection, and no certainty as to how it would have ended. However, in neither of these situations was the outcome in Robert's own hands. He did his very best, using his own charm, and whatever political leverage he could discover, including a bizarre appeal to the Spanish ambassador, to persuade Elizabeth to marry him. However, the circumstances in which Amy died, at Cumnor Hall on 8 September 1560, nullified the effects of her death.[46] Instead of freeing him to marry the queen, it created an enormous scandal. Probably both Robert and Amy knew that she was mortally ill, and that she had planned to kill herself. Such an explanation would account for oddities in both their behav-

---

[45] *Cal. Span.*, Elizabeth, i. 262–4; Wilson, *Sweet Robin*, 135–6.

[46] The circumstances of Amy's death have been frequently and thoroughly investigated. The most likely explanation is that she was suffering from an advanced breast cancer, which would account for her known irritability, and for the extreme fragility of the spine which caused her death. If Robert had known of her condition (as he must have done) it would account for his having described her as 'doomed' shortly before her death, a remark which has often been given a sinister interpretation (G. Adlard, *Amy Robsart and the Earl of Leicester* (London, 1870); J. E. Jackson, 'Amye Robsart', *Wiltshire Archaeological Magazine*, 17 (1898), 58–93; I. Aird, 'The Death of Amy Robsart', *English Historical Review*, 71 (1957), 69–79; N. Fourdrinier, 'Amy Robsart', MS MC5/29 in the Norfolk County Record Office; Wilson, *Sweet Robin*, 118–43).

iours over the previous few days, but at the time it was inevitably believed that he had had her murdered. His eventual exoneration by an enquiry was received with the greatest scepticism, and a political course, which would have been perilous in any circumstances, became impossibly foolhardy. Elizabeth probably never made a conscious decision not to marry him, but gradually accepted the hopelessness of such a course. Robert himself refused to accept this for some time, and never entirely abandoned his pretensions until he was forced to acknowledge his union with Lettice Knollys in 1578. Similarly Elizabeth's disposition in 1562 was entirely her own doing, and one of a number of actions which must cast doubt upon her established reputation for political sagacity. Had she died, Robert would have been put in a very similar position to that which his father had occupied in July 1553, and it is impossible to know how he would have fared.

By contrast, John Dudley's power came at the end of his career, and was much more substantial. For about three and a half years he was the real ruler of England, and it was he who attempted to enforce Edward's strange succession settlement once the king's driving will was removed. Had he succeeded, not only would the future of the English monarchy have been changed, but the recently developed authority of statute would have been heavily undermined, with incalculable consequences. Although it is arguable that Robert's career was as important as his father's, it was so in a different way. John Dudley's ambitions, talents, and limitations determined the conduct of government during the second half of Edward VI's minority, whereas Robert's influenced (or did not influence) an adult ruler perfectly capable of making her own decisions. In spite of this John is much the more elusive of the two. For much of his career he can be only imperfectly glimpsed going about his business and acting in the king's service. Even when he was the pivot of the state, much about him remains elusive. He was a difficult, contradictory man, and even at the end of this study it is impossible to sum up his career in a few words, but he is one of that handful of men through whom the power structures of Tudor England can be approached and understood. It is facile to describe him as a transitional figure, but the term is nevertheless an apt one. Ostensibly a great magnate in the traditional mould, with a ducal title, great estates, and a vast household, the appearances of his career are deceptive. Not only was he a 'service peer', a characteristic which he shared with most of those of Henrician or Edwardian creation, but he made no attempt to imitate the political style of an earlier generation. It is a mistake to describe him as leading an 'aristocratic reaction' in the reign of Edward VI. Like the duke of Suffolk before him, and the earl of Essex after him, he was a creature of the court and of the council. Unlike the duke of Gloucester in the 1470s, or the duke of Buckingham in the early years of Henry VIII, he had no power base outside the central government. Nor did he seek one. One of the most conspicuous features of his career, and one which has been frequently noted, is the lack of any attempt to build up a coherent and stable estate. John Dudley dealt in land as a modern business man might deal in shares. Even his 'title' lands in the midlands and north-east of England, so eagerly sought, were manipulated and disposed of. It is often difficult to identify the advantages which this trading brought, but they must have been mainly financial. To Dudley land was a source of income and prestige, but not of power in the traditional sense. Charles Brandon had also received and disposed of land freely, but in his case that had been determined by the king's priorities rather than his own. Dudley set his own agenda, working hard to obtain lands which he desired, but often selling them on after a short interval. Thomas Cromwell, who was similarly a powerful man without roots, had done the same, and it may well have been Cromwell upon whom Dudley modelled himself. If so, his eventual fate was ironic, because he also fell victim to the inconsistencies of royal favour. Like Cromwell, he gambled on the indispensability of his services, and lost. There are some striking similarities between the letter which Cromwell wrote to Henry after his condemnation, and that which Northumberland addressed to the earl of Arundel. For each rejection by the monarch spelled more than physical death, it represented the negation of the principles to which he had devoted his life. Each was, no doubt, egotistical and self-serving, but each had also dedicated his public life to the service of the Crown. Neither could have lived in peaceful retirement, and the crude political correctives of the sixteenth century provided the necessary punctuation for their restless and ambitious lives. John Dudley died execrated, and until very recently no attempt has been made to rehabilitate his memory, but that probably tells us more about the evolution of English history than it does about the duke of Northumberland.

Appendices

ABBREVIATIONS

BL Add. MS	British Library, Additional Manuscript
APC	*Acts of the Privy Council*, ed. J. Dasent *et al.* (London, 1890–1907)
Cal. Pat.	*Calendar of the Patent Rolls*, Edward VI, ed. R. H. Brodie (London, 1924–9)
E	Public Record Office, Exchequer classes
HMC	*Historical Manuscripts Commission Reports*
L. & P.	*Letters and Papers of the Reign of Henry VIII*, ed. J. S. Brewer *et al.* (London, 1862–1932)
SP	Public Record Office, State Papers class
VE	*Valor Ecclesiasticus*, ed. J. Caley and J. Hunter (London, 1810–34

I JOHN DUDLEY'S LANDS

Date	Lands gained	Lands relinquished	Particulars	Reference
1510			By the terms of his father's will lands in Cheshire were left to his use.	SP1/2, fos. 5–8 *L. & P.*, i. 559
1511–12	At the time of his indictment Edmund's lands were valued at 500 marks (£333. 6s.8d.) p.a. These lands were all restored by the act of restitution, except such as were assigned to use or specifically excepted. The value of the residue, which he inherited in 1525, can be estimated at £200 p.a.		The statute which restored him in blood granted his wardship to Sir Edward Guildford, without suing livery No inventory survives, either for Edmund at the time of his attainder, or for John on his majority	3 Henry VIII, c. 19
1 May 1527		Braye and Swayveling (Hants)	Sold to John Mylle *et al.*	*L. & P.*, iv. 3142
1527			Petition of John Maryng claims that John Dudley holds Manwood (Sussex) and Norwood (IoW) obtained fraudulently by Edmund Dudley.	*L. & P.*, 4, 3727
Mar. 1532	Messuage or mansion in Warwick called 'le Stewards place' Gardens and waters in Weggenoke park		Fees and annuities jointly with Sir Francis Bryan. Goes with the offices of Constable, Keeper, and Master of the Hunt.	*L. & P.*, v. 909 (15)

Date	Property	Detail	Note	Reference
Mar. 1532	Messuage of 100 acres in King's Norton; 20 acres in Feckenham, 2 burgages in Worcester; 140 acres in Clevys (Worcs.)		During the minority of Anthony Norton, with wardship	*L. & P.*, v. 909 (5)
1532–3	Lands (unspecified) to the value of £6,000 (c.£300 p.a.) by foreclosure of mortgage on John Lord Dudley (see May 23, 1537 below)		Letters of complaint from Lord Dudley to Cromwell	*L. & P.*, v. 1727 / *L. & P.*, vi. 467
1533			Cromwell had a valor of Sir John Dudley's lands, but it does not survive	*L. & P.*, vi. 299, p. 132.
25 Feb. 1535	There was a dispute with John Guildford over Sir Edward's inheritance after his death. How much Sir John gained is not clear			*L. & P.*, viii. 264
1536		Unspecified. £124. 10s. 3d. p.a.	Sold to Sir Edward Seymour	*HMC*, 58, ix. 324. Seymour papers
6 Feb. 1537		Irem Acton	Sold to Mr Popley	*L. & P.*, xii. 353
23 May 1537	Dudley, with castle, Segelly, Ettingsall, etc. (Worcs.) sold by Lord Dudley to Roger Brown of London to the use of Sir John Dudley (£4,000)	Drayton Bassett sold to George Robinson for £2,000. Painswick etc. offered as security for the balance	Foreclosure of mortgage on Lord Dudley. Drayton Bassett deal void if Lord Dudley pays Robinson £1,000 by Michaelmas	*L. & P.*, xii. 1263
9 June 1538	Site of the late abbey of Halesowen (Salop) and manors belonging to the house Valued at £293. 0s. 2½d.		Grant in fee	*L. & P.*, xiii. ii. 491 (1) / *VE*, iii. 206–8

Date	Lands gained	Lands relinquished	Particulars	Reference
27 July 1538		Drayton sold to 'Mr. Pope': various lands in Gloucester-shire offered to Thomas Cromwell	To pay debts	*L. & P.*, xiii. i. 1473
(A bargain with Cromwell is discussed, but the outcome is uncertain. See entries for Jan. 1539 below)				
Before Dec. 1538		Iddesley, Rings Ashe, Charle-ton (Devon), Trevispite (Corn.): value £60–80 p.a.	Sold to the marquis of Exeter	*L. & P.*, xiii. ii. 990
n.d.	(Feckenham)		Sought by exchange with the king	Thynne MSS, i. 9
1538	Acton Burnell		Bought of the duke of Norfolk for £98	*L. & P.*, xiii. ii. 1215
2 Jan. 1539		Little Halden, Halden Park, etc. (Cinq Ports) Eastguld-forde etc. (Sussex), 11 other properties, mainly Kent	Part of Jane Guildford's join-ture. Sold to Lord Cromwell	*L. & P.*, xiv. i. 9
Jan. 1539		Magna Pepinbury (Kent), Bullocksystowne (Sussex)	Part of Jane Guildford's join-ture. Sold to Lord Cromwell	*L. & P.*, xiv. i. 191 (1)
Feb. 1539	Halesowen properties in Salop and Worcester enfoeffed to Edward Blunt and George Willoughby, to the use of John and Jane Dudley			*L. & P.*, xiv. i. 403 (21)
Feb. 1539	Penkridge (Staffs.)		Purchased jointly with Edmund Sutton from Sir John Lister *et al.*	*L. & P.*, xiv. i. 403 (3)
Feb. 1539		Halden and other lands in	Sold to Lord Cromwell for	*L. & P.*, xiv. ii. 782

Date	Lands		Nature of transaction	Reference
		Kent and Sussex	£3,490 in two instalments (see July 27, 1538 above)	(340)
Mar. 1539		Lichfield and other lands of Dudford Priory	To Sir Andrew Dudley	L. & P., xiv. i. 651 (8)
Jan. 1541	Acton Burnell and other lands in Shropshire		Purchased from the duke of Norfolk (see 1538 above)	L. & P., xvi. 503 (22)
10 Jan. 1541 / Mar. 1541	Walsall (Staffs.), lands of Dudley Priory in Staffs. and Worcester. Other monastic lands in Northumberland and Northants		Grant in farm, no request, terms unspecified	E318/392 L. & P., xvi. 678 (47)
May 1541		Tithes of corn from the lands of Dudley Priory	Sold to Thomas Ryggway of Shipley	L. & P., xvi. 878 (42)
10 Jan. 1542		Acton Burnell (Salop) etc.	Sold to Fulk Crompton	L. & P., xvii. 71 (5)
Mar. 1542	Kayo (Surrey)		Purchased from William Byrche	L. & P., xvii. 220 (50)
May 1544	Hospitals of Burton Lazarus (Leics.), St Giles in the Fields (London)		Grant in fee for service	L. & P., xix. i. 610 (8)
1 June 1545	Eversley Wood, Ashwood, etc. (Kent)		Grant for services and £160. 16s. 8d.	L. & P., xx. i. 847
20 Sept. 1545		Kayo (Surrey)	Sold to Sir William Paget	L. & P., xx. ii. 469 (68)
10 Dec. 1545	Birmingham, Richards castle (parcel of the lands purchased of the king). Marfield (Salop), Kidderminster, etc.		Request to purchase	E318/393

Date	Lands gained	Lands relinquished	Particulars	Reference
18 Dec. 1545	Birmingham (Warks.), Richards Castle (Hereford), etc.		Grant, for service and £69. 2s. 0½d.	L. & P., xx. ii. 1068 (41)
Feb. 1546		Marfield and other lands in Shropshire	Sold to Roger Smith of Bridgenorth	L. & P., xxi. 302 (65)
1 Mar. 1546	Subsidy assessment for John, Viscount Lisle at £1,360 in lands			E179/59/54
26 Mar. 1546		Wymondham (Norfolk)	Sold to Robert Knight al. Kett	L. & P., xxi. i. 504 (47)
5 Apr. 1546	Site of the priory of St John, Clerkenwell, and other lands of the priory		Request for gift	E318/715
1 May 1546			Grant for service and £1,000 plus £6. 13s. 4d.	L. & P., xxi. i. 970 (1)
29 June 1546		Spardon, Choddesdon, and other lands in Derbyshire	Sold to the king	L. & P., xxi. i. 1150
6 July 1546		St Giles in the Fields	Sold to Wymondham Carew	L. & P., xxi. i. 1383 (110)
25 Nov. 1546	Inheritance of Elizabeth[a], Viscountess Lisle (mother)		Livery of lands	L. & P., xxi. ii. 476 (97)
Jan. 1547		Unspecified; given to the king in recompense of debt	Overplus £114. 3s. 2d. paid	L. & P., xxi. ii. 775, fo. 105
27 Mar. 1547	Manor, castle, and town of War-wick, and a long list of lands in eleven counties.		Request for gift	E318/2042

Date	Property / Description	Transaction	Reference
22 June 1547	Value £498. 18s. 8d. p.a.	Grant, of £300 p.a., in fulfilment of a promise by Henry VIII, and following his elevation.	*Cal. Pat.*, i. 252
22/23 June 1547	Site of St John Baptist, Ludlow	Grant, terms unknown, sold to William and Edward Foxe	*Cal. Pat.*, i. 4
11 July 1547	Site of the monastery of St John, Colchester, etc.	Sold to Sir Francis Jobson	*Cal. Pat.*, i. 204
30 Aug. 1547	Lincoln Place, Holborn	Purchased from the bishop of Lincoln, jointly with Sir Edward North	*Cal. Pat.*, i. 183
11 Dec. 1547	Rents and properties in Westinghanger (Kent) and in other parts of Kent, Warks., Salop, Derby, and Suffolk	Surveys and valuations no request	E318/2044
22 Dec. 1547	£108. 9s. 5d. p.a.	Grant, for services against the Scots	*Cal. Pat.*, i. 170
25 Dec. 1547	Ramborough (Suffolk)	Sold to Sir Edward North	*Cal. Pat.*, i. 200
n.d.	Subsidy assessment of 1 Edward VI shows the earl of Warwick at £1,200 p.a. in lands		E179/69 51
20 Feb. 1548	Haywood Barnes (Ches.)	Sold or given to Henry Broke (Steward of Household)	*Cal. Pat.*, ii. 87.
27 June 1548	Chedworth (Glos.), site and demesne of Penkridge (Staffs.) and other land in Worcester, Hereford, and Surrey (see entry for Feb. 1539 above)	Request to purchase	E318/2045

Date	Lands gained	Lands relinquished	Particulars	Reference
17 Aug. 1548			Grant; for £1,286. 5s. 7d. in Augmentations	Cal. Pat., ii. 29
24 July 1548		10 acres of marsh in Poplar	Sold to Sir Francis Jobson	Cal. Pat., i. 277
22 June 1549		(Manors of Odingsly and Feckenham (Worcs.) and other lands 'as would content my lord for Ballsalle' c.£120 p.a.)	Request to exchange for lands in Kent	Thynne MSS, i. 19
9 July 1549	Old Stratford, Stratford borough, Bishops Hampton, etc.	Richards Castle, etc.	Exchange with the bishop of Worcester	Cal. Pat., ii. 255
10 July 1549	Manor of Westinghanger (Kent), lands in Caernarfon, Denbigh, Flint, Warwick, Hereford, Devon, and Avon		No request lands assigned by the king to the earl	E318/2047 E318/2048
20 July 1549		Saltwood, Southborough, and other lands in Kent	Lands assigned by the earl to the king	E318/2048
12 July 1549		1,000 acres of land in Kent	Sold to Sir George Harper, Thomas Culpepper, and William Isley	Cal. Pat., ii. 338
19 July 1549	Lands in Warwick and Oxford, value £210. 6s. 3d. p.a.	Westinghanger and other lands in Kent	Exchange with the king	Cal. Pat., iii. 2
21 July 1549		Petersloo priory and other lands in Devon and Denbigh	Sold to Sir Richard Sackville	Cal. Pat., iii. 61

Date				
21 July 1549		Lands in Flint	Sold to Peter Mostyn	*Cal. Pat.*, iii. 58
22 July 1549		Kenilworth monastery, etc.	Sold to Andrew Flammock	*Cal. Pat.*, iii. 58
3 Jan. 1550	Lordship of Minster Lovell and other lands in Oxon., Herts., and Gloucester. Value £470. 9s. 7d. p.a.		Request to have in exchange	E318/2046
6 Jan. 1550		Castle, lordship, manor and, town of Warwick	Exchange	*Cal. Pat.*, iii. 71
8 Jan. 1550		Stowe (Glos.)	Sold to George Willoughby	*Cal. Pat.*, iii. 61
n.d. 1547–51	(Manors of Claverdon and Henley in Arden (Warks.))		No request	E318/2053
22 Apr. 1550	Manors of Alnwick, Warkworth, Rothbury (Northumberland), Topcliffe (Yorks.), Coxford (Worcs.). Value £693. 6s. 10d. p.a.		For service gift in fee simple	APC, iii. 11
20 May 1550			Total value £660. 0s. 0d. p.a.	*Cal. Pat.*, iii. 371
20 May 1550	(Mines in Denbigh and properties in nine other counties)		Request to have in gift	E318/2049
22 June 1550	Unspecified	Lands at Hatfield	Exchange with Elizabeth	APC, iii. 52
25 July 1550	Lordship, castle, town, and manor of Warwick, and other lands. Value £473. 5s. 7d. p.a.	Prudhoe, Rothbury, Warkworth, etc. (Northumberland)	Exchange with the king	*Cal. Pat.*, iii. 364
26 July 1550		Battle, Pangbourne, etc.	Sold to the duke of Somerset	*Cal. Pat.*, iii. 351

Date	Lands gained	Lands relinquished	Particulars	Reference
10 Sept. 1550	Manor and lordship of Tonbridge (Kent). Value £105. 5s. 6d. p.a.	Lordship and manors of Wressell and Newsham (Yorks.)	Exchange with the king	_Cal. Pat._, iii. 277
27 Nov. 1550	Manor of Halden and certain lands in Kent		Purchased from Harper, Culpepper, and Isley	_Cal. Pat._, iii. 243
9 Dec. 1550	Priory of Penmon and Ynys Seiriol (Ang.)		Lease for 21 years, paying £31. 2s. 0d. half-yearly	_APC_, iii. 178 / Royal MS 18C 24
15 Mar. 1551	Manor of Chelsea value £30. 3s. 1d. p.a.	Manor and park of Esher (Surrey)	Request to exchange	E318/2056 / Royal MSS 18C 24
14 Apr. 1551		Manors of Whitby Larepool, Whitby Lathe, and other lands in Yorkshire	Sold to Sir John York Licence to alienate £40. 13s. 4d.	_Cal. Pat._, iii. 351
17 May 1551				Royal MS 18C 24
18 May 1551	Manor of Otford, farm of the honour (Kent)	Manors of Langby and Burford (Oxon.). Forest of Wychwood	Request to exchange with the king	E318/2043
19 May 1551	Value £49. 3s. 8d. p.a.		Grant	_Cal. Pat._, iv. 180
21 May 1551		Lands in Nottinghamshire	Sold to Sir John Beaumont	_Cal. Pat._, iv. 61
n.d. (before Nov. 1551)	(Parcel of the College of Penkridge. Woods in Herts., Surrey, and Warwick)		No request	E318/2051

Date	Description	Transaction	Reference
30 Dec. 1551 5 Jan. 1552	Abbey of Tynemouth and lands in Northumberland, Yorks., Wilts., and Staffs. £695. 9s. 9d. p.a.	Grant and exchange, paying £114. 0s. 5d. p.a.	Royal MSS 18C 24 *Cal. Pat.*, iv. 117
14 Feb. 1552		No request	E318/1819
5 Jan. 1552	Lands in Alnwick, Warkworth, etc. (North.) Value £233. 6s. 8d. p.a.	Grant; for his honour and the surrender of an annuity of 500 marks	*Cal. Pat.*, iv. 185
10 May 1552	Knole, Sevenoak, Tonbridge, etc. (Kent)	Licence to alienate to Henry Sidney, etc. to the use of Jane Dudley	*Cal. Pat.*, iv. 431
15 Nov. 1552	Manor of Braudenborough and other lands in Wilts., Yorks., Northumberland, Middx., and Norfolk. Value £398. 15s. 7d. p.a.	Grant and exchange	E318/1820
21 Nov. 1552	Site and demesne of Tynemouth, lordships of Prudhoe and Rothbury, etc.	£1252. 6s. 3d. paid in Augmentations	*Cal. Pat.*, iv. 368
23 Nov. 1552	Wormegay (Norfolk)	Sold to Thomas Mildmay	*Cal. Pat.*, iv. 272
n.d. (1551–3)	Manors of West Coker, etc., in Somerset	Granted to John and Jane	E318/58
n.d. (1551–3)	Castle, borough, and barony of Alnwick and other properties in Northumberland and Durham	Grant to John, duke of Northumberland	E318/57

Date	Lands gained	Lands relinquished	Particulars	Reference
18 Feb. 1553	Manor and castle of Tonbridge (Kent)		Grant	*Cal. Pat.*, v. 179
2 Mar. 1553	Manor and park of Knole Value £104. 15s. 5d. p.a.	Manor and park of Otford	Exchange with the king	*HMC* 80, Sackville (Knole) MSS, i. 316
2 March 1553	Lordship of Stratford and other lands in Warwick. Value 1,000 marks p.a. (£666. 13s. 4d.)	Manor and castle of Tonbridge	Exchange with the king	
30 Apr. 1553	Lordship of Barnard castle and other Duchy of York land in the bishopric of Durham		Grant in socage to pay the full value yearly in Augmentations	Royal MS 18C 24
3 May 1553				*Cal. Pat.*, v. 174
8 May 1553		Manor and park of Halden in the parish of Tenterden (Kent)	Covenanting an estate to Sir Henry and Mary Sidney	*HMC* 77, De Lisle and Dudley MSS, i. 15
16 June 1553	Manors of Feckenham, Ordingley, and Upton in Severn (Worcs.), and other lands in Worcs.,	None specified	No request; by exchange	Royal MSS 18C 24
19 June 1553	Bucks., Yorks., Middx., Suffolk, and Norfolk; value £300 p.a.		Gift; for £46. 19s. 2d. in Augmentations	E318/1821
26 June 1553	Feckenham, Ordingley, Bromsgrove, etc. (Worcs.). Value £400 p.a.		Grant; 'for the better support of his charges'	*Cal. Pat.*, v. 171

4 July 1553	Wotton Bassett, Balsall (Warks.), etc. Value 400 marks p.a. Clypston (Notts.) value £24. 14s. 2d.	Grant Jointly with Sir Henry Sidney	*Cal. Pat.*, v. 242
Sept. 1553	After his trial and attainder, the duke's lands were valued at £4,300 p.a.		LR2/118

Notes

John Dudley's land transactions were exceedingly complex, and this list cannot claim to be complete, particularly for the earlier part of his career. It is also very difficult to tell which transactions involved a real acquisition of ownership, and which existed only on paper. In many cases Dudley disposed of property almost as soon as he acquired it, and seems to have been brokering. The nature of the interest acquired also varied; some were fee simple; some free socage. For some discussion of this, see B. L. Beer, *Northumberland* (Kent, Ohio, 1973), 183–6.

[a] Elizabeth had died in about 1526. Her second husband, Lord Lisle, had then held a life interest in her property. He died in 1543, but by then John had sold the reversionary rights to most of the inheritance (M. L. Bush, 'The Lisle–Seymour Land Disputes', *Historical Journal*, 9 (1966), 255–74).

II JOHN DUDLEY'S OFFICES AND PREFERMENTS (EXCLUDING COMMISSIONS)

Date	Office, etc.	Fee	Reference	Comment
4 Mar. 1523	Knighthood	—	Add. MS 10110, fo. 236	For gallantry, during the campaign in France
Mar. 1532	Constable of Warwick castle	£10 p.a.	L. & P., v. 909 (18)	In survivorship with Sir Francis Bryan
	Constable of the lordship and town of Warwick	10 marks p.a.		
	Keeper of the manor of Gooderest	4d. a day		
	Keeper of the Park of Weggenoke	6d. a day		
	Master of the hunt	6d. a day		
Apr. 1533	Archbishop's cupbearer at Anne Boleyn's coronation	—	Add. MS 21, 116, fo. 506 L. & P., vi. 562	Served at the queen's table
June 1534	Master of the Tower armoury	100 marks p.a.	L. & P., vii. 823 L. & P., xiii. i. 1309	Surrendered by June 1538
Feb. 1537	King's Chief Trencher	£50 p.a.	L. & P., xii. 539 (29)	Surrendered 12 Jan. 1552
7 Mar. 1537	Vice-Admiral	Unspecified	L. & P., xxii. 601	Instructions only
Nov. 1539	Master of the Horse to Anne of Cleves	?	L. & P., xiv. ii. 572	Discharged by July 1540
12 Mar. 1542	Created Viscount Lisle	—	Add. MS 6113, fo. 89 L. & P., xvii. 163	'by the right of his mother'
10 Nov. 1542	Lord Warden of the Marches (Scotland)	66s. 8d. a day	L. & P., xvii. 1063	w.e.f. 21 Nov.
17 Jan. 1543	Lord Admiral	£93. 6. 8. per month	L. & P., xviii. i. 100 (27) L. & P., xix. ii. 419	Surrendered Feb. 1547

Date	Office	Value	Source	Notes
23 Apr. 1543	Sworn of the Council		*L. & P.*, xviii. i. 450	Delayed by absence in the north
23 Apr. 1543	Knight of the Garter		*L. & P.*, xviii. i. 451	Surrendered 10 Mar. 1547
Aug. 1543	Steward of the manors of Bromsgrove, Kings Norton, etc. Steward of Feckenham. Ranger of the Forest	'usual profits'	*L. & P.*, xviii. ii. 107 (12)	
30 Sept. 1544	Captain of Boulogne and Senechal of the Boulonnais	40s. a day	*L. & P.*, xix. ii. 337.	
Before 1545	Gentleman of the Privy Chamber	£50 p.a.	Lansdowne MS 2, fo. 34	
28 Mar. 1546	'Lieutenant General of the army and armada upon the seas in outwards parts against the French'	?	*L. & P.*, xxi. i. 504 (41)	*Ex officio* as Lord Admiral?
Sept. 1546	Reversion of the Captaincy of Beaumaris castle and town	40 marks p.a.	*L. & P.*, xxi. ii. 200 (5)	Held by Sir Richard Bulkley
16 Feb. 1547	Created earl of Warwick	£20 yearly from the port of London	*Cal. Pat.*, i. 173–4	
Jan. 1547	Executor of Henry VIII's will	£500 legacy	Rymer, *Foedera*, xv. 117	See 'other benefits'
17 Feb. 1547	Lord Great Chamberlain		*Cal. Pat.*, i. 180	Succeeding the Earl of Hertford
Mar. 1548?	President of the Council in the Marches of Wales	£1,040 p.a. (incl. exp.)	*Cal. Pat.*, iii. 58	No patent of appointment
15 Oct. 1549	One of the Lords of the Privy Chamber		*APC*, ii. 344	Following the overthrow of the Protector
19 Oct. 1549	Lord Admiral	200 marks per month	*APC*, ii. 347	Vacant since January
Oct. 1549	Lord President of the Council		*APC*, ii. 347	
20 Feb. 1550	Lord Great Master	£200 p.a.	*Cal. Pat.*, iii. 189	Effective from Feb. 1550

Date	Office, etc.	Fee	Reference	Comment
27 May 1550	Governor of the county of Northumberland and Warden of the East and Middle Marches	£1,000 p.a.	*Cal. Pat.*, iii. 404 *APC*, iii. 88	Appointment cancelled 19 July 1550
26 Dec. 1550	Keeper of the manor of Esher	£10 p.a.	Royal MS 18C 24, fos. 26ᵛ, 63ʳ	In survivorship with Lord Lisle
	Lieutenant of the chase at Hampton Court	12*d.* a day		Surrendered 20 Mar. 1551
	Five other offices	One at 4*d.*, 4 at 2*d.* per day 'all fees and profits'		
17 Apr. 1551	Marshall of England		Royal MS 18C 24, fo. 80ᵛ *Cal. Pat.*, iv. 126	
20 Oct. 1551	Warden-General of the Marches against Scotland	2,000 marks p.a. (£1,333. 13s. 4*d.*)	*Cal. Pat.*, iv. 195	
30 Dec. 1551	Constable of Beaumaris castle and captain of the town	(see above)	Royal MS 18C 24, fo. 172ᵛ	
13 Apr. 1552	Chief Steward of the East Riding of Yorks. Steward of Holderness and Cottington, and of all the king's lands in Augmentations	£5. 6s. 5*d.* p.a.	Royal MS 18C 24, fo. 196ᵛ *Cal. Pat.*, iv. 344	
16 June 1552	Steward of the lands in Cumberland, late of Holme Cultram priory	£18. 3s. 4*d.* p.a.	Royal MS 18C 24, fo. 223ᵛ	
2 May 1553	Chief Steward of all the king's lands in Cumberland, Westmorland, Yorks., etc., belonging to the diocese of Durham. Keeper of Durham Castle	£50. 13s. 4*d.* p.a.	*Cal. Pat., v.* 175 Royal MS 18C 24, fo. 339ᵛ	'to have the leading of all the king's men'

III JOHN DUDLEY: ANNUITIES AND OTHER BENEFITS

Date	Grant	Circumstances	Reference
Mar. 1532	Wardship of Anthony Norton (see also land grants)		L. & P., v. 909 (5)
3 July 1543	Licence to export 400 tons of tallow and 400 dickers of calfskin at 10 skins to the dicker	For services as Lord Admiral	L. & P., xviii. i. 981 (25)
April 1544	Annuity in Augmentations	Unspecified	L. & P., xix. i. 368, fo. 43
May 1546	Wardship of Margaret Whorwood	Grandaughter of William Whorwood, and daughter of Anne, later wife of Ambrose Dudley	L. & P., xxi. i. 963 (27)
1546 n.d.	Annuity of 500 marks (£333. 6s. 8d.)	From the king's revenues in North Wales	Cal. Pat., iv. 185
Dec. 1546	3,000 fothers of lead at £4. 6s. 8d. a fother	Surrendered Jan. 1552 Payment to be made at the end of six years (£13,000)	Royal MS 18C 24, fo. 159 L. & P., xxi. ii. 647 (16)
30 Dec. 1546	Legacy of £500 under Henry VIII's will	Increased from £200	L. & P., xxi. ii. 634
7 July 1547			APC, ii. 106
9 May 1550	Licence for a weekly market at Bishops Hatfield; and two fairs on St Luke's day and St George's day		Cal. Pat., iii. 416
10 Oct. 1551	50 marks (£33. 6s. 8d.) out of the customs of Newcastle (£40)	On creation as duke of Northumberland	Cal. Pat., iv. 115
16 June 1552	Joint release of debts totalling £2,094. 17s. 3d.	Going back to 1541	Royal MS 18C 24, fo. 139v Cal. Pat., iv. 347
16 June 1552	Wardship and marriage of William Flammock		Royal MS 18C 24, fo. 224v

IV CALENDARS OF TWO REPORTS SUBMITTED BY QUEEN MARY'S COMMISSIONERS, APPOINTED TO WIND UP THE AFFAIRS OF THE DUKE OF NORTHUMBERLAND

A. PRO LR2/118

A brief declaration made by the Lord Rich and other the Queen's Majesty's commissioners appointed for the collection and sale of the goods and chattels of the late duke of Northumberland and other his confederates attainted of High Treason from the beginning of the commission, viz. 28th August to 13th September 1553.

Ready money: found at Durham Place—nil

found by Thomas Mildmay at the duke's apprehension in Cambridge, which he hath delivered by virtue of the queen's warrant as well to her Grace's own hands as to the hands of Edward Peckham to her Highness's use—£1,998. 18s. 2d.

Plate: £2,702. 9s. 10d., in addition to 651 oz. delivered to the duchess by Sir William Petre and certain parcels found at Cambridge, remaining in the hands of George Gate of the Guard.

Debts due to the duke: £866.13.4.

Money raised by the sale of stuff: £334. 13s. 3d.

[Similar accounts then follow for the marquis of Northampton, Sir Andrew Dudley, Sir John Gates, and Sir Thomas Palmer]

The clear yearly value of the lands:

of the duke	£4,300
of the marquis	£2,800
Sir Andrew Dudley—besides the lands of the bishop of Winchester—£160	
Sir John Gates	£796. 4s. 0d.
Sir Thomas Palmer	£309. 2s. 10d.
bishopric lands	£426. 2s. 1d.

Accounts of plate:

The duke	10,180 oz.
The marquis	369 oz.
Sir John Gates	646 oz.
Archbishop of Canterbury	46¾ oz.

Sums of money due (to Northumberland):

Henry Alcock of Leicester, by obligation, to be paid at Christmas 1 Edward VI— £36. 6s. 11d.

William Hide and John Bullan, to be paid at Christmas 23 Henry VIII by obligation—£412

John Eglesfield of Leckenfield in the county of York to be paid before 1st. May 7 Edward VI, by obligation—£133. 6s. 8d.

Gilbert Grice of Yarmouth, to be paid at Michaelmas 1551, by obligation— £30. 6s. 8d.

Thomas Pobled and John Maynard to be paid at Easter 2 Edward VI, by obligation—£766. 13s. 4d.

Total: £1,478. 13s. 7d.

Money coming by the sale of goods:
  The duke of Northumberland at Syon and Durham House—£589. 21d.

Payment of wages:
  The duke of Northumberland as appeareth by commandment of the Queen's Majesty—£135. 15s. 4d.

Goods appointed and given of the Queen's Majesty's liberal gift:
  The duchess of Somerset for part of the goods of the duke of Northumberland brought from Kenilworth and given to the said duchess—£30. 16s. 4d.

fo. 35   The duke of Northumberland his household servants (wages)

Gentlewomen:	Mrs Marten	16s. 8d.
	Mrs Bridget	16s. 8d.
	Mrs Parson	16s. 8d.
	Mrs Verney	16s. 8d.
	Mrs Geldyforth	16s. 8d.
	Mrs Mardlyn	16s. 8d.
Gentlemen:	Charles Tirell	40s. 0d.
	Edward Pecock	33s. 4d.
	Edmund Bridges	25s. 0d.
	Thomas Poste	25s. 0d.
	Richard Bradley	25s. 0d.
	John Bridgewater	40s. 0d.
	Thomas Freeman	20s. 0d.
	John Winslade	16s. 8d.
	Francis Percy	16s. 8d.
	Thomas Eire	16s. 8d.
	John Palmer	16s. 8d.
	John Huggins	16s. 8d.
	Andrew Sturton	16s. 8d.
	Richard Wentworth	16s. 8d.
	John Crane	16s. 8d.
	Michael Apsley	50s. 0d.
	John St John	16s. 8d.
	Edward Arrington	16s. 8d.
	Rowland Foster	16s. 8d.
	John Rogers	16s. 8d.
	James Pringle	16s. 8d.
	Henry Killigrew	16s. 8d.
	Thomas Dudley	16s. 8d.
	Charles Hopton	16s. 8d.
	Mathew Rochelye	16s. 8d.
	George Grenville	16s. 8d.
	George Lecke	25s. 0d.
	Peter Norwich	16s. 8d.

	Roger Standforth	16s. 8d.
	John Newporte	16s. 8d.
	Walter Reading	16s. 8d.
	John Gwyn	16s. 8d.
	Edward Ratcliffe	16s. 8d.
	George Tuckey	16s. 8d.
	Harry Percy	16s. 8d.
	Hugh Powell	16s. 8d.
	Thomas Stanhope	16s. 8d.
	James Guildford	16s. 8d.
	Henry Baskerville	16s. 8d.
	John Zouche	16s. 8d.
Grooms of the duke's Chamber		10s. 0d.
Grooms of the duchess's Chamber		7s. 0d.
Poticary	Thomas Smith	20s. 0d.
Keeper of the Household Books		
	Richard Herne	15s. 0d.
Footmen	4@	10s. 0d.
Wardrobe of the duchess's robes 3@		10s. 0d.
Yeomen ushers of the Chamber 26 (various)		
Purveyors		5d.
The Pantry		3d.
The Cellar		5d.
The Buttery		5d.
The Ewery		3d.
The Bakehouse		4d.
The Kitchen		14d.
The Larder		2d.
The Skullery		3d.
Keeper of the poultry		
Wardrobe of the beds		5d.
Brewers		2d.
Hall and woodyard		3d.
Porters		2d.
Slaughterhouse		3d.
'Cutours'		2d.
Laundry		4d.
'Granatour'		
The hunt		2d.
Drummer and Pipe		2d.
Riders		9d.
Grooms of the stable		12d.
Armourer		20s. 0d.
Sadler		
Gardeners		2d.
Grooms of the stable at Warwick		13d.
Launderers to the Ewery, pastry and cellar		4d.

Farrier

Under carter

Rewards for six servants, for their attendance upon the commissioners at Durham Place

[Similar household lists follow for the other attainted persons. Cranmer's numbers 69, headed by John Marshall, his Steward]

Of the duke's goods:

Sir Thomas Pope	£16. 14s. 0d.
The earl of Devon	£44. 13s. 4d.
The earl of Arundel	50s. 0d.
Sir Robert Southwell	£3. 14s. 8d.
Anthony Southwell	100s. 0d.
George Tirrell	£50. 2s. 8d.
Sir Humphre Ratcliffe	40s. 0d.
Mr White, Lord Mayor of London	33s. 4d.
Mr Garter	40s. 0d.
Mr Buckenham, Clerk Controller	£42. 0s. 0d.
Robert Bedell of the Inner Temple	10s. 0d.

fo. 91   Account of all the plate delivered to the duchess of Northumberland.

fo. 93   Account of household stuff delivered to the duchess of Northumberland.

fo. 98   Warrant for the discharge of the duke's servants at Syon. Issued by the council, 23 August 1553.

fo. 105   'The names of all such as did belong to the stable'

Charles Tirrell   Gentleman of the Horse
Roger Legh   Clerk of the Stable
2 yeomen
2 yeomen riders
24 grooms

fo. 107   Certificate that 7 hogsheads of wine have been delivered to the queen's use.

fo 116   John Empson's account of the apparel of the duke of Northumberland.

B. PRO E154/2/39

Inventory of the goods of John, late duke of Northumberland made by Lord Rich, Sir Robert Southwell, Sir John Huddleston, Sir Thomas Pope, and Sir Thomas Stradling [no date]

Commissioned to sell goods etc. and pay wages of servants.

At Durham Place

Five undischarged obligations, totalling £1478. 13s. 4d. [see LR2/118 above] 'Delivered to the Lord Treasurer to the Queen's Majesty's use'

Gold plate   94G oz.

Other plate at Durham Place, Syon, and the Tower: 4,891¼ oz.

Parcel gilt plate: 561 oz.

White plate: 3357 oz.

All the above delivered to Richard Wilbraham, Master of the Jewel House.

234½ oz. of gilt plate ⎫ delivered to the duchess of Northumberland.
417 oz. of white plate ⎭

326½ oz. delivered to Mark Anthony by the council's warrant.

43 oz. delivered to Mrs Clarencius to the queen's use.

158 oz. delivered to Fisher the goldsmith by the council's warrant.

97 oz. delivered to Sir Henry Sidney by the council's warrant.

Sum total of the plate: 10,180 oz.

A list of items of linen 'reserved for the Queen's Majesty and delivered to Mrs. Clarencius'

Another list 'delivered to the Duchess of Northumberland by the Queen's warrant'

The duke's wardrobe:

Miscellaneous items delivered to Mrs Clarencius for the queen's use

Some items given to the earl of Devonshire

Parliament robes given to the duke of Norfolk

Further items 'to the Queen's use'

Some old items given to the commissioners' servants

Other items sold to the value of £8. 17s. 8d.

The duchess's wardrobe:

'Delivered to the Duchess to her use by commandment of the council'

'In a chest in Page the Keeper's house'

Items of cloth delivered to Mrs Clarencius to the queen's use.

The duke's underchamber

Various items sold (£40. 4s. 6d.), given away, or stolen (2¼ yards of white sarcenet)

'certain other books and one patent sealed with the seal of the Duchy of Lancaster' conveyed with other evidences to the court of Augmentations

The duke's coronet given to the duke of Norfolk

His rapier given to the earl of Devon

[The furniture is mostly left *in situ* at Durham Place]

Collar of the Order of the Garter given to the duke of Norfolk

One gown is listed as being 'with the Duke at the Tower'

One room is described as 'The Earl of Huntingdon his chamber'

'Mr Arblaster's chamber'

Various items taken away by him and ordered to be returned to the queen's use

'Mr Wynstanley's chamber' and 'Mr Blount's chamber'

Various items delivered to them as their own goods

'Found at Nicholas Boreman's house without Temple Bar in London'

Various items of clothing given to two of the queen's servants

Kitchen equipment sold to Lord Lumley
'A butt of malmsey and a butt of sack half wasted—spent'

Stable equipment 'taken away by the Duchess'

p. 20 The House at Syon
Household stuff sold to divers persons

£168. 13s. 9d.	(hangings etc.)
£30. 10s. 0d.	(coverlets)
£25. 22s.	(carpets)
110s. 4d.	('sparvers and testams')
£10. 16s. 4d.	(quilts)
£88. 3s. 8d.	(beds and bolsters)
67s. 4d.	(mattresses)
74s. 4d.	(fustians)
25s. 0d.	(pillows)
£14. 7s. 8d.	(chairs and stools)
76s. 4d.	(cushions)
£14. 4s. 2d.	(bedsteds tables and chests)
£37. 13s. 2d.	(brass and ironwork)
£4. 11s. 0d.	(glasses)
34s. 0d.	(sheets and napery)
£57. 5s. 4d.	(lead)
36s. 8d.	(horseharness)

(A few items retained for the queen's use)

Household stuff delivered to sundry persons by the council's warrant

Carpets, tapestries etc. from several listed rooms delivered to the duchess

The contents of Lord Ambrose's chamber delivered to him for his furniture at the Tower

Stuff from Lady Mary Sidney's chamber delivered to Sir Henry Sidney

Contents of the duke's bedchamber delivered to the duchess

Wardrobe contents mainly delivered to Mrs Clarencius to the queen's use

28 yards of Holland cloth delivered to Lady Margaret Dudley[1]

Contents of the Steward's room delivered to him as his own.

Contents of the armoury delivered to Sir Richard Southwell (70 sheeves of arrows, 26 bows, 52 javelins, 6 boarspears, 41 morris pikes, 99 demilances, 22 white almain rivetts, 32 black corselets, 32 black bills and poleaxes; some horse harness)

Kitchen stuff delivered to the duchess

Grain, wine, etc., delivered to the queen's purveyor

Household stuff at Syon delivered to George Tirell, the Keeper there

p. 37   'The goods of the said Duke found at St. Johns in London brought from Kenilworth by Clement Throgmorton Esq.'

Delivered to Francis Newdigate for the use of the duchess (quilts, cushions, etc.) to the value of £30. 16s. 4d., the sale of which is cancelled

Sold to Sir Edward Waldegrave (hangings, etc.) worth £31. 16s. 0d., cancelled,
given by the queen

	Totals: Specialties	£1,478. 14s. 7d.
	Plate	10,180 oz.
	Goods sold	£598. 21s.

p. 41   Sum total of the goods of the marquis of Northampton (listed)

	Specialties	£2,000
	Plate	369½ oz.
	Goods sold	£65. 7s. 0d.

The bulk of Northampton's goods at Eston in Essex given to Sir John Huddleston,
and separately inventoried

p. 42   The goods, etc., of Sir John Gates, found at his house at Pirgoe in Essex

[Most of which is noted as sold to Sir Edward Waldegrave, Sir Robert Rochester, Sir
Henry Cotton, and Mr Stradling]: a small amount given to Lady Gates

Goods of Sir John Gates found at St Stephen in Westminster

(Sold to Sir Edward Hastings)

	Total:	Plate	27 oz.
		Goods sold	£321. 4s. 10d.

p. 50   The goods of Sir Andrew Dudley

	Specialties	£300
	Ready money	£1,200
	Goods sold	£95. 22s.

p. 57   The goods of Sir Thomas Palmer

	Specialties	£276. 13s. 4d. and 20 ewes
	Plate	646½ oz.
	Ready money	£161. 17s. 7d.
	Goods sold	£121. 18s. 6d.

p. 62   The earl of Warwick his goods

Found at Mr Jobson's house at Westminster

| | Goods sold | £7 |

The Lord Robert Dudley's goods, found at Mr Jobson's

| | Goods sold | £6. 13s. 4d. |

p. 63   The goods of the late archbishop of Canterbury

30 bills of obligations, mostly for small amounts, totalling £1,214. 4s. 2d.

[The contents of the chapel are noted as 'conveyed and stolen away']

[Some of the kitchen contents are noted as 'given to the bishop's wife'.[2] Similarly
some of the napery, etc.]

The contents of the Armoury

(124 sallets, 130 pairs of splints, 143 breasts and backs, 51 swords, 85 yew bows,
60 wich bows, 90 sheeves of arrows, 2 iron guns with wheels, 3 guns of iron called
¾ bases, 3 small pieces of iron with 9 chambers, 2 little barrels of gunpowder and
5 half hakes)

	Totals:	Plate	—
		Specialties	£1,214. 4s. 2d.

Goods sold   £196. 2s. 8d.

Goods also sold from Beckesborne and Ford, houses of the archbishop of Canterbury

The bishop's palace at Canterbury
          Total goods sold now   £328. 14s. 6d.

Note

LR2/119 and 120 are also detailed inventories of the duke of Northumberland's possessions, but there is no comparable inventory of his lands, apart from a survey of the manor of Birmingham (E36/167)

[1] This was probably the wife of Lord Henry Dudley, rather than Northumberland's daughter of the same name, who seems to have died in infancy.
[2] This entry seems to refute the generally held view that Cranmer sent his wife to Germany before his arrest (J. Ridley, *Thomas Cranmer* (Oxford, 1966), 354). There is also a list of 'stuff appointed for Mrs. Cranmer' (bedding, blankets, pots, and pans, etc.) (E154/6/41, fo. 7).

Bibliography

PRIMARY SOURCES

A. Manuscripts

Public Record Office

SP1	State Papers, Henry VIII, General series
SP2	State Papers, Henry VIII, Folios
SP10	State Papers, Domestic, Edward VI
SP11	State Papers, Domestic, Mary
SP12	State Papers, Domestic, Elizabeth
SP15	State Papers, Domestic, Addenda, Edward VI to James
SP46	State Papers, Domestic, Supplementary
SP68	State Papers, Foreign, Edward VI
C24	Town depositions
C65	Parliament rolls
C66	Patent Rolls
E101	Accounts various
E154	Inventories of goods and chattels
E179	Lay subsidy rolls
E315	Augmentations Office, miscellaneous books
E318	Particulars for grants
E351	Pipe Office, declared accounts
KB8	Court of King's Bench, Baga de secretis
LC2	Lord Chamberlain's Office, records of special events
LC5	Lord Chamberlain's miscellanea
LR2	
PROB 11	Prerogative court of Canterbury, registered copy wills

British Library

Additional MSS   6113, 6128, 9069, 10169, 30198, 32649, 32650, 32654, 34628, 45131, 46354, 48126, 70984

Additional Charters   981

Cotton MSS   Titus B ii, B xiii, F iii
Vespasian D xviii, F xiii
Nero C x
Caligula B vii, E iv
Claudius E vii
Otho E x
Galba B xii

Egerton MSS   2603

Harleian MSS   36, 284, 306, 353, 354, 523, 787, 1294, 2194, 7383

Lansdowne MSS   2, 3, 127, 523, 285, 238, 1236

    Lansdowne Charter 14
    Royal MSS   C16, 17B/39, 18C/24
    Sloane MSS 4149
    Stowe MSS 652
    Wyatt MSS 23

London Guildhall Library
    Repertories
    Journals

Inner Temple Library
    Petyt MSS   47, 538

Longleat
    Dudley Papers ⎫
    Seymour Papers ⎬ on microfilm, at the Institute of Historical Research
    Thynne Papers ⎭

House of Lords Record Office
    Original Acts

Library of the Society of Antiquaries
    MS129A

Birmingham Reference Library
    Hagley Hall MSS   351613, 351614, 346500

Bodleian Library, Oxford
    Additional MS   C94
    Rawlinson MS   846

B. Contemporary published works

Foxe, John, *The Acts and Monuments of the English Martyrs* (London, 1563), ed. S. R. Cattley and George Townsend (London, 1837–41).

Grafton, Richard, *A Chronicle at large* ... (London, 1568), ed. H. Ellis (London, 1809).

Hakluyt, Richard, *The principall navigations ... of the English nation* (London, 1589), ed. W. Raleigh (Glasgow, 1903–5).

Hall, E., *The unione of the two noble and illustre famelies of York and Lancastre* (London, 1542), ed. H. Ellis (London, 1809).

Harrison, James, *An exhortacion to the Scottes* (London, 1547).

Holinshed, Raphael, *Chronicles etc.* (London, 1577), ed. H. Ellis (London, 1807–8).

The saying of John, late Duke of Northumberland upon the scaffolde (London, 1553), ed. W. K. Jordan and M. R. Gleason, *Harvard Library Bulletin*, 23 (1975).

Patten, William, *The expedicione in Scotlande of ... Edward, Duke of Somerset* (London, 1548), in E. Arber (ed.), *An English Garner* (London, 1877–96), iii. 51–155.

Pettie, G., *The civile conversation of S. Guazzo* (London, 1586).

Pole, Reginald, *Pro ecclesiasticae unitatis defensione* (Rome, 1536), ed. J. G. Dwyer (Westminster, Md., 1965).

(Edward, Duke of Somerset) *Epistola exhortaria ad pacem ... missa ab ... Protectore Angliae ... ad populum regni Scotiae* (London, 1548).

—— An Epistle or exhortation to unitie and peace sente from the Lorde Protector (London, 1548).

Thomas, William, *The Pilgrim* (London, 1552), ed. J. A. Froude (London, 1861).

—— *The Historie of Italie* (London, 1549), ed. G. B. Parks (New York, 1963).

C. Calendars and modern editions

Acts of the Privy Council, ed. J. Dasent *et al*. (London, 1890–1907).

Bale, John, *The vocacyon of Johan Bale to the bishoprick of Ossory* (London, 1553).

Brigden, S. E. (ed.), 'The letters of Richard Scudamore to Sir Philip Hoby', *Camden Miscellany*, 30 (1990), 73–86.

Brodie, D. M. (ed.), *Edmund Dudley's Tree of Commonwealth* (Cambridge, 1948).

Byrne, M. St Clare, *The Letters of Henry VIII* (London, 1968).

—— *The Lisle Letters* (London and Chicago, 1981).

Calendar of State Papers, Scotland, ed. J. Bain *et al*. (Edinburgh and Glasgow, 1898–1952).

Calendar of the Patent Rolls, Edward VI, ed. R. H. Brodie (London, 1924–9).

Calendar of State Papers, Domestic, Edward VI, ed. C. Knighton (London, 1992).

Calendar of State Papers, Foreign, 1547–1553, ed. W. Turnbull (London, 1861).

Calendar of State Papers, Spanish, ed. Royall Tyler *et al*. (London, 1862–1954).

Calendar of the Patent Rolls, Henry VII (London, 1914–16).

Calendar of State Papers, Venetian, ed. Rawdon Brown *et al*. (London, 1864–98).

Chronicles of London, ed. C. L. Kingsford (London, 1905).

Cockayne, G. E., *The Complete Peerage*, rev. V. Gibbs (London, 1910–49).

Corbett, J. S. (ed.), *Fighting Instructions, 1530–1816*, Navy Records Society, 29 (1905).

Cranmer, Thomas, *Works*, ed. J. E. Cox (Parker Society, 1844–6).

Dictionary of National Biography

Dickens, A. G. (ed.), *Tudor Treatises*, Yorkshire Archaeological Society Record Series, 125 (1958).

Dugdale, William, *Origines Judicales* (London, 1680).

Elton, G. R., *The Tudor Constitution* (Cambridge, 1982).

Fortescue, Sir John, *De Laudibus Legum Angliae*, ed. S. B. Chrimes (London, 1942).

Frere, W. H., and Kennedy, W. M., *Visitation Articles and Injunctions of the period of the Reformation* (Alcuin Club, 1910).

Gasquet, F., and Bishop, E., *Edward VI and the Book of Common Prayer* (London, 1890).

Godwin, Francis, *Rerum Anglicarum Henrico VIII, Eduardo VI* (London, 1653).

Guaras, Antonio De, *The Accession of Queen Mary*, trans. R. Garnett (London, 1892).

Hay, D. (ed.), *The Anglica Historia of Polydore Vergil*, Camden Society, 3rd series 74 (1950).

Haynes, S., and Murdin, W. (eds.), *A Collection of State Papers ... left by William Cecil, Lord Burghley* (London, 1740–59).

Hayward, John, *The Life and Raigne of King Edward VI*, ed. B. L. Beer (Kent, Ohio, and London, 1993).

Historical Manuscripts Commission Reports: Marquis of Bath (Longleat; Dudley, Seymour, and Thynne Papers); Salisbury (Hatfield); Rutland; Sackville (Knole); Pepys (Magdalene College, Cambridge); Montague of Beaulieu; More-Molyneux (Losely); Corporation of Gloucester; De Lisle and Dudley.

Hughes P. L., and Larkin, J. F., *Tudor Royal Proclamations* (New Haven and London, 1964–9).

Inquisitions Post Mortem of the Reign of Henry VII (London, 1898–1956).

Jordan, W. K. (ed.), *The Chronicle and Political Papers of King Edward VI* (London, 1970).

Journals of the House of Commons (London, 1803–52).

Journals of the House of Lords (London, 1846).

Leadam, I. S. (ed.), *The Domeday of Enclosures, 1517–8*, Royal Historical Society (London, 1897).

Lefèvre-Pontalis, G., *Correspondance politique de Odet de Selve* (Paris, 1888).

Lumby, J. R. (ed.), *Bacon's History of the Reign of King Henry VII* (London, 1892).

Letters and Papers of the Reign of Henry VIII, ed. J. S. Brewer *et al.* (London, 1862–1932).

Loades, David, *The Papers of George Wyatt*, Camden Society, 4th series, 5 (1967).

Lodge, E., *Illustrations of British History* (London, 1838).

Muller, J. A., *The Letters of Stephen Gardiner* (Cambridge, 1933).

Nichols, J. G. (ed.), *The Diary of Henry Machyn*, Camden Society, 42 (1848).

—— *The Chronicle of Queen Jane and of the First Two Years of Mary*, Camden Society, 48 (1850).

—— *The Chronicle of the Greyfriars of London*, Camden Society, 53 (1852).

—— *The Literary Remains of King Edward VI* (Roxburghe Club, 1857).

'The Letters of William, Lord Paget of Beaudesert', ed. B. L. Beer and S. I. Jack, *Camden Miscellany*, 25 (1974).

Pocock, N. (ed.), *Records of the Reformation: The Divorce, 1527–1533* (Oxford, 1870).

—— *The Troubles connected with the Prayer Book of 1549*, Camden Society, 37 (1884).

Pollen, J. H. (ed.), *Papal Negotiations with Mary, Queen of Scots*, Scottish Historical Society, 37 (1901).

Proceedings and Ordinances of the Privy Council of England, 1386–1542, ed. N. H. Nicolas, London, 1834–7.

François de Rabutin, *Commentaires des guerres en la Gaule Belgique, 1551–59*, ed. C. G. de Taurines (Paris, 1932).

Reports of the Deputy Keeper of the Public Records, Reports, III and IV.

Robinson, H. (ed.), *Original Letters Relative to the English Reformation* (Parker Society, 1846–7).

Rymer, T., *Foedera, conventiones etc.* (London, 1704–35).

The Scottish Correspondence of Mary of Lorraine, Scottish Historical Society, series 3: 10 (1927).

Short Title Catalogue of books printed in England, Scotland and Ireland, and of English books printed abroad, 1475–1640, ed. A. W. Pollard and G. R. Redgrave, Bibliographical Society (London, 1926); rev. W. A. Jackson and F. S. Ferguson (London, 1976, 1986).

The State Papers … of Henry VIII (London, 1830–52).

Statutes of the Realm, ed. A. Luder *et al.* (London, 1810–28).

Tawney, R. H., and Power, Eileen, *Tudor Economic Documents* (London, 1924).

Teulat, A. (ed.), *Relations politiques de la France et de l'Espagne avec l'Écosse au XVIe siècle* (Paris, 1862).

Tytler, P. F., *The Reigns of Edward VI and Mary* (London 1839).

Valor Ecclesiasticus, ed. J. Caley and J. Hunter (London, 1810–34).

Venn, J., *Alumni Cantabridgiensis* (Cambridge, 1922–7).

Vertot, R. A. de, *Ambassades des Messieurs de Noailles* (Leyden, 1743).

Wingfield, Robert, 'Vitae Mariae Reginae', ed. D. MacCulloch, *Camden Miscellany*, 28 (1984).

Wood, A., *Athenae Oxoniensis*, ed. P. Bliss (London, 1813–20).

Wriothesley, Charles, *A Chronicle of England during the Reigns of the Tudors, from 1485 to 1559*, ed. W. D. Hamilton, Camden Society, NS 11, pts. i and ii (London, 1875–7).

SECONDARY SOURCES

A. Books

Adlard, G., *Amy Robsart and the Earl of Leicester* (London, 1870).

Beer, B. L., *Northumberland: The Political Career of John Dudley, Earl of Warwick and Duke of Northumberland* (Kent, Ohio, 1973).

—— *Rebellion and Riot: Popular Disorder in England during the Reign of Edward VI* (Kent, Ohio, 1982).

Bernard, G. W., *War, Taxation, and Rebellion in Early Tudor England* (Brighton, 1986).

Bindoff, S. T., *et al.*, *The House of Commons, 1509–1558* (London, 1982).

Brigden, S. E., *London and the Reformation* (Oxford, 1989).

Burnet, G., *The Historie of the Reformation of the Church of England* (London, 1694).

Bush, M. L., *The Government Policy of Protector Somerset* (London, 1975).

Challis, C. E., *The Tudor Coinage* (Manchester, 1978).

Chrimes, S. B., *Henry VII* (London, 1972).

Connell-Smith, G., *The Forerunners of Drake* (London, 1954).

Cornwall, J., *Revolt of the Peasantry, 1549* (London, 1977).

Dewar, M., *Sir Thomas Smith: A Tudor Intellectual in Office* (London, 1964).

Dickens, A. G., *The English Reformation* (London, 1989).

Dietz, F. C., *English Public Finance, 1485–1641* (London, 1964).

Dodds, M. H., and Dodds, R., *The Pilgrimage of Grace and the Exeter Conspiracy* (Cambridge, 1915).

Donaldson, G., *Scotland: James V to James VII* (Edinburgh, 1978).

Elton, G. R., *The Tudor Revolution in Government* (Cambridge, 1953).

—— *Policy and Police: The Enforcement of the Reformation in the Age of Thomas Cromwell* (Cambridge, 1972).

—— *Reform and Renewal: Thomas Cromwell and the Common Weal* (Cambridge, 1973).

—— *Reform and Reformation: England, 1509–1558* (London, 1977).

Emmison, F. G., *Tudor Secretary* (London, 1971).

Fox, A., *Reassessing the Henrician Age: Humanism, Politics and Reform, 1500–1550*, with J. Guy (Oxford, 1986).

Fraser, Antonia, *The Six Wives of Henry VIII* (London, 1992).

Froude, J. A., *The Reign of King Edward VI* (London, 1909).

Gairdner, James, *Lollardy and the Reformation in England* (London, 1908–13).

Gammon, S. R., *Statesman and Schemer: William, First Lord Paget of Beaudesert* (Newton Abbot, 1973).

Gould, J. D., *The Great Debasement* (Oxford, 1970).

Graves, M. A. R., *The House of Lords in the Parliaments of Edward VI and Mary: An Institutional Study* (Cambridge, 1981).

Gunn, S. J., *Charles Brandon, Duke of Suffolk, 1484–1545* (Oxford, 1988).

—— and Lindley, P. G., *Cardinal Wolsey: Church, State and Art* (Cambridge, 1991).

Guy, J. A., *Tudor England* (Oxford, 1988).

Harbison, E. H., *Rival Ambassadors at the Court of Queen Mary* (Princeton, 1940).

Heal, F., *Of Princes and Prelates: A Study of the Economic and Social Position of the Tudor Episcopate* (Cambridge, 1980).

Hicks, M., *False, Fleeting, Perjur'd Clarence* (Bangor, 1992).

Hoak, D. E., *The King's Council in the Reign of Edward VI* (Cambridge, 1976).

Hurstfield, J., *The Queen's Wards: Wardship and Marriage under Elizabeth* (London, 1958).

Ives, E. W., *The Common Lawyers of Pre-Reformation England* (Cambridge, 1983).

—— *Anne Boleyn* (Oxford, 1986).

James, M. E., *Change and Continuity in the Tudor North: The Rise of Thomas, First Lord Wharton* (York, 1965).

Jordan, W. K., *Edward VI: The Young King* (London, 1968).

—— *Edward VI: The Threshold of Power* (London, 1970).

Knecht, R. J., *Francis I* (Cambridge, 1982).

Kreider, A., *English Chantries: The Road to Dissolution* (Cambridge, Mass., 1979).

Land, S. K., *Kett's Rebellion* (Ipswich, 1977).

Lehmberg, S. E., *Sir Thomas Elyot: Tudor Humanist* (Austin, Tex., 1960).

—— *The Reformation Parliament, 1529–1536* (Cambridge, 1970).

—— *The Later Parliaments of Henry VIII, 1536–1547* (Cambridge, 1977).

Loach, J., *Protector Somerset* (Bangor, 1994).

Loades, D., *Two Tudor Conspiracies* (Cambridge, 1965).

—— *Mary Tudor: A life* (Oxford, 1989).

—— *The Reign of Mary Tudor* (London, 1991).

—— *The Tudor Navy: An Administrative, Political and Military History* (Aldershot, 1992).

—— *The Tudor Court* (Bangor, 1992).

—— *The Politics of Marriage: Henry VIII and his Queens* (Stroud, 1994).

—— *Lectures on the Reign of Edward VI* (Bangor, 1994).

McConica, J., *English Humanists and Reformation Politics* (Oxford, 1965).

MacCulloch, D. N. J., *Suffolk and the Tudors: Politics and Religion in an English County, 1500–1600* (Oxford, 1986).

Maclean, J., *The Life of Sir Thomas Seymour, Knight, Lord Seymour of Sudeley* (London, 1869).

Mattingly, G., *Renaissance Diplomacy* (London, 1955).

Miller, Helen, *Henry VIII and the English Nobility* (Oxford, 1986).

Muller, J. A., *Stephen Gardiner and the Tudor Reaction* (New York, 1926).

O'Day, R., and Heal, F. (eds.), *Continuity and Change: Personnel and Administration of the Church of England 1500–1642* (Leicester, 1976).

Pollard, A. F., *England under Protector Somerset* (London, 1900).

Read, C., *Mr. Secretary Cecil and Queen Elizabeth* (London, 1955).

Redworth, G., *In Defence of the Church Catholic: The Life of Stephen Gardiner* (Oxford, 1990).

Reid, R. R., *The King's Council in the North* (London, 1921).

Richardson, W. C., *The Report of the Royal Commission of 1552* (Morganstown, W. Va., 1974).

Ridley, J., *Thomas Cranmer* (Oxford, 1966).

Rose Troup, F., *The Western Rebellion of 1549* (London, 1913).

Roskell, J. S., *The Commons and their Speakers in English Parliaments, 1376–1523* (London, 1965).

Rowse, A. L., *Tudor Cornwall* (London, 1969).

Russell, F. W., *Kett's Rebellion in Norfolk* (London, 1859).

Sandford, Francis, *A Genealogical History of the Kings of England* (London, 1677).

Scarisbrick, J. J., *Henry VIII* (London, 1968).

Slavin, A. J., *Politics and Profit: A study of Sir Ralph Sadler, 1507–1547* (Cambridge, 1966).

Smith, L. B., *A Tudor Tragedy* (London, 1961).

—— *Henry VIII: The Mask of Royalty* (London, 1971).

—— *Treason in Tudor England: Politics and Paranoia* (London, 1986).

Spalding, J. C., *The Reformation of the Ecclesiastical Laws of England, 1552*, Sixteenth Century Essays and Studies, 19 (Kirksville, Mo., 1992).

Starkey, D., *The Reign of Henry VIII* (London, 1985).

Stow, John, *The Annales of England* (London, 1592).

Strype, John, *Ecclesiastical Memorials* (London, 1721).

Sturge, C., *Cuthbert Tunstall* (London, 1938).

Tawney, R. H., *The Agrarian Problem in the Sixteenth Century* (London, 1912).

Thompson, G. S., *Lords Lieutenant in the Sixteenth Century* (London, 1923).

Torrance, T. F., *Space, Time and Incarnation* (London, 1969).

Warnicke, R. M., *The Rise and Fall of Anne Boleyn* (Cambridge, 1989).

Wernham, R. B., *Before the Armada: The Emergence of the English Nation, 1485–1588* (New York, 1966).

Whitaker, E. C., *Martin Bucer and the Book of Common Prayer* (London, 1974).

Willen, D., *John Russell, First Earl of Bedford: One of the King's Men* (London, 1981).

Williams, P., *The Tudor Regime* (Oxford, 1979).

Wilson, D., *Sweet Robin: A biography of Robert Dudley, Earl of Leicester* (London, 1981).

Wolffe, B. P., *The Crown Lands, 1461–1536* (London, 1970).

Zagorin, P., *Rebels and Rulers, 1500–1660* (Cambridge, 1982).

Zeeveld, W. G., *Foundations of Tudor Policy* (Cambridge, Mass., 1948).

B. Articles and Theses

Adair, E. R., 'William Thomas', in R. W. Seton Watson (ed.), *Tudor Studies* (London, 1924).

Adams, S., 'Faction, Clientage and Party: English Politics, 1550–1603', *History Today*, 32 (1982), 33–9.

—— 'The Dudley Clientele in the House of Commons, 1559–1586', *Parliamentary History*, 8 (1989), 217–39.

—— 'The Dudley Clientele, 1553–1563', in G. W. Bernard (ed.), *The Tudor Nobility* (Manchester, 1992).

Aird, I., 'The Death of Amy Robsart', *English Historical Review*, 71 (1957), 69–79.

Alsop, J. D., 'The Revenue Commission of 1552', *Historical Journal*, 22 (1979), 511–33.

—— 'The Theory and Practice of Tudor Taxation', *English Historical Review*, 97 (1982), 1–30.

—— 'Innovation in Tudor Taxation', *English Historical Review*, 99 (1984), 83–93.

Alsop, J. D.,'A Regime at Sea: The Navy and the 1553 Succession Crisis', *Albion*, 24 (1992).

Beer, B. L., 'Northumberland: The Myth of the Wicked Duke and the Historical John Dudley', *Albion*, 11 (1979), 1–14.

—— 'Episcopacy and Reform in Mid-Tudor England', *Albion*, 22 (1991).

Bernard, G. W., 'The Downfall of Sir Thomas Seymour', in G. W. Bernard (ed.), *The Tudor Nobility* (Manchester, 1992), 212–40.

Blanchard, I. S. W., 'Population Change, Enclosure and the Early Tudor Economy', *Economic History Review*, 2nd series, 23 (1970).

Boscher, P. G., 'Politics, Administration and Diplomacy: The Anglo-Scottish Border, 1550–1560', Ph. D. thesis, University of Durham, 1985.

Braddock, R. C., 'The Rewards of Office Holding in Tudor England', *Journal of British Studies*, 14 (1975), 29–47.

—— 'The Character and Composition of the Duke of Northumberland's Army', *Albion*, 8 (1987), 1–11.

Brodie, D. M., 'Edmund Dudley: Minister of Henry VII', *Transactions of the Royal Historical Society*, 4th series, 15 (1932), 133–47.

Buckley, H., 'Sir Thomas Gresham and the Foreign Exchanges', *Economic Journal*, 34 (1924), 589–601.

Bush, M. L., 'The Lisle–Seymour Land Disputes: A Study of Power and Influence in the 1530s', *Historical Journal*, 9 (1966), 255–74.

—— 'The Problems of the Far North', *Northern History*, 6 (1971).

Condon, M. M., 'Ruling Elites in the Reign of Henry VII', in C. Ross (ed.), *Patronage, Pedigree and Power* (Gloucester, 1979), 109–42.

Cooper, J. P., 'Henry VII's Last Years Reconsidered', *Historical Journal*, 2 (1959), 103–29.

Cornwall, J., and MacCulloch, D., 'Debate: Kett's Rebellion in Context', *Past and Present*, 93 (1981), 160–73.

Davies, C. S. L., 'Slavery and Protector Somerset: The Vagrancy Act of 1547', *Economic History Review*, 2nd series, 19 (1966), 533–49.

—— 'The Pilgrimage of Grace Reconsidered', *Past and Present*, 41 (1968), 54–76.

Elton, G. R., 'Henry VII: Rapacity and Remorse', *Historical Journal*, 1 (1958), 21–39.

—— 'Henry VII: A Restatement', *Historical Journal*, 4 (1961), 1–29.

—— 'Thomas Cromwell's Decline and Fall', in *Studies in Tudor and Stuart Politics and Government*, i (Cambridge, 1974), 189–230.

—— 'Taxation for War and Peace in Early Tudor England', in J. M. Winter (ed.), *War and Economic Development* (Cambridge, 1975).

—— 'Politics and the Pilgrimage of Grace', in *Studies in Tudor and Stuart Politics and Government*, iii (Cambridge, 1983), 183–215.

Emmison, F. G., 'A Plan of Edward VI and Secretary Petre for Reorganising the Privy Council's Work, 1552–3', *Bulletin of the Institute of Historical Research*, 31 (1958), 203–7.

Fisher, F. J., 'Influenza and Inflation in Tudor England', *Economic History Review*, 2nd series, 18 (1965), 120–9.

Fourdrinier, H., 'Amy Robsart', typescript, *c*.1957, MS MC5/29, in the Norfolk County Record Office.

Goring, J. J., 'Social Change and Military Decline in Mid-Tudor England', *History*, 60 (1975), 185–97.

Gunn, S. J., 'The Duke of Suffolk's March on Paris in 1523', *English Historical Review*, 101 (1986), 596–634.

—— 'The Accession of Henry VIII', *Historical Research*, 64 (1991), 278–88.

—— 'The Courtiers of Henry VII', *English Historical Review*, 108 (1993).

Harrison, C. J., 'The Petition of Edmund Dudley', *English Historical Review*, 87 (1971), 82–99.

Harriss, G. L., 'Thomas Cromwell's "New Principle" of Taxation', *English Historical Review*, 93 (1978), 721–38.

Hicks, M., 'Attainder, Resumption and Coercion, 1461–1529', *Parliamentary History*, 3 (1984), 15–31.

Hoak, D. E., 'Rehabilitating the Duke of Northumberland: Politics and Political Control, 1549–1553', in J. Loach and R. Tittler (eds.), *The Mid-Tudor Polity, 1540–1560* (London, 1980), 29–51.

—— 'The King's Privy Chamber, 1547–1553', in D. J. Guth and J. W. McKenna (eds.), *Tudor Rule and Revolution* (Cambridge, 1982), 87–108.

—— 'Two Revolutions in Tudor Government: The Formation and Organisation of Mary I's Privy Council', in C. Coleman and D. Starkey (eds.), *Revolution Reassessed* (London, 1986), 87–115.

—— 'The Secret History of the Tudor Court: The King's Coffers and the King's Purse, 1542–1553', *Journal of British Studies*, 26 (1987), 208–31.

Holmes, P. J., 'The Great Council in the Reign of Henry VII', *English Historical Review*, 101 (1986), 840–62.

Horowitz, M. R., 'Richard Empson, Minister of Henry VII', *Bulletin of the Institute of Historical Research*, 55 (1982), 35–49.

Ives, E. W., 'Faction at the Court of Henry VIII: The Fall of Anne Boleyn', *History*, 57 (1972), 169–88.

—— 'Henry VIII's Will: A Forensic Conundrum', *Historical Journal*, 35 (1992), 779–804.

Jackson, J. E., 'Amye Robsart', *Wiltshire Archaeological Magazine*, 17 (1898), 58–93.

King, J. N., 'Freedom of the Press, Protestant Propaganda, and Protector Somerset', *Huntington Library Quarterly*, 40 (1976), 1–10.

Kipling, G., 'Henry VII and the Origins of Tudor Patronage', in G. F. Lytle and S. Orgel (eds.), *Patronage in the Renaissance* (Princeton, 1981), 117–64.

Loach, J., 'Pamphlets and Politics, 1553–8', *Bulletin of the Institute of Historical Research*, 48 (1975), 31–44.

Loades, D., 'The Last Years of Cuthbert Tunstall, 1547–1559', *Durham University Journal*, 66 (1973), 10–21.

—— 'The Dissolution of the Diocese of Durham, 1553–4', in *Politics, Censorship and the English Reformation* (London, 1991), 167–79.

MacCulloch, D. N. J., 'Kett's Rebellion in Context', in P. Slack (ed.), *Rebellion, Popular Protest and the Social Order in Early Modern England* (Cambridge, 1984), 39–76.

McCoy, R. C., 'From the Tower to the Tiltyard; Robery Dudley's Return to Glory', *Historical Journal*, 27 (1984), 425–35.

Malkiewicz, A. J. A., 'An Eyewitness Account of the Coup d'Etat of October 1549', *English Historical Review*, 70 (1955), 600–9.

Manning, R. B., 'Violence and Social Conflict in Mid-Tudor Rebellions', *Journal of British Studies*, 16 (1977).

Miller, H., 'Henry VIII's Unwritten Will: Grants of Land and Honours in 1547', in E. W. Ives, R. J. Knecht, and J. J. Scarisbrick (eds.), *Wealth and Power in Tudor England* (London, 1978), 87–105.

Murphy, J., 'The Illusion of Decline: The Privy Chamber, 1547–1558', in D. Starkey (ed.), *The English Court from the Wars of the Roses to the Civil War* (London, 1987), 119–46.

Parry, G. J. R., 'Inventing the Good Duke of Somerset', *Journal of Ecclesiastical History*, 40 (1989).

Potter, D. L., 'Documents Concerning the Negotiation of the Anglo-French Treaty of March 1550', *Camden Miscellany*, 28 (1984), 59–180.

Slack, P., 'Social Policy and the Constraints of Government, 1547–1558', in J. Loach and R. Tittler, *The Mid-Tudor Polity* (London, 1980), 94–115.

Slavin, A. J. 'The Fall of Lord Chancellor Wriothesley: A Study in the Politics of Conspiracy', *Albion*, 7 (1975), 265–85.

Somerville, R., 'Henry VII's "Council Learned in the Law"', *English Historical Review*, 54 (1939), 427–42.

Starkey, D., 'From Feud to Faction: English Politics, *c.*1450–1550', *History Today*, 32 (1982), 16–22.

—— 'Intimacy and Innovation: The Rise of the Privy Chamber, 1485–1547', in id. (ed.), *The English Court from the Wars of the Roses to the Civil War* (London, 1987), 71–118.

Stone, L., 'Patriarchy and Paternalism in Tudor England: The Earl of Arundel and the Peasants' Revolt of 1549', *Journal of British Studies*, 13 (1974), 19–23.

Sturge, C., 'John Dudley, Earl of Warwick and Duke of Northumberland', Ph.D. thesis, University of London, 1927.

Tighe, W. J., 'The Gentlemen Pensioners, the Duke of Northumberland and the Attempted Coup of 1553', *Albion*, 19 (1987), 1–11.

Tittler, R., and Battley, S. L., 'The Local Community and the Crown in 1553: The Accession of Mary Tudor Re-visited', *Bulletin of the Institute of Historical Research*, 136 (1984), 131–40.

Weikel, A., 'The Marian Council Revisited', in J. Loach and R. T. Tittler (eds.), *The Mid-Tudor Polity* (London, 1980), 52–73.

Wolffe, B. P., 'Henry VII's Land Revenues and Chamber Finance', *English Historical Review*, 79 (1964), 225–54.

Wyndham, K. S. H., 'Crown Land and Royal Patronage in Mid-Sixteenth Century England', *Journal of British Studies*, 19 (1980), 18–34.

Youings, J. A., 'The South-Western Rebellion of 1549', *Southern History*, 1 (1979), 99–122.

Index